ROLES
IN
THE LITURGICAL
ASSEMBLY

ROLES
IN
THE LITURGICAL
ASSEMBLY

*the
twenty-third
Liturgical Conference
Saint Serge*

translated by Matthew J. O'Connell

PUEBLO PUBLISHING COMPANY • NEW YORK

Design: Br. Aelred Shanley

Originally published in French as *L'assemblée liturgique et les différents rôles dans l'assemblée* © 1977 Edizioni Liturgiche, Rome.

English translation © 1981 Pueblo Publishing Company, Inc. 1860 Broadway, New York, NY 10023. All rights reserved.

Printed in the United States of America.

ISBN: 0-916134-44-X

CONTENTS

Preface   ix

Allmen, Jean-Jacques von
The Communal Character of Public Worship
in the Reformed Church   1

Adronikof, Constantin
Assembly and Body of Christ: Identity or Distinction   13

Arranz, Miguel, S.J.
The Functions of the Christian Assembly
in *The Testament of Our Lord*   29

Botte, Bernard, O.S.B.
Christian People and Hierarchy in the *Apostolic Tradition* of
St. Hippolytus   61

Braniste, Ene
The Liturgical Assembly and Its Functions
in the *Apostolic Constitutions*   73

Cazelles, Henri, P.S.S.
The Old Testament Liturgical Assembly and the Various
Roles Played in It   101

Cothenet, Edouard
Earthly Liturgy and Heavenly Liturgy according to the
Book of Revelation   115

Dalmais, Irénée-Henri, O.P.
The Structures of the Liturgical Celebration as an Expression of Ecclesial Communion in the Coptic Church   137

Heitz, Serge
Reflections on the Contemporary Liturgical Assembly   155

Kniazeff, Alexander
The Role of the Deacon in the Byzantine
Liturgical Assembly   167

Koulomzine, Nicolas
Liturgical Roles in the Assembly of the Primitive Church
according to Father Nicolas Afanassieff   187

Kovalevsky, Maxime
The Role of the Choir in Christian Liturgy   193

Neunheuser, Burckhard, O.S.B.
The Relation of Priest and Faithful in the Liturgies of
Pius V and Paul VI   207

Renoux, Charles
Liturgical Ministers at Jerusalem
in the Fourth and Fifth Centuries   221

Triacca, Achille M., S.D.B.
Methexis in the Early Ambrosian Liturgy 233

Vogel, Cyrille
Is the Presbyteral Ordination of the Celebrant a Condition
for the Celebration of the Eucharist? 253

Walter, Christopher, S.J.
The Bishop as Celebrant in Byzantine Iconography 265

Westphal, Gaston
Role and Limit of Pastoral Delegation to Laymen for the
Celebration of the Eucharist
in the Protestant Reformed Churches 275

Abbreviations 291

Notes 295

PREFACE

As everyone knows, the basic purpose of Christian public worship is to enable the Mystical Body of Christ to take palpable form in the liturgical assembly; the liturgy renders the *Ecclesia* visible.[1] Insofar as the Church is the "mystery"[2] of our union with Christ as foreseen and willed by the Father and as made a reality by the power of the Spirit, it can only be described by a plurality of different but complementary analogies.[3] The mystery of the *Ecclesia* is extremely rich in meanings and cannot be expressed in a single formula.

Such a formula would have to express simultaneously the function Christ has for the Church and in the Church and, at the same time, the function of the Holy Spirit.[4] These functions are given concrete shape and visibility in the liturgical assembly. The latter is thus the effective sign of the "covenant" that is constantly being made a reality, and the embodiment of the active emergence of a community that perdures through time and space. Once again, then, it is clear that to study the nature of the liturgical assembly is to understand more fully the inner nature of the *Ecclesia* and vice versa.

On the other hand, the many "incarnations" and "epiphanies" of the one Church in many liturgical assemblies[5] help us to see that the liturgical assembly is in fact a community "called together" here and now by the Blessed Trinity so that the *Ecclesia* may be progressively established as "people of God and worshiping community."[6] In studying the Church, then, the most reliable procedure from the methodological standpoint and the simplest and most fruitful from the practical, pastoral and liturgical standpoints is to look at the liturgical assembly, where we see that the primary purpose of Christian public worship is the "edification" or building up of the community,[7] and to study its dynamics as the effective embodiment of the *Ecclesia*.

In the liturgical assembly the faithful are called together by the Father, in the Spirit of the glorified Christ, by means of the "pastors" whose function is to be the voice, here and now, of the Spirit. Once *called together*, the liturgical assembly *calls to mind* the wonderful things God has done for it and *calls upon him* with praise, thanksgiving and petitions to the Father who expresses his overflowing goodness and love for us in his Son. Once reminded of God's magnificent plan of salvation, the liturgical community realizes that it continues and perpetuates the liturgical assemblies of all the ages past. It also discovers that by the power of the Spirit it is able to activate in itself the profound dynamisms that were at work in the first Christian community and were summed up in dedication to the teaching of the apostles, fellowship, the breaking of bread and prayer.[8] As a result of all this, the liturgical assembly becomes increasingly conscious that it renders visible, at this point in space and time, the comprehensive unity of those whom the Father, by the power of the Spirit, has called forth from the human race to be one with Christ, the eternal high priest.[9]

In the *Ecclesia*, then, all power and grace comes from liturgical activity, and conversely everything is directed to the sacred liturgy. The liturgy is the point of departure, the generative power, and the wellspring of vital energy for all activity in the Church, and, at the same time, the goal to which all this activity tends.

A study therefore of the various roles taken in the liturgy which the assembly celebrates will be a study of how the various members are to interact in the life of the Church in order that everything may contribute in an orderly way to growth toward full stature in Christ.[10] In the liturgical assembly we discover, in its essentials, the full transforming power of active participation: the close and profound *methexis* of the "divine mysteries." The liturgical celebration brings to light the principle of the identity and unity that binds together the various functions and charisms by means of which and in which the complex structure of ecclesial activity is formed into a single whole. Under the guidance of its pastors, the liturgical assembly, with its many functions, contributes in an ordered way to the fruitful action of the community. Each individual plays a part, and this part is not to be confused with that of others nor to be usurped by others.[11]

In the ordered integration of all its functions the unique nature of the *Ecclesia* shines forth clearly: the Church as a single living body, hierarchically structured and drawing its life from the gifts of the Spirit.

The essays collected here undoubtedly make a notable contribution to a deeper understanding of the set of problems I have briefly outlined in this preface.

As a service to the Church of Christ we offer here the papers[12] presented at the very interesting Twenty-third Week of Liturgical Studies at the Saint-Serge Institute in Paris.[13] These papers, we are convinced, will prove very useful to all who look for an ecumenism that is both authentic and effective. As for those who attended the Week, the volume will surely help them profit more fully by the very intense work done during the "fiery" days of the meeting (and what a warming experience those days in Paris were!). A report, at least in summary form, of the comments made and of the replies given by the authors of the papers would also have been useful, but for technical and editorial reasons which readers will readily imagine for themselves this proved impossible.

Achille M. Triacca
Pontifical Salesian University, Rome
December 25, 1976

Jean-Jacques von ALLMEN

The Communal Character
of Public Worship
in the Reformed Church

While the public worship of the Reformed Church is everywhere recognizable by certain constant features, it has nonetheless been modified and adapted in many ways since the sixteenth century. The purpose of these changes has been to align the liturgy with the tastes or attachments of various past ages and of our own day. There can be no question in a short paper like this one of reviewing the history of the communal character of Reformed worship. A historical survey is nonetheless required, but I shall limit it to the sixteenth century. On the basis of the survey I shall, in my concluding remarks, indicate some of the reasons why the Reformed Church is in a better position today than ever before to express and intensify the communal character of its public worship.

What does Reformed theology understand public worship or liturgy to be? It is the gift bestowed on the faithful whereby they are able "zealously to frequent the sacred assemblies, especially on the day of rest, in order to listen to the word of God and participate in the holy sacraments, to pray publicly to the Lord, and to contribute as Christians should to the needs of the poor."[1] Public worship therefore comprises four elements: the hearing of God's word, the reception of the sacraments, the public prayer of the Church, and the sharing of one's goods with the less fortunate. This definition, frequently repeated,[2] makes public worship an eminently communal action.

Because they are convinced that Christian worship is what we have just seen it to be, the Reformers make at least the following seven demands of their liturgical program. All the requirements have for their purpose to make it clear that while a minister of Christ is needed in order to validate worship as specifically Christian, the worship itself is not his business alone but that of the entire people of God.

First requirement: The liturgy must be celebrated in the language of the people. While "it is legitimate for individuals to pray privately in any language they like, provided they understand it . . . public prayers in Christian churches must be offered in the vernacular and must be intelligible to each person."[3]

Second requirement: Since it is by his word that the Lord gathers, builds up, protects and guides his people, this word must be communicated in a serious and generous manner. This is a matter less of having many readings from scripture than of explaining and applying the scriptures. This accounts for the primary importance of the homily or sermon, which becomes the key element in traditional Reformed worship. But, contrary to what has often been asserted, the cardinal place given to preaching does not condemn the assembly to a passive role. As K. Barth remarks in his commentary on the Scottish Confession of 1560, "There is simply no activity that is more intense, absorbing or moving than listening to God's word: listening to it in the way it deserves—ever anew, ever better, with ever greater fidelity and clarity. This activity gives divine service its content."[4]

Third requirement: If the eucharist is to be celebrated as Christ instituted it, the faithful must be acknowledged to have the right and duty of communicating. This leads, for pastoral reasons, to the suppression of eucharistic celebrations in which the faithful do not participate by receiving communion. I shall not go into historical details about the frequency of celebration of the Supper in the Reformed Church.[5] I simply make two points: on the one hand, the separation between the Lord's day and the Lord's Supper was meant to be only a provisional measure in the eyes of the Reformers;[6] on the other hand, in many Reformed churches the eucharist was initially celebrated much more often and regularly than the three or four times a year which gradually became the rule (a rule to which, in any case, there have always been exceptions).

Fourth requirement: There is to be an end to the distinction made between clergy and people in regard to participation in the Lord's Supper; that is, there is to be an end to the practice of having only the members of the clergy take communion under both kinds. Christ instituted the Supper under two kinds; the people must therefore have a right to the chalice. This requirement has everywhere been strictly met.

Fifth requirement: The people are to be actively involved in the celebration of the liturgy by means of antiphonal singing, as at Zürich, or by the singing of psalms and canticles, as in the Strasbourg–Geneva tradition.[7] For this purpose the one hundred and fifty psalms, the two tables of the Law, the Apostles' Creed, the Lord's Prayer, and the Canticle of Simeon were all translated in verse form.[8] "Each person should be a participant," said Calvin in the *Letter* to the reader at the beginning of his *Forme des prieres*,[9] and singing was meant especially to foster such participation. For "we know from experience that singing has great power to move and inflame the hearts of people so that they will invoke God and praise him with a more intense and ardent zeal."[10] Unlike the Lutheran Reform, which led to an extraordinary flowering of hymnology,[11] the Calvinist Reform was content with the psalms and the versification of *biblical* texts (the Apostles' Creed being regarded as such). Calvin was convinced that "God puts these words in our mouths, as if he himself were singing in us in praise of his glory."[12]

Sixth requirement: The long-standing and widespread custom of saying certain prayers silently must be suppressed. On the contrary, the minister is to say the prayers "in a loud voice" or "in a loud and solemn voice."[13]

Seventh and final requirement: The minister is to wear no liturgical vestments that distinguish him from the people. Admittedly, he will wear a robe different from that of the faithful generally, but it is the robe proper to his state, his robe as a scholar, and not any priestly vestment that smacks of the old covenant.[14]

These seven requirements of the reformed Reform have the effect of declericalizing public worship. Yet nothing could be more wrong than to think that these requirements call into question the Church's need of receiving from God ministers who will gather, exhort, teach and guide the Christian people in the name of and by the authority of the Lord. Here is one of the basic statements made in the Second Helvetic Confession: "We did not eliminate the Church's ministry when we eliminated from the Church of Christ the priesthood as found in the Roman Church."[15] The pastor is a necessity if worship is to be Christian worship. We may say that he puts the seal of Christian authenticity on it. It is he who invokes God at the beginning of the celebration. It is he who "announces the absolution in the name of the Father, the Son and the Holy Spirit"[16] to the faithful after they have confessed their sins. It is he who offers the prayers to God in the name of the people. It is he who (in the Calvinist tradition) reads the scriptures, and it is he who preaches. It is certainly he who presides over the eucharist and distributes the bread of life to the faithful.[17] It is he who pronounces the excommunication of unrepentant sinners, and it is he who receives them back into the peace of the Church[18] when they have done penance. Finally, it is he who "sends" the Church out into the world as he bestows the blessing of the Lord upon it. Consequently, to emphasize the communal aspect of worship is not to question whether the ministry is needed for the Church to be the Church.[19]

The presence of the pastor-president, then, is indispensable if public worship is to be the worship Christ instituted for his Church. This does not mean, however, that the pastor becomes the master of the celebration. That is to say: he cannot design it to suit his pleasure, since he is bound by the official liturgical books, which belong not to him but to the Church. True enough, some parts of the liturgy are expressly left "to the discretion of the minister": for example, in the Genevan liturgy, the epiclesis in which the pastor asks "God for the grace of his Holy Spirit, so that God's word may be faithfully expounded, to the honor of his name and the building up of the Church, and so that it may be received with the humility and obedience it deserves."[20] By and large, however, the minister must follow the order of worship and the received prayers.[21]

Against this background we must now consider briefly the two major liturgical traditions of the Reformed Church and the way in which each, in the beginning, made public worship an action of the *community*. By "two traditions" I mean, of course, the tradition of Zürich, which goes back to Zwingli, and the tradition of Strasbourg, the main lines of which Calvin took over and which became the main liturgical tradition of the Reformed Church.[22] In a paper like this it is not possible to go into great detail, to compare different editions of the same liturgy, and so on. I shall concentrate on the main elements and on parish worship in which the Supper is celebrated.

The eucharistic liturgy of Zürich forms, in principle, a single whole. More accurately, it should be said that at Zürich the Sunday liturgy of the word formed a self contained whole, so that it did not give the appearance of lacking its climactic element when the Supper was omitted. But when the Supper was in fact celebrated, it was always preceded by a liturgy of the word, and this latter included a sermon.[23] In other words, the eucharist in this case *continued* the worship that had begun with a liturgy of the word; the eucharist did not begin a new liturgy.

Zwingli wanted a celebration that would clearly manifest the thanksgiving and jubilation[24] that should mark the Lord's Supper. It must be acknowledged that he succeeded in a way that greatly surprises the reader who approaches these texts prejudiciously and thinks Zwingli suspect in matters of sacramental theology. The worship he required and in fact established calls for three kinds of liturgical agents: the pastor, the deacons, and the people.

The *pastor*, who stands near the communion table and facing the people, presides over the entire celebration. He says the prayers of the Church and urges the community to humble itself; he intones the three compositions which will be recited antiphonally by the assembly: the Gloria, the Apostles' Creed, and, at the end of the service, Psalm 112 (LXX); he recites the Lord's Prayer, enacts the Lord's Supper, and sends the people away with God's blessing.

The *deacons*—who are sometimes also called lectors—assist the pastor, one of them standing at his right, the other at his left. They read the two texts that are constitutive of the eucharistic liturgy: 1 Corinthians 11.21-29[25] and John 6.47-63 (after this second reading the lector kisses the gospel). After the reading of the epistle they say, together with the assembly, "Glory to you, Lord," while in preparation for the reading of the gospel they give the traditional greeting, "The Lord be with you," and receive the reply, "And with your spirit." Last, but not least, the deacons bring the eucharistic species and distribute them to the faithful, who remain seated in their pews.

Finally, the "liturgy" of the *people* (we are using liturgy in the sense given the term by Clement of Rome[26]) is likewise full and rich. After all, according to the teaching of Zwingli, the assembled Church becomes by means of the eucharistic celebration, the very body of Christ. The people with their "Amen" make their own the prayers said in their name. They join the deacons in responding to the reading of the epistle with the acclamation, "Glory to you, Lord," and before the reading of the gospel they answer the lector's greeting with their "And with your spirit." The men on one side of the church and the women on the other recite alternately (this kind of antiphonal singing is characteristic of the eucharistic liturgy that Zwingli wanted) the Gloria, the Apostles' Creed and Psalm 112, all of which the pastor has intoned. At communion the faithful serve themselves from the unleavened bread which the deacons present to them in wooden bowls.[27] We may add, finally, that the people kneel for the prayers.

Such is the liturgical action of the community as Zwingli wanted it to be; this is what he planned should be introduced at Zürich on Easter day 1525. He did not succeed completely. The municipal councils of the city did not want to have the people overly involved in the liturgical action; consequently the alternating recitations by men and women, as well as the other antiphonal forms, were dropped in favor of recitations or antiphonal singing involving only the pastor and deacons.

And yet this partial frustration of the reformer's intentions does not lessen the high quality and interest of his liturgical program, which was devised to turn the liturgical assembly into a community fully involved in the praise, jubilation and thanksgiving of the celebration.[28] I would even go so far as to maintain that we may legitimately ask whether Zwingli's eucharistic *liturgy* really requires Zwingli's eucharistic *theology*. And I think we may well answer in the negative: the liturgy of Zürich would be completely compatible with a much "higher" eucharistic doctrine than the one generally attributed to the Zürich reformer (wrongly attributed to him, say the experts on Zwingli[29]).

The Calvinist version of Reformed worship likewise aims at forming "a celebrating community."[30] Zwingli spoke of thanksgiving and jubilation. Calvin, for his part, also speaks of joy: "Not without reason does the Holy Spirit so carefully exhort us in the holy scriptures to rejoice in God and to order all our other joys to this one as to its true goal."[31] Yet how different the atmosphere is in the liturgy of Calvin! Teachings, exhortations, admonitions, penitential and doctrinal warnings, and bits of catechetics almost strangle the element of thanksgiving in the liturgy—at least by the norms of modern liturgical taste. Twenty years later, when the Second Helvetic Confession says the prayers must not be too long "so that the greater part of the time during sacred assemblies may be given over to the exposition of Gospel teaching,"[32] it seems to be describing worship at Geneva rather than at Zürich, even though its author was Bullinger, chief pastor at Zürich.

At Geneva, and wherever the Genevan tradition (which we are describing here solely from the viewpoint of the *communal* character of its worship) has become traditional, there are, as at Zürich, three distinct "liturgies": that of the pastor, that of the deacons, and that of the people. We may observe, first of all, that by comparison with Zürich the liturgy of the word is more structured. The *pastor*, who presides over the entire divine service, stands at the communion table and invokes the presence of God. He himself says all the prayers, including the "Amen."[33] He directs the ceremony of public repentance and gives the absolution to the people. He then reads the scriptures and, from the pulpit, preaches the sermon. Finally he blesses the congregation and dismisses it. On days when there is no eucharistic service, he also recites the Apostles' Creed and the Lord's Prayer.

The *deacons* have essentially two functions: they distribute the chalice after having received from it themselves (after the pastor, who receives communion first).[34] Their other function is to take up the collection[35] that renders possible the service activities of the Church and meets the administrative needs of the community.[36]

On days when the Supper is not celebrated, the chief function of the *people* is to be the *ecclesia docta*, or "Church that receives instruction," while their formal liturgical participation is reduced to the singing of a few psalms and the Decalogue. On days when the Supper is celebrated, their role is more varied. It is the people who sing the Lord's Prayer and the Apostles' Creed (both in verse form). As at Zürich, they kneel for the prayers. The deacons do not, as in the liturgy of Zwingli, come to distribute the species to the faithful as the latter remain seated in their pews; rather, the faithful approach the holy table where the pastor gives them the (leavened) bread, and the deacon gives them the cup of blessing.

Whereas Zwingli eliminated from the liturgy the kind of singing hitherto customary and replaced it not by canticles but by the kind of alternating recitations we have already mentioned,[37] the Geneva model prefers a people who sing rather than speak. What they sing is texts from scripture or the Apostles' Creed which faithfully sums up the teaching of the word of God. Here, by way of example, is the verse form of the Apostles' Creed:

> I believe in God the Father almighty
> who created earth and the splendid heavens,
> and in his only Son, Jesus Christ,
> our Lord: conceived by the Holy Spirit,
> and born of Mary wholly Virgin;
> unjustly caused to suffer under Pilate,
> crucified, dead upon the cross,
> entombed, descended into hell;
> from death he took back his life on the third day
> and ascended to the heavenly dwelling place,
> where he sits at the right hand of the Father,

the eternal Father who is almighty and rules all things.
From there he will come again to earth
to judge the living and the dead as well.
In the Holy Spirit my faith is firmly placed;
I believe in the holy and catholic Church;
a true union, shared by all,
between the saints and the faithful;
the full forgiveness of our sins
and the resurrection of the flesh.
Finally, I believe in eternal life.
Such is my faith, and I wish to die in the same.[38]

At this point, we really should follow the course of these two liturgies through the subsequent history of the Reformed Church, but this would take us too far afield. I shall therefore limit myself to a few quite summary reflections.

If my information is correct, the Zürich tradition soon lost its vitality. There were two main reasons for this. First, there was the refusal of the political authorities to permit the alternating recitals and antiphonal singing of men and women. As a result, all of the properly communal elements in the liturgy were clericalized, since the alternation of men and women became an alternation of pastor and deacons. The congregation was thus reduced to complete silence,[39] since the liturgy of Zürich had already eliminated the singing of psalms and canticles by the assembly.

There was a second, and more theological, reason: the extreme infrequency of the celebration of the eucharist (four times a year!), which prevented the people from acquiring a real knowledge of the liturgy. Yet if a liturgy is to be truly the action of the community, then those who celebrate it must be familiar with it and, indeed, know it very well.

The liturgy of Geneva, on the other hand, became classic and was regularly celebrated. But its very regularity also made its limitations stand out clearly. Three noteworthy efforts have been made to bring about the needed changes. All three have aimed at increasing the participation of the faithful. First of all, at the beginning of the eighteenth century, there was the proposed Liturgy of Neuchâtel, which was composed or inspired by Jean-Frédéric Ostervald,[40] who has rightly been called the second reformer of Neuchâtel. He said: "The people should not be present at the service as mere listeners or spectators, nor should they follow in a purely mental way what the ministers of the Church say; rather, they too must have a speaking part."[41] Ostervald's effort deserves the greatest respect, even if it did not fully attain the goal it set for itself.

A second effort to infuse new life into the Reformed liturgy is connected with the name of Eugène Bersier.[42] In large measure he made his own the program drawn up by Ostervald, but, like Ostervald, he was not able to strip the traditional Reformed liturgy of its highly clerical character. The third attempt at liturgical reform is the one we are presently engaged in, as the result especially of initiatives taken by the Vaudois group, *Eglise et Liturgie*, and by the Taizé Community. This third attempt has a great chance of succeeding, and this for four reasons.

First, and perhaps foremost, because the problem has at last been tackled from the proper angle, namely, with the problem of the frequency of eucharistic celebration as the starting point. The eucharist must be given back its place as the climax of the Sunday liturgy. It is the renewal of the sacramental life that will make possible an effective renewal of the communal character of the liturgy.

The second reason for hope is that the effort to renew the Reformed liturgy—at least in the French and English speaking worlds—follows in the wake of the biblical, patristic and liturgical renewals to be found in all the Western Churches. The effort also benefits by the very important impulse given by Vatican II, which has made its own most of seven requirements listed at the beginning of this paper.

A further important reason is that the confessional Churches are, explicitly or implicitly, exchanging experiences and programs in their common quest for a greater fidelity. A very important factor in frustrating the efforts of Ostervald and Bersier is that what they were pushing seemed "Catholic," and people wanted to assert their confessional uniqueness in a form of worship that was as distinct as possible from the worship of the other confessional Churches. This was true on both sides of the line, of course. This reflex of fear or revulsion—"But that's Catholic!" or "That's Protestant!"—has still not completely disappeared, but it has weakened sufficiently that it no longer sabotages projects for liturgical change that are moving in the direction of the great "catholic" tradition.

Finally, if even among us the communal character of the liturgy is gradually finding better expression, one reason is that dechristianization has reduced the number of participants in public worship. Those who do participate are people who are ready to *take an active part* in the celebration. As long as attendance at worship and the taking of eucharistic communion were duties imposed by ecclesiastical discipline, that is, as long as the "faithful" were forced to attend services (as was the case, for example, in the cantonal Protestant Churches of Switzerland), it was still possible to treat them as an *ecclesia docta* but not as an *ecclesia celebrans*. *Pastoral* conditions, then, are no longer those that prevented the Reformers, and J.F. Ostervald and E. Bersier at a later time, from celebrating the liturgy in the way they desired and the way it should be celebrated.

Pastoral conditions today are such that we can expect of the faithful the authentic involvement in the liturgy which is a condition for rediscovering the communal character of public worship.[43] The fact that these conditions are also found today at the more vital levels of the Roman Catholic Church, the Anglican Church and the Lutheran Churches is an added reason for hope, since the liturgical effort is closely connected with the efforts made in behalf of the *unitatis redintegratio*, "the restoration of unity." This is all the more true since illicit liturgical improvisations are quickly running out of steam and are, in any case, very often a sign that pastors or priests are forgetting that the worship over which they are called to preside is not their own but belongs to the Church.

Constantin ANDRONIKOF

Assembly and Body of Christ: Identity or Distinction

St. Ephraem offers us a bit of very sound advice when he tells us to be believers "without delving curiously into the utterly divine and holy doctrine which this faith teaches us." Jeanne Léon Bloy offers a shrewd definition of this kind of curiosity: "The attempt to gain knowledge of the original instead of being content with the image."

Nonetheless, I shall not follow the bidding of this master of prayer, and I leave it to your wisdom to decide whether I am indulging in a curiosity that is imprudent even if it be not out of place here.

For, as a matter of fact, eucharistic theology and ecclesiology (especially that dealing with the "Mystical Body"), both of them drawing their sustenance from the reality given us in the liturgy, confront us with a contradiction that will not leave the mind at peace.

13

The contradiction can be set forth in logical form:

Thesis A: 1) The assembly is the Church; but
2) the Church is the Body of Christ, and
3) the assembly partakes of the Body.

Therefore a) the assembly partakes of the Church, that is,
b) of itself.

In the case of this Thesis A we are led to conclude that there is no transformation (*metochē*) of the assembly into the Body, since change is a passage from one entelechy or "act" to another and since the assembly, being already the other, cannot *become* the Body by participation in a whole which it already is. There is therefore no communion or partaking at all, inasmuch as the likeness (*homoiōma*) or identity (*tautotēs*) of which the Fathers speak exists prior to the eucharistic action. All that is left is a static tautology which is completely unexplainable and deprives liturgical action of all power and meaning, since it reduces it to an autophagy or eating of the self, something blasphemous, something even sillier than it is heretical, something devoid of even the slightest symbolic value.

Let us now turn to

Thesis B: 1) The assembly partakes of the Body;
2) it thereby *becomes* the Church–Body.

From this it follows that the assembly looks to the Church as its ultimate state and that in itself it is only a process for attaining this goal. It also follows that prior to the eucharist the assembly is not the Church–Body; that in the eucharist it becomes and is the Church–Body; and that after the eucharist it begins a new phase in which it is once again not the Church–Body prior to the following eucharist.

Thesis A is absurd and can be rejected without any difficulty, even of a logical kind. Thesis B, however, implies some very difficult problems. These can be glimpsed in the conclusions just drawn.

As a consequence of all this, we are led to look a little more closely at what effectively happens to the assembly as it celebrates its liturgy.

On the one hand, we can say, with Florovsky among others, that "in the eucharistic prayer the Church comtemplates itself, and conceives of itself, as the one, integral Body of Christ."[1] The writer is here relying especially on the well-known interpretation that Simeon of Thessalonica gave of the prothesis: "In the divine figure and action of the holy proskomide we see Jesus himself after a fashion, and we contemplate the one Church. . . . There is a great mystery here. . . . God among men and God among the gods who have received deification from him who is true God by nature. . . . The future kingdom is here, and the revelation of eternal life."[2]

Before Simeon, all the Fathers who discuss participation (*metoche, koinonia, communio, communicatio*, etc.) are in agreement that the holy sacraments establish the Church and give it its unity. Tertullian, for example, says that due to these sacraments "we are a single Church."[3] Or Cyprian: the Church is "the sacrament of unity" or "of unanimity."[4] Or Augustine who, citing 1 Corinthians 10.17 ("We are all a single body because we all participate in this single bread"), says: "If you receive as you should, you are what you receive."[5] St. Hilary had already said in quite realistic language: "He [Christ] is in us by reason of his flesh, and we are in him; what we are is in God along with him"[6]; or again: "The sacrament of the flesh and blood truly make us one in nature (*naturalis unitas*)."[7]

John Chrysostom cites 1 Corinthians 10.16 and contrasts *metoche* with *koinonia* in order to make clearer the reality of the union effected:

"'Is not the bread we break a communion in the body of Christ?' Why does he [St. Paul] speak of 'communion' (*koinonia*) and not of 'participation' (*metoche*)? Because he wants . . . to show how close the union is (*pollen ten synapheian*). We do not simply participate and take a part (*metechein*); we commune with him in unity (*toi henousthai koinonoumen*). But Paul goes on to say: 'since the bread is one, we who are many are a single body' (1 Cor 10.17). Why speak any longer simply of 'communion'? He says: we are this very body. After all, what is the bread? It is the body of Christ. And what do the communicants become? They become the body of Christ."[8]

Chrysostom had also asserted: "We become a single mass with him, a single body of Christ, and a single flesh."[9]

The expressions used by Cyril of Alexandria are no less forceful than those of Chrysostom: "We have become concorporeal with him and with one another (*heautoi syssomous kai allelois*). This is why the Church is called the Body of Christ, and each of us his members (Eph

5.23). Since we are all united to the one Christ by means of his sacred body . . . we should think of our members as belonging more to him than to us."[10]

"We become concorporeal with him through reception of the mystical eulogy [i.e., the eucharist]."[11] Citing John 6.56, "He who eats my flesh . . . dwells in me and I in him," Cyril expresses his thought even more precisely: "Christ does not say that he is in us by a relation of an affective kind, but by physical participation (*kata methexin physi-ken*)."[12]

Allow me to refer again to this commentary of Cyril on John because it emphasizes the role the Spirit plays in the *koinonia* with God and because this kind of emphasis is not very often found in theology: "When we receive into ourselves the same unique Spirit . . . we are as it were mingled with one another and with God. . . . Just as the power of the sacred flesh renders its recipients concorporeal with one another, so too, in my view, the one Spirit who comes to dwell in all, brings all into a spiritual oneness."[13] Cyril concludes: "We are all one in the Father and the Son and the Holy Spirit . . . by an identity of nature . . . and by communion in the sacred flesh of Christ and by communion in the one Holy Spirit."[14]

Cyril of Jerusalem, in his turn, does not hesitate to say that "because we have participated in the body and blood of Christ . . . we become Christ-bearers. . . . According to Blessed Peter, 'we become sharers in the divine nature' (*theias koinonoi physeos*)."[15]

As is his custom, St. John Damascene states things very precisely. Through the eucharist, he says, the assembly "participates in the two natures: corporeally in the body, spiritually in the divinity (*ton duo physeon metechomen, tou somatos somatikos, tes theotetos pneumatikos*)."[16] Finally, it is this that constitutes the Church: "We call the eucharist a *koinonia*, and that is what it truly is, since through it we are in communion with Christ."[17]

All this, then, is solidly established fact. On the other hand, we are faced with the paradox that the liturgy which the assembly celebrates does not look at things this way at all, or rather that it adopts an entirely different perspective. The liturgy thinks of *metoche* and *koinonia* not as a goal already reached and a state bringing satisfaction with it, but as an eschatological and soteriological *movement* toward a fulfillment still to come. The eucharistic liturgy is a continual, never

16

finished, bringing of Christ to his fullness (Eph 4. 13). The assembly is part of a *process* whereby the Body gradually reaches completion so that the Head may *become* all in all through the action of the Holy Spirit and in accordance with the *plan* of salvation. The assembly effects the sacrament of unity *in-its-becoming*, or the very thing which is the object of the Son's prayer: "that they may become perfectly one (*ut sint consummati in unum; hina ōsin teteleiōmenoi eis hen*)" (Jn 17.23), and it does so by the power of the Spirit.

In addition, a whole series of Fathers and Doctors of the Church who have analyzed the liturgy in a more detailed way conceive it precisely as what we have been saying it is: as the unfolding of the mystery of the Church, as an inauguration and development of new life, so as to bring about the *eschaton* and the *teleiotēs*.[18] The eucharist with its eschatological orientation is the paschal mystery, that is, the *passage* from the old to the new, the transformation of the old Adam into the glorified Church of the Body, the progressive growth of god-manhood to the full stature of Christ. That is why the eucharist is both memorial and prophecy, the experience of the here-and-now assembly and the anticipation of the Church of the final age. "Receive me as a participant in your mystical supper today" and "Receive us all into your kingdom" (Anaphora of St. Basil).

The theologians of the liturgy constantly return to this point: "an image of the ineffable plan carried out by Christ"[19]; "the mystery that recapitulates the entire economy of salvation."[20]

Given this perspective, Palamas is correct in not separating the eucharist from baptism: these basic sacraments "recapitulate the entire economy of the God-man."[21] And for Cabasilas the eucharist "is the one mystery that completes all the other sacraments . . . since these cannot complete the initiation apart from the eucharist."[22]

We must note, however—and here we find a suggestion of our initial contradiction—that Cabasilas unhesitatingly makes his own the traditional doctrine regarding the essence of the eucharistic mystery: "The [holy] mysteries signify the Church, again, because the Church is 'the body of Christ' and because [the faithful] are 'the members of Christ' (1 Cor 12.27)." In a well-known passage Cabasilas goes on to describe the reality in precise terms: "The Church is signified (*sēmainetai*) in the mysteries, not as in symbols (*en symbolois*), but as the members are signified in the heart . . . as the branches are signified in the vine. For there is here not simply a community in name nor a likeness of analogy, but there is a real identity (*ou gar onomatos entautha koinōnia, monon ē analogias homoiotēs, alla pragmatos taut-otēs*)."[23]

But this "real identity" between the Church and the Body of Christ in the eucharist is not quite coextensive with the *participation* of the assembly in the ongoing soteriological process. By its eucharistic action, in which time is transcended, the assembly actualizes the economy and brings it into a purer state, but it does not bring the economy to its final perfection in the age of the kingdom. The economy continues to unfold; it remains as a work to be done. The prayer of the assembly carefully takes this fact into account, both in its semantic content and in its grammatical structure. "Behold, the mystery of your economy is fulfilled, as far as this is in our power. We have remembered your death; we have seen the figure (*typon*) of your resurrection; we have been filled with your infinite life; we have enjoyed inexhaustible happiness which we pray you will judge us worthy to possess *in the age to come*."[24]

In other words, though "the powers of hell shall not prevail" against the Church, the assembly nonetheless prays for the Church to reach its fulfillment in eternity. We may recall how Irenaeus described this economy of salvation, which is the human person's progressive entry into communion with God.[25] For (he says) salvation is communion with God through Christ in the Spirit.[26] There is but a single redemptive sacrifice of the Lamb, but our own sacrifice must be constantly repeated by the assembly until all sacrifices are done away with. "[God] says that this bread, which is part of his creation, is his body that *gives growth* to our bodies," as members of the Church of the pleroma. That is why "as often as the commemoration is celebrated, the work of redemption is accomplished (*quoties . . . commemoratio celebratur, opus . . . redemptionis exercetur*)."[27]

But it is in virtue of the action of the acting Church (*ex opera operantis Ecclesiae*) that the assembly celebrates its eucharist as the seed of redemption, as the power that produces incorruptibility, as the dynamic source of deification by the Spirit and the Word—this eucharist which "enables us to bear fruit in the form of good works (*karpophorountas en ergois agathois*),"[28] because it is "the food of salvation"[29] and "the hope of everlasting resurrection."[30] The community is thereby involved, in view of eternity (*ad aeternitatem*), in that process of Christian rebirth which St. Leo the Great sums up in lapidary form: "Just as the Lord became our flesh by being born, so we for our part have become his body by being reborn."[31]

"Let the grace of the Holy Spirit come upon us and upon this offering . . . so that this bread may become the holy body . . . and this cup the precious blood of our Lord Jesus Christ, and that it may be for whoever eats and drinks . . . the great *hope of resurrection* from the dead, the salvation of soul and body, and a *new life in the kingdom* . . . and that we may come to enjoy the future blessings which do not pass away."[32]

Consequently the Fathers use terms, familiar to all of us, that bring out the *inchoative* nature and dynamic character of the eucharistic action done by the assembly: *symbolon, eikōn, antitypon* (*Didascalia, Didache, Apostolic Constitutions*), *phainomenon* of the flesh and blood (Cyril of Jerusalem and Macarius of Egypt), when referring to the gifts; *pharmakon uthanasias* or *antidotos tou me apothanein* (Ignatius of Antioch), *sperma tes athanasias* (Cyril of Alexandria), *pharmakon zoes* (Euchology of Serapion of Thmuis), when referring to communion, which brings about *koinonia, synaxis* (Denis the Areopagite, John Chrysostom, and others), or simply *life* (Ambrose, Cabasilas). "The food [i.e., the sacrament] is given spiritually (*pneumatikos*) . . . that it may serve spiritually (*pneumatikos*) as a safeguard for resurrection to eternal life."[33]

This, then—and not the doctrine of the Church as Body—is the content of the liturgical texts; what the assembly says in prayer makes no reference to this doctrine. And while the effect of the economy of Christ (as stated by Cabasilas in his summary of tradition) is "nothing else than the descent of the Holy Spirit on the Church,"[34] the epiclesis over the assembly asks only for "the *first-fruits* of the inheritance *to come*, the *beginning* of the eternal blessings" (Anaphora of St. Basil).

Just as the assembly *commemorates* in the anaphora an event that has not yet taken place in time (namely, the parousia), so also it celebrates in the midst of our present temporal duration a being, an existence, that is not only still to come but is eternal by nature, namely, the kingdom. The assembly experiences in time and space a figure of itself, the model of which is transcendent. During the time of the eucharist the assembly is the Church; it exercises a royal priesthood; it asserts that it is the flock of the One Shepherd, the communion of saintly celebrants gathered around the One High Priest, the temple of the Holy Spirit in which the Father's will is done on earth as it is in heaven.

But the assembly does this *in symbol*. For in fact the assembly remains in the world and is subject to the categories of space and time. It is not in fact coextensive with the Spouse of Christ who has reached full stature, nor with the universal and eternal Jerusalem. All the members of the assembly will in fact die some day. The assembly is still located within history; it still has a destiny to fulfill, a temporal duration to live through. It is not holy, it is not incorruptible, and it is risen only in hope, that is, *potentially*. It has only "the guarantee of the Spirit," it is only "the first-fruits of creation."[35] It does not yet share in "the glorious freedom of the children of God." The Spirit must still "intercede for the saints"; these are indeed "called according to the plan of God," but the plan had not yet been implemented on a universal scale. The assembly must still—and repeatedly—gather to pray and groan "while awaiting adoption." In addition, "it is not in his very nature that the Spirit descends" on the eucharistic assembly; rather it is a power emanating from him that descends to carry out everything and bring it to fulfillment."[36]

Certainly, as St. Paul says, we have been saved, but only in hope.[37] In every assembly, the Church must still "wait perseveringly" for "the measure" to be filled up, so that she may finallly become herself. At that future moment and after delays which even the God-man cannot know but which he nonetheless will crown at the *last* judgment, the Church and the assembly will be coextensive, and the mystical marriage will take place.

In other words, through the sacrament and in prayer the Church experiences the *eschatological* tension proper to the Church. The Church is what the assembly aims at being. By communion in eternal life the assembly is the *symbol here and now* of the Church . . . for a while. But this "while" is the time of the liturgy, that is, a time which is itself symbolic of the promised eternity. Thus our contradiction assembly–Church, Church–Body of Christ, is resolved, or, better, transcended, in the *eschaton*.

The work (*ergon*) that is the liturgy (*leitourgia = laou ergon =* work done by the people) is, of course, utterly real, while nonetheless being symbolic in the sense I have indicated (the dichotomy between realism and symbolism, as Berengarius conceived it and the Roman Council of 1059 condemned it—though in the name of a contrary and equally exaggerated dualism—is foreign to the Orthodox tradition). But this work, though real, is imperfect in relation to the Church in its fullness: the temple wherein the work is carried on is not yet the Lord himself; the assembly is not yet the city wherein stands "the throne of God and the Lamb"; the worship it offers is not yet that of "the marriage supper of the Lamb" (Rev. 21.22; 22.1; 19.9). Indeed "the time is near" (Rev. 22.10), but the assembly is still living in *the time of the coming* or drawing near, and those who are holy must continue to be holy (cf. Rev. 22.11).

The Church is indeed the Spouse, but she herself must "prepare herself" and "be clothed with fine linen, pure and bright," which is "the righteous deeds of the saints" (Rev. 19.7-8). The assembly makes this preparation of the Church a present reality by carrying out, at a moment in time, mysteries laden with eternity.

In *this* sense, then, it is legitimate to see a distinction between the assembly and the Church defined as Body of Christ. The distinction or difference is due to the fact that the assembly is the Church only in the stage of becoming and not in the eternity of resurrection and deification. By sharing in the Body and Blood and thus rendering its members "one in body and one in blood" with Christ,[38] the assembly constantly actualizes—i.e., makes real and effective here and now—the spiritualization of its being, but this is precisely a process that must constantly be repeated and renewed because it is incomplete by comparison with the perfection of the God-man whose incarnation was effected by the Spirit; it is a process that will be complete only in the "moment" of eternity when that perfection is attained.

This difference is itself a mystery; it expresses an ontological opposition (similar, for example, to that involved in the coexistence within us of sin and the kingdom). It can, however, be made more accessible to the mind if we compare it with the symbolism which creates a gap between the immanent *typos* or *antitypon* or *eikon*, on the one side, and, on the other, the Son who sits at the Father's right hand. At the farthest limits of symbolism (limits reached in every celebration of the eucharist) all distance is eliminated; immanence and transcendence fuse; the assembly becomes the Church. The Church, in turn, be-

21

comes the kingdom. But the assembly does not remain at this farthest limit. I am tempted to say that the assembly experiences this boundary situation *mystikos* and *pneumatikos* (according to the patristic tradition), but not *physikos* (despite some expressions used by the Fathers). The flesh of the assembly is not risen; its entire being, along with its entire historical development (still incomplete), is only in movement toward deification. And yet this being is already transformed.

The human mind cannot escape the inner wrenching which the analysis of the contradiction or conflict produces in it, because in making the analysis the mind necessarily remains under the sway of a dialectic whose terms are time and eternity. More precisely, the two terms with which the dialectic must work are, on the one hand, the unfolding duration within which the assembly is necessarily located and which has death for its end, and, on the other hand, the fullness of time that comes at the end of the entire *kairos* which it is the Church's task to "make the most of" (Eph 5.16): the fullness of time when the Church will receive "all the fulness of God" (Eph 3.19), the Day of God when all things will be made new and time will be abolished in the eternal existence which time symbolizes by means of the liturgy. The assembly, meanwhile, are those who are "waiting for and hastening the coming of the day of God. . . . according to his promise"(2 Pet 3.12-13).

Consequently, we must use our present category of corruptible time in order to grasp the transtemporal symbolism of ecclesial communion with the Source of Life. In the anamnesis of the liturgy the assembly recapitulates past and present, and locates and justifies them in and by the future. But this terminology, which seems clear enough, is in fact misleading and has no symbolic value, since it is entirely subordinate to the logical dimensions of time, that is, by definition, to finite dimensions, whereas participation in the Body and Blood is both spiritually and corporeally a transtemporal participation. The communion (*metoche*) of the assembly does have an immanent aspect, but its *koinonia* is with transcendence by means of a transformation (*metabole*), since it makes us "sharers of the divine nature" and since this divine nature is eternal in its being, or, in the terminology of logic, it is extratemporal, metatemporal, or, to speak most exactly, atemporal.

As envisaged in the plenitude it will have in the final age, that is to say, as envisaged with its Head and all its members, the Church is the eternal ideal for which the assembly strives. The assembly symbolizes this Church in time (both linear and liturgical) as well as in space (since the assembly constitutes a sacred space, all the more so when it is in a church).

Such reflections inevitably raise a number of difficult problems, especially the problem of the duration of the transformation of the assembly into the Church, i.e., into the Body of Christ (everyone knows of the controversies in the West on the permanent or temporary character of the transubstantiated species). If we follow the argument I have been proposing, we will be led to conclude that the *metabole* is only an instant in duration. Otherwise, the assembly would coincide in a definitive, i.e., eternal and infinite, way with the Church. Then we would be back in the absurd contradiction of an "autoeucharist." This provisional aspect of communion may shock a particular kind of pious sensibility, but it seems nonetheless clearly suggested by the texts of the Bible, the liturgy and the Fathers, some of which have been cited.

Once again, if at the consummation of all things the Church is in fact the Body of Christ and the Bride of the Lamb, this state of hers is the result of a *growth*. The assembly pursues this process of growth in a manner that is continuous as far as the cycles of liturgical time are concerned, but that is discontinuous in terms of historical time; in terms of the duration that ends in death the process is one of discrete acts. And, let me repeat, the process occurs *in symbol*. In this sense, the assembly is existentially a phenomenon, while the Church is essentially a noumenon—not in a transcendental sense (none of this has anything to do with Kant) but in an ideal (though not Platonic or gnostic) sense that is related to the Wisdom of God, to the incarnate Word, and to god-manhood.

Similar remarks must be made with regard to space. The Church can be compared with the continuum of the *saecula saeculorum* or endless ages, that is proper to the created order when it reaches its consummation, or to the cosmos of the heavenly Jerusalem. The assembly would then be the quantum of sacred space that symbolizes *the* Temple which is the Lord (Rev 21.22). Or again, we may borrow an analogy from wave mechanics and say that the assembly is a tridimensional particle that can be located in time (by its act of commemorating and by its existence here and now), but a particle allied with the immemorial wave that is the Church.

Putting the matter in christological and pneumatological terms, I would say that if the Church is the perfect Body of the God-man, the assembly is a stage of the communication of properties (*communicatio idiomatum*) to each of its members and to the Church as a whole, by assimilation to the model of divine humanity, i.e., the Son. In other words, the assembly brings the theanthropic energy to bear here and now by appropriating to itself the power of the Spirit. The Spirit is free, of course, to act when and where he chooses, but the assembly has the assurance of the promise that he will carry out the mystery of the deification of human nature through participation in the divine nature. The assembly thus brings the Church into being by causing it to become the Body of Christ.

The fact that the assembly commemorates this becoming of the Church and brings it to pass "now," shows that this becoming is incomplete. Consequently, each assembly *prepares* for the Church, that is, for what the assembly itself potentially is, or what it is by participation *sub specie aeternitatis* but not *naturaliter in aeternitate*. St. Cyril of Alexandria put it this way: "In receiving within us, both corporeally and spiritually, the true Son who is one in substance with the Father . . . we receive the glorious privilege of participating and communing in the supreme nature."[39]

The mystery of the assembly thus becomes (relatively) explicable only by reference to the goal toward which it is moving. The assembly is the eschatological movement by means of the participation of the celebrants here and now, toward the eternal and complete *koinōnia* and *klēronomia*. However, the distinction thus established between assembly and Church applies to each member, as far as his or her degree of sanctification or of deification by adoption is concerned. The members, as a group and individually, live in active expectation of the consummation of theanthropic fullness (the fullness of godmanhood), that state in which perichoresis (circuminsession) becomes, via the spiritual body, a genuine communion with the divine nature in whatever way God has in store for his image.

This gradual transformation is effected by assimilation of the "sacred mysteries" which transform the communicants (according, as we have already seen, to a constant teaching that runs from Augustine and Cyril of Jerusalem down to John Damascene and Cabasilas). Nonetheless, as we have also pointed out, this action is neither complete nor definitive in its effects. The assembly is the Church–Body of Christ only in its transtemporal "entelechy." It is not continuously identical with this Church in its present course through time nor in the earthly state of each of its members, since these must all die, and so on. This is what has led us to say that the assembly is the symbol of the Church and thus to justify the propositions of Thesis B which were our point of departure.

It is necessary here to point out the parallelism with the other "basic sacrament," namely, baptism. In baptism we are baptized into the death of Christ and we receive the anointing of the Holy Spirit. In the eucharist we share in the life of Christ and are reborn by the power of the Holy Spirit. The dialectic operative in baptism, as indicated by St. Paul, is operative in the eucharist as well. "If we have been united with him in a death like his, we *shall* certainly be united with him in a resurrection like his" (Rom 6.5). In other terms, "if . . . we were reconciled to God by the death of his Son, much more . . . shall we be saved by his life" (Rom 5.10). These two actions, "the death leading to resurrection" and "the lifegiving life," are the object of the anamnesis that embraces both past and future, just as they are the content of the hope which the community experiences, because it has "access to this grace in which we stand" and knows that "hope does not disappoint us, because God's love has been poured into our hearts through the Holy Spirit who has been given to us" (Rom 5.2, 5) in baptism and now in the eucharist. And if the individual dies alone, he or she is restored to life by the assembly in the Church.

In all this, however, we are dealing with a *hope*. "Hope" expresses very exactly the symbolic distance or eschatological tension between the assembly and Church. In the kingdom, on the other hand, once the fullness of Christ has been achieved, the Lord himself shares the meal with the assembly which *has become* the Church, his Body. All the "symbols" will then have completely, and permanently, acquired their integral ontological density.

As a conclusion to this exposition, which has perhaps been overly compresséd, it would be appropriate to show from the text of the liturgy that it is this tension (which is eschatological because it is soteriological) and not the claimed perfection of the Church–Body that forms the essential content of the assembly's prayer. But is such illustration really necessary? We know the text almost by heart. Nevertheless, for the sake of all possible completeness I shall remind you of a few passages. But, first, a brief reference to the cultic typology of the Letter to the Hebrews will help to clarify my purpose.

The liturgy of the former covenant had only "a shadow of the good things to come instead of the true form of these realities (*ouk auten ten eikona ton pragmaton*)." Therefore, it could "never, by the same sacrifices which are continually offered year after year, make perfect (*teteleiosai*) those who draw near. Otherwise, would they not have ceased to be offered? If the worshipers had once been cleansed," would their sanctification not have been complete (Heb 10.1-2)? When Christ comes, he "abolishes the first [kind of worship] in order to establish the second" (Heb 10.9). It is true, however, that this Old Testament typology is valid, once adaptations have been made (which is to say, in a certain degree), for the second form of worship.

In the latter we certainly possess "the true form (*auten ten eikona*)" of the realities, but we cannot say that we possess the eternal realities of this "true form." Just as the former worship is a type of the worship that replaces it, so the latter becomes the experiential symbol of the "realities," or, in other words, the dynamic process for attaining to these realities. This is precisely what the Letter to the Hebrews tells us. For although the text says that "by a single offering he [Christ] has perfected for all time those who are sanctified," it goes on to state a paradox which coincides exactly with the one that has been occupying our attention here: "Therefore, brethren, since we have confidence to *enter* the sanctuary by the blood of Jesus, by the new and living *way* which he *opened* (*enekainisen, initiavit*) for us through the curtain, that is, through his flesh . . . let us hold fast the confession of our *hope* . . . not neglecting to meet together (*ten episynagogen*) . . . but encouraging one another, and all the more as you see the Day drawing near" (Heb 10.14, 19-20, 23, 25).

Following the same typological parallel, we can say that "the outer tent" or "Holy Place" is comparable to the assembly in the transcended time and space of this world, while the inner tent or "Holy of Holies" is comparable to the Church in the eternity of the kingdom.

In this sense, we can say, with the Letter, that all this "is symbolic for the present age" (Heb 9.9)

A quick recall of the liturgical texts will make it clear that the assembly is located in the dimension of promise and hope, and not in the eternal pleroma of the Church, though this is symbolized here below. Here are some phrases from the Anaphora of St. Basil:

"Receive us all into your kingdom . . . cleanse us . . . and teach us to perform the holy [mystery] *(hagiosynēn)* in order that in receiving a portion of the gifts that have been consecrated to you *(tēn merida tōn hagiasmatōn sou)* we may be united to the holy Body and holy Blood of your Christ . . . and become the temple of your Holy Spirit. . . . Grant that until our final breath we may worthily receive a portion of your consecrated gifts as an *introduction* to eternal life and a favorable plea before the awesome judgment seat . . . so that we may share in your eternal blessings" (Prayer before the Our Father).

The same soteriological perspective is to be found in the thanksgiving. For example: "Set us on the right path . . . watch over our lives"(St. John Chrysostom). "You have made us worthy of participating in your mysteries" and not of "having become your Body." After communion, which we pray may "become for us faith unashamed, love without hypocrisy," etc., in our subsequent lives as sinful human beings who are trying to become holy, we sing: "The invisible Trinity has saved us." The verb here is in the past tense, as though salvation were a *fait accompli*. But then, in the litany, we go right on to pray: "Help us, save us!" In other words, we still need to be saved.

We also pray, even more specifically: "Let this entire day be perfect." For there is a danger that this day, the very day on which we have remembered the great Day, will not be perfect. "Let us put our whole life in Christ's hands": for we still have to live out our lives and they are not wholly and purely the life of Christ in us. In the prayer "behind the ambo" we ask: "Do not abandon us who hope in you," and before the dismissal we exclaim: "Glory to you, Christ God, our hope!": in other words, an abandonment remains possible (even if only during the inevitable moments of the death agony) and we can do nothing but hope.

"Here we have no lasting city, but we seek the city which is to come. Through him [Christ] then let us continually offer up a sacrifice of praise to God" (Heb 13.14-15).

27

Miguel ARRANZ

The Functions
of the Christian Assembly
in The Testament of Our Lord

"Testament or words which our Lord Jesus Christ spoke to his apostles after his resurrection from the dead, written down by Clement of Rome, a disciple of Peter, in eight books." This is the improbable title of the appendix, known as the *Clementine Octateuch,* to the Peshitta or Syriac Bible. However, only the first two books of the *Octateuch* contain this apocryphal testament of Jesus. A colophon at the end of the second book informs us that the *Testament* ends here: "End of the second book of Clement, translated from Greek into Syriac by James, an unworthy man, in the year 998 of the Greeks (687 of our calendar)."

Despite its bold title the work was not ranked with other and better known books on the liturgy, such as the *Didache of the Apostles,* the *Apostolic Tradition,* the *Didascalia,* or the *Apostolic Constitutions.* And

29

yet, as witness of a very ancient liturgical practice, the *Testament* deserved to be regarded more highly.

Modern liturgical scholars, however, have given the work a great deal of attention, chiefly because of its close relations with the *Apostolic Tradition*. In his edition of the latter Dom Bernard Botte frequently cites the Testament.[1] The late Father Jean-Michel Hanssens, in the two editions of his *La Liturgie d'Hippolyte*,[2] goes further and presents a Latin synopsis of the parallels between all the documents related to the *Tradition*; among these our *Testament* occupies an important place. We shall take these scholarly works into account throughout our presentation, but this essay is meant less as a new study of the *Testament* than as a simple and summary reading of the text from the viewpoint of ecclesiastical functions within the Christian assembly.

It is not possible here to take account of all that has been said about the *Testament*. Patrology manuals and specialized dictionaries will supply ample bibliography on the subject.[3]

By way of background we may recall simply that under one or other name the work exists in Syriac, Coptic, Arabic and Ethiopic versions. The Syriac version, in a manuscript preserved at Paris, was known to Renaudot[4] and de Lagarde[5] in the eighteenth and nineteenth centuries, respectively. However, it was the Syro-Catholic Patriarch Ignatius Ephraem II Rahmani who in 1899 published the Syriac text of the first two books of the *Octateuch* or, in other words, the complete *Testament*; he followed a codex preserved in Mosul and accompanied his edition with a Latin translation.[6]

The learned studies of A. Vööbus[7] and R.-G. Coquin[8] have done much to define, somewhat negatively, the critical value of Rahmani's edition, without, however, denying its importance. As far as the relations between the *Testament* and similar documents (*Didache, Didascalia, Apostolic Constitutions, Canons of Hippolytus*) are concerned, Rahmani himself took account of them in the introduction to his work, and no one since then has cast doubt on these relations. The date Rahmani assigned to the *Testament* is much less widely accepted. Intoxicated, it seems, by his discovery Rahmani regarded the work as dating from the second century; this was surely to make it far too old.

Two years later, F. X. Funk published an erudite book of over three hundred pages that was devoted entirely to a critical study of the *Testament*; he rejected Rahmani's dating of the work and assigned it to the fifth century.[9] Countless monographs were written on the *Testament*. Immediately after Rahmani's edition appeared, and before Funk published his study, many prestigious scholars such as Harnack, Baumstark, Ehrhard, Morin, and Parissot wrote on the subject—an indication of the immense interest the work has created.[10] But after Funk had published his seemingly definitive conclusions, interest in the *Testament* fell off. In 1913 F. Nau published a French translation of the entire *Octateuch*; we shall be using this translation as the basis of our summary.[11]

In 1905 Funk claimed that both the *Testament* and the *Apostolic Tradition* depend on the eighth book of the *Apostolic Constitutions*. The studies of Schwartz and Connolly have since restored the *Apostolic Tradition* to its proper place,[12] but the *Testament* has unfortunately been forgotten.

Funk's view, assigning the *Testament* to the fifth century, prevails today over Rahmani's opinion that the work originated in the second century. But not everyone accepts Funk's dating. Among Russian scholars M. Skaballanovich is not convinced by Funk's arguments and assigns the *Testament* to the third century[13]; N. Uspensky takes a more radical view: after comparing the arguments of Funk and Rahmani, he decides on the second century as the proper date.[14] The Rumanians[15] and the Greeks[16] follow Western scholars in accepting the fifth century.

In connection with the Nineteenth Liturgical Week at St.-Serge I myself had occasion to study a specific point in the *Testament*: the deacon's instructions or exhortations before the anaphora.[17] It seems clear to me from my research that the two basic views on the date of the *Testament* are not incompatible, for, while the final redaction of the document took place in the fourth or fifth century (as indicated by enough points of internal criticism), yet the anaphora itself, as well as the general structure of the Mass, represent a stage of development that relates them closely to the eucharist in the *Apostolic Tradition*. An anaphora without a *Sanctus* and intercessions belongs to an archaic form of the eucharist; according to L. Bouyer, such a form antedates the fusion of the eucharist celebrated in house churches with prayers deriving from the synagogue.[18] Such a eucharist is certainly older than the one we find in the *Apostolic Constitutions*; the latter belongs to the group of fourth-century anaphoras of the Antiochene type.

If we compare the *Testament* and the *Apostolic Tradition* as a whole we will doubtless discover that from its twentieth chapter on the *Testament* follows the *Apostolic Tradition* very closely. Even here, however, the *Testament* adds new expansions and texts that explain certain overly concise passages of the *Apostolic Tradition*, though it does not indulge in the degree of elaboration that makes the eighth book of the *Apostolic Constitutions* an original work.

The main subject of the *Testament* is the constitution or order of the Church as a whole. Ordinations and baptism, however, receive the lion's share of attention, as is the case in the *Apostolic Tradition* as well. The eucharist is described only in connection with the ordination of a bishop or the participation of the newly baptized in the mysteries.

There is an introduction consisting of fourteen short chapters; this is quite original, and there is no trace of it in the *Tradition*. It shows the Lord conversing with the apostles and prophesying to them what the life of the disciples will be like. The prophecy resembles the gospels rather than the Apocalypse; it puts no emphasis on the extraordinary, and we can scarcely regard it as belonging to the genre of "catastrophe" writing. Despite his boldness in having the Lord speak in the first person, the author of this section of the *Testament* evidences a degree of prudence that is uncommon in this type of apocrypha. He adds little or nothing to the gospels, and he departs very little from them. This disposes us to accord him a degree of trustworthiness that the literary genre he has chosen would tend to make us refuse him.

In chapters 15 and 16,[19] the apostles (Peter, John, Thomas, Matthew, Andrew, Matthias, and the others) and the devout women (Martha, Mary, and Salome) question the Lord about the responsibilities and ministries to be established in the Church which they are to spread. This is a pious strategem meant to justify the claim to apostolicity which documents of this genre make: *Didache, Tradition, Didascalia, Constitutions*. The apostles ask questions of the Lord and pass on his answers to us via Clement who acts as secretary. It is important here to note the role played by the women; it helps us understand the role of widows and deaconesses in the early Church. These women doubtless obeyed to the letter Paul's injunction that "women should keep silent in the churches" (1 Cor 14.31), but though they were silent, they were not therefore inactive.

In chapter 17,[20] the Lord answers the disciples' question about the ecclesiastical rule (QONUNO 'IDTONOIO) governing the ordination and appointment of the person who is to preside over a Church. The whole of the next chapter (18) is an exhortation to preserve a double *arcanum* (or secrecy). Some of the things Jesus will reveal are reserved to ministers alone; the rest is meant for the entire Church but not for those outside the Church. As a matter of fact, the subsequent chapters do not distinguish between what is reserved to ministers and what is meant for the Church at large, since all the ordinations are performed in public and with the participation of the people. The only secrecy that is maintained seems to be secrecy with regard to nonbelievers.

Chapter 19[21] is the last that is proper to the *Testament*; chapter 20 corresponds to chapter 1 of the *Tradition*. Chapter 19 (with the Lord still speaking) explains the structure of the church building. Neither the building nor the liturgy celebrated in it can be very old. There is already mention of a heavenly liturgy. The chapter clearly suggests the influence of the liturgy of the Temple, or rather the liturgy of Exodus and Leviticus, which the Christians of the fourth century had rediscovered. Modern critics who date the *Testament* in the fifth century are certainly correct if this chapter is taken as the sole norm for judgment. We believe, however, that other elements in the *Testament* are much older. One merit of chapter 19 is that it tells us of the places occupied in each church by ministers, faithful and catechumens.

From chapter 20[22] to chapter 47, which is the last in the first book of the Syriac *Testament* (other versions do not divide the *Testament* into two books), the author deals with the ecclesiastical functions or ministries of bishops, priests, deacons, confessors, widows, subdeacons, readers, and virgins. In this section, the *Testament* follows the *Tradition* (chapters 2–14[23]) closely and is in agreement as well with the parallel documents: the *Canons of Hippolytus*, the eighth book of the *Constitutions*, and the *Epitome* or *Constitutions through Hippolytus*. I mentioned earlier J.-M. Hanssens' synoptic tables for all these documents.[24] Similar tables had already been drawn up by the Anglican bishop, Arthur Maclean, one of the English translators of the *Testament*.[25] In addition to documents closely related to the *Tradition*, Maclean also studies the documents related to the *Didache* and to the document known as the *Apostolic Church Order*.

The second book of the *Testament*, the beginning of which corresponds to chapter 15 of the *Tradition*,[26] is a treatise on the catechumenate, baptism, and the first steps taken by the new Christians.

In this paper we shall be examining the second part of the first book, which deals especially with ministries. We shall not neglect interesting details scattered throughout the second book, but neither shall we simply combine the data from the first and second books, since it is possible to observe some points that are incompatible and may suggest a diversity of sources. Our purpose is to draw as clear a picture as we can of the various people whom the *Testament* speaks of as being in the service of the community. We shall not fail to note what the *Tradition* and other parallel documents have to say on certain points, especially when the *Testament* seems obscure. On the other hand, we also wish to bring out the original, and sometimes eccentric, content of a document that we have chosen as our subject precisely because of its originality. This is why we shall avoid any unnecessary recourse to the *Tradition*.

It seems clearly proven that the *Testament* derives from the *Tradition*; evidently, too, the final redaction of the *Testament* must be assigned to the fourth or fifth century (because of certain passages, e.g., chapter 19 on the church building). It is surprising, nonetheless, that the many archaisms in the document seem not to have been a problem for the final editor. In any case, liturgists are not displeased that a document whose content is ancient should be of such a relatively recent date. This is because the document bears witness to a longer survival than expected of liturgical rites and usages which are quite primitive at first sight and which overturn not a few preconceived ideas on the liturgical (and theological) mentality of Christians in the first centuries.

In our presentation we shall avoid, on the one hand, a mere series of quotations from the text, since the result would be a rather wearisome anthology, and, on the other, an overly elaborate summary of the author's thought. In general, we shall give an abridged version of F. Nau's *Octateuch,* but we shall also have before us at all times Patriarch Rahmani's Latin translation and the Syriac text itself. Thus we can shift from Nau to Rahmani whenever the former seems to be getting lost in vague paraphrases, while we can depart from both when this seems necessary. Both translators tended to be a bit too free with texts which the liturgical science of their day did not enable them to understand fully. Once again, however, we must remind the reader that the aim of this essay is not critical assessment but simply to make known the content of the text.

After these preliminary remarks, we may now turn to the description given in the *Testament* of the various service functions in the Church.

THE FIRST BOOK OF THE *TESTAMENT OF OUR LORD*

1. Bishops
"Jesus also tells us: Since you too have asked me about the ecclesiastical norm, I shall speak to you and make known to you how you are to ordain (Syriac verb TAKES, from the Greek TAXIS) and appoint (PQAD) him who presides over the Church, and to observe the perfect, just, and good rule on every point, thus pleasing the Father who has sent me (I, 18)."[27]

According to chapter 20,[28] a bishop (EPISQOPO) is chosen by all the people, according to the will of the Holy Spirit. The man chosen must be blameless, pure, calm, humble, free of anxiety, vigilant, not a lover of money, without fault, not quarrelsome, merciful, skilled in teaching, not garrulous, a lover of what is good, a lover of work, concerned for widows, orphans, and the poor, an expert in the sacred mysteries, not desirous of roaming and of gadding about with worldly people, peaceable, perfect in virtue, as befits one to whom the rank or place of God has been entrusted. It is preferable that he not be married or at least that he have been married only once, so that he can sympathize with the suffering of widows. He should be of mature years (Rahmani: middle-aged) and not young.

All must agree to his ordination (chapter 21[29]) and bear a common witness to him together with all the priests and neighboring bishops.

The bishops impose hands on him, while the priests simply stand beside them and pray in silence.

Two formulas follow: the first, spoken by all the bishops, is a kind of declaration; the second is a prayer spoken by a single bishop in the name of the others. These formulas contain, to some extent, a definition of the bishop's function. Here is the first: "We impose hands on this servant of God who has been chosen by the Spirit in order that the Church may be in a solidly grounded and devout state of order [Syriac KATASTASIS, which is evidently borrowed from Greek] and that he may exercise the absolute and indivisible rule of God ["the Church, the government of which is monarchic," is Rahmani's translation, and it is closer to the Syriac than Nau's]."

In the prayer, which can be called an ordination prayer even though it seems to play a secondary role in relation to the formula spoken by all the bishops, the celebrant asks for the graces which the man chosen needs for carrying out his new task. According to this prayer, which is much like the one in chapter 5 of the eighth book of the *Constitutions*, the bishop is obliged to feed the holy flock of God, to exercise high priesthood by serving God day and night, to offer the gifts (QURBONO) of holy Church, to loose all bonds (the reference is to the apostles), to pray with the people, and to be afflicted because of sinners.

Chapter 22[30] lists a new series of episcopal duties: to be regular in his service at the altar (Syriac NADBAH: altar or holy place; Hebrew MIZBEAH: altar of sacrifice) and to persevere in prayer day and night, but especially at the appointed hours of the night. These hours of the night are: the first hour, midnight, and the first glimmer of dawn. The daytime hours are: early morning (the first hour of the day in the Coptic and Arabic versions), the third, sixth, ninth, and twelfth hours, and the hour when the lamps are lit. At each hour he will be well to offer ceaseless prayers for the people and for himself. Let him remain alone in the house, i.e., the church. If he cannot spend the entire night there, let him at least pray at the hours mentioned.

In addition, the bishop should fast three times a week throughout the year; he should also fast for the three weeks following his ordination. Let him taste no wine but that from the cup of offering; this, whether he be sick or in good health. Let him never eat meat, not because eating meat is blameworthy but because he who loves weakness should not eat fortifying foods. Avoiding meat will also make him more alert.

The sacrifice is to be offered only on Saturday or Sunday and on fastdays (cf. a different translation in Nau). In the evening he is to teach the mysteries to those he knows have ears to hear. If he is ill, let him get well quickly lest he become feeble and the assembly cease to be held. When he teaches in the church, he is to speak energetically like a man who knows how to offer the witness of his teaching; he is to speak of everything of which he has good knowledge and memory. He should take pains to implore the Lord that his words may produce the fruits of the Holy Spirit in his hearers. Let him dismiss the catechumens after authoritatively teaching them the thoughts and exhortations of the prophets and apostles so that they will have a good knowledge of him in whom they believe. He is to teach the mysteries to the faithful.

Chapter 23[31] gives us a rather specific description of the eucharist and of the functions in it of the various members of the clergy. A veil is to be hung across the door (of the sanctuary, Rahmani adds) during the celebration; chapter 19 has already told us about this veil. The bishop officiates beyond the veil, together with the priests, deacons, canonical widows, subdeacons, deaconesses, readers and charismatics. The bishop stands at the front of this group; the priests form two groups behind him; the widows stand behind the group of priests on the left, while behind the right-hand group of priests stand the deacons, readers, subdeacons and deaconesses, in that order. This text suggests that the widows were very numerous, i.e., as numerous as the deacons, subdeacons, readers and deaconesses taken together. In this second listing the charismatics are missing, while the readers, who had been named after the deaconesses in the first list, are here placed before the subdeacons. The priests impose hands on the offering at the same time as the bishop.

In this eucharist the deacon issues a proclamation before the anaphora (encouraging some to participate and discouraging others). Toward the end of the anaphora he likewise urges all the faithful to be at peace with one another.

Communion is distributed according to the rank held by the various categories of clergy and faithful. Here is the order given: bishops, priests, deacons, widows, readers, subdeacons, charismatics, newly baptized persons, children, the elderly, young unmarried people, then the rest of the people. Among the women, deaconesses come first.[32] In this third list of categories the reader continues to follow upon the deacon, while deaconesses seem to precede laymen.

Let us return to the bishop. Chapters 24 and 25 deal with the consecration of the oil used for healing the sick and the sanctification of penitents (i.e., those who have returned) and with the consecration of water; these rites seem to be performed after the Mass, as is the case in the *Tradition*, though only for the oil. Chapter 26[33] is devoted to the early morning prayer, the "praise at dawn," at which the bishop presides; it is to last until sunrise. This office is not to be found in the *Tradition* or in any of the parallel documents. The bishop summons the people and pronounces the first three prayers of praise. After four psalms and canticles, there are three concluding prayers of praise; these can be said either by the bishop or by one of the priests. N. Uspensky, in his dissertation on the office of the nocturnal vigil in the Byzantine Churches, has studied these sets of three prayers which the *Testament* gives for various moments of the day.[34] They are recited three times a day, and are still to be found among the Ethiopians under the name of "Prayers of the *Testament*." In my view, these prayers are closely related to the Jewish *berakhoth* of the *Shema' Israel*.

After this office at dawn come (in chapter 27[35]) the readings of the Mass and the sermon which is given by the bishop or a priest. These are followed in turn by the prayer of the catechumens and the laying of hands on them.

Chapter 28[36] gives the text of the explanation of the mystery (ROZO: mystery, symbol, secret, or simply Mass); the explanation is given by the bishop or, in his absence, by one of the priests. The text presents a kind of christological creed, fully orthodox in content, which explains the entire economy of salvation. When the people have been instructed on the mysteries, the eucharist is celebrated (the Greek word for eucharist is used in the Syriac text).

2. Priests

According to chapter 29,[37] the entire people must approve of any priest (QASHISHO: elder, old man) who is to be ordained. He must have the ability to read in public; he must be humble, mortified (poor,

38

according to the Syriac; a lover of the poor, according to the Coptic and Arabic), and not avaricious; he must have worked a good deal in the service of the sick. He must be a man who has been tested and is pure and beyond reproach; a father to orphans, a servant of the poor; diligent in attendance at services in the church; devout and gentle. He must be all this in order to be worthy to receive revelations from God concerning all that is useful and suitable, and in order to merit the gift of healing as well.

The ordination prayer in chapter 30[38] is spoken by the bishop who alone imposes hands on the ordained, while the other priests touch him and support him. This prayer likewise contains some points that sketch an image of the priest for us. He must receive the spirit of grace, counsel and strength, the spirit of a "presbyterate" or elder-ship that does not fail. He must be a balanced individual (calm, according to Nau; consistent, says Rahmani), loving the faithful but also able to reprimand and so to lead and govern the people as did the elders chosen by Moses. The prayer asks that he be filled with the wisdom and the hidden mysteries of God, so that he may be able to shepherd the people in holiness and with a pure and sincere heart, and so that he may be able to praise, bless, preach, give thanks, and sing the doxology at all times, night and day, as he endeavors joyously and patiently to be a vessel of the Holy Spirit and one who always clings to and carries the cross of Christ.

Chapter 31[39] lists some further obligations of the new priest: he is to be diligent in attendance at the altar; he is to pray and work without ceasing (the text is obscure in the Syriac; Rahmani translates: devoting himself laboriously and uninterruptedly to prayer). He may take his rest at times in one of the cells that are part of the Lord's house (Rahmani translates: withdrawing to a house, he may at times rest from his duties in the house of the Lord), but he may not omit or shorten any of the times of prayer. He is to fast three days a week throughout the year.

Next comes a very prudent rule that applies to bishop and priest alike: if the priest or bishop is inspired to speak, let him speak; otherwise let him not cease from his work or think little of it. If he is inspired to visit his missions (his pilgrimages, according to the Syriac; Rahmani's Latin has *mansiones suas*) and preach the word there, let him go; otherwise let him spend his time interceding with God in

39

prayer. Let him speak to those to whom he should speak, but as one who always bears the burden and yoke of him who was crucified for him. He should pray for all the people. A bishop or priest is not to be worried about clothing or food; God will provide these in the way he judges best. If someone offers him food or a garment and then someone else offers him still more, he should accept from the first whatever is suitable and necessary, but then not accept anything more that would be superfluous. A priest must remain firm and upright in faith; he should examine the heart of each person (Rahmani prefers: Let the heart of each person be examined; but the context suggests rather that the priest takes the initiative); he should not allow weeds to grow amid the good grain. He is to be constantly instructing the faithful so that they may walk in the full light; a priest's teaching should be properly adapted, peaceful and restrained, but it should also make an appeal to fear and trembling. The same holds for the bishop. Neither priest nor bishop may mingle talk of empty things with their teaching, but are to say all that their hearers should then go and observe.

The greater part of chapter 31 deals with the ministry of preaching and with the discernment of the spirits at work in the faithful; this discernment will help the priest direct his preaching. All this presupposes a man who is dedicated to prayer and not lacking in the charisms.

Accompanied by a deacon, the priest is to enter the homes of the sick and visit them. He must try to tell them what is appropriate and useful, especially if they are believers; this last qualification presumes that he visits nonbelievers as well. He should make the entire assembly aware of those who are sick and poor.

After some advice to a priest who is himself ill, a final counsel is given: priests should in every respect be models for the faithful in the work of sanctification. The priest is to offer praise and thanksgiving as the bishop does.

Chapter 32[40] deals with a special obligation of the priest: the daily praise of God in the church. Three prayers are given here which closely resemble the prayers at the beginning of the "praise at dawn" over which the bishop presides and which is followed by the Sunday eucharist. Daily praise is preceded by a dialogue such as opens the eucharistic Preface; evidently, the participation of the people is taken for granted. No psalmody is prescribed, but room is made for possible discourses by prophets; this detail takes us back to the very earliest days of the Church.

The last part of the chapter treats of the duty of midnight prayer on the part of the priests and of the more perfect individuals among the people. No text is given for this prayer.

3. *Deacons*

Chapter 33[41] discusses the kind of man who is to be a deacon (MSHAMSHONO: servant, minister, administrator). A deacon should be a man of good life: pure, if he is chosen because of his asceticism; married only once, if a married man is chosen. He should not be taken up with worldly affairs or with art, nor be wealthy nor have children. If he has been married and has children, the latter too must be of such a character that they can serve the Church.

A deacon's ministry (chapter 34[42]) consists first and foremost in making known or announcing whatever the bishop commands. He is an adviser to all of the clergy, and a symbol, so to speak, of the Church. He takes care of the sick, sees to the needs of strangers, helps widows, is a father to orphans, visits the homes of the poor to see whether anyone there is indigent, sick, or distressed. He also visits catechumens in their homes, in order to encourage the hesitant and instruct the ignorant. He prepares the dead for burial and provides burial for strangers; he takes under his wing those who have left, or been exiled from, their native land; he makes known to the community the situation of those in need of help. But he should not importune the bishop; it is enough that he render the bishop an account of everything on Sundays.

When the community assembles, he should go through the church and see to it that there is no one there who is arrogant or frivolous, no one who is a busybody or a gossipmonger. In the sight of all he must rebuke and expel anyone deserving punishment; but if the person asks to be allowed to receive communion, he should grant him this consolation. If someone persists in his fault or lacks discipline, the deacon is to let the bishop know; the guilty party is then to be excluded for seven days, but then recalled, lest he be lost. If, after returning, he is obstinate and remains in his sin, he is to be excluded until such time as he repents for good, returns to himself, and asks to be readmitted.

If a deacon lives in a seaside town, he should take care to search the shore for anyone who may have suffered shipwreck, and should clothe the corpse and bury it. Similarly, he is to inquire at the inns whether anyone there is sick or in need or has died, and he will then let the community know in order that necessary steps may be taken. He should bathe those who are paralyzed or ill and thus alleviate their suffering. He should obtain for each person, through the community, whatever may be required.

The end of chapter 34 gives an overview of the church's ministers: 12 priests, 7 deacons, 14 subdeacons (Rahmani reads four, but thinks readers are meant), 13 widows (Rahmani reads three) "who take precedence." One of the deacons is assigned to take care of strangers. It is clear, of course, that one individual could not have carried out all the duties incumbent on the deacon. This text assures us that there was more than one deacon, while we shall see below that the sub-deacons were real helpers of the deacons.

Chapter 35[43] begins with a fine definition of a deacon: he is to be, in all matters, "the eye of the Church," and is to endeavor to be in every way a complete model of piety for the people. The remainder of the chapter contains the formulary for the deacon's proclamation or admonition by the deacon (MAUD'ONUTO); it is the text of a litany still used among the Ethiopians and reminds us of the "synapte of peace" among the Byzantines. It is preceded by some admonitions similar to those that precede the anaphora and are meant to exclude catechumens and persons judged unworthy. Among these admonitions there is also a kind of *Sursum corda*. All these elements place the prayer of the faithful on the level of the eucharistic anaphora. We have already had occasion to note the importance of the "prayer of the faithful" as a derivative of the Jewish Eighteen Blessings, which, in its turn, was a substitute for the ancient sacrifices that were no longer offered. The synapte or litany is set down without any mention of a celebration to which it might belong, but it certainly did form part of a celebration, since it presupposes the prayer of the bishop or priest as well as the prayer of the kneeling faithful. In the eighth book of the *Apostolic Constitutions* a similar litany occurs at Vespers, Matins and Mass. The synapte of the *Testament* is simpler than the one in the *Apostolic Constitutions* and also seems to be older. In the petitions for the various categories of church members, we are once again given an overview of the makeup of the community:

"Let us pray for the bishop, that our Lord may give him a long life in the faith, in order that he may distribute the word of truth and remain pure and blameless at the head of the Church.

"Let us pray for the presbyterate (QASHISHUTO) that the Lord may not take the spirit of priesthood from it but grant it zeal and devotion to the end.

"Let us pray for the deacons that the Lord may allow them to run a perfect race and perform all the works of holiness, and may remember their labors and their love.

"Let us pray for the elderly women [but Rahmani reads 'priestesses,' and refers to the *presbytides* of canon 11 of the Council of Laodicea], that the Lord may hear their prayer, preserve their heart in the grace of the Spirit, and help them in their work.

"Let us pray for the subdeacons, readers and deaconesses that the Lord may grant them the reward of their perseverance."

The litany goes on to pray for the laity, catechumens, the empire (MALKUTO), rulers, the entire world, sailors and travelers, the persecuted, the deceased, sinners, and all who are present.

It has been observed that the prayer for the persecuted would prove our document is very old and antedates the coming of peace for the Church. Yet we must not forget that this document, written in Syriac, may have in mind other persecutions—those by the Persians, for example—than those conducted by the Roman empire.

Chapter 36[44] describes in detail the functions of the deacon as he stands at the church door during the eucharist: he is to recognize all who enter and thus prevent spies from making their way in. He must not allow latecomers to enter, less they disturb those already praying; he can let them come in once the praise has been completed. At this point, the deacon taking part in the service will ask the assembly to pray for the latecomers; among other things, this will teach the negligent and lazy a lesson.

Another function of the deacon, described in chapter 37,[45] is to pass judgment on certain sins and decide who is to be admitted to communion and who, on the contrary, is to be forbidden entry into the Church, even if the individual has repented of his sin. The deacon takes charge of penitents and brings them to the bishop or priest for instruction.

The *Testament* thus has in view a Church in which the deacon passes judgment on the moral life of the faithful; in which there is an official penitential practice; but also in which we see the bishop and priests intervening only to enlighten and instruct the penitents. The prayer for the ordination of a bishop assigns the bishop the apostolic function of loosing all bonds, but the *Testament* provides no rite of absolution.

The chapter ends with the following recommendations: If the deacon cannot carry out his duties, let him at least devote himself to prayer and regard intercession, meditation, charity, the way ("religion," says Nau), and mourning as his work; let him keep holy fear before him, and he will be called a child of the light.

Chapter 38[46] deals with the ordination of a deacon. He is ordained by the bishop alone, since he is not ordained for priesthood (KAHNUTO, from *kohen*; same word in Hebrew, where it refers only to Jewish priests), but only for the service (TESHMESHTO D'DUIOLO) of the bishop and the Church.

The ordination prayer asks that God grant the deacon zeal, fortitude, gentleness, and the power to please him. The Lord it is who must make of the deacon a faithful and blameless servant, a man of gentleness, a friend of orphans, devout folk and widows, a fervent lover of what is good.

In this prayer, the only words referring to a liturgical function of the deacon at the altar are somewhat difficult to interpret. "Lord, enlighten this man whom you have chosen and appointed to serve your Church and, in the holiness of your sanctuary, to offer you what is offered you by the heirs of the princes of your priesthood." This translation of Rahmani suggests that it is the deacon who makes the offering; Nau's translation is even less clear. In my opinion, the Syriac text does not enable us to be more accurate. In the *Tradition* the parallel text says that the deacon presents the offering to the celebrant.[47] Chapter 10 of Book II of the *Testament* says the same.

4. *Confessors*
Chapter 39,[48] which deals with the "complete" confessor (i.e., the one who has suffered imprisonment and torture for the name of the

Lord), creates problems of translation that are due primarily to our excessively sacral concept of ministry. According to the *Testament*, no one is to impose hands on the confessor for either deaconate or priesthood (QASHISHUTO, which Nau translates as "clerical office"), because: *Habet enim honorem cleri, cum per confessionem a manu Dei protectus fuerit*, i.e., "he possesses the dignity of cleric, having been protected by God's hand because of his confession." Thus Rahmani. Nau's translation is more succinct: "the hand of God has already elevated him to the rank of confessor." In the *Tradition*, the parallel text is translated thus by Dom Botte: "If a confessor has been imprisoned for the name of the Lord, no one is to impose hands on him for deaconate or priesthood, since he possesses the dignity of priesthood by reason of his confession."[49]

The *Testament* and the *Tradition* are in agreement when it comes to promoting a confessor to the episcopate: in this case, he is to receive the laying on of hands.

But let us dwell on the rank of priesthood that the confessor possesses. The word for "rank" or "dignity" if TIMÎ in Greek, IQORO in Syriac; the root QOF RESH OLAF brings us back to the Syriac verb QRO (in Hebrew, QARA). There is question, then, not of a simple honor, but of a proclamation, an acknowledgment, an appointment, that recalls Luke 1.35: "The child to be born will be called . . . the Son of God."

In my opinion, the text should be read in a quite straightforward way, and we should not try to read into it, a priori, our theological notions. We could then accept, at least as a working hypotheses, the idea that in the *Testament* (and perhaps in the *Tradition* as well) the laying on of hands signifies not so much a sacramental action that transforms a man, causing him to pass from one state to another and giving him a character he did not have before, as an action that fills the candidate with the divine grace he needs in exercising the ministry to which he has been appointed or ordained. The appointment itself can take different forms: a divine revelation (cf. Acts 13: the appointment of Paul and Barnabas to their mission); election by the people and the agreement of neighboring bishops (as in the *Testament*, where the principal action seems to be an appointment of the candidate through the laying on of hands by all the bishops); or, as in the case of the confessor, the suffering a man has endured (for the authors of the *Testament* and the *Tradition*, this suffering amounts to an attestation that the man possesses the grace which the Church would have asked for him through the laying on of hands). The laying on of hands, then, would be the same as that practiced by our present-day charismatics: an outpouring—for whatever situation—of the grace of the Spirit. The episcopate, however, presupposes a grace superior to that won by suffering for the faith; since the spiritual qualities required for deaconate and priesthood are not enough in the case of a bishop, a further laying on of hands is necessary.

The case of a "lesser" confessor (i.e., one who has not been imprisoned but has simply been haled before a judge) confirms the interpretation just given of the "complete" confessor. The witness given by a "lesser" confessor does not prove he has the requisite qualities for deaconate and priesthood. Therefore, he receives the laying on of hands, but, in view of his merits, the prayer is somewhat shortened.

The *Canons of Hippolytus* are even more explicit. Here is the text as translated by J.-M. Hanssens:[50]

"If a man has been worthy of being imprisoned because of the faith and of suffering torment for Christ, when he is set free he has won the rank of priesthood in God's eyes, without any ordination being conferred by the bishop. Furthermore, his confession is his ordination. On the other hand, if a man has confessed the faith but has not undergone any torments, he is worthy of the priesthood but must be ordained by the bishop. If a slave has undergone torture for Christ, he too is a priest of the flock. Although he has not received the form of priesthood, he has nonetheless acquired its spirit; the bishop therefore omits the part of the prayer that refers to the Holy Spirit."

The eighth book of the *Apostolic Constitutions*, however, shows a further development in the line of the Church's classical practice: "The confessor is not ordained. . . . He is worthy of high rank. . . . If necessary, he is to be ordained bishop, priest or deacon. But if a non-ordained confessor claims a dignity of this type by reason of his confession, he is to be deposed and expelled, since he has rejected the directives of Christ and is worse than an unbeliever."[51]

5. Widows
In the documents making up the *Apostolic Order* (closely related to the *Didache*), widows occupy the fifth and final rung of the hierarchic

ladder, after the bishop, priest, reader and deacon.[52] In the *Tradition* and the *Testament*, widows come after confessors but before readers.

In chapter 23 we saw the widows standing behind the priests and beside the deacons during the eucharistic prayer; they received communion after the deacons. In chapter 35, in the deacon's synapte, they were called "priestesses," a term Nau translates by the neutral "elderly women" (*presbyteros* means "elder").

In chapters 40[53] and following, to which we now turn our attention, widows are normally ordained, although without any laying on of hands, and seem to have a real liturgical function involving precedence. In the eighth book of the *Apostolic Constitutions* widows are not ordained.

Like the chapters on the bishop, the priest, and the deacon, chapter 40 begins by describing the qualities required in a widow, since she is ordained after having been chosen. The conditions for her being chosen are the following. She must have been a widow for a long time; she must have had the opportunity to remarry but have refused it for reasons connected with the faith. She must be devout; she must have raised her children properly; she must love and honor pilgrims, be humble, gladly come to the aid of the afflicted. The saints must have had revelations regarding her. She must be able to carry and endure the yoke (of the Lord), pray unceasingly, be perfect in all respects, be ardent of soul, and have the eyes of her heart open to everything. She must be always pleasant and a lover of simplicity. She must possess nothing in this world but constantly carry the cross. She must have overcome all evil, be diligent at the altar day and night (we saw above that this same diligence at the altar is required of the priest and bishop but not of the deacon), and do her work gladly and unostentatiously. If she has one, two or three companions worthy of her, "I shall be in their midst" (at every point the Lord is regarded as the one speaking in the *Testament*). She must be perfect in the Lord as one visited by the Spirit.

After listing the qualifications required, the *Testament* goes on to indicate the widow's responsibilities. She is to perform devoutly and zealously whatever is commanded her. She is to exhort disobedient women, instruct ignorant women, convert sinful women and teach them to be chaste. She is to follow in the footsteps (*perquirat* is Rahmani's term) of the deaconesses. She will teach women entering (the church) how they are to behave, and exhort those leaving. She will patiently teach women catechumens how they should act; after their third reprimand she will no longer speak to the disobedient; she will love women who want to live in virginity and purity, and she will reprimand, though with restraint and modesty, those who travel the other path. She must be peaceful in her dealings with all. She is to rebuke especially those women who indulge in long and empty conversations; if they do not heed her, she is to take another older woman with her or else report the case to the bishop. She is to be silent in church and diligent in prayer; she is to visit the sick every Sunday, taking with her one or two deacons whom she is to assist. If she owns any material goods, she should use them to help the poor and the faithful; if she owns nothing, the church is to assist her. She is not to do any secular work in order to earn a livelihood; her works are to be those of the spirit. She will be diligent in prayer and fasting; she is not to look for anything extraordinary but to accept whatever the Lord gives. She is not to busy herself with her children, but must entrust them to the Church so that they may live in the house of God and become fit for the ministry of priesthood.

God will accept her prayers, for these are a holocaust and an altar ('OLOTO UMADBEHO DALOHO). If women are intemperate, irascible, drunkards, gossipers, inquisitive, disagreeable, or lovers of pleasure, the image of their souls that stands before the Father of lights will perish, and they will be led off to dwell in darkness. Our text continues with this theme and the theme of the future life; it emphasizes the point that each soul's image and type exists before God since the foundation of the world.

Chapter 41[54] describes the widow's ordination (METASRHONUTO, the same word used for the ordination of a bishop, priest or deacon). It consists in a prayer of the bishop, which he says in a low voice so as to be heard only by the priests; nothing is said of a laying on of hands. During the prayer the candidate remains on her knees at the entrance of the sanctuary. The *Tradition*[55] says that the widow is advanced to her rank by the word, without any imposition of hands; but the *Tradition* gives no prayer of ordination.

The prayer in the *Testament* for the ordination of a widow adds nothing to what has already been said in the preceding chapter.

Chapter 42[56] lists some further devotional duties of a widow after her ordination—probably for a limited period of time, since they are somewhat inconsistent with what has already been said. She is to accept no responsibilities but is to live in solitude and devote herself to prayer, since solitude, for a widow, is the basis of her holiness and way of life, enabling her to love no one but God.

At fixed hours, she is to offer praise, especially during the night and at dawn. If she is going through her period, she is to remain in the church but not to approach the altar: not because she is in any way defiled, but out of respect for the altar. After fasting and bathing, she continues (her service at the altar). When she offers thanksgiving and praise, if she has companions who are virgins and who are in agreement with her, it is good that these pray with her by answering "Amen." Otherwise she is to pray alone in the Church and in her home, especially during the night. The chief times for celebrating God's praises are Saturday, Sunday, Easter, Epiphany and Pentecost; on other days of the year she is to give thanks humbly by means of psalms, canticles and meditations. This is to be her work (Rahmani has: *itemque laboret*, i.e., she is not only to pray but to work as well).

Chapter 43[57] gives us the text for the widow's praise during the night and at dawn. The office consists of two prayers couched in the first person; in them praise mingles with personal intentions regarding her own ministry. For the other hours of the day we must suppose that the widow goes to the church, since no special prayers are given for these hours.

The tone of the nocturnal and dawn prayers is quite devotional. We may even think them fairly close to the spirituality of our own medieval mystics. Here are some examples:

"If you will have me, I will belong to you, O God. . . . In your goodness you have chosen me for your servant and have judged me worthy of being called a Christian. . . . Ground my heart immovably in you until it is filled with the Holy Spirit; strengthen me for building up your holy Church. . . . You who have taken care to change the very direction of my mind that I might serve you and you alone. . . . You who have dispelled all hesitation from your servant's heart . . ."

We shall end this section on widows by recalling that the title "widow" is a conventional one and that it surely comes from 1 Tim

49

5.3-16. The *Testament* speaks several times of "widows who have precedence." We have seen that one duty of widows is to be attentive to the deaconesses who likewise have a place at the altar and receive communion before the other women; the document says nothing, however, about the ordination of deaconesses or about their ministry. Are we to infer that deaconesses were but a class of widows who did not have precedence? Can widows and deaconesses be put into the same category?

In the ancient redaction of the Byzantine Euchology, down at least to the eleventh or twelfth century,[58] there is a ceremony for the ordination of a deaconess; it takes place before the altar and involves a laying on of hands and a recitation of ordination prayers parallel to those used for a deacon. The Byzantine deaconess received communion from the bishop's hand at the altar. Unfortunately, the manuscripts do not tell us what the functions of the deaconess were. In my opinion, the deaconesses were simply a category derived from the widows of the *Tradition* and the *Testament* (and from 1 Timothy), since it is quite unlikely that the Byzantines took the initiative and introduced an innovation in so important a matter as the ministry of women at the altar. According to some codices (e.g., *Coislin 213*), the deaconess must be a pure virgin; this means she could not be a widow.

6. Subdeacons

Chapter 44[59] tells us that the ceremony for the ordination of a subdeacon (HUPODIAKNO) consists of an exhortation addressed to him and unaccompanied by any prayer of ordination or any laying on of hands. In the *Testament* the subdeacon is presented before the reader and the virgin; the *Tradition*, however, gives him the last place in the hierarchic order, with even virgins coming ahead of him.

According to the *Tradition* the subdeacon is not ordained in the strict sense but is simply appointed to assist the deacon. According to the eighth book of the *Apostolic Constitutions* he receives an imposition of hands, accompanied by a prayer asking for the Holy Spirit in order that the ordinand may be able to handle the sacred vessels worthily.[60] The *Testament* gives no specifics about the role of the subdeacon. The only condition he must meet is that he be pure. The *Canons of Hip-*

polytus require an attestation of his good behavior if he is a celibate.

In the *Testament* the words by which the bishop appoints a subdeacon require of him an exemplary and almost ascetical manner of life: he is to serve and hear the gospel with devotion; cultivate self-knowledge in holiness; be pure and live ascetically; look about, be watchful, and listen in a modest fashion; not neglect prayer or fasting, so that the Lord may judge him worthy of passing to a higher rank. The priests then say: "Let it be done! Let it be done! Let it be done!"

7. Readers

As we noted a moment ago, the reader comes ahead of the subdeacon in the *Tradition*; in the documents making up the *Apostolic Order* the reader comes after the priest and before the deacon.[61] The *Canons of Hippolytus* require that the reader have the virtues of a deacon; according to these same *Canons* a man becomes a reader when the bishop entrusts him with the book of the Gospels. According to the *Tradition* the bishop gives the reader a book, but the book is not specified[62]; the same is true of the *Testament*. However, the Sahidic version of the *Tradition*[63] tells us that the book given him is that of the *Apostolos*. We may think this more normal, but the detail is perhaps simply an interpolation, and Dom Botte takes no account of it.

According to the *Tradition* the bishop says nothing at the moment when he appoints a reader. According to the *Testament* he uses a formula similar to the one he addresses to a subdeacon. The eighth book of the *Apostolic Constitutions* speaks of a laying on of hands and a very fine prayer that is very much like the one we find in the Byzantine Euchology; the prayer in the *Apostolic Constitutions* asks that the reader receive the Holy Spirit and the prophetic spirit.[64]

Let us look now at chapter 45 of the *Testament*.[65] A reader must be pure, peaceable, humble, prudent, talented, scholarly and very learned; he must have a good memory and be vigilant so as to be fit for a call to a higher rank. Here is the formulary for his ordination: "Christ has chosen you to be the minister of his words. Endeavor, therefore, to excel in this rank and even in a higher rank, in the presence of our Lord."

It is expected, then, that the reader will be able to ascend to a higher rung on the hierarchic ladder. Moreover, if we reflect on the knowledge, scholarship and memory the reader requires and if we take account of the fact that according to the ordination prayer the reader is a minister of the words of Christ, we can understand why the *Apostolic Order* puts the reader after the priest and before the deacon and why the *Canons of Hippolytus* prescribe that the book of the Gospels is to be given to him. Clearly, the reader could well be a direct descendant of the early teachers. His functions would have been taken over at an early date by the deacon as reader of the gospel and by the bishop and priest as commentators on scripture. In the *Testament* the priest is the prophet who speaks as circumstances require, but he is not yet given the role of commentator on scripture. In the fourth century the sermons of the Fathers are, in the main, commentaries on the Bible, but it may be that on this point, as on others, the *Testament* reflects a practice antedating the fourth century.

If we also take into account the single ordination prayer for the reader and the psalmist that is still used in the Byzantine Euchology, we will be surprised at the importance the text gives to functions to which little attention is paid today. The prayer is certainly a very old one and supposes a practice quite different from our present one. It is not the privilege of just any cleric (usually lacking any real training in scripture) to read the scripture or chant a psalm. Some Churches of the Reformation have retained the praiseworthy custom of having the scripture read by the most important persons present for the service; it is not beneath the dignity of an archbishop to read St. Paul at Mass.

8. Virgins

According to chapter 46,[66] virgins, be they men or women, are not ordained. It is by their own initiative that they dwell apart and take the title of virgin; no one imposes hands on them, because this particular order or state of life (TEGMO, from the Greek TAGMA) is of their own choosing.

What we have here is a class of individuals very similar to our own religious men and women; they live in the midst of the Christian community, without any apparent relationship to the monks living in solitude. Their manner of life is described as follows. Virgins must devote themselves to bodily mortification if they are in good health; they must be diligent in fasting and prayer amid tears and spiritual mourning. They are to live in expectation of their departure from the flesh and are to live each day as if it were to be their last. They will not yield to anger or intemperance, to drinking or gossiping, to secular concerns or empty distractions, but will live as men and women who have been nailed to the cross. Their hearts should dwell in heaven through humility and purity of heart and through meditation on the sacred books, on the teachings of faith and its sweet consolations. Then, when they pray they will obtain what they ask for. They should not rebuff the faithful who seek to be attentive to them, in order that through them the faithful too may obtain a share in life.

They are to be solidly grounded in charity, gentleness and true and perfect grace. They should admonish and instruct the neophytes, inspire the young with their understanding, knowledge and gentleness, and be a model of holiness for them.

All this seems to be addressed first of all to men, since the *Testament* adds that female virgins are to do the same. All of them are to speak and act in an orderly manner and in the light of grace and knowledge, in order that they may truly be the salt of the earth. They are to cover their heads in church so as to hide their hair. They must win the respect of all, so that other women may desire to imitate them.

9. Charismatics

Chapter 47,[67] which is the final chapter of Book I and a very short chapter at that, deals with the charisms. It tells us that if anyone of the faithful has the gift of healing or knowledge or tongues, no one is to impose hands on such persons, since their power is enough to make them stand out; they are, however, to be honored.

The *Tradition*[68] speaks only of the gift of healing; the *Canons of Hippolytus* likewise speak only of this gift, but prescribe the ordination of a healer. Book VIII of the *Apostolic Constitution* allows for exorcists and healers, but without any ordination. Oddly enough, the *Constitutions* and the *Tradition* suppose that it is through a revelation that the healer receives the gift of healing.

THE SECOND BOOK OF THE *TESTAMENT*

The second book of the *Testament* is simply a continuation of the first and deals chiefly with catechumens and neophytes. Here again it follows the *Tradition* closely, although the latter, not being divided into books, passes quite naturally from charismatics to catechumens.[69]

The second book presents first the catechumen and, in the process, the perfect model of a believer. Limitations of time and space prevent us from examining this, the basic part of an ecclesiology, namely, the part treating of the faithful. As a matter of fact, the *Testament* itself has already pushed the faithful into a subordinate position in order to concentrate on the ministries of the Church.

We may allow ourselves, however, at least to list the subjects dealt with in the second book of the *Testament*, all of them certainly deserving of detailed study:

> Catechumens and their families.
> The professions or trades forbidden to catechumens.
> The professions allowed conditionally.
> The instructor of the catechumens.
> Female catechumens and faithful.
> The role, in baptism, of bishop, priest, parents of children too young to answer for themselves, deacon, and widows.
> Neophytes, child choristers, the sick, parents of unbelievers.
> Clerics invited to meals; those who offer them.
> The dying who make their wills.
> Girls to be married.
> Those who receive communion without having fasted.
> Those who are prevented from coming to church.
> The sick, the dying, the deceased.
> The hours for prayer, and other obligations of Christian life.

We shall now try to glean from Book II only what has to do with the ministries. This may help shed a little light on passages of Book I that are too succinct or incomplete.

According to both the *Tradition* and the *Testament* candidates for the catechumenate[70] are brought to the teachers, who examine them. The *Canons of Hippolytus* mention only deacons as instructors in the catechumenate, whereas in Book VIII of the *Apostolic Constitutions* the deacons bring the candidates to the bishop or priests.[71] We may recall that Book I of the *Testament* says nothing about teachers. In Book II the teachers are to question the candidates and bring out their dispositions; according to Book I this would have been the role either of the priests, as being prophets, or of the deacons as administrative aides of the bishop and overseers of the community.

Once a candidate is admitted, the bishop is to take charge of his instruction which seems to take the form of an orderly reading of the Bible: first, the prophets; then, if the catechumen makes progress, the letters; then the gospel; and finally the body of doctrine. The revelation of certain mysteries is reserved until after baptism. The bishop is also to be concerned about the catechumen's married life. The catechumenate lasts for three years. Catechumens who are virgins have a special place alongside Christian virgins (chapter 4).[72]

Chapter 5[73] deals with the laying of hands on the catechumens by the bishop or a priest. The prayer accompanying this imposition of hands asks understanding, perfection and faith for the catechumens, but it says nothing of the Holy Spirit. The imposition takes place daily, after the prayer for the catechumens that follows upon the gospel.

Exorcism (chapter 7[74]), which also consists of a prayer and an imposition of hands, takes place on the day of baptism. The prayer is a lengthy one and does not mention the Holy Spirit. If a candidate resists the exorcism (by manifestations of inability to accept it), he is to be led aside by the deacons; later on, he is to be exorcised by the priests until he is purified (of the evil spirit).

Chapter 8[75] explains the ritual of baptism. Before the baptism the bishop prays over the two oils of thanksgiving and exorcism. He then receives each candidate's renunciation of Satan; at this point the women are covered with a veil held by the widows, since they have already stripped off their garments. The bishop seems to be the one who does the exorcistic anointing, but the text is not very clear.

Baptism is conferred by a priest who imposes hands, questions the candidate three times about his trinitarian faith, and immerses him three times; the deacon goes down into the water with the candidate.

A second anointing, with the oil of thanksgiving, is done by a priest or a widow, but in both cases it is the priest who pronounces the formula.

Chapter 9[76] speaks of an imposition of hands that takes place after entry into the church and is done by the bishop. The accompanying prayer is the first to ask the gift of the Holy Spirit for the baptized person; it alludes to the descent of the Spirit on the apostles and prophets. The bishop anoints the baptized person once more, makes the sign of the cross on his forehead, and gives him the kiss of peace.

The eucharist is now celebrated (chapter 10[77]). During it the deacon presents the offering to the pastor who pronounces the prayer of thanksgiving.

We were given a description of the eucharist in Book I, chapter 23, in connection with the ordination of a bishop. The passage in Book II adds some further details: here the deacons carry fans (*rhipidia*); the deacons also distribute communion, although not to the priests, to whom they simply present the uncovered vessels so that they may take communion themselves. It is also noted, in passing, that a deacon administers baptism in case of necessity when no priest is available.

During this eucharist the priests instruct the new Christians about the resurrection. The resurrection is not to be mentioned before baptism, for, says the author of the *Testament* (who always puts what he has to say in the mouth of the Lord) resurrection is the new name which no one knows except the person who has received the eucharist; the allusion is to the message of the angel to the church of Pergamun in Revelation 2.17.

In chapter 11[78] we learn that people can give alms for widows, poor women, and those individuals, namely, the clergy, who are continually taken up with the affairs of the Church. This alms is called "the bread of the poor"; the name evidently supposes that the clergy are poor.

Next there is a description of an evening office. The deacon brings in a lamp, as is done in the Roman liturgy of the Easter Vigil. The children sing psalms; perhaps they are the children of the clergy, the priests and widows, who, as we have seen, are in the service of the Church. In the *Tradition*[79] this evening office introduces the community meal; the *Testament* speaks of the latter in the next chapter.

Chapter 13[80] discusses meals at which the bishop is an invited guest. Rahmani calls these meals "agapes," but the word does not appear in the text. The meal begins with a breaking of bread

(BURKTO), which the *Tradition*[81] insists is not to be regarded as a eucharist but simply as a symbol of the Lord's body; it is then said that catechumens may not take part in this supper of the Lord. The *Testament* likewise prohibits the catechumen from taking part, but, unlike the *Tradition*, does not deny that the blessing in question may have been the eucharistic breaking of bread. In my opinion, this whole section may well be very ancient, and, while the celebration of the eucharist proper was no longer connected with community meals in the period when the *Tradition* and the *Testament* received their final form, the texts themselves could nonetheless be relics of an earlier time when meal and eucharist were not separated. This would be why the *Tradition* calls this community meal a "supper of the Lord."

Chapter 15[82] shows us a community that has a common coffer to which the faithful contribute in a significant way. Thanks to it the church is able to make sizable outlays, such as are required, for example, for the support of orphans.

Chapter 19[83] deals with the superintendence which the deacons, aided by the readers and subdeacons, exercise during services. They must see to it that the children behave properly and do not go to sleep during the vigils, especially the Easter Vigil.

The degree of participation in the Easter Vigil depends on the individual's state of life. Workers, catechumens and married women keep watch for only a part of the night. Others spend the entire night in church: bishop, priests, widows, virgins, elderly women (*presbyterae*, "priestesses," for Rahmani), the newly baptized. All, however, are urged to fast until the moment of the eucharist, when the whole body of the Church is to receive the new food. The deacon brings communion to the sick; priests bring it to sick priests, deaconesses to sick women. Chapter 20[84] seems to be dealing only with Easter.

Chapter 21[85] says that the bishop, the leader of the priests (*summus sacerdos* or "high priest," according to Rahmani) may personally visit the sick if he so desires.

Chapter 22[86] recommends antiphonal singing both in the church and outside it. In the church it is the virgins and the children who respond to the psalmist or leader of song.

The church is to take care of the deceased if there is no one else to perform this duty (chapter 23).[87] If individuals die and do not leave their property to the Church, the church is to give these goods to the poor, for the sake of the souls of the deceased. This same idea that material goods can be of profit to the souls of the deceased has already appeared in chapter 15.

Chapter 24[88] lists the times at which the faithful are to pray through the day: on rising from sleep, at the third, sixth and ninth hours, in the evening, at midnight and at dawn. They may pray in the church or in their own homes.

A final chapter, the twenty-fourth,[89] contains advice for Christian life: instruction and mutual correction, concern for the catechumens, universal love and Christ's promises (always with Christ speaking) to remain with the faithful. The Lord's final precept is that each of the faithful should be careful to participate in the eucharist before eating ordinary food, in order that nothing they eat may harm them. In the *Tradition*[90] the reference is clearly to the eucharist which people reserve in their homes and which they receive before any other food; the *Canons of Hippolytus* bear witness to the same practice.

If we go back now to chapter 18 and the community meals, we may perhaps take it that the blessing, which replaced the eucharist, at the beginning of the meal was due to a recent interpretation. For it would be surprising that the eucharist which is prescribed before the meals of the ordinary faithful in their homes should be missing from a community meal that is called a "supper of the Lord" and is presided over by the bishop, and should be replaced by a mysterious bread which the catechumens are not allowed to eat. We might well raise the question here of a *eucharistia minor* or *eucharistia maior* against the background of *Didache* IX-X. But we must, instead, bring this entire essay to an end.

CONCLUSION

The *Testament* is one of the apocryphal writings in the Syrian and Alexandrian tradition. When it was translated from Greek into Syriac in the seventh century it may have been thought to be Antiochene in origin. However, its dependence on the *Apostolic Tradition* of Hippolytus (also known as the *Egyptian Church Order*) suggests rather an

Alexandrian origin, unless the *Tradition* is really a Roman document, something by no means impossible. In any case, the christological creed preceding the eucharist and the rest of the prayers and texts seem completely orthodox. If the book belonged in fact to a sectarian community that based its life on ancient traditions abandoned by the other churches, these Christians seem at least to have been neither gnostics nor heretics.

It is not easy to determine the antiquity of the document, since in it we find parts that are very old (perhaps from the second century, as Rahmani insisted in his edition) and other parts that are much more recent (probably postdating the liturgical renewal of the fourth century). The final redaction is surely late, but the editor seems to have been very careful not to revise old parts of the text, even to the point of allowing some contradictions to stand.

We may therefore suppose that the *Testament* preserves echoes of very early Christianity and gives us a picture of a community profoundly faithful to the gospel ideal and to apostolic traditions, especially those of St. Paul.

A bishop who is first and foremost a man of prayer and the father of his community; a presbyterate entirely devoted to prayer, prophecy and instruction; deacons who are real servants of the community and strangers and who are in the full sense the bishop's factotums; a ministry of widows and perhaps of deaconesses who are very active pastorally and even liturgically; other auxiliary ministries devoted to various services for the common good; charismatics with the gift of healing; virgins giving the example of a consecrated life; and, finally, a community of believers who have undergone a strict testing before being admitted to the catechumenate and who have prepared themselves for three years for baptism. Such is the ideal and, doubtless, somewhat idealized picture of a Christian community leading a simple life (without naivete but also without paraevangelical complications) that is portrayed for us in the mysterious document, so close to the New Testament, that bears the name *Testament of Our Lord Jesus Christ*.

Bernard BOTTE

Christian People and Hierarchy
in the Apostolic Tradition
of St. Hippolytus

The *Apostolic Tradition* [1] is a complex document and cannot be properly understood unless this complexity is borne in mind. At first glance, we might be tempted to regard it as a ritual, for it contains many liturgical prayers and descriptions of ceremonies. But when we read the chapter "On professions and trades" in connection with preparation for baptism, we realize that the author is not a master of ceremonies preoccupied with the proper performance of ritual, but a pastor concerned with the concrete situations in which his flock lives. Neither is the *Apostolic Tradition* a theological treatise, although the prayers reveal a theological depth that continually catches our attention. None of these aspects must be neglected.

How, then, can we describe the Church as it appears in the theology of St. Hippolytus? It is first and foremost a charismatic Church.

We must not lose sight of the fact that the *Apostolic Tradition* was preceded by a treatise *On the charisms*.[2] We know but little about this lost treatise, except that it dealt with the gifts or charisms by means of which God restores to man the likeness to his Creator which he had lost by sin. The *Apostolic Tradition*, which opens with the consecration of bishops,[3] clearly presents the institutional aspect of the Church. We must therefore avoid opposing the charismatic and the institutional as though they were irreconcilable.

By any accounting, the charismatic Church is not an anarchic Church. When St. Paul lists the charisms, he puts "apostles and prophets" together at the head of the list[4] (the two groups are joined with a single definite article in Eph 2.20), and gives the apostle the right to regulate the use of the charisms in the assemblies. St. Paul has no liking for disorderly gatherings, and the entire passage on the manner in which assemblies should be conducted ends with the praise of the greatest of all God's gifts: "So faith, hope, love abide, these three; but the greatest of these is love."[5]

On the other hand, it would be a misconception to think of the institutional Church as simply a juridical organization based on arbitrary norms. It is not election by the people that makes a man a bishop. Rather, he must receive the laying on of hands from other bishops[6]; it is the latter who communicate to him the gift of the Spirit which Christ received from his Father and passed on to his apostles. In virtue of the ordination prayers the bishop is a charismatic, just as are the priest and the deacon. Each receives a gift suited to the functions that are properly his.[7]

The Church as seen in Hippolytus is truly the Church of the Holy Spirit, for the same Spirit inspires each of its members no less than its hierarchy. The Christian receives the gift of the Spirit in the rites of initiation, during which he is anointed, and even anointed twice according to Hippolytus[8]; we shall return to this point later on.

The Christian people offer the eucharistic sacrifice. In the prayer of episcopal ordination it is said that the bishop, as a high priest, offers the gifts of holy Church.[9] Obviously, these gifts can only come from the faithful. There is no room in Hippolytus' liturgy, however, for an offertory procession such as we find in the time of St. Gregory. The gifts must therefore have been brought at the beginning of the meeting and given to the deacon who in turn brings them to the altar at the time of the eucharist.[10] Nor is there a question of any other gift than the bread and wine, the material for the eucharist. When the eucharist begins, the congregation answers the bishop's greeting and the opening dialogue.[11] When the prayer of thanksgiving ends, it is probably the people who answer with an "Amen."[12]

Apart from the eucharist there are only two public services or offices, one in the morning, the other in the evening. It seems that a system of "stations" or meeting places was in use; each evening the bishop determined where the next morning's gathering would take place. The faithful were invited to this morning assembly, and the church is twice said to be the place where the Spirit flourishes.[13] In the evening there was the *lucernarium* or ceremony of "lamp-lighting" over which the bishop presided.[14] Apart from these two gatherings there was no other public ceremony. The hours for prayer of which the *Tradition* speaks were for private prayer. There were prayers during the day, at the third, sixth and ninth hours (each commemorating a point in the passion of Jesus), and prayer around midnight.[15] These prayers became public or communal only in monastic communities; from the monastic office they then passed into the clerical office. But in the time of Hippolytus all this was in the distant future.

The ordinary faithful play an important role in recruiting for the community. It does not seem that in Hippolytus the normal function of the bishop is to spread the gospel among the pagans; instead, the faithful bring him any candidates for baptism. The faithful vouch for the good behavior and upright intentions of the candidates,[16] and when the time for baptism draws near, they are again called on to bear witness.[17] The bishop's role in the process is to examine the candidates and supervise their formation, either directly or through other ministers.

The reader of the *Tradition* will note that the catechumenate is not simply a course of instruction. The instruction is accompanied by sacramental activity. Thus after the instruction the catechist prays and lays hands on the candidate; he does so whether or not he is a cleric.[18] It is thus clear that an ordinary Christian can act as catechist.

The length of the catechumenate comes to us as a surprise: it normally lasts three years. There can be no doubt that such a rigorous practice was the result of experience. To understand it, we must try to visualize the situation of the community. We are at the end of the second and the beginning of the third centuries. The gospel has emerged from its original Jewish setting and entered the pagan world. But the paganism it encounters is no longer that of the official cults of the Greco-Roman cities. The Mediterranean world has since been invaded by the Eastern religions: the cults of Mithras, Isis, Cybele.

We tend to think of gnosticism as a Christian heresy, and indeed there was a Christian gnosticism. In the first book of his *Adversus haereses* Irenaeus tries to construct its genealogy, with Simon Magus as the fountainhead. It is highly unlikely that the genealogy is accurate, but this is unimportant. The significant thing is that gnosticism antedated Christianity and that, whatever be the genealogical relations among the systems, they all show certain essential tendencies that were incompatible with Christianity. The first such tendency is a metaphysical dualism: matter is essentially evil. This means that the Incarnation was impossible: God, who is good, cannot enter into a union with matter. All the sects won over to gnosticism were therefore docetic; that is, they maintained that Jesus could not have had a real body and that he simply created the illusion of a body.

A further consequence of this dualism was the denial of the unity of revelation; the Old Testament had to be rejected. This runs counter, of course, to an essential datum of the Christian faith, for which God the Father, to whom Jesus appeals, is the God of Abraham, Isaac, and Jacob. Jesus is always presented as the Messiah whom the prophets had promised. For St. Paul, Abraham is the father of all believers, and it is in his posterity, that is, in Jesus, that all the nations will be blessed.[19] Gnosticism is thus the destruction of genuine Christian faith. The success of the gnostic sects was a threat against which the leaders of the churches had to be on guard when they recruited catechumens.

There was still another danger. The correspondence of Pliny the Younger with Trajan shows that Christianity was experiencing an extraordinary growth in certain regions of the empire.[20] But the same documents make it clear that a large number of Christians denied their faith under the pressure of persecution. We all know the problems this kind of apostasy caused the Church. Was it possible to allow such apostates to be reconciled? The bishops thus had a stake in admitting only sure candidates as neophytes. That is why the catechumenate was so prolonged. Besides, the ideal of the apostolic Church was not to acquire as many individual converts as possible, but to create, first and foremost, communities that would be closely united around their bishops. The letters of St. Ignatius of Antioch show that the Church is regarded as a eucharistic community gathered around a single altar,[21] and St. Hippolytus is a witness to the same tradition.

I mentioned earlier that lay people could exercise certain ministries connected with preparation for baptism, especially those of sponsor and catechist. It is now time to explain the meaning of these practices. In the apostolic Church the formation of catechumens and neophytes was not yet the business of a single ministry, but was the concern of the entire community. The local Church was seen as a living body that grows through the action of the Spirit whom Jesus has given to his apostles and whom the latter in turn had transmitted to their successors, the bishops. The growth had two aspects: a quantitative and a qualitative. Quantitative growth occurred through the spiritual birth of new Christians, men and women born of water and the Spirit.[22] The very existence of the community was at stake here, and all its members had an interest in recruiting and forming new Christians.

Qualitative growth occurred through the spiritual progress of all the baptized. In the second stage of their initiation the faithful had received the gift of the Spirit. This gift is the root of the charisms, that is, those various gifts which individuals receive for the benefit of the entire community. As we pointed out, Hippolytus twice bids all come to the church on time, adding that it is there that the Spirit flourishes. This "flourishing" can only refer to the development of the charisms. Furthermore, in the third stage of their initiation the faithful have been introduced to the eucharistic mystery.[23] From then on it was their duty to seek nourishment from the bread of life which is the flesh of Christ. This food would make the life of Christ intensify in them. The Church of Hippolytus is thus a living Church, an expanding Church, that cultivates its own organic growth under the action of the Spirit who gives it life.

The organization of the catechumenate is still in its beginnings in Hippolytus, but we can already distinguish two main stages. First, there are the simple catechumens, whose instruction will normally go

65

on for three years.[24] Second, there are those who are preparing directly for the next occasion of solemn baptism.[25] Hippolytus gives this latter group no special name, but he does allude, as it were, to the name that will be given to them at a later period. St. Ambrose tells us that the candidates for proximate baptism are called *electi* at Rome and *competentes* in the other Churches. This accords with what we find in the Roman rite that depends on the Gelasian Sacramentary: *Orate, electi* ("Pray, chosen ones"). Now in Hippolytus there is the statement that a "choice" is made of those who are to receive baptism shortly.[26] It is unlikely that this similarity of vocabulary is purely accidental. The name *electi* itself may refer secondarily to the eternal choice made by God, but the immediate reference is probably to a choice made by the bishop and the leaders of the community. The passage in Hippolytus supplies a further point of information: at the moment when the candidates are chosen, they do not as yet have any knowledge of the gospels; from now on they are allowed to hear them.

What was the subject matter of the catechesis in its first stage? Undoubtedly the Old Testament. The convergence of all the sources, liturgical and patristic, indicates that the initial catechesis always began with Genesis. We must even ask ourselves whether this practice was not inherited from Judaism. Philo of Alexandria, a Jewish writer contemporary with Jesus, devoted his entire activity to commenting on the Law, and his work had a profound influence on Christian exegesis. In the patristic *catenae* or "chains" the series of citations from the Fathers often ends with one from "Philo the Jew," or "Philo the bishop," or simply "Philo," but it is always the same writer that is meant. All the Fathers of the first six centuries were influenced by Philo, either directly, as in the case of Origen or St. Ambrose, or indirectly.

For a long time scholars misunderstood the real nature of Philo's work, regarding him as a philosopher in search of a system. Recent studies, however, have shown that Philo is anything but a philosopher. He is a devout man who wants to present the Jewish religion to the Hellenistic world in a form which the latter can understand. But the Jewish religion is the Law of Moses. Thus it is Jewish exegesis that Philo is in fact communicating in what outwardly is a philosophical garb. Recent studies have also shown that Philo's interpretation is akin to rabbinical exegesis. We may therefore think

66

that Philo is simply a representative of the way in which Jewish prose-lytes were prepared.

The Church, then, was continuing the Jewish tradition. This kind of fidelity to Jewish tradition was not an accident but had a profound theological significance. In response to the negations of the gnostics the universal Church was obliged to assert the unity and continuity of revelation. The Church was aware of being the people of God—but a people that began with Abraham. Abraham is the father of all believers; God promised him that all the nations of the earth would be blessed in his descendants.[27] And St. Paul adds: "'And to your off-spring,' which is Christ."[28] It is impossible to separate Jesus from Abraham. The God whose people we are is the God of Abraham, Isaac and Jacob, the God of our ancestors. If Jesus were not the offspring of Abraham, if he were not the one who comes to fulfill the Law and answer the appeal repeated century after century: "Come, Lord, and do not delay,"[29] he would be nothing or, rather, he would be simply an impostor.

We must now look at the baptismal ritual in the *Apostolic Tradition* and gather from it what information we can regarding the author's conception of the Church.

The rite, presided over by the bishop, begins with the blessing of the water[30] and the blessing of the holy oils: the oil of exorcism and the oil of thanksgiving or blessing.[31] No document from the apostolic age mentions a ritual anointing as part of the ceremony of Christian initiation. The rite of anointing belongs to the tradition of ancient Israel. Thus the Old Testament describes Saul being anointed king by Samuel the prophet,[32] Aaron being anointed high priest by Moses,[33] and the stone at Bethel being anointed by Jacob.[34] The sense of these anointings is easy to grasp: the ability of oil to penetrate symbolizes the divine power that enters into the persons or things men are trying to consecrate.

This symbolism of consecration can be present, however, without there being any material rite of anointing. In the messianic texts of the Old Testament the Messiah, who is the "Anointed One" par excellence, does not receive an anointing with oil. This is true of the text from Isaiah which Jesus applies to himself: "The Spirit of the Lord is upon me, because he has anointed me to preach good news to the poor."[35] And for the text about the stump of Jesse: "There shall come forth a shoot from the stump of Jesse, and a branch shall grow out of his roots. And the Spirit of the Lord shall rest upon him, the spirit of wisdom and understanding."[36] In the gospel scene which may be regarded as the messianic enthronement of Jesus the Spirit descends on him in the form of a dove.[37]

In the Judeo-Christian tradition, then, there is an affinity between the rite of anointing and the idea of consecration and consequently between anointing and the Spirit of God who is the normal agent of the divine action: the Spirit effects a spiritual anointing. The same holds for Christian initiation. The thing that distinguishes Christian baptism from Jewish rites of purification is that the former is a baptism in the Spirit. Jesus teaches Nicodemus the necessity of rebirth from water and the Holy Spirit.[38] John the Baptist says that he himself baptizes with water but that the one coming after him will baptize with the Holy Spirit.[39] St. Paul, in reminding Christians of their baptism, observes that they have been "sealed" with the Holy Spirit (*esphragisthēte, signati estis*).[40] The Holy Spirit has imprinted a seal on them. However, this seal or "anointing" is now not purely of the spiritual order. Rather, the symbolism of anointing influenced the rite so that at a very early period a bodily anointing with oil became part of the baptismal rite. This occurred everywhere in the Church, although the precise liturgical form differed. Thus in the patriarchate of Antioch the anointing took place before baptism. In the Africa of Tertullian's time, on the other hand, it took place after baptism. Hippolytus is the first that we know of to adopt both anointings, but to do so he had to change their meaning. The first is an anointing for exorcism,[41] the second an anointing of thanksgiving, that is, of blessing or consecration.[42]

Between the two anointings come the renunciation of Satan and the profession of faith that accompanies the act of baptism. There is no baptismal formula of the type: "I baptize you . . ." or "So-and-so is baptized . . ." To be baptized in the name of the Father and of the Son and of the Holy Spirit means to be baptized by professing faith in the three divine Persons.[43] The reader will observe that the baptismal creed of Hippolytus contains no abstract truths such as the resurrection of the flesh, the forgiveness of sins, and eternal life, as later creeds will. Similarly, the Church is mentioned but not as an article of faith. The third part of the formula is: "Do you believe in the Holy Spirit within the holy Church?": not *eis ten ekklesian* (the Church as an object of belief, parallel to the Holy Spirit), but *en te hagia ekklesia* (a locative dative).[44] This last phrase can be understood in two ways. It can be taken as the conclusion to the entire creed: it is in the Church that we believe in the three divine Persons. Or the phrase is to be connected only with the third part of the creed: we believe in the Holy Spirit who is in the Church. Whatever be the interpretation adopted, the creed of Hippolytus has two characteristic marks: It expresses not a belief in abstract truths but a personal attachment to God; and this personal attachment is impossible except in and through the Church.

The act of baptizing is immediately followed by an anointing with the oil of thanksgiving or blessing. Tertullian had already written: "The flesh is anointed in order that the soul may be consecrated" (*caro ungitur ut anima consecretur*).[45] However, there are two stages in this anointing. As the neophyte emerges from the baptismal pool, he is welcomed by a priest who anoints his entire body except for his head. After putting on his clothes, the candidate approaches the bishop who anoints his head and then signs him on the forehead.[46] The two stages make up one continuous action, and it is useless to ask whether the postbaptismal anointing belongs to baptism or to confirmation. The question will arise later on, but Hippolytus does not raise it.

The signing does not complete the initiation. As we pointed out a moment ago, the individual's union with God is possible only in and through the Church. In order that the initiation may be complete, the neophyte must become part of the eucharistic community. The community must receive him with the holy kiss to which he has a right from now on; the neophyte now joins the community in offering the eucharistic sacrifice.[47]

The neophyte's first eucharist contains a special rite. At communion time three priests present three chalices. One contains water that commemorates the water of baptism; a second contains the wine that has become the blood of Christ; the third contains a mixture of milk and honey.[48] This third cup reminds us of the exhortation in the first Letter of St. Peter: "Like newborn babes, long for the pure spiritual milk."[49] The neophytes are infants who require a special nourishment if they are to grow spiritually. But we also think that the milk and honey symbolize the land promised to the people of God.[50] The initiation is now complete.

I might sum up the impression I receive in rereading these pages of the oldest Christian baptismal ritual by saying that it reminds me, first and foremost, of the dignity proper to a Christian. There is no trace of puritanism in this ritual. Christians had, of course, been sinners just like everyone else. The chapter on professions and trades says repeatedly: "Let him cease from this work or be sent away."[51] No one is rejected because of his or her past conduct, but all must learn to behave henceforth as Christians. This does not mean simply behaving like honest citizens; it means learning and practicing the specifically Christian virtues. Even when they were preparing for baptism, their sponsors had to attest that the candidates were practicing the works of charity.[52]

But, more than this, a change has now taken place in these individuals. They are not simply making moral or psychological progress. No, the Holy Spirit has transformed them. They have been buried in death with Christ and have come forth from the tomb with him in order to live a new life with him.[53] They have received the Spirit of adoptive sonship, and by his power can now cry: "Abba, Father!"[54] They have a new relationship with God: they are his children, they are the brothers and sisters of Christ. Their food now is the flesh and blood of Christ, and they must change and become like him. We are reminded of St. Leo's exhortation to the Romans of the fifth century: "Christian, recognize your dignity (*agnosce, O Christiane, dignitatem tuam*)! Now that you have become a sharer in the divine nature, do not turn back to your former vile state by acting unworthily."[55] St. Leo is only echoing St. Paul: "You were bought with a price. So glorify God in your body."[56]

There is no Christian, whatever his Church or confession, who does not feel some nostalgia when he reflects on the rich simplicity of the faith in apostolic times. But the supreme expression of this apostolic faith is the eucharistic mystery. We who share a single bread and a single cup all form a single body.[57] The Second Vatican Council grasped this fact, and the whole thrust of its reform has been to turn our Sunday gatherings into genuine communities of faith, prayer and love, after the model of the communities of the apostolic age.

Is it possible, now that ten years have passed, to pass some judgment on the road traveled since Vatican II? Any answer must be a qualified one, in which times and places are distinguished. It is no secret that the years immediately after the Council were years of blithe anarchy for the Catholic Church. I know of no one blither than the Walloon parish priest who wanted to dramatize the entry of Jesus into Jerusalem. All the men of the parish, young and old alike, refused to take part in the procession. He then turned to the female half of the community and found a devout young lady who was ready to play the part of Jesus. But the girl was stuck-up and thought that an ass was not a mount worthy of a woman nowadays; she demanded a horse. Thus the parishioners were surprised to see a kind of triumphant Joan of Arc riding into their church. The bishops were perhaps taken aback by this and similar occurrences, but they had the good sense not to regard such exuberance as a great tragedy; they retained their confidence in the prudence of a clergy whose dedication was beyond question. More recently, there have been signs of a solid renewal taking place. The Sunday Mass broadcasted by France-Culture and accompanied by a fine scriptural sermon can be cited as a model. The Masses broadcasted on Sundays by RTB in the little parishes of the Naumur diocese are also very well done.

It must be admitted, however, that not every one has as yet understood the real message of the Council. This year (1976), on the first Sunday of Lent, the parishioners of a church regarded as pioneering arrived for Sunday Mass to find that there would be no fore-mass: no prayers, no readings. The whole of it would be replaced by a discussion. Chairs were placed in a circle and a discussion was begun on a subject that had nothing to do with Lent. Some of the parishioners naturally protested: By what right are we being deprived of the word of God?

The Council wanted an extension and enrichment of the readings from scripture; there were too few of them in the Missal of Puis V. The lectionary compiled in response to this desire of the Council contains a three-year cycle and makes it possible for the faithful to hear the more important passages of the Old and New Testament. Providing, of course, that they are in fact read. But some priests systematically omit the Old Testament readings. In addition, these passages require explanation, but explanation is rarely given; instead, when read at all, the passages serve as a springboard for speaking of something completely unrelated. The victims, in this case, are the faithful, and it is the duty of the bishops to come to their defense.

It must be admitted that some priests have forgotten the teaching of Vatican II or else that they never really understood it. They seem to think that the Council erased the slate of the past and that they can now invent whatever they please. True enough, in his *aggiornamento* John XXIII meant to eliminate routines that had lost their meaning. But this purification had for its whole purpose to bring out what is essential, i.e., what assures that the faith is authentically apostolic. That is the principle on which all ecumenism is based: that each Church, by following its own true tradition, should get back to the essentials of the faith of the apostles. Only by following this path can we fulfill the desire of the Lord: "that they may be one," Father, "even as we are one."[58]

Abbaye de Mont César
Louvain

Ene BRANISTE

The Liturgical Assembly
& Its Functions
in the Apostolic Constitutions

I. INTRODUCTION: THE ORIGIN, CONTENT, AUTHOR, PERIOD AND
PLACE OF REDACTION OF THE *APOSTOLIC CONSTITUTIONS*
The compilation generally known as the *Apostolic Constitutions*
(*Diatagai ton hagion apostolon dia Klementos ton Romaion episkopou*) is the
most complete and important canonical and liturgical collection
among the various literary documents that make up the set of
"pseudoapostolic" writings composed between the end of the first
century (appearance of the *Didache*) and the end of the fifth century
(probable date of the *Canons of Hippolytus*).[1]

The *Apostolic Constitutions* were the work of an anonymous compiler of Syrian origin, who made the collection toward the end of the
fourth century. Like all the other "pseudepigrapha" ("falsely as-
cribed writings"), this one claims the authority of the apostolic college

73

which supposedly dictated their directives and passed them on to the Church, i.e., primarily to the bishops, through Clement, their disciple and bishop of Rome.[2] The collection contains many regulations, norms and directives of a disciplinary, doctrinal, moral and liturgical kind for which an apostolic origin is claimed. The whole is divided into eight books of unequal length and value; these in turn are sub-divided into chapters whose number and length differ from book to book.[3]

From the end of the fourth century on, many Christian writers of the East know and cite the *Apostolic Constitutions*, which they regard as apostolic in origin and as having been passed on by Clement of Rome. In its second canon the Council *In Trullo* (692) says that here-tics have introduced falsehoods into the compilation; the Council does not, however, doubt the supposed apostolic origin of the collec-tion. That is why the reading, use, and diffusion of the document through a large number of manuscripts did not come to a halt after the Council *In Trullo*. Photius, patriarch of Constantinople, seems to have been the first to doubt the apostolic origin of the *Apostolic Con-stitutions*, as he tried to determine which texts the Fathers of the Council *In Trullo* had regarded as falsified by heretics; this great scholar does not in fact pay much attention to these heresies.[4]

The apostolic origin of the *Apostolic Constitutions* continued to be accepted even after the first printed editions and Latin translations had appeared in the sixteenth-century West, where the compilation had hitherto been unknown. Only toward the middle of the last cen-tury did scholars begin to voice doubts in this regard. Since that time a great deal of study and research has been done in the effort to identify the real editor (or compiler) of the collection; Clement of Rome could certainly not have been this real editor. All this study led to the conclusion that the collection contains very little that could be regarded as the original work of the unknown editor. The collection is, on the whole, a compilation inspired by certain older disciplinary writings (first to third centuries) that were regarded as apostolic in origin. The editor simply adapted and codified this material, altering and adding to the texts in order to make them fit the situation of the Church in his day and his geographical area.

The first six books represent an expanded redaction of a work dis-covered around the middle of the last century: the *(Syriac) Didascalia*

Apostolorum. This last was probably composed in Syria between 215 and 250, but has come down to us only in Coptic, Arabic and Ethiopian versions or adaptations and in some Latin fragments based on a Greek original that has been lost.[5]

The first section of Book VII (chapters 1–32) of the *Apostolic Constitutions* is an amplification of the well-known, postapostolic but anonymous little work entitled *Didache of the Twelve Apostles* (*Didachē tōn dodeka apostolon*),[6] while the second part of the book (chapters 33–38) is a personal addition by the compiler, who likewise makes interpolations in the first six books. The eighth book, which is the most important from the liturgical standpoint, is inspired in its first two chapters by the book *On charisms* (*Peri charismatōn*) of Hippolytus, priest of Rome. For the rest of Book VIII the compiler used the *Apostolic Tradition* (*Apostolikē Paradosis*) of the same writer. The *Tradition*, which used to be known as the *Egyptian Church Order*,[7] is probably the most ancient set of ecclesiastical regulations that we have and is also the common source of all other similar documents.

Unlike the *Didascalia, Apostolic Tradition, Canons of Hippolytus,* and *Testament of Our Lord*, which have been preserved only in translations and adaptations, the *Apostolic Constitutions* have fortunately reached us in their original (Greek) text. The sections of interest to the liturgist provide us with a good deal of information (scattered throughout the entire work) about the liturgical functions of the various ranks of the clergy,[8] advice about churches,[9] feasts and fasts,[10] regulations for the daily divine Office and the Mass[11] and for the sacraments of Christian initiation (baptism, confirmation, and the eucharist), ordinations, and so on.[12] The information on the Church's worship is the most important part of the entire document; it also facilitates the identification of the mysterious compiler hidden behind the name of St. Clement of Rome, as well as the more or less probable determination of his country of origin and the period when he did his work. The date generally accepted for the appearance of the collection is between 380 and 400.[13]

In drawing up his rule for the Church's liturgical life, the compiler—as I pointed out above—used older writings that reflect the period when Christian worship was developing (therefore, the second and third centuries) and that therefore required to be adapted to the later stage which the liturgy of the editor's time and area had reached. This is why, alongside information taken from older documents and reflecting liturgical practices prior to the fourth century (as, e.g., prayers for the faithful being persecuted, for those in the prisons and mines, etc.), the *Apostolic Constitutions* contain data and directives proper to the stage the Christian liturgy had reached toward the end of the fourth and the beginning of the fifth century (the Office of Mass and baptism, the number and dates of the feasts, the discipline of the catechumenate, the names and functions of certain minor orders of clergy, various terms and phrases in the text, prayers, various liturgical formulas, etc.).

If we compare the liturgical formulas and rites for the Mass and baptism as described in the *Apostolic Constitutions* with those given in other written sources for the history of Christian worship in the fourth century (e.g., the well-known catecheses of St. Cyril of Jerusalem, the exegetical and liturgical homilies of St. John Chrysostom, [14] or the baptismal homilies of Theodore of Mopsuestia[15]), we can infer, first of all, that the compiler of the *Apostolic Constitutions* can only have been a Syrian and a native of Antioch or its vicinity, for it is the cultic traditions of Antioch that he has taken as his model.

In the second place, if we keep before us certain doctrinally incorrect expressions and formulas that occur in the liturgical prayers and disciplinary directives of the *Apostolic Constitutions* and that also occur in the interpolated passages of the Letters of St. Ignatius of Antioch, [16] we can conclude that the anonymous redactor of the *Apostolic Constitutions* is identical with the interpolator of the Ignatian letters. The writer in question is an Arian, a Semiarian or an Apollinarist. More concretely, he has been identified by some with bishop Euzoius "of the imperial church of Antioch" (36–370), a former Arian turned Homoean and supposedly the driving force behind the entire body of pseudoapostolic literature of which the *Apostolic Constitutions* are a part, [17] and by others with Acacius of Caesarea[18] or Silvanus of Tarsus. [19]

Finally, because of details in the formulas expressing the trinitarian theology of the *Apostolic Constitutions*, details found also in the surviving writings of Eunomius, an Anomaean who became bishop of Cyzicus ca. 361,[20], Mgr. Georg Wagner, bishop of Eudoxia, is inclined to think that Eunomius himself may have been the redactor of the *Apostolic Constitutions*. According to St. Jerome, [21] Eunomius was still living in Cappadocia in the last decade of the fourth century (392) and authoring many writings against the faith of the Church. One of these, says Mgr. Wagner, could well have been the *Apostolic Constitutions*, in which Eunomius would be attempting to formulate some of his sectarian ideas and transmit them to later generations in the guise of more ancient documents which the Church regarded as being apostolic in origin.[22]

But the unknown redactor clearly was not trying to defend his sectarian ideas. His aim was to draw up a body of regulations for the life of the Church in his day and to give these directive apostolic authority. The few traces of heresy may have already been part of the original documents which the compiler used, or he himself may have introduced them as he modified the older texts. In either case, they do not greatly prejudice the documentary value, canonical[23] or liturgical, of the collection. The *Apostolic Constitutions* are regarded as one of the most important literary sources for the ecclesiastical discipline and worship of the Eastern Church toward the end of the fourth century.[24]

The document supplies a great deal of valuable information especially for reconstructing the Mass as celebrated toward the end of the fourth century in the area of the old patriarchate of Antioch. The eucharistic service is described twice: first, and briefly, in Book II, chapter 57, and a second time in Book VIII, chapters 5–15, where the rite for the consecration of a bishop is followed by the oldest complete formulary of the Mass that we have. The chapters not only describe the sequence of parts for the service, but also give the texts of the prayers, diaconal litanies, and liturgical formulas spoken by deacon, priest or bishop. This is the so-called "Clementine liturgy," after Clement of Rome whom the compiler of the *Apostolic Constitutions* presents as the scribe who takes down the instructions of the Apostles. The first of the two descriptions (II, 57) is of the regular liturgical assemblies held on feast days (including Sundays)[25]; the second description is of an exceptional Mass celebrated at the consecration of a bishop and more solemn in character.

Like every set of regulations, these two descriptions "always express to some extent an ideal that does not necessarily correspond to the reality."[26] At the same time, however, even if scholars generally regard the descriptions as "ideal formularies" which supply "models"[27] rather than formulas actually used, the two descriptions of liturgical assemblies in the *Apostolic Constitutions* do reflect faithfully enough the liturgical practice of the major churches of Syria, Antioch, Laodicea, Tyre, Caesarea, Jerusalem, and perhaps even Constantinople. This applies to the sequence of component parts, the shape of the rites, the readings and prayers, their style and general themes, etc.[28] This is the main reason why the Clementine liturgy has attracted the attention of liturgists, who regard it as a very important document for the history of the Syrian liturgical rite.[29] These two descriptions of liturgical assemblies, supplemented by further details in other books and chapters of the compilation, will serve us as our chief source of information in this essay.

II. THE LITURGICAL ASSEMBLIES DESCRIBED IN THE *APOSTOLIC CONSTITUTIONS*

1. Specific aspects of the Eastern Church's life and the development of its Christian worship during the second half of the fourth century
In speaking of the liturgical assemblies of the local Church, and especially of assemblies for Mass, the anonymous compiler of the *Apostolic Constitutions* habitually uses the phrase "the assembly of the faithful" (*to ton piston synathrousma*) or the biblical expressions "the Church of God" (*he tou Theou ekklesia*)[30] and "the body of Christ" (*to soma tou Christou*).[31] As everywhere else in the Church, these assemblies comprise the members of the clergy and the faithful.

The gradual evolution of Christian worship (the pace had quickened since the peace established by Constantine), the growing number of Christians once the time of persecution had passed, the increasingly numerous and larger churches that were being built everywhere, the more developed organization of the catechumenate and the discipline of public penance, the ever-changing conditions in which the Church lived its life, and so forth: all these had caused the establishment of new and many-faceted functions and services in liturgical assemblies at the time when the *Apostolic Constitutions* were compiled.

Some of these functions and services had been taken on by the various classes of clergy in the strict sense (bishops, priests, deacons) or by ministers lower in rank (minor orders) of the kind that had already been in existence before the peace of Constantine (deaconesses, subdeacons, readers, exorcists, porters). The number of individuals serving in these various ranks had kept pace with the increasing number of faithful. But, in keeping with the biological principle that "a function creates its own organ,"[32] new functions also led to the creation of new kinds of ministers who took their place among the minor orders; an example of such a new ministry is the *cantor*.

The sacramental functions of the three classes of clergy proper in liturgical assemblies had been more or less precisely defined since the end of the first century and the beginning of the second.[33] The roles of the lower ranks of ministers had likewise been determined when these first made their appearance in the life of the ecclesial communities. However, at the time with which we are now dealing, the usurpation of diaconal functions by persons in minor orders was making it necessary for ecclesiastical authorities to intervene with a firm hand so as to restore order and determine more specifically the rights and obligations proper to each kind of minister. We find these clarifications in the canons of various councils[34] and in the disciplinary directives and rules of the various anonymous but supposedly apostolic Church Orders.

It is this situation that explains the great number and variety of such rules in the *Apostolic Constitutions*,[35] as well as the important role which all the disciplinary compilations of this type have played, down to the present day, in the Eastern Churches,[36] where such regulations have proved constantly necessary for order and discipline. Chapters 28 and 46 of Book VIII of the *Apostolic Constitutions* are especially interesting and significant. The first of these two chapters contains a summary but very unambiguous statement of the liturgical rites and functions of the various ranks of the clergy, while the second, with an eye on those who "dare to confuse the degrees and to violate the ordination given to each person by arrogating to themselves dignities not bestowed on them,"[37] contains a good deal of advice and exhortation concerning respect for the Church's assignment of the various functions.

2. The members of the clergy proper and their functions in the liturgical assemblies described in the Apostolic Constitutions
a. The bishop (ho episkopos, ho archiereus)
As head of the local Church, the bishop enjoys a primacy in the respect given him by all the members of the clergy and the entire body of the faithful. He has the right to convoke, gather or reunite the *ekklēsia* or ecclesial community that is under his direction, and he takes the initiative in such convoking, that is, in bringing into existence the "liturgical assembly," which meets in the cathedral church and over which he presides as principal celebrant of the Mass: "And you, O bishop, when *you gather the Church of God . . .*" (II, 57, 2).

In other words, the bishop, acting in the name of Christ, transforms an assembly into a eucharistic synaxis and a visible manifestation of the Church of God, or an "epiphany" of the Church, to use the language of modern theologians.[38] Because he possesses full and supreme sacramental power in the Church, his main function is to offer sacrifice for the people, as did the high priest in the Old Testament; concretely, his chief role is to celebrate the holy eucharist. This is why his place in the church is close to the altar of sacrifice, in the sanctuary.

"You bishops are priests and Levites for your people. You officiate at the holy Tabernacle, in the universal holy Church, and you remain near the altar of sacrifices of the Lord our God and offer him *bloodless sacrifices of praise*[39] through Jesus, the high priest (Heb 4.14). You are prophets . . . mediators between God and his faithful, receivers and messengers of the word, experts in scripture, the voice of God and witnesses of his will. You carry the sins of all and are responsible for all" (II, 25).

Book VIII, chapters 4 and 5 describe the rite of election and consecration of a bishop. The first manifestation of the new degree of priesthood that is now his is the celebration of Mass together with the college of priests.[40] This is why both descriptions of the liturgical assembly in the *Apostolic Constitution* are of Masses presided over and celebrated by the bishop himself along with all the members of the clergy.[40a]

The bishop is not only the head of this assembly; he is also responsible for good order in the Church and for the religious welfare of his spiritual flock, "as a pilot (is responsible) for a great ship" (II, 57).[41] He is therefore obliged to give subordinate ministers directives that will assure proper order, silence and discipline in the church during divine service, "for the Church is a school not of disorder but of good order" (VIII, 31).

From his seat in the center of the sanctuary (*hē anō kathedra*, "the chair on high"), he oversees the entire assembly and the progress of the service, especially during the first part of the liturgy, the Mass "of the catechumens." Then, once the Mass "of the faithful" has begun, he approaches the sacred altar and, according to custom, says aloud the great prayer of the holy sacrifice (the *anaphora* or *eucharistic canon*), for which the Clementine liturgy provides a lengthy formulary (VIII, 12). The bishop likewise says all the prayers and liturgical formulas for the greeting and blessing of the faithful, the *catechumens*, the *candidates for baptism* (*competentes*, *photizomenoi*), the *penitents*, and *energumens* ("demoniacs"); all these groups, except the faithful, are sent from the church one by one at the end of the liturgy for the catechumens. Model texts for these prayers are given in VIII, 6–9 and 11.

The bishop gives the sermon (homily) that follows upon the reading of the gospel; when the concelebrating priests also preach, the bishop is the last to rise and speak (II, 57). Prayers are said for the bishop during the diaconal litanies (ectenies) and in the course of the eucharistic anaphora (VIII, 10 and 12–13).[42] When the time for communion arrives, the bishop is the first to receive (VIII, 13), and it is he who then offers the sacred bread to all the members of the clergy and all the faithful.

If a bishop of another diocese visits one of his colleagues, he will be invited to speak to the people and even to celebrate the holy sacrifice if he is willing; if he does not wish to celebrate, he should at least give the blessing to the people (II, 58).[43]

b.Priests or presbyters (hoi presbyteroi, hoi hiereis, presbyteri, sacerdotes)
Priests play a somewhat subdued role in the assemblies described in the *Apostolic Constitutions*. There were many priests in each local church, just as there had been in apostolic times (Jas 5.14: "Is any among you sick? Let him call for *the elders* [the *presbyters*] of the

church"). In cathedral churches the priests had their place in the sanctuary on either side of the bishop's chair; they sat on the "second seats" (*deuteroi thronoi*), facing the people.

One of the priests might read the gospel (if a deacon did not do so); then, in some churches, all the priests present arose and preached before the bishop arose in his turn (II, 57).[44] When the time for the kiss of peace came, the priests and deacons gave this greeting to the bishop; then they washed their hands in water brought to them by the subdeacons, as a sign of purity of soul. During the eucharistic anaphora, they surrounded the bishop at the altar of sacrifice, standing on his right and left "like so many pupils around their teacher," and saying the prayers in a low voice or silently while the high priest prayed aloud (VIII, 12). Both the deacons, in the great litany that began the Mass of the faithful, and the bishop during the eucharistic anaphora prayed for the presbyters (VIII, chapters 10, 12, and 13). At communion time they received the sacred species immediately after the bishop (VIII, 13).

The rite of presbyteral ordination is also described (VIII, 16).[45]

c. Deacons (hoi diakonoi, diaconi)

At this period of history the deacons had many more functions in the liturgical assembly than they have today in the Eastern Churches which have retained this clerical order. Despite canon 15 of the local council of Neocaesarea (315), which decreed that there be only seven deacons in each city, no matter how large a city it might be,[46] the number of deacons kept on growing in response both to the development of the liturgy and to new needs in the social and religious life of the Church. At the same time their traditional importance within the Christian communities likewise increased, so that in the lists of clerics in the *Apostolic Constitutions* the deacons are sometimes listed immediately after the bishop. They had the right to sit near him, "as Christ sits near the Father" (II, 26). They acted as "the ears and eyes and mouth of bishop, as his heart and soul, in order that he might no longer be obliged to concern himself with many things but might limit himself to the most important ones (II, 44; III, 19).

Just as the Son is the angel and prophet of the Father,[47] so the deacon is the angel and prophet of the bishop (II, 30). This is why, if need arose and the bishops and priests were absent, the deacon was given power to excommunicate ministers of lesser rank (subdeacons, readers, cantors, and deaconesses; cf. VIII, 28). The bishop ordained the deacons in the presence of all the priests and other deacons (VIII, 17-18).[48]

The eucharistic service as described in this compilation supposes that there was a rather large number of deacons in the cathedral churches of Syria at this period; this inference is based on the many functions deacons had to exercise in the liturgical assemblies. In their role as "sailors" and "commanders of the rowers in the ship of the Church," they received from the bishop—the captain of the ship—the command, first of all, "to determine the places to be occupied in the church by the brothers and sisters, as well as by the navigators, and to do so with all care and propriety" (II, 57). In principle, the deacons had their own place in the sanctuary, near the bishop and priests. Some at least of the deacons in fact stood there, robed "in less elaborate garments" (ibid.) as befitted men who were helpers of the bishop and priests. Other deacons, however, had to be almost constantly on the move throughout the church: leading newcomers to their places, keeping an eye on the people, rebuking the unruly and restoring order, so that discipline and silence might reign in the church during the service. At the proper time, one of the deacons went to the ambo and read the gospel, unless a priest did so on any given occasion (ibid.).

The deacons recited all prayers in litanic forms (the ectenies) and saw to it that various categories of people left the church who were obliged to do so at the end of the liturgy of the catechumens. Before the eucharistic anaphora some of the deacons deposited on the altar the offerings of bread and wine which the faithful had brought for the eucharist, while other deacons concentrated on the behavior of the faithful. While the bishop recited the anaphora, two deacons stood at the altar and waved fans (*rhipidia*) made of thin parchment or peacocks' feathers or linen (VIII, 12). The others remained at the doors for men, to see that no one entered or left the church (VIII, 11). It was also the deacons who welcomed the faithful from other places who might arrive during the liturgy of the word; after checking the letters of recommendation or approbation which these strangers carried[49] and after verifying their orthodoxy, the deacons brought them into the church to the place reserved for persons of their condition or rank. The same procedure was followed in receiving members of the clergy from other communities.

At the consecration of a bishop, deacons held the open book of the gospels above the head of the consecrand (VIII, 4). They likewise took part in the ordination of the clergy of all ranks (VIII, 16ff.). Prayers for them were said during the diaconal litanies and in the diptychs of the eucharistic anaphora (VIII, chapters 10, 12, 13). When the time came for the clergy to communicate, the deacons received the sacred species from the bishop, after the priests (as they do to-day). At the communion of the laity one of the deacons offered them the sacred cup from which the faithful took a little of the precious blood directly; the deacon said: "Blood of Christ, cup of life," and the communicant answered "Amen." When all had communicated, the deacons took what remained of the eucharist and deposited it in the pastophorion (a kind of sacristy) or in the prothesis (a chamber off the sanctuary) (VIII, 13; cf. chapter 28).

Another function of the deacons was to distribute to the clergy, in accordance with the directives of the bishop or priests, the offerings the faithful had brought to the church (VIII, 31). They also presented to the priests or bishop pagan candidates for the catechumenate and the reception of baptism (VIII, 32).

In the *Apostolic Constitutions* we find hardly any reference to the *archdeacon* or his function, although this function was a very important one in the churches of the Eastern Syrians.

3. Minor Orders

As is generally known, at this period of history the lesser liturgical ministers played a very important part in liturgical assemblies, by reason both of their large numbers and of the functions they exercised. In the liturgical service described in the *Apostolic Constitutions*, the following five subordinate ranks are mentioned, each having its proper activities: subdeacons, readers, cantors, deaconesses, and porters.

a. Subdeacons

The *subdeacons* (*hoi hypodiakonoi, subdiaconi*) mentioned in literary documents from the third century on,[50] are called *hyperetai* (ministers, servants) in canons 20-22, 24 and 43 of the council of Laodicea (ca.

362),[51] in which their rights and functions in the liturgy are determined in a more precise way. In the *Apostolic Constitutions* they are designated at times by their ancient name of *hyperetai*[52] and at other times by the name *hypodiakonoi* (subdeacons),[53] which will henceforth be the accepted term for them in Orthodox liturgical vocabulary down to the present time. The anonymous compiler continues the effort of the council of Laodicea to define the rights and duties of subdeacons in the Church's assemblies for public prayer, over against those of the deacons and other ministers of lower rank.

Subdeacons, for example, do not have the right to celebrate baptism. They can be ordained only by the bishop (III, 11),[54] and we are even given a prayer formula for the cheirothesia of subdeacons (VIII, 21).[55] Like all others in minor orders, the subdeacons are subordinate to the deacons, and the latter have the right to excommunicate them, if need arises, in the absence of bishop and priests (VIII, 28).

At liturgical assemblies and during the Mass of the faithful, subdeacons guarded the doors where women entered, in order to prevent anyone from entering or leaving the church. One of the subdeacons brought the priests the water for washing their hands (VIII, 11, 11). At communion time they came forward immediately after the deacons (VIII, 13, 14). After Mass when the offerings meant for the Church's ministers were being distributed, subdeacons received the tenth part which each minister of minor rank was assigned (VIII, 31). The subdeacons, along with the others in minor orders, were prayed for both in the diaconal litanies and in the general intercessory prayers for the Church (the diptychs) which the bishop recited at the end of the eucharistic anaphora (VIII, 10, 9; VIII, 12, 43).

b. Deaconesses

Deaconesses (*hai diakonoi, virgines canonicae*) were the only women admitted to the ranks of the lower clergy in the early Church. At the same time, however, they were also the oldest of the minor orders. The name of Phoebe, deaconess of the church at Cenchreae (Rom 16.1), has come down to us from the apostolic age. Literary documents from the period which saw the compilation of the *Apostolic Constitutions* have preserved the memory of deaconesses famous for their piety and learning: such women as Olympias, Procula and Pentada, collaborators and correspondents of St. John Chrysostom[56];

Marthana of Seleucia, friend of Egeria, the pilgrim from the West,[57] eulogized by Basil of Seleucia (fifth century)[58]; Macrina, the devout sister of St. Basil the Great and St. Gregory of Nyssa; and others.

Their admittance to the ranks of the lower clergy by means of a special consecration (cheirothesia), which is attested in earlier documents,[59] is confirmed by the *Apostolic Constitutions*. They are mentioned here in some lists of the lesser clergy, usually after the latter and before the various classes of women: elderly women, virgins, etc. (cf. II, 26). Once they are given the unusual honor of being mentioned, in a forced trinitarian parallelism, immediately after bishop and deacon. In this passage it is said that the bishop is to be honored like God the Father, the deacon like Christ who did only what pleased the Father, and "the deaconess you are to honor in the image of the Holy Spirit, since she does and says nothing apart from the deacon, just as the Paraclete does and says nothing on his own as it were; rather, in glorifying Christ, he waits upon the latter's will" (II, 26).

This extravagant comparison of the deacon with Christ and the deaconess with the Holy Spirit (Bardesanes had already made it and the *Didascalia* had repeated it) is one manifestation of the subordinationist doctrine held by the compiler (probably Eunomius). It can be explained by the latter's Syrian origin, since only in Syriac is the name of the Holy Spirit a feminine one, thus allowing Syrians to compare the Spirit to a woman, in this case a deaconess.[60]

Deaconesses were recruited solely among spotless virgins or at least among widows who had been married only once and had remained faithful and deserving of respect (cf. 1 Tim 5.9).[61] They received their consecration from the bishop (III, 11); no minimum age was required.[62] We are given a prayer formula for their cheirothesia, which took place in the presence of the priests, deacons and deaconesses (VIII, 19–20). After reciting the consecratory prayer, the bishop anointed the forehead of the new deaconess with sacred oil (III, 16).

The deaconesses did not have the right to perform baptisms by themselves (III, 11) or to perform any of the sacramental actions reserved to priests or deacons.[63] They simply assisted priests and bishops in the baptism and confirmation of women "for propriety's sake" (VIII, 28). At the prebaptismal anointing of women "the deacon is simply to anoint their foreheads with sacred oil; then the deaconesses are to complete the anointing, so that the transmission of the incorruptible seal may take place in all decency (III, 16). Similarly, for reasons of modesty and the avoidance of subsequent suspicions, any women wishing to visit a deacon or bishop could be brought into his presence only by a deaconess (II, 26).

In the liturgical assemblies the deaconesses stood near the doors used by women and kept watch at them (II, 57; cf. VIII, 28).[64] They welcomed all women, whatever their social status or age and no matter where they came from, locally or from foreign parts, and led them to the places appointed for them (II, 58). At communion time, they stood in line after the rest of the lower clergy and after the ascetics (cf. below), and received communion first among the women, i.e., before the virgins and widows (VIII, 13). Like the other lower clergy they received a share of the offerings distributed to the clergy after Mass (VIII, 31).[65]

The great importance accorded to deaconesses in the early Syrian Church caused their order to have a longer life among the Western Syrians than in the other Eastern Churches.[66]

c. Readers

Readers (*hoi anagnōstai, lectores*), who are listed as a minor order from the end of the second century and the beginning of the third,[67] had one of the most necessary and useful of all functions in Christian liturgical assemblies: the reading of the sacred books. This explains why they appear early on in the liturgical life of the Church; it also explains why this clerical order has survived, in different forms and with different names, in almost all the Christian Churches of our day. It explains, too, why readers are always mentioned when lists are given in the *Apostolic Constitutions* of the clergy generally and of the minor orders in particular (on at least ten occasions).

We know of no debates or controversies about the usefulness of their liturgical function. They were first in the hierarchy of minor orders until subdeacons made their appearance; henceforth they vied for priority until the subdeacons won out for good. This is why in the lists of lesser clergy in the *Apostolic Constitutions* they are sometimes named immediately after the deacons (and before the subdeacons) as was traditional (II, 26; 28; III, 11), and sometimes after the sub-deacons (VI, 17; VIII, 10; 12; 13; 31).[68]

Many of the directives given with regard to readers in the *Apostolic Constitutions* are to specify their assignments, rights and duties in the religious life of Christian communities and in the Church's worship. For example, the bishop alone can bestow their order upon them; we are even given a prayer formula for their cheirothesia.[69] They had no right to officiate at baptisms (III, 11). They could marry only once, either before or after entering the ranks of the clergy (VI, 17). In liturgical assemblies they exercised their function from the ambo which was located at the center of the church; they read all the passages from the Old and New Testaments (except for the gospels) that formed the main part of the liturgy of the catechumens (II, 57). Prayers were offered for them in traditional intercessory formulas during the great litany (collect) at the beginning of the Mass of the faithful and in the diptychs of the eucharistic anaphora (VIII, 10; 12). At communion time they followed the subdeacons (VIII, 13) and, like the rest of the lower clergy, they had a share of the food brought for the agape tables (II, 28)[70] as well as of the offerings of bread and wine that had not been used in the eucharist (VIII, 31).

d. Cantors

During this period cantors (*hoi psaltai, hoi psaltodoi, psalmistae, cantores*) formed a distinct order among the lower clergy, having taken over some of the functions hitherto exercised by readers, namely, those concerned with singing in church. They had been mentioned previously in canons 15, 23 and 24 of the council of Laodicea (ca. 362) where they were prohibited from wearing the *orarion* (*stola*, stole) during divine services. The *Apostolic Constitutions* mention them when dealing with minor orders that have more or less precisely determined functions. For example, they are listed (after the readers) among the clerics who are recommended to the laity for attention and respect (II, 26) and who have a claim on the offerings which the faithful make for the support of the clergy (II, 28) and on the offerings (eulogies) which the faithful bring to the church (VIII, 31).

Like all the lesser clergy, cantors can be ordained only by the bishop.[71] They do not have the right to baptize (III, 11) and can marry only once, either before or after entering the clergy (VI, 17). Like all the other minor orders they are subordinate to the deacons, who can excommunicate them, if need arises, in the absence of priests and bishop (VIII, 28).

In the liturgical assemblies the cantors had a still rather limited role, since the short responses to the litanies and various formulas spoken by the deacons were given by all of the faithful.[72] However, they were in charge of the psalms sung in responsorial fashion between the scriptural readings in the liturgy of the catechumens: they did each verse solo, and the faithful joined in with an *akrostichon* or refrain.[73] Intercession was made for them whenever the Church prayed to God for the members of the clergy generally, in the great deaconal litany and in the diptychs of the eucharistic anaphora (VIII, 10; 12). At the communion time they received the sacrament after the readers (VIII, 13).

e. Porters

Porters (*hoi pylōroi, ostiarii*), that is, watchmen or overseers of the church doors during services, formed the final rank of the lower clergy that is acknowledged in the *Apostolic Constitutions*. They had already been listed among the lower clergy in a law of 337 (*Theodosian Codex* XVI, xii, 24) and in canon 24 of the council of Laodicea. Their function, though modest, was nonetheless fairly important in a period when the discipline of "the secret" (*disciplina arcani*) as well as the disciplines of the catechumenate and public penance were still in force, and it was necessary to know who entered and left the church, especially during liturgical assemblies.

Apart from services they had the same moral and disciplinary rights and duties as all the others of the lesser clergy (II, 26; 28; III, 11; VI, 17). During liturgical assemblies they were required to stand at the doors where males entered, and to keep an attentive watch over these doors, especially during the celebration of the holy sacrifice (II, 57). They are not mentioned among the lesser clergy in connection with the public prayer for the latter in the great diaconal litany or in the diptychs. At communion time they probably came up after the cantors, although they are not mentioned at this point in the description of the Clementine liturgy (VIII, 13). Neither are they mentioned among the liturgical ministers whose sacramental roles are described in chapter 28; nor is any prayer given for the bestowal of their order in the chapters on the cheirotonia and cheirothesia of the various ranks of the clergy (VIII, 16ff.)

f. Exorcists

Exorcists (*hoi eporkistai, exorcistae*) are mentioned among the lower clergy from the second century on,[74] and played an active role in the preparation of candidates for baptism and in the supervision of energumens during services, but they are not listed among the members of the clergy in the *Apostolic Constitutions*. A single text discusses the point (VIII, 26): exorcists are not ordained because the power to exorcise (to banish evil powers and the devil's action) was still regarded as a charism, an exceptional gift which God gives not by human appointment but by the inspiration of the Holy Spirit.[75] This is why no mention is made of them either in the description of the baptismal rite (VIII, 39–45) or in VIII, 28 where the sacramental role of each order of the clergy is described. An exorcist could, however, enter the ranks of the clergy if he fulfilled the conditions required for being chosen a deacon, a priest or even a bishop.

4. The faithful (laity) in the liturgical assembly
a. General considerations on the participation of the faithful in the Church's worship during the early Christian period

The faithful (*hoi laikoi*) who make up "the people" (*ho laos*) or "the Church of God" (*hē tou Theou ekklesia*) as a religious community play an important part in the liturgical assemblies of this period. Their importance is owing to their large numbers and to their active participation in the services celebrated by the clergy. "You too, the laity, the Church chosen by God, must heed this, for the people too were named of old the *people of God*[76] and a *holy nation* (Ex 19.5-6). Therefore you are *God's holy Church, written in heaven, a royal priesthood, a holy nation, a people acquired* [by God] (cf. Heb 12.12; 1 Pet 2.9), *a bride adorned* by God (Rev 21.2), a great Church, a faithful Church (II, 26)."[77]

The participation of the faithful in the liturgical assemblies of the period was an ongoing feature; at the same time it was *total* or quasi-unanimous from the numerical standpoint. Only the sick, prisoners, or those prevented by causes over which they had no control absented themselves from Mass; even to these people, however, the deacons brought the sacred species after Mass.[78] At this period, the liturgical assembly, gathered around the bishop (or presiding priest whom he delegated) who was flanked (assisted) by the clerics of all ranks, provided the liveliest image of that complete unity in prayer, worship and love that characterized the early Church. The most severe penalty—"excommunication"—inflicted on the faithful meant in practice that they were excluded from the community when it assembled for the public worship of the Church.[79]

Furthermore, participation in the liturgical gathering was at that time essential and characteristic for Christian life generally. The awareness the faithful had of belonging to the *ekklēsia*, i.e., a new religious society different from the pagan world around it, found its outward expression especially in attendance at liturgical gatherings and principally the eucharist. The fact of assisting at one and the same altar of sacrifice was the most important proof of unity with the bishop and with the Christian community over which he presided. On the other hand, a person's absence from the place of assembly for public prayer was the clearest evidence that he had separated himself from the unity of the Church.[80]

This is why the *Apostolic Constitutions* insist on the duty of the faithful to gather daily in the church for morning prayer and the evening office. There is the conviction that the liturgical assembly in fact represents the *Church* as the visible community or body of Christ and that only if the community thus assembles in the sacred building for the celebration of the eucharist, which is the center of the Church's religious life, will the unity and permanence of the Church be assured. Failure in this duty was equivalent to separation from the body of Christ; it meant the scattering of the Church and the breakdown of its spiritual unity.[81] II, 59, addressed to the bishop, is concerned entirely with his duty of seeing to it that the Church "assembles" at the liturgical synaxes on weekdays as well as on Sundays.

Christian participation in liturgical assemblies was a real and conscious affair at this period. It was a participation enlightened by the knowledge of doctrine and liturgical symbolism that had been gained through mystagogical initiation before and after baptism. This knowledge and initiation were the object (content) of the well-known homilies and catecheses left us by the great teachers of the period when the discipline of the catechumenate was being developed: St.

Cyril at Jerusalem, St. John Chrysostom at Antioch, St. Ambrose at Milan, Bishop Theodore at Mopsuestia, and others.

The participation of the faithful in the Mass was also *effective* or *active* and found outward expression especially in these three actions:

1) All of the faithful brought to church an offering of bread and wine that would provide the matter for the eucharistic sacrifice and symbolize the offering of their personal lives.

2) Everyone received communion as a matter of course (at each Mass).

3) All took part in the singing of the hymns and responses, with the children always to the fore.[82] As we noted above, the cantors were in charge only of the psalms sung between the scriptural readings at the beginning of the liturgy of the catechumens. The entire people associated themselves with the prayers the deacon said in litanic form (the ectenies): "And let all of the faithful offer heartfelt prayer for them [the catechumens] by saying: 'Lord, have mercy!'. . . And to each prayer formula recited by the deacon . . . the people are to respond with: 'Lord, have mercy!' with the children taking the lead" (VIII, 6, 4 and 9).[83]

b. Order and discipline in the liturgical assembly

This massive participation of the Christian people in the liturgy meant that very large crowds of the faithful regularly gathered in the vast cathedral churches (basilicas in style), both in Syria and in other Christian areas. Given the size of the churches, the large number of participants in the liturgical assemblies, and the differences among them in sex, age, profession, social class, and religious and moral life, it was not unnatural that from the moment they entered the building they should be separated into groups according to age and sex, with each group having its precisely determined place in the church. The task of distributing places and watching over order and discipline within each group fell to the deacons, subdeacons, deaconesses and porters.

"Bishop, when you bring together the Church of God, you shall, like the pilot of a great ship, take steps to assure good order in the assemblies by commanding the deacons, like so many sailors, to determine the places to be occupied by the brothers and sisters, as well as by the navigators, and to do so with all care and propriety.

"First of all, the church is to be oblong (rectangular) in shape, like a ship, and is to face East, with the *pastophoria* (themselves also facing) East on each side. At the center (of the apse) the bishop's chair is to be placed, and the priests (the *presbyterion*, the presbytery or college of priests) are to sit on his right and left. The deacons are to stand nearby, robed in less elaborate garments, for they are like sailors and commanders of the rowers.[84]

"Under the direction of the deacons the faithful (*hoi laikoi*) are to be given their places in the other part of the church,[85] in complete silence and good order. The women are to sit apart and in silence.[86] . . . The porters (*hoi pyloroi*) must stand at the doors intended for men, and the deaconesses at the doors for women, and observe who enters the ship. . . . When they find someone who is not in his or her proper place, the person is to be reprimanded by the deacon . . . and led to his or her place. For the church is not only like a ship; it is also like a fold, and just as the herders group all the mute animals— the sheep and the goats—by sex and age, and each animal gathers with its fellows, so too in the church the youngest are to sit all on one side if possible, and if there is no room, they are to stand; the older people are to take their places in good order, with fathers and mothers keeping their standing children close to them. Similarly, let the young girls have a separate place if possible; if not, let them stand behind the women. Let the married women and those with children have their own area. But let the *virgins* and *widows* and *elderly women* be in the front rows.

"The deacon is to take charge of these places, so that all who enter (the church) may go to their proper place and not remain at the entrance. So too, the deacon is to keep an eye on the people, so that no one may whisper or laugh or doze or make gestures, for in church everyone should behave respectfully and keep his ears attentively open to the word of God (II, 57)."

The passage just cited is the first description given in the *Apostolic Constitutions* of a liturgical assembly. The emphasis is on measures taken to assure order; these were quite necessary in order to provide an atmosphere of silence and self-control in the church during the liturgy of the catechumens, which was attended not only by the faithful but by the *catechumens* (those preparing for baptism), the *energumens* or *possessed* (who were in the care of the exorcists), the *candidates for proximate baptism (phōtizomenoi, illuminandi, competentes)*, and the *penitents*.[87] All of these groups usually remained in the antechamber to the nave (the narthex or vestibule of the church), where they were permitted to listen to the scripture readings and the sermon (homily) which made up the first part of the "liturgy of the word." The same permission was given to pagans (*apistoi*) who were not yet registered among the catechumens but wished to hear the gospel message. For this reason these individuals are sometimes called "hearers" (*ak-roōmenoi, audientes*); they are not to be confused with the category of catechumens or penitents that bear the same name. Canon 14 of the Council of Nicaea had prescribed an apprenticeship of three years for such "hearers" before they were registered among the catechumens. They were obliged to leave the church immediately after the sermon (homily). Therefore, when the deacon ascended the ambo for the recitation of the litanies, he first announced: "Let no hearer, no unbeliever (remain in the church)!"[88]

When the hearers had left and silence had been restored in the church, the liturgy of the catechumens continued with the litanies (recited by the deacons) and special prayers (recited by the bishop or presiding priest) for the four categories of people mentioned above; each group left the church in turn after receiving the bishop's blessing.[89]

With this the liturgy of the catechumens ended and the Mass of the faithful began; only believers could take part in the latter. The faithful, now the only ones present in the church, presented their offerings of bread and wine for the eucharist[90] and could receive communion.

c. Privileged groups among the faithful at the liturgical assemblies
During the Mass of the faithful at this period liturgical assemblies were marked by the presence of certain groups of the faithful (the laity), male and female, who occupied places of honor (the places closest to the sanctuary) in the nave, either because of their advanced years or because of their piety or because of the useful services which they were giving the Church and which were rewarded in the form of the special honor and attention accorded them in the local communities, both in the church building and outside of it.

The first were the *ascetics* (*hoi* or *hai asketai*), who are also known to us from other documents,[91] which call them *ascetics* or *solitaries* (*monazontes*) or *continent ones* (*apotaktites, apotactitae, continentes*).[92] These persons were quite numerous in the Christian East at this period and were a kind of monk (anchorite) still in the world; far from withdrawing into the desert, they lived in the midst of society but practiced continence, fervent prayer, fasting and asceticism, and were also distinguished by their special zeal in attending the daily services of the Church.[93] Most of these individuals were men, but women were not lacking.

The fact that women ascetics were in a minority is the reason why they were often confused with another privileged group in the Christian communities of that era, namely, the *virgins* (*hoi* or *hai parthenoi, virgines*). These were recruited primarily among young women who, without withdrawing into a monastery (convent), led an abstemious life, practiced chastity, regularly attended liturgical assemblies, and were at the disposal of the Church for the various services they could provide other Christian women. However, there were also men who adopted this manner of life and who were also called *virgins* (*hoi parthenoi*).

Other distinct groups in the early Church were *widows* (*hai cherai, viduae*) and *elderly women* or *presbytides* (*hai presbytides*); a further group at times were the *orphans* of the community, to whom the Church gave care and protection. Christian widows and elderly women were very numerous at this period and received no aid or assistance from the slave-based society of the pagan world; from the apostolic period on, they came under the protection of the Church, which devoted special concern to them and to which they in turn devoted all their active energies by performing various services and living in simplicity, purity and piety. It was from among these women that ordained *deaconesses* were recruited.

The compiler of the *Apostolic Constitutions* devotes an entire book (III) to widows. In it he gives them advice regarding a life of virtue and emphatically recommends them to the attention and care of the clergy and faithful. These women made a special vow to remain widows and chaste, and formed a kind of intermediate group between the clergy and the laity, although they received no cheirothesia. Especially in liturgical assemblies *widows* had a place of honor in the nave of the church. This is why they are sometimes given the honorary title of "front-seaters" (*prokathēmenai, praesistentes*). They may have exercised certain functions in maintaining order and discipline in the women's section of the church. The council of Laodicea had, however, forbidden the introduction of these women into the ranks of the clergy by a cheirothesia,[94] and the *Apostolic Constitutions* made this conciliar directive its own, both for *widows* and for *virgins*.[95] The moral requirements we have already seen are repeated for the virgins; they are to be examples to the faithful of virtue and purity (IV, 14).

The widows, elderly women and virgins all enjoyed the material benefits and honors flowing from their privileged position in the Christian communities. The compiler of the *Apostolic Constitutions* speaks of this privileged position in terms that are sometimes exaggerated: "You must honor *widows* and *orphans* after the image of the altar, and respect *virgins* as you do censer and incense" (II, 26).[96] Widows, elderly women and virgins are consistently listed immediately after the members of the clergy whenever the latter are recommended to the attention and respect of the faithful.[97] The *elderly women* were invited to the agapes (communal meals organized by the community) and were given a share of the food brought to these meals (II, 28).[98]

At the liturgical assemblies, the *ascetics, widows, elderly women* and *virgins* "had their places in front of everyone else" (II, 57) and prayers were offered for them in the great diaconal liturgy at the beginning of the Mass of the faithful and in the intercessory prayers which the bishop said during the eucharistic anaphora (VIII, 10; 12). At communion time, the *ascetics, virgins* and *widows* came forward immediately after the clerics in minor orders, i.e., immediately after the *deaconesses* (VIII, 13).[99]

Confessors still living after the persecutions also received particular respect at the liturgical assemblies, but they were accepted as consecrated only if they had been admitted to some rank of the clergy.[100]

Special attention was also given to the *children* of the Christian communities. These children attended the liturgical assemblies in large numbers and took an active role in the services (VIII, 6, 9),[101] thus forming part, as far as they could, of the *ecclesia orans* or praying Church. Among these children *orphans* were the object of special attention and concern on the part of the Church; the *Apostolic Constitutions* devote an entire book (IV) to them.

The solicitude and attentiveness of the ecclesial communities to these various groups within the body of the faithful did not betray any tendency or intention of creating or maintaining privileged classes within the Christian Church that could be compared with classes in the pagan society of the age. The Church's concern was rather a way of acknowledging and rewarding the services which some of its members gave (virgins and widows, for example) or a way of expressing a natural respect for the exemplary life of others (the ascetics, for example). At the same time, this attention represented one of the ways in which the Church came to the aid of those in need of it (orphans, sick people, elderly women, and so on).

The assemblies, moreover, were characterized by a great spirit of democracy. Thus clerics were forbidden to manifest any haughtiness toward the faithful because of the clerical rank: "The bishop must not exalt himself over (become proud toward) deacons and priests, nor priests in regard to the people, for the Church is made up of all these" (VIII, 1, 20).

Church authorities and all of the clergy showed the same attentiveness and consideration to all the faithful no matter what the age or social condition of these might be. For example, if a distinguished person, local or foreign, happened to come while a service was going on, the service was not interrupted on his account; he was welcomed by the deacons and led to his appropriate place, while the bishop remained seated where he was or continued any liturgical action he might be performing.[102] People of more modest condition, be they local or foreign, old or young, were treated in that same manner; in their case too, "the deacon is to find places for them, and to do it gladly, that he may not give the impression of being partial to some and that his service may be pleasing to God. The deaconess is to act in the same way toward women who may come, be they rich or poor" (II, 58, 6).

III. CONCLUSION: DO THE *APOSTOLIC CONSTITUTIONS* HAVE ANY VALUE FOR US TODAY?

In the ecumenical atmosphere of reform and renewal that dominates theology today, students of documents originating in the Christian Church's distant past do not seek a knowledge of the past solely for its own sake and in response to purely archeological or scientific concerns. They are also looking to the Church's past life for information, suggestions and experiences that can be renewed or reapplied to the Church of our day. A dialogue of the present with the past is being carried on. The past cannot, of course, be brought back to life, but it can still provide us with instruction and can shed light on the paths we are now taking into the future, just as the dim light of oil lamps on the tombs of our ancestors gently dispels the nocturnal darkness of cemeteries.

In this perspective, what does the study of the *Apostolic Constitutions* teach us?

We are now beyond any doubt living through a period that is quite different from the one we have been speaking of in this presentation. The ever-changing conditions of the Church's life since the fourth century, the abolition of the practice of public penance, the disappearance of the catechumenate as infant baptism became the rule—these and other causes led to the decay of the minor orders of clergy and even to the disappearance of some of them. At the same time and in the same measure, the number of the faithful taking part in the liturgical assemblies fell off, as did their active participation in the divine services, that participation which had been the Church's chief source of strength and greatness in the period under discussion.

As we have been seeing, the compiler of the *Apostolic Constitutions* has, first of all, left us two valuable descriptions of the Christian liturgy of his day: one in II, 57, the other in VIII, 6–13 (the latter being also known as the Clementine liturgy). Along with the parallel and slightly later (fifth century) description of the liturgy in the *Testamentum Domini* (I, 19; 23; 27; 28; 35), which Father Arranz has examined for us, the *Apostolic Constitutions* are the most complete and valuable literary source Christian antiquity has left us for restoring the image of the liturgical assembly in Syria toward the end of the fourth century. This image may still be regarded as a suggestive model, an "ideal" for the whole of Christendom in our time.

98

Few Christian writers give us such an explicit picture of what a liturgical assembly of that age looked like and how the various categories of the Church's laity took part in divine services.

Secondly, the *Apostolic Constitutions* provide us with a good deal of useful information and a good many canonical regulations and directives regarding the rights, duties and functions of the different orders of the clergy. The compiler either derived these regulations and directives from the earlier documents which were his sources of information, or else he formulated them himself.

All this information shows us that clerics, especially those in minor orders, were numerous indeed; it also tells us of their various ranks and liturgical functions, which were more or less specifically determined. We are dealing with a period in which the competition in the primitive Church between charismatics (itinerant missionaries) and the clerical hierarchy (exercising permanent administrative functions in each local Church)[103] had long since been resolved in favor of the hierarchy. For all the functions arising in the course of the natural development of religious life in the Christian communities the Church had gradually established appropriate clerical degrees or orders, all of them integrated into an increasingly clear-cut and complex institutional hierarchy. (This statement is valid even if the Eastern Church never developed the kind of extreme "clericalism" for which some Churches would later be blamed.[104]) Down to the time of which we are speaking the local Churches of East and West had not developed any ministries without functions; all ranks of the clergy really carried out the functions for which they had been established. Correspondingly, the Church did not hesitate to get rid of certain minor orders which no longer had any useful functions, for example, the gravediggers (*fossores* or *cursores*) of the age of persecutions.

In keeping with the title of my paper, I have been emphasizing chiefly the liturgical role of the deacons and of the lower clerical orders generally. But those in the Catholic Church who have since the Second Vatican Council been promoting the "restoration of the permanent diaconate" could easily find in the *Apostolic Constitutions* many details, directives and suggestions that would be useful and relevant today, regarding the service ministry which these orders exercised in the social life and missionary activity of the fourth century Church.

A third point worth our taking away with us is the redactor's great concern for the order and discipline that should reign in liturgical assemblies. The ultimate purpose of such order and discipline was the creation of an atmosphere that would foster the unanimous, real and active participation of the entire community—the clergy and all classes of the faithful—in the celebration of the holy sacrifice and in sacramental communion with Christ. No less noteworthy is the compiler's insistence on the obligation which all the faithful and all the members of the clergy have of remaining within the Church unity that has the bishop for its focal point and is directed and represented by him. This obligation is still a basic principle in contemporary Orthodox and Catholic ecclesiology.

Another point that is an impressive example to us is the spirit of solidarity, brotherhood and communion that united all the members of each local Church with one another and found expression not only in the assistance and support, material and moral, which the community gave to its needy members, but also in the public prayer of the Church. In the liturgy prayers were offered for the members of the clergy and the various privileged groups mentioned earlier, but also for married men and women, neophytes, infants, the sick, travelers, exiles, prisoners, those in slavery, and so on. Even if the texts which the *Apostolic Constitutions* give for these prayers (especially the great collect and the intercessions during the eucharistic anaphora of the Clementine liturgy) were not actually used in any local Church, they are nonetheless models for our present-day Churches, for they show the authentically universal (ecumenical) range of intentions that marked the public prayer of the Christian Church of that age.

In any case, inasmuch as this document is a source for the history of the Christian liturgy and a treasury of information about the past, it is of immense value to the liturgical and disciplinary life of the contemporary Church. In the judgment at least of liturgists and canonists, this fact enables us to forgive the anonymous compiler for introducing some dim hints of doctrinal heresy and thus drawing down on his head a condemnation at the bar of Church history.

Bucharest

Henri CAZELLES

The
Old Testament Liturgical Assembly
and the Various Roles
Played in It

It is rather obvious that during the long period when the Old Testament, with its foreshadowings of New Testament realities, was being composed, the shape and structure of the liturgical assembly did not remain constant and unchanged. Therefore, too, the assembly did not always call for the same services and the same ministries.

What we find in the beginning are family or tribal gatherings. In the archaic passover ritual of Exodus 12, it is an elder (v. 21), or in practice the head of the family (v. 26), who sacrifices and roasts the lamb before that springtide departure for new pastures which circumstances will transform into a ritual celebrating a liberation. The father was likewise responsible for the sacrifices which Jaussen described in his *Coutumes des Arabes au Pays de Moab*. But the sacrifice might also be connected with a pilgrimage to a holy place that was "three days" distant, as the stereotyped formula puts it (Gen 22.4; Ex 5.3; Num 10.33). The holy place might be a bare, uninhabited mountain, or it might be a more narrowly circumscribed spot, a *haram*, a house—temple, set amid a grove of trees. In this second instance, the place has a caretaker, and the caretaker is the servant of the god. That is why a very ancient text speaks of Moses as "entrusted with all my house" (Num 12.7).

LOCAL SANCTUARIES

These sacred places were local Canaanite sanctuaries at the time when the patriarchs and their descendants began to visit them in order to worship their own God there. We do not know what family was in charge of sanctuary at Gilgal that played so important a role before the coming of the monarchy. It is possible, but not at all certain, that Phinehas was caretaker of the sanctuary of Baal-peor. We are better informed about the sanctuary of Laish–Dan, because, according to Judges 18.30, it was served by a descendent of Moses (and not of Manasseh) by way of Gershom. The most important thing here was not the sacred place as such but the idol kept there before being transferred (Judg 18.17). The caretaker is called a *kôhen* (i.e., "priest") and a "father." He stands at the entrance of the gate (v. 17); he consults God (vv. 5-6). The "voice" in 18.3 can be understood as referring to prayers said (or sung) aloud.

If we move on to Shiloh (still in the premonarchic period), we find Eli exercising priesthood there, this time in a house–temple of the Lord (1 Sam 1.7, 24). The *kôhen* watches over the house and lives in it (1 Sam 3). He sits at the door of the temple (1.9) and keeps an eye on the faithful in order to maintain proper order, especially at the autumn festival when the grape harvest can lead to drunkenness (1.13). He is the intermediary through whom offerings and gifts (e.g., the offering of little Samuel by his parents) can be put at the service of the Lord (1.26-28; 2.11). It is not the *kôhen* but the believer himself who offers the sacrifice (1.3, 4, 21). The priest and guardian of the sanctuary of which God is the master has the right to a share in the sacrificial victim, but he can abuse this right (2.12-17).

SEASONAL GATHERINGS

The local sanctuaries must have functioned in the way just described until the Deuteronomic reform. We have an echo of this older practice in the agrarian rituals described by Jeremiah, whose family officiated at Anathoth (Jer 14.1-9). In Deuteronomy 26.1-11 the believer brings the first-fruits in a basket, and the *kôhen* accepts them "before the altar of the Lord" (26.4). Deuteronomy 33.8-10 lists the functions of the Levitic priesthood; the list is pre-Deuteronomic in part. According to it, the *kôhen* is first and foremost the one who possesses the sacred oracular lots, the Urim and Thummim, by means of which the secrets of God are revealed; they are in the hands of the "godly one." It is possible that observance of the word and the covenant is a Deuteronomic adaptation. These Levitical priests place incense before God and put the *kâlîl* (probably a name for the holocaust) "upon thy altar," but they do not offer sacrifice.

Such rituals were especially suitable for the seasonal festivals at which the first-fruits of the barley (feast of Unleavened Bread), the wheat (Pentecost) and the vineyards (feast of Tents, in the autumn) were offered. The Canaanites and the Israelites of the settlement had already celebrated these three great feasts before the latter became associated with the history of salvation.

THE *QÂHÂL*

There were, however, other liturgical assemblies that did not depend on the seasonal cycle as celebrated either by nomads (Passover) or settlers. The tribes were summoned to assemble by the sound of the horn (*shôphar*), and the gathering was held in the name of the God of hosts (*sabaoth*). This assembly was often held at the sanctuary of Gilgal, from which we see Joshua repeatedly setting out. This kind of assembly is a *qâhâl*, a word which scholars are more and more inclined to connect with *qôl*, the "voice" of the *shôphar* (cf. Ex. 19.16; 20.18; Amos 2.2; 1 Kings 1.41; etc.). This *qâhâl*, which the Septuagint translates as *ekklēsia*, is also held at Shiloh (Josh 18.1), at Bethel (Judg 21.2), at Ephes-dammim (1 Sam 17.1), at Abel of Beth-maacah (2 Sam 20.14), and finally at Jerusalem (1 Kings 12.21). For the

Deuteronomist, however, the great day of *qâhâl* was at Horeb (Deut 5.19; 9.10; 10.4; etc.), and he lays down rules for admission to this *qâhâl* (23.2-9). When the temple is dedicated, a real *qâhâl* assembly takes place at the autumn festival (1 Kings 8.2). "For the Lord and for Gideon" shout the soldiers of Gideon when the trumpets sound for the attack on Midian (Judg 7.18). This liturgy for departure into battle will be transferred to the temple where Psalm 20 celebrates the beginning of a campaign, and Psalm 21 offers thanksgiving after the victory. It is probable that, as in 1 Kings 22, prophets spoke in God's name and promised victory.

ROYAL ASSEMBLIES

The great liturgical celebrant in these circumstances is the military leader: Gideon, for example, who leads his three hundred warriors to victory in the name of God (Judg 7.15), or Ehud after he passes the sculptured stones at Gilgal (3.19, 26-28). With the way paved for it by such judges as Gideon and Jephthah, a royal priesthood was introduced into Israel, modeled on Melchizedek and the kings of the ancient East. David orders the transfer of the ark, performs a ritual dance before the Lord, then blesses the people and offers them sacrificed food (2 Sam 6.14-19) after having offered holocausts to the accompaniment of ovations and the blowing of the horn. Solomon will do the same at the dedication of the temple. In 1 Kings 8.6 we are told that the assembly (*'edah*; in Greek *synagogē*) offers sacrifice along with the king; but at the transfer of the ark no one but David is mentioned as providing liturgical service. The priests are simply the guardians of the ark (1 Kings 8.10) and cannot even "stand" in the sanctuary.

Kôhen will be the title given to Abiathar and Zadok (2 Sam 8.17) as well as the sons of David (v. 18); Zadok and Abiathar are mentioned with Ira in 2 Samuel 20.25-26 and by themselves in 1 Kings 4.4. Their function is to protect the ark and the place where it is kept (2 Sam 15.24, 29). It is probable that like Pharoah and the other kings of the period the king of Jerusalem had the title "priest" (according to Melchizedek), but that he excercised his priesthood through the mediation of these *kôhanîm*. The great royal ritual was used as the coronation festival and very probably also at the autumn festival which reactualized the enthronement. The fall of the monarchy, however, led to a profound alteration of the biblical description of the autumn festival, and the liturgical assemblies for the enthronements in 1 Kings 1 and 2 Kings 11 took place in exceptional circumstances which permit only an imperfect glimpse of the ritual. The role of the priest with the horn of oil emerges clearly (1 Kings 1.39). The role of the prophet is less clear (the prophet is Nathan in 1 Kings; cf. also Is 6); his function was probably to proclaim the man whom the national God has "chosen" (cf. Neh 6.7).

The principal royal feast was the feast of Tents which was held at the full moon of the first autumn month and marked the beginning of the new year. It was the time when the winter's store of food was gotten in, and when prayers were offered for the return of the lifegiving rains and the renewal of the strength and powers of king, people and nature. There are still echoes of all this in the Jewish liturgy of Rosh ha-Shanah. The feast involved singing, processions and hornblowing (cf. Mowinckel's studies). There were certainly cantors. It was at this time that the formation of the royal Davidic psalter began and perhaps of the psalter of Asaph as well (Asaph's activity is documented chiefly after the return from exile). As R. de Vaux has shown, Heman, Calcol and Darda (1 Kings 4.31) were choristers.[1] Religious music has its place on Zion as it did in the sanctuary at Bethel (Amos 5.23). Liturgical vestments—which were in fact a royal costume which the clergy of Israel no less than of Egypt wore because they represented the king—were so important that the "keeper of the wardrobe" is mentioned in connection with the temple of Jerusalem (2 Kings 22.14) and with the house of Baal in Samaria (2 Kings 10.22). As late as under Pilate the keeping of the vestments will cause a problem.

Insofar as they were caretakers of the sanctuary, the priests shifted this duty to gatekeepers. The lists of those returning from exile speak of "Solomon's servants" (Ezra 2.55) and of "oblates" (*nethinim*, v. 58), similar to young Samuel. The temples of Babylonia had similar "oblates" (*shirkutu*). The oblates of Jerusalem were not necessarily Israelites.

REFORMS

The Deuteronomic reform and the renewal of the covenant by Josiah, with the accompanying restoration of Passover, upset the established liturgical order of things. The kings intervened in matters liturgical until the Torah of Ezekiel sharply curtailed their rights (Ezek 45–46). Thus, after Ahaz had been to Damascus to pay homage to the Assyrian conqueror, he had the priest at Jerusalem replace the bronze altar which Solomon had erected (cf. 1 Kings 8.64); he also introduced a new pattern of sacrifices: morning burnt offering and evening cereal offering; holocaust and offering of the king, and holocaust, offering and libations of the people (2 Kings 16.10-15). The mention of these last seems to suppose a liturgical assembly, even if the offerings made by landowners were predominant.

In the Deuteronomic reform, which comes about a hundred years after the changes Ahaz had made, it is the priest who receives the offering of first-fruits and gives meaning to the rite in an important profession of faith (Deut 26.1-14). The great liturgical gatherings, which now can take place only at the Jerusalem temple, are always held at the seasonal feasts, but the spring Passover, commemorating the liberation from Egypt, replaces the autumn festival which had been much too Canaanite in character. In theory, the king continues to be the principal celebrant, and in fact Josiah presides over the Passover of 2 Kings 23. In the Deuteronomic law, however, his liturgical role is not mentioned, even in connection with the start of military campaigns; instead, scribes (shôterim) stand near the priest (Deut 20.2-9). Before anything is said of military commanders, the scribes remind the soldiers of those who can claim exemption, and the priest encourages the troops with an exhortation. It is also the priest who gives the blessing in the name of the Lord (cf. Deut 18.5), whereas in the time of David and Solomon it was the king who gave it. No longer is it said, as in 1 Sam 2.35, that the priest comes in and out before the anointed king; all that is said now is that the priest "stands and ministers in the name of the Lord" (Deut 18.5).

These liturgical assemblies are joyous affairs and have as their focal point a sacred meal for which the landowner is responsible; he must invite not only his own family but also those who are economically insecure: servants, widows, orphans, Levites and strangers (16.11).

Once again it is not the clergy who offer the sacrifice. The task of the clergy is primarily to assure proper order in the gathering, as the priest Amaziah does at Bethel when he finds Amos exaggerating (Amos 7.10ff.), and as Pashhur and the Jerusalem clergy will do in dealing with Jeremiah, especially after the latter's discourse in the temple (chaps. 7 and 26). We know from the prophets, however, that the clergy themselves could be involved in orgies (Is 28.7; cf. Hos 4.18).

The fall of Jerusalem and the burning of the temple put an end to the old liturgy, but the latter was not forgotten. Even during the time of the exile there were certainly assemblies held on the ruins of the temple. In Jeremiah 41.5 a group of eighty men from Shechem, Shiloh and Samaria present offerings and incense in the ruined temple. The Book of Lamentations likewise seems to suppose a liturgy held among the temple ruins (2.10, 19; 3.41), but it is not a fully developed liturgy: no dancing (5.15), no priest, no prophets (2.9, 14).

ASSEMBLIES IN EXILE
It is possible that the exile saw the beginning, under the priest-prophet Ezekiel, of new assemblies for liturgical prayer apart from the temple; these would be the originating source of the later synagogal liturgy. (Such liturgies are attested as early as the third century, but for Egypt.) People gathered around Ezekiel, who had been a priest in the Jerusalem temple which he had known quite well before the exile; they thought highly of what he had to say (Ezek 33.22). They listened to God's word to the accompaniment of music, even if at times they hung their lyres on the willow trees in protest (Ps 137). The sabbath became the great feast day, in deliberate opposition to the seasonal rituals of the Babylonians. The exilic edition of the Decalogue requires Israelites to "make" the sabbath "sacred." This day is placed at the head of the liturgical calender in Leviticus 23 and is called a day of "holy convocation," which seems to imply an assembly gathered around the exiled priests, who represent the only institution to survive the collapse of the state.

After the return from exile the restoration of the temple marks the beginning of the great liturgy that draws together the scattered families of Israel. This is the liturgy that is presented to us in the final redaction of the Pentateuch. This is the liturgy that Ben Sirach and Aristeas will celebrate, and it will leave a permanent mark on the Jewish soul.

Ezekiel's distinction of priests and Levites is now applied (chap. 44). Caravans of Jews return with Sheshbazzar, Zerubbabel, Ezra and Nehemiah, and Israel continues its worship as if there has never been any break. It would be imprudent to rely on Ezra 3 in describing a liturgical assembly around an altar that had been rebuilt in the second month of the second year of the first return. The passage is already speaking of a new temple being built and of Zerubbabel whose activity is in fact attested only eighteen years later. What we may have here, in Ezra 3, is a picture painted by the chronicler, whose liturgical preoccupations run through his entire reinterpretation of the history and life of God's people. On the other hand, Asaph's group must have returned to its duties as cantors at an early date and must have begun the adaptation of old psalms from the period of the monarchy to the new conditions in which the Jews were living (Ps 67 on the harvest). One of the most liturgical of these psalms is 118 with its procession.

THE GREAT ASSEMBLY AFTER THE RETURN

When the people gather for a major assembly in the time of Ezra or Nehemiah (Neh 8), the assembly is called a *qâhâl* (vv. 2, 17); the technical term *'edah*, which is habitually used in postexilic texts to describe liturgical assemblies occurring on fixed dates, is not used here. Ezra seems to preside, either because he is a priest or because he is a scribe (*sôpher*). In accordance with Deuteronomy 31.10 he reads the Law, as prescribed for the feast of Tents; during the reading the Levites at his left and right translate the Hebrew text and explain its meaning (v. 8). They are already practicing the art of the homily. Then Ezra blesses the Lord, and all the people say "Amen, Amen," and bow to the ground. They weep and grieve, but the Levites bid them rejoice instead, and the liturgy ends (v. 12) with a joyous meal in the spirit of Deuteronomy.

The narrative then turns to the feast of Tents which, in accordance with the very ancient rite described in Leviticus 23, involves booths or huts built of branches and foliage (vv. 15-16). In this celebration the priests and Levites have no special role. A new New Year's ritual is grafted on to the old autumn festival; it is now the new moon and not the full moon that marks the beginning of the new year. The festival closes on the twenty-fourth of the month with a penitential ceremony that includes a confession of sins; the service is an anticipation of *Yôm kippur*, which will be celebrated on the tenth of the month. The priests are not involved in the penitential ceremony; it is the Levites who urge the people to pray and repent and then to bless the Lord (9.4-5). We can see a revision of the Levites' role taking place when Numbers 6 reserves to priests the right to bless (at least to bless the people) and when Psalm 133 reserves the ritual of anointing (the sign of blessing) to the beard and robes of Aaron.

LITURGICAL FUNCTIONS IN THE REBUILT TEMPLE
Before the time when the Book of Chronicles is accepted and canonized, the temple liturgy with its psalms is carried on in accordance with the principles set down in the Torah of Ezekiel. The priests are the ones who draw near to God whose glory rests upon the temple building. The priests are the ones who have the privilege of "using" the blood (de Vaux's phrase[2]). Blood is life and belongs to God, but, according to Leviticus 17.14, God grants that the blood may be used on the altar for the rite of *kipper*, that is, for expiation or, better, for healing and curing.

In the first redaction of Ezekiel's Torah the consecration of the altar was still entrusted to men who are priest-Levites (with no distinction made between the two offices); this is in keeping with the theology of Deuteronomy. But the text has been corrected to make it consistent with the second redaction which supposes the distinction (43.19) and reserves the function in question to the descendants of Zadok. In the Torah of Ezekiel, nothing is said of an assembly and little of the prince; the people are mentioned once, but a good deal is made of the sanctuary. The priests descended from Zadok wear special vestments and are bound by special rules of purity. They offer not only the blood but the fat.

The Levites, on the other hand, are the guardians of the temple and especially of its gates. But they serve the people as well, and it is they who have the task of slaughtering the victims for the holocausts and communion sacrifices. However, in the final redaction of the sacerdotal code this last-named regulation is not retained; in accordance

109

with older tradition, the lay offerer immolates the victim himself (Lev 1.5) after it has been found acceptable but before the priests, now called "the sons of Aaron," offer the blood.

Except for the ritual of priestly investiture and the description of the great day of the *Kippurim*, we have few descriptions of liturgical assemblies in postexilic texts of the Torah, even in connection with occasions on which the glory of God appears (Ex 16 and Num 14). However, we can get an idea of what such assemblies were like from Leviticus 9. Once he has been invested, the high priest offers sacrifice for himself and then for the people; he performs the rites involving the blood and makes the smoking offering of fat, then gives the blessing that precedes the theophany. The Letter to the Hebrews makes many references to this ritual.

The Levites in Numbers 1–10 are only sacristans in charge of the furnishings and their transport (Num 4). They are given no liturgical function at the assembly, and chapter 16 is a cogent reminder that Levites—Korah, in this instance—are not to touch the incense. The Book of Chronicles introduces a new situation which the Sadducees did not like but which the Pharisees regarded as normative. This book assigns an important role to the high priest, as when Azariah, accompanied by eighty priests, withstands Uzziah as the latter is about to burn incense in the great hall of the temple: "It is not for you, Uzziah, to burn incense to the Lord, but for the priests, the sons of Aaron, who are consecrated to burn incense. Go out of the sanctuary, for you have done wrong, and it will bring you no honor from the Lord God" (2 Chron 26.17-18).

The priests are divided into twenty-four classes which take turns serving in the sanctuary; when their period of service is over, they go back to their priestly towns. But there are also Levitical families, which David divides into three classes (Gershom, Kohath and Merari); they now emerge from the sacristy and are given a role in the sanctuary. They have charge of the courts and chambers of the Lord's house and see to "the cleansing of all that is holy" (1 Chron 23.28). They also have charge of the showbread (v. 29) and of every holocaust offered to the Lord on the sabbaths, new moons and liturgical feasts (*mô'adim*), according to a set ritual (v. 31).

The cantors now become Levites, and some of them are regarded as prophets (chap. 25). They are accompanied by the music of lyre, harp, cymbal and often trumpet as well. Like the priests, they are divided into twenty-four classes, with twelve cantors in each class. Gatekeepers are likewise now considered to be Levites (1 Chron 26; this is in line with Ezek 44.11), as are those in charge of the temple treasuries; but at this point we are removed from the liturgical assembly proper.

This entire personnel springs into action at the transfer of the ark and the Lord's taking possession of his temple; this was an event calling for an annual celebration. The chronicler was forced, however, to respect certain historical facts set down in the Book of Kings. Thus he notes that the priests have sanctified themselves without regard to the order of their classes (2 Chron 5.11). It is noteworthy that the high priest is not mentioned, but in fact when the chronicler speaks of the role of the king, it is in fact of the king's successor, the high priest, that he is thinking. The priests, playing their trumpets and singing their praises, surround the Levitical cantors who are gathered in their full complement; in the spirit of Hosea 14, singing as the expression of the heart is regarded as more important than the holocausts.

When the chronicler describes the great penitential ceremony and Passover under Hezekiah and later Josiah and gives these kings a preponderant role, it is of the high priest that he is really thinking. At the assembly, which is here once again called a *qâhâl* (2 Chron 30.13, 25), it is the king who intercedes for lay people who are not sanctified according to the rules of the sanctuary (v. 19). A high priest comes on the scene only to give instructions where to put surplus contributions (31.10).[3] It is Levites who perform the rituals of purification (29.5ff.), while those who bless the people are called "priests and Levites" (30.27). We are told that the Levites did a better job of sanctifying themselves than the priests did (29.34), and they take part in the dismemberment (*haphshit*) of the holocausts. The priests retain the function of pouring the blood on the altar, but in 2 Chronicles 29.25-28 the holocaust is to some extent conditioned by the singing of the Levites. In connection with the Passover the chronicler even gives us the detail that the priests receive the blood from the hands of the Levites (30.16).

IN THE SERVICE OF THE ASSEMBLY

The last great liturgical assembly before the destruction of the temple occurs at the Passover celebrated by Josiah. The king prescribes the service which priests and Levites are to perform for the people. His instructions represent a reform. After having restored the functions of the priests, the king turns to the Levites who are no longer needed for carrying the ark as they had been in the desert (cf. Numbers). He says to them: "Stand in the holy place according to the groupings of the fathers' houses of your brethren and according to the fathers' house of the Levites." (2 Chron 35.5).[4] The Levites are the most active group: they prepare for the Passover, roasting the lambs for the lay families, then for the priests and their brother Levites, the cantors and gatekeepers, who must remain in their proper places. The Levites exercise a real deaconate since they prepare or, in another translation, "distribute" the consecrated food (35.15). The term "to serve" is not used, but the LXX version of Ezra and Maccabees does use *diakonein* to translate the Hebrew liturgical term *shereth* that is used in some of these texts (1 Chron 23.13, of Aaron; 2 Chron 23.6, of the priests and Levites).

In the liturgy described by Aristeas there is again question more of *leitourgein* than of *diakonein*. But the priests do the immolating, and what the author seems to admire more than anything else is the sheer feat of strength which the killing of so many victims represents (*Letter* VII, 92).

In Ben Sirach (ca. 180 B.C.) the high priest is the focal point of the liturgy, whether the author is speaking of Aaron (45.6-22) to whom he gives more verses than he does to Moses, or whether he is offering a more vivid description of the high priest Simon II (chap. 50), a man closer to his own day. In 50.15-16 we see him officiating (TOB) or presiding over the liturgy, exercising the priesthood, blessing the people in the Lord's name, offering holocaust, incense and commemorative perfumes, performing the rite of expiation (vv. 14-15) in behalf of the people. "How splendid he was as he looked down from the sanctuary, when he emerged from the curtained shrine" (v. 5, Jerusalem Bible, following Hebrew text). Some of the images used are similar to those the author had already employed in chapter 24 to describe the Wisdom (itself liturgical in character) that comes forth from God.

Chapter 50 gives us a glimpse of the functions exercised by the other officiants. The high priest receives the holocausts from the other priests who are stationed around him like a crown. All the sons of Aaron stand before the assembly: they carry in their hands the offerings for the Lord; they play the trumpet; they make a great noise to be heard for remembrance before the Most High. The cantors sing a sweet melody, and the people twice fall to the ground to worship the Lord and receive the blessing.

Neither Sirach nor Aristeas speak of the Levites, being perhaps hostile to them. We may note, in this connection, that Josephus (*Antiquities* II, 216) regarded Agrippa II's granting of the white robe to the cantors as one of the causes for the destruction of the temple. In any event, the destruction of the temple put an end to these assemblies. In the Letter to the Hebrews Christians will speak of a liturgy that is centered upon Christ as high priest, temple and victim and that has the Apostles as its consecrated ministers (according to Jn 17.20). The Pharisees will develop a synagogal liturgy of a different kind.

Ecole Pratique
Institut Catholique des Hautes Etudes

Edouard COTHENET

Earthly Liturgy
and Heavenly Liturgy
according to the Book of Revelation

At least in the West, the faithful gathered for worship seem no longer to have any awareness of the presence of the angels. And yet the liturgy itself, which is by nature conservative, continues to have us recite or sing the Sanctus, while solemnly inviting us to join the heavenly spirits in their praise! But who pays any real attention to these antiquated formulas? What a difference between us and the early Church which found satisfaction in listing the various choirs of angels and liked to inflate the numbers of the heavenly spirits (myriads of myriads!).

As a matter of fact, the danger at that time was of going to the other extreme from us: the danger St. Paul signals as *thrēskeia tōn aggelōn* (worship of angels, Col 2.18). Was there not the risk of giving the Powers, Thrones and Dominations so important a place that the mediation of Christ would be downgraded? This was a very real danger in Jewish Christianity, as Cardinal Daniélou, among others has shown.[1] For, alongside orthodox speculations on *Christos aggelos* we find the tendency to make Christ nothing more than a superior angel.

The Book of Revelation of St. John originates in a Jewish Christian milieu, but it does not fall into this trap. For, while it follows the lead of apocalyptic literature and shares its delight in imagining the heavenly liturgy, it is distinguished by a solid christology.[2] It has even been said that, next to the fourth Gospel, it is the New Testament book most explicit on the divinity of Christ.

I shall try, therefore, to do justice to the double perspective of Revelation: a liturgical perspective in which the worship offered on earth is linked with the sacrifice of praise being offered in the heavenly temple, and a christological perspective which shows the unique role of Christ as source of creation (3.14) and Lamb who has won the victory by the sacrifice of his blood (5.6). To this end, after a brief survey of the data provided by Revelation, I will seek out the source of this current of thought, especially at Qumran, and then, finally, I will comment on the scene of the enthronement of the Lamb in the heavenly court.

I. THE LITURGICAL DATA OF THE BOOK OF REVELATION[3]

Of all the New Testament books Revelation is undoubtedly the one that supplies the most extensive data regarding the Christian liturgy. Hymns and doxologies ring out from one end to the other of this message which is too often depicted as being the revelation of God's wrath. John was writing in Asia Minor where at a very early date the Holy Spirit moved Christians to "address hymns to Christ as to a God."[4] Consequently he did not invent the hymns and doxologies out of whole cloth but used existent formulas or composed new ones in the style with which he was familiar. It is difficult, of course, to prove this for individual texts, but we can nonetheless admit that by and large Revelation reflects the liturgical life of the end of the first century.

The very first chapter is significant in this regard, for it is on the Lord's Day (1.10) that the exile of Patmos receives his inaugural vision: the Son of Man, who holds seven stars in his hand, commissions

John to send exhortations, reproaches, and encouragement to the churches of Ephesus, Smyrna, Pergamum, Thyatira, Sardis, Philadelphia and Laodicea. Each of these letters contains references either to baptism or to the eucharist, as P. Prigent has shown in his little book *Apocalypse et liturgie* [The Apocalypse and the Liturgy].[5]

The visions proper begin with a heavenly liturgy to which I shall return at greater length; it depicts the worship of the Creator and the enthronement of the Lamb.

As in a medieval mystery play the action unfolds on two levels: now in heaven, where God dwells in what is at once a palace and a sanctuary, and now on earth. Angels supply constant communication between the heavenly "dwelling" and the earthly "dwelling," thus bringing out the unity of the history of salvation which St. Augustine in his *The City of God* describes as beginning with the creation of the angels on the first day.

Sometimes the angels praise the Creator on their own behalf (e.g., 4.8), sometimes they act as mediators for the human race. The angel of incense, for example, fills his golden censer with the prayers of all the saints (8.3; cf. 5.8).[6]

Prayer of praise takes first place in Revelation. From time to time, however, the heavenly liturgy echoes the dramatic events occurring on earth. At the breaking of the fifth seal, for example, the souls of those martyred for their witness to the word of God seem to awaken. They cry out in a loud voice:

O Sovereign Lord, holy and true,

how long before thou wilt judge

and avenge our blood on those who dwell upon the earth? (6.10)

Because prayer in heaven matches the prayer of the faithful on earth, this urgent appeal of the martyrs in Revelation reflects and supports the pleading of Christians subjected to persecution. We may recall here the parable of the self-righteous judge and the importunate widow: "Will not God vindicate his elect, who cry to him day and night?" (Lk 18.7).

A refrain runs through the succession of plagues: "Thou art just, O Lord!" (cf. Rev. 15.3; 16.5, 7; 19.2). We are reminded of Greek tragedies, in which the chorus intervenes to express the feelings and thoughts of the spectators as the drama unfolds. In Revelation it is not only the angels who have this function, but also the elect, who have

117

crossed the sea of glass mingled with fire and now sing the song of Moses, the servant of God, and the song of the Lamb (15.3).

In order to describe salvation in its stage of fulfillment the seer transposes to heaven the Jewish liturgy for the feast of Tents.[7] Of all the solemnities of the Jewish year this was the one most strongly marked by joy and hope; according to a common saying, "The man who has never seen the joy of the night of this feast has never seen real joy in all his life."[8] During the processions, in which the faithful carried in their hands a citron branch, the sign of eternal life, and a palm, the sign of victory, they sang Psalm 118: "Save us, we beseech thee, O Lord! O Lord, we beseech thee, give us success! Blessed be he who enters in the name of the Lord!" (vv. 25-26). It was easy, therefore, to transpose the ritual for the feast of Tents and with its aid, to suggest the joy of heaven, as the seer of Patmos does in chapters 7 and 21.

These two passages are also marked by an ecclesial perspective. In chapter 7 the Church appears to be made up, as it were, by the remnant of Israel (the 12,000 from each tribe) and by the elect who are drawn from every nation on earth. In chapter 19 the bride of the Lamb is clothed in "fine linen, bright and pure." "The fine linen is the righteous deeds of the saints" (19.8). What an invaluable sign of the relation between liturgy and everyday life! The righteous deeds in question are listed for us in the letters to the seven churches: the faith that resists the seductions of false prophets, the spirit of service, spiritual poverty, the perseverance that enables the believer to hold out to the end, and so on.

Without any pretence at exhausting the subject, we may point out a last echo of Christian prayer; it occurs at the very end of Revelation: "The Spirit and the Bride say, 'Come.' And let him who hears say, 'Come.' And let him who is thirsty come, let him who desires take the water of life without price. . . . He who testifies to these things says, 'Surely I am coming soon.' Amen. Come, Lord Jesus!" (22.17, 20).

The cry, "Come!" corresponds to an invocation which was dear to the primitive community: *Maranatha* (1 Cor 16.22; *Didache* X, 6). Following G. Bornkamm, P. Prigent says we should see in this ending a transposition of the eucharistic liturgy which begins with an exhortation to receive God's grace: Let him who is thirsty come (v. 17).[9] A warning follows: it is usually directed to Christians who are unfaithful to the grace of their baptism (1 Cor 16.22a; *Didache* X, 6), but it is directed here at those who distort the text of the book of revelations. The promises are called to mind by the water of life, the tree of life (cf. 2.7, and note *e* in the [French] Ecumenical Translation of the Bible), and entry into the holy city (v. 19b).

This liturgical warning is balanced by the promise of Christ: "Surely I am coming soon." This represents the reminder of the eschatological dimension which is inseparable from any eucharistic celebration (1 Cor 11.26). A final invocation brings out the intense expectation that gains new vitality from every encounter with Christ: "Amen. Come, Lord Jesus."

After these rather brief indications I must now ask why John gives the heavenly liturgy such an important place in his work. What religious current is it that supplies the idea of heaven and earth being thus associated in praise, petition and thanksgiving?

II. COMMUNION WITH THE ANGELS

Several times in the psalter we find an invitation issued to the sons of the Most High to join in the praise being offered by Israel. Take Psalm 29 as an example: "Ascribe to the Lord, O heavenly beings [LXX: sons of God], ascribe to the Lord glory and strength. Ascribe to the Lord the glory of his name; worship the Lord in holy array" (vv. 1-2). There follows a description of the terrifying effects of the Lord's voice as it speaks in the unleashed storm. It is a grandiose vision that ends in the calm of the temple liturgy: "In his temple all cry, 'Glory!' The Lord sits enthroned over the flood. . . . May the Lord bless his people with peace!" (vv. 9-11).

I cannot review in detail here the mythological origins of this conception of the heavenly court where God makes his plans for history (see, e.g., the vision of Micaiah during the campaign of Ahab and Jehoshaphat against the Aramaeans, 1 Kings 22.19-23) or listens carefully to the reports of his angels and the Accuser (as we see him doing in the prologue to the Book of Job). In comparison with its polytheistic neighbors Israel shows great restraint in this regard; the oneness of God required this kind of moderation.

It is only in the final centuries before the Christian era that angelology and demonology develop. Apocalyptic literature is a reliable witness to this; we may think, for example, of the struggle between

Michael and the prince of Persia in Daniel 10.13, a struggle to which
Revelation will refer (12.7). It is also an angelic interpreter who encourages the seer and explains to him the messianic significance of his
visions (Dan 7.16ff.; 8.16ff.; 9.21ff.; 12.6ff.). But despite the importance thus given to the angels as mediators of revelation, we cannot say that in the Book of Daniel there is a real communion in
worship between the inhabitants of earth and the sons of the Most
High.

The situation is quite different in Qumranian circles, as A. Jaubert
especially has shown in her book *La notion d'Alliance dans le Judaïsme*
[The Idea of Covenant in Judaism].[10] To make our study complete, we
would have to follow her in citing related, though non-Qumranian,
texts such as the *Testaments of the Twelve Patriarchs* or the *Book of
Jubilees*. We may note that according to the latter the angels are the
most faithful observers of the Law: they are circumcised on the eighth
day and observe the sabbath and all the feasts prescribed by Moses.[11]
In order, however, not to make too many demands on the reader's
attention, I think it preferable to restrict myself to a passage from the
Hymns (*Hodayôt*) of Qumran. A commentary on it that is based on
other texts will show us the cultic background of the visions in Revelation.

> I give Thee thanks, O Adonai,
> for Thou has redeemed my soul from the Pit
> and from Sheol of Abaddon (20) Thou has made me rise to
>   everlasting heights,
> and I have walked in an infinite plain!
>
> And I knew there was hope
> for him whom (21) Thou hast shaped from the dust
> for the everlasting assembly (*lswd 'wlm*).
> Thou hast cleansed the perverse spirit from great sin
> that he might watch with (22) the army of the Saints (*sb'
>   qdwsym*)
> and enter into communion (*yhd*) with the congregation of
>   the sons of Heaven (*bny smym*).
> And Thou hast cast an everlasting destiny for man
> in the company of the Spirits (23) of Knowledge (*rwhwt d't*)

that he might praise Thy Name in joy[ful] concord (*yhd*)
and recount Thy marvels before all Thy works. [12]

According to G. Jeremias, [13] this passage belongs to the songs of the community, which are distinct in their overall tone from the hymns in which the Master of Justice communicates his own experience and refers to his role as spiritual leader. As often happens in the canonical psalter, the "I" in the passage I have translated is therefore a collective "I," that is, it is the community that is giving thanks for the protection which it has enjoyed and which is a proof of its vocation. Let me anticipate and call attention immediately to the two uses here of the term *yhd* (community) which recurs over and over in the *Rule of the Community* as a way of designating the group and expressing its ideal of the spiritual life: "And they shall eat in common, bless in common, and deliberate in common." [14]

According to the Hymn a communion (lines 22 and 23) is established between the faithful of the group and the everlasting assembly, the army of the saints, the sons of heaven. The reference is clearly to the same heavenly beings who constitute the great assembly (*swd*) in the presence of God, that is, the army of Yahweh Sabaoth. The passage is inspired especially by Psalm 89.5-8: "Let the heavens praise thy wonders, O Lord, thy faithfulness in the assembly of the holy ones! . . . A God feared in the council of the holy ones, great and terrible above all that are round about him. O Lord God of hosts, who is mighty as thou art, O Lord?"

Several critics have expressed the view that the psalmist of the *Hodayôt* was voicing the hope of heavenly immortality, of a future participation in the life of the angels. They can cite in support of this view the ideas developed in the Wisdom of Solomon.

However, following G. Lambert, G. Vermès and M. Delcor, I think that the text is concerned rather with the present religious experience of the group; the group already forms, with the sons of heaven, a single praising community. There are several points that support this interpretation.

The term translated "watch with" (*m'md* in line 21) means, etymologically, to "stand" and describes the posture of the servant who stands before his master, ready to carry out his orders. It is often used in either a military or a cultic context.

The scroll of the War Rule refers several times to the position or post that the combatants must keep (VII, 3, 17; XVI, 5); these fighters are assured of help from "the Valiant of the gods" in the struggle against the spirits of ungodliness (XV, 14). M. Delcor writes: "We might suppose that to the psalmist the expression means that the faithful of the community keep watch like soldiers at their posts. This would fit in well with the expression 'the army of the saints' or 'the eternal army' with which our phrase is connected. Yet I prefer to assign it a cultic origin that has left its traces in the specification 'watch before God' in *Hymns* XI, 13 (cf. 1 Chron 23.28; 1 QSa I, 22)."[15]

The foregoing interpretation finds a strong confirmation in another passage from the Hymns of Qumran:

> Thou hast cleansed man of sin because of Thy glory
> that he may be made holy (11) for Thee from all unclean
> abomination
> and from (every) transgression of unfaithfulness,
> that he may be joined wi[th] Thy sons of truth
> and with the lot of (12) Thy Saints
> that this vermin that is man
> may be raised from the dust to [Thy] secret [of truth]
> and from the spirit of perversity to [Thine] understanding;
> (13) and that he may watch before Thee with the everlast-
> ing host
> and together with [Thy] spirits [of holiness],
> that he may be renewed with all [that is] (14) [and] shall be
> and with them that know, in a common rejoicing.[16]

Here again the mention of the vermin might suggest that the psalmist is thinking of the general resurrection, as in Daniel 12.2. But in the context the reference is to conversion which is thought of as a resurrection. The new initiates entering the community are compared to dead persons who have been raised to life[17]; they enter into communion with heavenly beings so as to form a community (*yhd*) that praises and glorifies God.

There is another text, unfortunately a mutilated one, that can help us understand these mystical perspectives of Qumran. I refer to the *Songs for the Sabbath Burnt Offering* which J. Strugnell has published.

Document B draws its inspiration from the vision of the divine chariot (*merkabah*) in Ezekiel 1, a vision which was the subject of esoteric speculations that were regarded as dangerous, as this text from the Mishnah shows: "The forbidden degrees may not be expounded before three persons, nor the Story of Creation before two, nor [the chapter of] the Chariot before one alone, unless he is a Sage that understands it of his own knowledge."[18]

The Talmud relates some delightful little stories by way of commenting on this passage. I repeat one of them as evidence that the idea of a communion with the angels is not limited to Qumranian circles: Rabban Johanan ben Zakkai was journeying by donkey, in the company of Rabban Elazar ben Arakh. The latter wished to offer an explanation of the *Merkabah*; at this Rabban Johanan got down from his donkey, saying: "It is not fitting that I listen to the glorification of my Creator while I am mounted on my donkey." They sat down beneath a tree; a fire came down from heaven and surrounded them, and the angels of the service leaped before them as guests at a wedding rejoice before the new husband."[19]

Let us return to our text in the *Songs for the Sabbath Burnt Offering*. It falls into two sections: one dealing with the *Merkabah* and adding new details to the already rather complicated picture in Ezekiel, and the other depicting the liturgy in the camp of God. "The Cherubim above the heavens bless the likeness of the Throne of the Chariot [and] acclaim the [majes]ty of the firmament of light beneath the seat of His glory. And when the wheels turn, angels of holiness come and go between His glorious wheels like visions of fire. Spirits of supreme holiness surround them. . . . Spirits of the living [G]od unceasingly accompany the glory [of] the marvellous Chariot."[20]

The end of the text is unfortunately mutilated seriously. It seems to set up a correspondence between the worship in heaven and that of the "recruits" on earth: "The sound of joyous shouting ceases in all the camp of God and also the wind[s] of [d]ivine blessing, [and] a voice of praise [. . .] from the midst of all their battalions in [. . . and] all the numbered ones cry out, e[a]ch, each, in [his] place."[21]

Despite its obscurity this *Song for the Sabbath Burnt Offering* supplies us with information regarding the idea much in favor among the people of Qumran, namely, that their community is the true temple of God. For Ezekiel, the vision of the divine Chariot on the banks of

123

the river Chebar meant that God was not restricted to a particular country or a particular place, however holy, but that he freely chose where he would dwell. The desolating vision of the divine glory abandoning the temple is followed by a promise: "I have been a sanctuary (*miqdash*) to them [the exiles] for a while in the countries where they have gone" (Ezek 11.16).

I shall not repeat myself here on this point which I discussed last year in my conference on the attitude of the primitive Church toward the temple.[22] In any event my present concern is to see how, in continuity with the vision of Ezekiel, the entire community exercises the priestly office of praise because it participates in the liturgy of the heavenly army. As A. Jaubert rightly observes, this conception explains for us the importance given to the 364 day calender which insures that the feasts will always recur on the same day of the week. The organization of the liturgy must, if it is to be valid, correspond to the order of creation, which in turn guarantees the order of the covenant. The final part of the *Rule of the Community* is very enlightening on this point: prayer is organized according to the daily rhythm of light and darkness and according to the succession of the seasons and new moons.

> For the whole of my life the graven Decree (*hoq*) shall be upon my tongue
> as a fruit of praise and the offering of my lips.
> I will sing in Knowledge. . . .
> When day comes and the night, I will enter the Covenant of God,
> when night and morning depart, I will recite his precepts (*huqyw*),
> and for as long as they are, I will establish in them my realm of no return.[23]

The participation of the entire community in the worship offered by the angels seems to be an argument showing the "spiritualization" of worship and the "common" possession of priesthood: such is the interpretation of G. Klinzing, for example.[24] We should bear in mind, however, that Exodus 19.6 on which the theologians would later rely in speaking of the *regale sacerdotium* (royal priesthood) or the priesthood of the faithful is not used in the Qumran texts thus far published.[25] The Qumran movement was founded by priests, after all, and was not prepared to set aside the special role of priests in teaching and in offering sacrifice. If the members of the community abstained for the time being from taking part in the temple ceremonies, this was because the priests officiating there were illegitimate and not because the Qumran movement in any way disparaged sacrifices as such.[26] When the *Temple Scroll* is published, we will be able more accurately to determine the expectations of the community on this point. For the moment we may note that in the *Rule of the Congregation* the priestly Messiah takes priority over the Davidic Messiah.[27] In the Revelation of John, however, Christ unites in his own person all the functions: royal, priestly, and prophetic.

III. THE MYSTERY OF CREATION
AND THE ENTHRONEMENT OF THE LAMB

Between the letters to the seven churches and the description of the sets of seven (seals, then trumpets), chapters 4 and 5 of Revelation form a dramatic unit that can be compared to a medieval mystery play. The unit contains two sharply contrasting scenes. First, there is a kind of timeless vision in which stative verbs predominate: the subject is the mystery of creation and the cosmic praise offered to him who has brought all things into being. The sudden mention of a sealed scroll in the sovereign's right hand stimulates new interest and leads to a second, highly dramatic scene focused on learning who will be capable of reading the scroll and thus becoming lord of history.

In his book *Apocalypse et Liturgie* P. Prigent has greatly helped us in understanding the cosmic liturgy of chapter 4.[28] We can therefore be brief in dealing with it; the second scene calls for lengthier discussion.

Cosmic Liturgy

In his vision John draws inspiration from Ezekiel's description of the divine chariot. But unlike the author of the *Songs for the Sabbath Burnt Offering* who adds further details to his model, John simplifies and goes straight to the essentials. He does, however, add a new group of characters: the twenty-four elders. We must ask what their presence signifies.

The main purpose of Ezekiel's vision of the chariot was to show God's mobility, as it were, that is, the freedom with which he intervenes. But in the static picture with which we are dealing here the description is concerned primarily with the celebration of the wonders of creation (cf. v. 11). P. Prigent in his discussion of the chapter attaches a great deal of importance to the mention of the sea, clear as crystal, that is connected with the throne of God and with the four living creatures. This kind of description was familiar to the Jews. According to Rabbi Eliezer (ca. 90 A.D.), on the second day God created the firmament that stands above the heads of the four living creatures (in Ezek 1.22). "If this firmament did not exist, the world would have been drowned in the waters above and below it. But this firmament keeps the waters separate (Gen. 1.6ff.)."[29]

This kind of speculation had been anticipated long before. According to the Yahwist document God had promised, after the deluge, that he would henceforth respect the regular course of the seasons (Gen 8.22). This cosmic covenant is matched by the covenant concluded with the posterity of Abraham and with David: "Thus says the Lord: If I have not established my covenant with day and night and the ordinances of heaven and earth, then I will reject the descendants of Jacob and David my servant and will not choose one of his descendants to rule over the seed of Abraham, Isaac, and Jacob. For I will restore their fortunes, and will have mercy on them." (Jer 33.25-26).

It is permissible, then, to interpret Revelation 4.1-8 as a revelation of God as Creator: God manifests himself as the one who has separated the waters by means of the firmament and surrounds himself with heavenly servants who maintain the stability of the universe.

More important for our purpose here is a study of the hymnic formulas in this chapter. It is possible to discern in them an echo of the earthly liturgy, either Jewish or Christian?

Let us note, first of all, the specific form taken by the *Trisagion*[30] that is sung by the four living creatures: "Holy, holy, holy is the Lord God Almighty, who was and is and is to come!" (4.8).

As in the Jewish tradition the seraphim of Isaiah have been assimilated to the cherubim of Ezekiel. The expanded form of the divine name, "He who was and is and is to come," occurs constantly in Revelation and has its basis in targumic usage.[31] The liturgical use of the *Quedushah* seems to be attested from the beginning of our era in the morning prayer, the *Yotzer:*

"Blessed are you, Lord, our God, king of the universe, who form light and create darkness (cf. Is 45.7), who make peace and create all things; in mercy you give light to the earth and to all who dwell on it, and in your goodness you renew the created world every day and continually. . . .

"All the spirits who serve him stand on the heights of the universe and with awe proclaim aloud and with one voice the words of the living God and eternal King. . . .

"They all take on themselves the yoke of the kingdom of heaven, each from the other, and encourage one another to bless their Creator; with calmly joyous spirits, in pure words and according to a holy melody they all respond with one voice in awe and say with reverence. . . ."

At this point the entire congregation joins the *Sheliach Sibbur* and sings the *Qedushah* with him: "Holy, holy, holy is the Lord of hosts; all the earth is filled with his glory."

Then the *Sheliach Sibbur* takes up his prayer again: "And the Ophanim and the holy *Haioth*, with a noise as of mighty waters, rise up facing one another, give praise and say: . . ."

Here again all join in the chant: "Blessed be the glory of the Lord, from his place" (Ezek 3.12).[32]

The heavenly liturgy in Revelation 4 follows the same plan. After four living creatures have sung the *Qedushah*, the twenty-four elders answer with their praise: "Worthy art thou, our Lord and God, to receive glory and honor and power, for thou didst create all things, and by thy will they existed and were created" (Rev 4.11).

There has been a great deal of discussion about the identity of these twenty-four elders (*presbyteroi*) with their white garments and golden crowns (4.4). Many commentators think the reference is to a higher class of angels, but nowhere are heavenly beings described in this way. P. Prigent follows A. Feuillet and maintains that the reference is to the just of the Old Testament.[33] This view is a very probable one. Christ promises his followers that they will share the banquet in the kingdom of heaven with Abraham, Isaac and Jacob (Mt. 8.11). In addition, the number twenty-four matches the number of the priestly classes (1 Chron 24.1-19) that took turns officiating in the temple. The elders in Revelation have a priestly role, inasmuch as they offer the prayers of the saints in golden censers (5.8). J. Colson sees the twenty-four elders as a reflection of the presbytery that according to Ignatius of Antioch (*Ad Magnesios* XIII, 1) surrounds the bishop like "a precious spiritual crown."[34] Whatever judgment we pass on this particular hypothesis, we must recognize the fact that the acclamation of God the Creator by the elders is purely Jewish in its tone.

The Enthronement of the Lamb

While P. Prigent has shed light on the origins of the heavenly liturgy of Revelation 4 and made a valuable contribution to the history of the *Trisagion* in the Christian liturgy, he has hardly carried his demonstration over to chapter 5. It is appropriate that we here analyze this chapter on its own account and that we then inquire into its correspondence with the christological hymn in Philippians 5. We shall then have some idea of the liturgical background of our passage.

The "mystery" of the enthronement of the Lamb unfolds in two stages: first, there is the ceremony of investiture, involving the transmission of a book; then the conquering Lamb receives the homage of the entire court: the living creatures and the elders (vv. 8-10), the angels (vv. 11-12), and the whole of creation (v. 13). The final doxology (vv. 13-14) forms an inclusion with the beginning of chapter 4.

In writing this chapter John is inspired chiefly by the vision of the son of man in Daniel 7[35]: in both passages there is an investiture with a royal power that is worldwide in scope and lasts for ever. But the substitution of the figure of the Lamb for that of the Son of man changes the theological meaning of the vision. Other changes accentuate the victory as something unforeseen and mysterious.

The books in Daniel 7.10 were the heavenly records in which God keeps an exact account of the good and bad actions of men. In the Apocalypse there is but a single scroll, and the description of it corresponds to that of the scroll given to Ezekiel when he was called (Ezek 2.9ff.).[36] The reference in v. 5 to the messianic prophecies shows that the book is the scriptures, the meaning of which remains veiled until the coming of Christ (cf. Lk 24.25; 2 Cor 3.14).

After the description of the scroll, v. 3 sounds like an admission of defeat: "And no one in heaven or on earth or under the earth was able to open the scroll or to look into it." This threefold division of the world is found again in Philippians 2.10. In our present context, it indicates a totality: not even the four living creatures, who are the thronebearers and the guardians of the cosmic order, can claim the right to open the scroll. Like the author of the Letter to the Hebrews, John wishes to exalt Christ above the angels (Heb 2.5-9).

It is a *presbyteros* or elder, and not an angel, who consoles the seer (v. 5). If the choir of elders does indeed represent the just of the Old Testament, then there could be no happier thought than to have one of them remind the seer of the messianic promises.

Verse 5 sounds like a triumphal fanfare: "Lo, the Lion of the tribe of Judah, the Root of David, has conquered!" Here we have two celebrated titles which bring to mind the epical age of David and indicate that messianism involves expectations that are both religious and political. The two titles are also well chosen inasmuch as the prophecy of Jacob (Gen 49.9) was very popular,[37] while that of Isaiah about the descendant of Jesse calls to mind the gifts of the Spirit that are promised to the coming Messiah (Is 11.1ff.).[38]

"And between the throne and the four living creatures and among the elders, I saw a Lamb, standing as though it had been slain (*esphagmenon*), with seven horns and with seven eyes, which are the seven spirits of God sent out into all the earth" (Rev. 5.6). The figure of the Lamb (*arnion*) dominates the remainder of Revelation (it is mentioned twenty-nine times). I shall not here review the entire dossier on the point.[39] What the vision is meant to emphasize is the fact that the Lamb is victorious as a Lamb that is immolated. Dodd's idea that in some circles the ram is an apocalyptic symbol of strength and victory does not account for the paradox which we have in this scene. What we are seeing here is radical interpretation of scripture by scripture itself, and specifically of certain messianic promises by other messianic texts. It is this that justifies my interpretation of the scroll as referring to the Old Testament which remained sealed until the day when Christ would unveil its meaning. It is not therefore a mighty warrior who wins the victory, but a sacrificial lamb which remains silent as it is dragged to slaughter (Is 53.7 LXX: *sphagēn*). According to A. Feuillet the title Root (*riza*) of David would remind readers of the figure of the Servant seen as the (Davidic) root that emerges from a waterless soil.[40] This association would confirm the link between the vision in Revelation and Isaiah 53.

A. Feuillet is correct in emphasizing the importance of the prophecy of the Suffering Servant for an understanding of the New Testament texts on redemption. He has not, however, drawn attention to the link in the chain connecting the prophecy of Isaiah with the Christian faith. Behind the figure of the Servant we glimpse the intercession of Moses and the suffering of Jeremiah, but such language remains rather theoretical unless it is associated with the dramatic experience of martyrdom that Israel acquired in the time of Antiochus Epiphanes and with the further understanding of sacrifice that was acquired by meditation on the sacrifice of Isaac, the beloved son (Gen 22.2 LXX: *ton huion ton agapeton*). In recent years a number of studies have emphasized the importance of the *aqedah* (or: binding) of Isaac,[41] which was commemorated especially during the night of Passover. In a development of the data provided by the biblical text, the Palestinian Targum makes the merits of Isaac a pledge that the prayers of the people will be heard: "And now when his [Isaac's] sons are in the hour of affliction, remember the *aqedah* (binding) of their father Isaac and listen to the voice of their supplication and hear them and deliver them from all affliction."[42]

In the same line of thought, the various sacrifices prescribed by the Law are seen as memorials of the *aqedah* of Isaac. Here is how the same Palestinian Targum justifies the sacrifice of the seven-day-old lamb: "The lamb was chosen to recall the merit of the unique man [i.e., just man], who was tied on one of the mountains like a lamb as burnt offering upon the altar. But (God) delivered him in his good mercies, and when his sons pray they will say in their hour of tribulation: 'Answer us in this hour and listen to the voice of our prayer and remember in our favour the *Aqedah* of Isaac our Father.'"[43]

The same explanation is given of the Passover lamb. The interesting point about this next text is that it links the sacrifice of Isaac with a heavenly vision and with an evocation of the angelic liturgy on the very night of Passover: "Our father Isaac was thirty-seven years old at the moment when he was offered on the altar. The heavens came down and lowered themselves, and Isaac saw their perfections, and his eyes grew dim because of their sublimities (from this moment on). And he called Esau, his elder son, on 14 Nisan and said to him: 'My son, this night the heavenly (beings) sing the praises of the Master of the world, and the treasures of the dew are opened.'"[44]

The Lamb who conquers at the cost of his blood not only fulfills the mysterious prophecy of Isaiah (chap. 53) but is also the true antitype of Isaac to whose merits Jews appealed in their liturgies. The Lamb of Revelation has not only generously offered his life; in a true sense he has sacrificed it by carrying the gift of himself to the extreme. The seven eyes, which elsewhere express the omniscience of God (Zech 4.10), here show the universality of the Lamb's action. As always in John, the sending of the Spirit is connected with the sacrifice of Christ (Jn 7.37-39; 20.22).

Having been presented to the entire heavenly court, the Lamb will be invested with supreme authority by reception of the scroll: "He went and took the scroll from the right hand of him who was seated on the throne" (5.7).

In succession, the dignitaries now pay homage to him who henceforth shares the throne of God. After a liturgical prostration and an incensation the four living creatures and the twenty-four elders intone the coronation hymn which begins with the word *axios* that is still used in the rite of episcopal consecration: "Worthy (*axios*) are thou to take the scroll and to open its seals, for thou wast slain and by thy blood thou didst ransom (*egorasas*) men for God from every tribe and tongue and people and nation, and hast made them a kingdom and priests (*basileian kai hiereis*) to our God, and they shall reign [or: are reigning] on earth" (5.9-10).

The verb "ransom" (*agorazein*) alludes to God's ransoming of his people when they were slaves in Egypt (cf. 1 Pet 2.9) and to his acquisitions of Israel as his special people through the covenant at Sinai.[45] Here we see at work the Exodus typology that is so basic to the expression of the idea of redemption in the New Testament (see, e.g., Col 1.13; Rev 15.3). After being rescued from the power of darkness the people become God's inheritance; they become a kingdom and priests (cf. Ex 19.6).

What is new here in comparison with the ancient texts is that the ransom no longer benefits only a single people but now embraces all human beings "from every tribe and tongue and people and nation."

This kind of formula, which is borrowed from Daniel 7.14, occurs frequently in Revelation as a way of underscoring the universality of the Church (cf. 7.9; 10.11; 14.6).

Doubt is possible regarding the reading in v. 10. The French Ecumenical Translation of the Bible prefers the future ("they shall reign"), which fits in with the vision in 20.6. A. Feuillet chooses the present tense ("they reign" or "they are reigning"), as being the *lectio difficilior*.[46] The royal investiture of the Lamb is matched by the spiritual reign of believers who are already appointed "priests and kings" because they are associated with the sacrifice and the victory of Christ.

The Lamb, who is chosen in advance as the victim for the great exodus (cf. 1 Pet 1.20), is not only the Lord of the Church but the Master of the entire universe. This is the point of the final verses where all creatures "in heaven and on earth and under the earth and in the sea" pass before the Victor (v. 13). Even the four cherubim, the throne-bearers and the guardians of the cosmic order, bow down and say their Amen. The praise which was initially directed to the Creator of all things is now directed as well to the Lamb who shares the throne of almighty God: "To him who sits upon the throne and to the Lamb be blessing and honor and glory and might for ever and ever!" (5.13).

Comparison with the Christological Hymn in Philippians 2.5-11
The full significance of the universal homage we have been discussing will become clearer if we compare the scene in Revelation with other New Testament compositions, especially 1 Timothy 3.16 and Philippians 2.5-11, in which a number of exegetes have seen the outline of a hymn of royal enthronement. For brevity's sake we shall be satisfied here with a comparison of Philippians 2 and Revelation 5.

The christological hymn in Philippians 2[47] had two main parts: the first speaks of the kenosis or self-emptying of Christ who carries obedience to the point of death on the cross; the second describes the intervention of God who confers on Jesus the Name that is above every name and establishes him as Kyrios of the universe. The commentators have devoted their efforts chiefly to explaining the difficult phrases about the preexistence of Christ and the nature of his kenosis. The second part of the hymn, therefore, has not always received the attention it deserves.

The influence of Isaiah 52.13–53.13 on the christological hymn in Philippians 2 is undeniable. The *morphē doulou* (the form of a servant) corresponds to the figure of the Servant, while the exaltation bestowed by God sums up 52.13: "Behold, my servant shall prosper, he shall be exalted and lifted up, and shall be very high." On the other hand, the idea of sacrifice and atonement, which is developed in Isaiah 53, is missing in Philippians 2 but is to be found in Revelation 5. The mastery of the universe that is forcefully brought out in Revelation 5 is similarly emphasized in Philippians 2 but is missing in Isaiah 53. Evidently, then, the dependence of Philippians 2 and Revelation 5 on Isaiah 53 does not explain the similarities between the two New Testament texts. These are to be explained rather by the importance assigned to the messianic enthronement of Jesus in early preaching (cf. Acts 2.36). With their faith in the exaltation of Christ as their basis, and making use of royal psalms such as Psalms 2 and 110 or prophetic texts such as Daniel 7, the first Christians took the acclamations they offered Christ at their gatherings and made them part of a heavenly liturgy of enthronement.

The development of this genre is an answer to a typical problem of that age: the relation between Christ and the Powers. The latter, according to the texts, make their appearance as rulers of the cosmic order or as guardians of the Torah. On this subject I can only refer you to M. Cambe's recent article, "Puissances célestes."[48] Although it is difficult for us moderns to think of them as personal entities, the Powers are constantly on the horizon, as it were, of the christological texts not only of St. Paul but also of the Catholic Letters and the writings of Jewish Christianity. Thus, according to 1 Peter 3.22 Christ has gone to heaven and is at God's right hand, while angels, authorities and powers are now subject to him.[49]

In order to account for these ideas, there is no need to appeal to the gnostic myth of the Primal Man who descends to earth in order to gather sparks of light imprisoned in matter and then to return to heaven (the thesis defended, with variations, by Dibelius, Lohmeyer, Käsemann). The contrast of humiliation and exaltation which provides the structure for Philippians 2 is to be found everywhere in the

Bible (e.g., Mt 23.12; Lk 1.52; Rom 12.16; Jas 1.3; etc.) The sapiential writings, in particular paved the way for christological developments on the preexistence of Christ and his dwelling on earth. Think, for example, of Proverbs 8.22-31; Sirach 24.1-22; Baruch 3.38; and others.

On the other hand, the exaltation of Christ above the Powers is a response to specific needs. In the Jewish Christian communities the purpose is to show in what sense Christ reigns and what is the meaning of the time between his resurrection and the parousia. The use of Psalm 110, which is combined with Psalm 8 because of the associations of the verb *hypotassein* (Ps 8.6), plays an important role in this demonstration. We may cite a text from 1 Corinthians in which the preoccupations of Jewish Christian eschatology are discernible: "For he must reign until he has put all his enemies under his feet. The last enemy to be destroyed is death. 'For God has put all things in subjection under his feet'" (1 Cor 15.25-27).

In Hellenistic circles the point of the argument is different. The concern of the faithful here is not to know how the messianic prophecies are fulfilled, but what Christ's relation is to the mysterious forces that rule the universe. Everyone knows how widespread the cult of *Tychē* or *Good Luck* had become at this period, and what an interest there was, in some circles, in cosmogony and astrology. The faith had to be related to these expectations and concerns. E. Käsemann is quite correct when he writes, in commenting on the end of the christological hymn in Philippians 2: "Christ had taken the place of *Anankē* [Necessity]. He is now the *Pantokrator* [Ruler of the Universe] whom all powers and forces serve; under his absolute power he brings together all the things that had previously tended to split apart and be in conflict as opposing powers and fields of force. As Lord of the three orders of the cosmos he is the one who reconciles all things in himself, as we are told in Colossians 1.20."[50]

CONCLUSION

The study of Revelation 5 and the comparison of the passage with various early hymns (Phil 2.6-11; 1 Tim 3.16; 1 Pet 3.18, 19, 22; etc.) allow the inference that there was in existence a liturgical schema for speaking of the heavenly enthronement of Christ. The whole concept of Christ's enthronement in heaven was meant to strengthen faith in the lordship of Jesus and to enkindle confidence in his unlimited power. Thus St. Paul exclaims: "Who shall separate us from the love of Christ? . . . I am sure that neither death, nor life, nor angels, nor principalities, nor things present, nor things to come, nor powers, nor height, nor depth, nor anything else in all creation, will be able to separate us from the love of God in Christ Jesus our Lord" (Rom 8.35, 38-39).

Within this genre Revelation 5 is set apart by its dramatic character. John's vision has for its literary basis the enthronement of the Son of man in Daniel 7, but paints an even broader picture by introducing various classes of actors. The multitude of angels, the twenty-four elders, the four living creatures all acknowledge the supremacy of Christ and urge the faithful to turn to him and to him alone. Following Isaiah (chapter 53), John introduces an element of pathos into the scene: the victory is not won by the use of a great army but in the loneliness of sacrifice. It is the blood of Christ that ransoms and establishes the new people of priests and kings for the glory of God.

Just as, in P. Prigent's hypothesis, chapter 4 of Revelation represents a transposition of a Jewish liturgy in praise of the Creator, so chapter 5, in my view, represents a development, along the lines of a drama, of the theme of the early hymns. John corrects in some measure the enthusiastic views of his day: for example, he rejects any and every kind of worship that might be given to the angelic interpreters (19.9-10; 22.8-9). Adoration is reserved for God and the Lamb.

We of the West have perhaps learned this lesson only too well and have lost sight of the cosmic and liturgical perspectives of Revelation. And yet communion between heaven and earth continues to have a profound meaning. Our keen sense of man's importance threatens to narrow the focus of our prayer to social and political causes alone. Our need is to rediscover the immensity of the cosmos, not as an abyss of glacial silence but as the place where God reveals his majesty: "The heavens are telling the glory of God, and the firmament proclaims his handiwork" (Ps 19.1).

Institut Catholique de Paris

Irénée-Henri DALMAIS

The Structures
of the Liturgical Celebration
as an Expression
of Ecclesial Communion
in the Coptic Church

There are doubtless few liturgical celebrations in which the communion of the faithful who are assembled and united in Christ finds such striking expression as it does in those of the Coptic Church. I am speaking not only of relatively small village communities but also of the much larger urban churches, such as the new Cathedral of Saint Mark at Cairo or the nearby Basilica of Saint Peter, the Boutrousieh.

A quick glance at such an assembly might give the impression of a family festival marked by friendly disorder and improvisation. A more careful examination, however, soon uncovers a structure, but one that seems almost spontaneous, in which each person knows what he should and may do in carrying out his own role. This situation is undoubtedly the fruit of a long tradition that has its roots in the very distant past; I would like to point out briefly certain components of this tradition.

Without dwelling on them at length, I must call at least passing attention to certain characteristics of the Egyptian mind that are recognizable throughout a multimillennial history: a very keen sense of the sacred as embodied in the most concrete realities of everyday life; a respect for and even an extreme sensitivity to the tradition received from the ancients; a temperament more inclined to meditative listening than to movement and gesture.

These traits would evidently be reflected in the various expressions—doctrinal, liturgical, spiritual, and social—of the Christian faith in Egypt. From at least the beginning of the fourth century these expressions claimed to represent apostolic tradition as received from St. Mark the Evangelist. We are, unfortunately, very poorly informed about the way in which the faith fused with Egyptian culture. In any event, the process seems to have been a very rapid one, both in the thoroughly Hellenized ambiance of Alexandria where the way had been prepared for the faith by the large Jewish community (the work of Philo is for us the most typical embodiment of that community's outlook), and in the countless villages of the Delta and the Valley which retained deep ties with the ancient Egyptian tradition.

It has long been observed that the great Alexandrian theologians effected a noteworthy development of the theology of "the Church as body of Christ." The development is already to be seen at the very beginning of the third century in the teaching of Clement of Alexandria and especially in the last books (VI–VII) of his *Stromata*. However, it is in Origen that this theology reveals its full power and develops its many and varied implications. The *Homilies on Joshua* (especially nos. VII and XXIII) as well as the *Homilies on Leviticus* provide us with plenty of evidence on this point. We shall cite here only this concise but very rich passage from the *Contra Celsum:*

"We answer, in accordance with the divine scriptures, that the body of Christ, to which the Son of God gives life, is the entire Church of God, and that the members of this body, this whole, are each and all believers. As the soul animates and moves the body which, without the soul, would be inert, so the Word gives strength and movement for the good of the whole body which is the Church;

138

he moves each member of the Church, and none of them does anything apart from him. All this, I think is consistent and forms a well-integrated whole"[1].

We all know how fully and richly this teaching will be developed in the theology of St. Athanasius[1a] and also in that of St. Cyril of Alexandria, which unfortunately has not been extensively studied from this point of view.[2] The Coptic communities do not explicitly refer back to this tradition and probably do not even have any habitual clear awareness of it; nonetheless they live by it. Whereas the traditions of Syria emphasize the perspectives afforded by pneumatology and eschatology and live their life as churches under the guidance and inspiration of the Spirit,[3] the Coptic Church for its part is eminently Christ-centered. It looks upon the incarnate Word—for whom its favorite name is "Emmanuel, our God, our King"—as the sustaining and animating principle of all its activity.

Against this background, it is not without significance that as a result of the decree which Patriarch Gabriel II ibn Turaïk (1131–45) issued shortly after his consecration as patriarch when he first visited the patriarchal monastery of St. Macarius, some words were introduced into the solemn profession of faith which the celebrant pronounces just before communion. The traditional formula read: "I believe and profess that this is the body of our Lord and Savior Jesus Christ, which he received from God through conception by the Holy Virgin Mary." To this the patriarch added: "which he unites to his divinity." Then, at the insistence of the monks who found this formulation too dualistic (and therefore suspect of "Nestorianism"), these further words were added: "without mingling and without confusion, and without alteration," that is, the very words of the Council of Chalcedon whose decrees the Coptic Church had always refused to ratify.[4] I note in passing the well-known fact that this liturgical formulary provided the basis for the "joint declaration on the faith" issued by Pope Paul VI of Rome and the Pope and Patriarch of Alexandria, Shenoute III (May 10, 1973).

INFORMATION DERIVED FROM THE LITURGY

In all probability there is unfortunately no chance of our ever discovering just how the great doctors and bishops who ruled the Church of Alexandria in its period of glory—the fourth and fifth centuries—gave structured expression to their faith in their liturgical celebrations. Their sermons and other writings do not provide us with even an approximate idea of what went on. In particular, we have no mystagogical catechesis such as has been preserved for the churches of Jerusalem, Antioch and Milan and the area of which Carthage was the primatial see. The oldest liturgical texts are either very fragmentary or are difficult to locate in a specific context; this is true, for example, of the collection entitled (quite arbitrarily) the *Euchologion of Serapion.*[5] They do not therefore allow us to establish the structure of the celebrations and the distribution of roles among the participants. At best, we may think that in the most solemn celebrations, or at least in those at which the "pope" of Alexandria, sometimes called "the Christian pharaoh," presided, some elements were introduced of the ceremonial formerly in use at the court of the Ptolemies and later taken over by the Roman emperors and their representatives in Egypt. Comparable practices were surely accepted, were they not, into the liturgical ceremonial of Rome or Constantinople?

MONASTIC TRADITIONS

At that same period, however, another type of Christian community came into existence in Egypt due to the efforts of St. Pachomius. Recent studies, especially those of Fr. Armand Veilleux,[6] have brought out the characteristic traits of these monastic communities which were so different from the more or less loosely knit groups of anachorites that had hitherto been formed with an "Abba" (Coptic: "Apa") as their center.

"To his disciples as well as to his biographers Pachomius is *the founder of the koinonia,* and this is his real claim to glory. . . . The thing that characterizes the Pachomian community is that it is no longer essentially a gathering of individuals around a father, but rather *a community* of brothers, a *koinonia* or fellowship. . . . The foundation of this common life was evidently fraternal charity, that oneness of mind and heart by which all men could recognize disciples of Christ. . . . This unanimity and union of hearts is not a simple 'brotherhood' of a purely 'spiritual' kind. It is something concrete; today we would say it has its 'material' dimension: it consists in serving one another in a concrete embodied way.

140

"This idea of service and even of servitude is at the basis of Pachomian cenobitism, as it would be later on of the Studite reform. In keeping with the notion of authority that was traditional in the first centuries of the Church's life, Pachomius sees his role of superior as one of service, and he will be very inflexible on this point whenever his disciples will try to give him any privileged treatment. . . .

"It is clear that the Pachomians thought of their monastery or *koinonia* as a Church or, more accurately, an 'ecclesial community". . . . In point of fact, the Pachomian *koinonia* is simply the kind of life established by the Apostles, with the original community of the faithful at Jerusalem as its ideal realization. . . . Similarly, right from the beginning Pachomius organized the life of the community he was trying to build, on this model which we might call 'liturgical'. . . .

"It can legitimately be said that the Pachomian community is a Church from two points of view. First, because it is an embodiment of the *mystery* of the Church, the mystery of divine life communicated to human beings. For, in this monastic *koinonia*, the Holy Spirit uses the proclamation of Scripture, meditation on it, the celebration of the mysteries, common prayer, and asceticism as means of carrying on the work of man's divinization by which the Church is built up. Second, the monastic *koinonia* is a Church because it is a concrete embodiment and visible manifestation of *communion*, or, in other words, a sacrament in which the Church expresses its own mystery—the mystery of Christ—in the midst of and over against the peoples of the earth.

"From an institutional point of view, a monastery is a local Church that is dependent on the bishop of the diocese, just like any other Coptic village of Upper Egypt. . . . Pachomian superiors are seen as having a charismatic calling as pastors and therefore prophets of the new covenant, a calling which they exercise in dependence on and under the control of the hierarchy. Apart from isolated instances in which a certain tension was felt, the bishops not only accepted but promoted the exercise of this charismatic function."[7]

I thought it worthwhile to quote Fr. Veilleux at such great length in order to highlight the salient traits of Pachomian monasticism. I have done so because this monasticism played and still plays a very important role in the life and structural development of the Coptic

141

Church and because there is such a close relation between the doctrine that sustains Pachomian monasticism and the doctrine, recalled earlier, that is at the heart of the Alexandrine tradition. This tradition has admittedly not always been preserved in its original purity and power; at an early date it lost some of its vigor and became somewhat inflexible. Moreover, contact with the rather different traditions of the monks of Lower Egypt as widely broadcast by visitors to these monks, especially Cassian,[8] led to a certain distortion of proper perspective. The rigid views of Shenoute, founder of the famous "White Monastery" (Deir-el Abjad) in the desert near Suhag-Akhmim, and man who seems to have played no small role in the development of the Coptic liturgy, must likewise be taken into consideration. But these various influences led to only minor alterations of a tradition solidly established in its substance.

INFORMATION DERIVED FROM THE CANONS

Only from the eleventh century on do we find ourselves on terrain where there are landmarks to show the way. For one thing, from this period on the *History of the Patriarchs of Alexandria*, by Severus ibn al-Muqaffa', bishop of al-Ashmunain, supplies us with contemporary testimonies on the life of the Coptic Church. More important still, from the eleventh to the thirteenth centuries the codification of canonical decrees furnishes us with exact information on the organization of the liturgy. This data is repeated and supplemented in the *Liturgical Regulations* which Patriarch Gabriel V (1409–37) promulgated on May 3, 1411, at an especially dark time in the life of his Church.[9] In principle, it is these norms that even today determine the manner in which the Coptic liturgy is celebrated, although allowance must of course be made for variations in local custom.

The first of the legislating patriarchs, and one whose concern was chiefly with matters liturgical, seems to have been Christodoulos (1047–77). His intention was not to innovate but simply to codify traditional practice on points that were probably the subject of dispute and abuse. Later compilers, and notably as-Safi ibn al-Assal in his classic collection (thirteenth century), claimed that this ancient discipline was based on collections of "Apostolic Canons" which were rather closely related to the texts that served as the basis for the

Apostolic Constitutions (Syrian in origin). It would therefore be unwise to go looking for specifically Egyptian elements in this discipline. On the contrary, it is perhaps safe to say that at a very early date the Coptic Church took the practice of its sister Church in Syria as the model for its own discipline, especially in liturgical matters.

Only a few specific points are treated in the thirty-one canons which Christodoulos solemnly promulgated on August 1, 1048, on occasion of the consecration of the church of St. Raphael Archangel at Alexandria. From these canons a few bits of information on liturgical celebrations can be derived.

"Canon 22: And it is not allowed to a priest, when he is not present at the Liturgy (*Kuddas*) from its commencement, to make the offering or to break (the bread), and he shall not at all touch the Sacred Body with his hands.

"Canon 23: And the priest shall not go out of the Haikal (Sanctuary) with the censer of incense after the reading of the gospel of the Liturgy (*Kuddas*) into the midst of the people, but he shall incense with it around the altar until the appointed time.

"Canon 27: And if the senior deacons are absent from the ministry of their churches, and are present on festivals and desire to officiate, this is not allowed to them; but those shall officiate who are assiduous in the ministry, even though they be their inferiors."[10]

It is clear that these few directives against flagrant abuses really tell us very little about the actual course of a liturgical celebration.

Nor is there much more to be gleaned from the ten canons on liturgical discipline which the great reforming patriarch, Gabriel II ibn Turaik, supposedly promulgated during a visit to Alexandria, probably toward the end of his term of office. The date given in the manuscripts (1154) is in fact almost ten years after his death. The directives concern the duties of the various ranks of the clergy, both in liturgical celebration and in everyday life. I shall cite only those that relate directly to the liturgy.

"1. It is obligatory for the priests of every church to keep to their ranks (*taxis*), and each of them shall serve the turn which is appointed to him each day. Each of them shall serve his day, and if it shall be weekly, both shall serve a week; and if one of them be absent, the other shall take his place; if both of them be absent, then the office (*taxis*) shall be (served) by him who is after them. And no one shall be absent from the church on the day of his celebration, except for an evident excuse, and none of them shall bestow his rank (*taxis*) on his son or on a near relative without the consent of him who is present with him [i.e., who serves with him] and who is higher than he is in the priesthood, because this raises discord and hatred; but as to the Gospel of the Morning Prayer and the books and the diptychs (*diptycha*), a near relative or a son shall read them, and none but they.

"2. The Liturgy (*Kuddās*) shall not be celebrated until after there have been read the Apostle (*Abustulus* [i.e., the Epistles of St. Paul]), the Katholicon (*Katalikūn* [i.e., the Catholic Epistles]), and the Acts (*Abraksīs*), and the Gospel proper to the day, if there are the books, and if there are not, then there shall be read all that is appointed from the lessons of these books. And the deacon shall not officiate, except that he shall read the Holy Gospel, unless a bishop be present and desire to honour him. As regards the rest of the lessons and the Gospel of the Morning Prayer, those of the priests who are present shall assist in the reading of them, and he who does not know how to read the Gospel shall not be allowed to officiate. As regards the deacons who have not officiated until now, none of them shall officiate until he reads well; but he shall study the writings (*chartes*) and the Gospel of the Morning Prayer; and when he is skilled in reading and is proficient in what he reads, there shall be prepared for him a letter in which there shall be the signatures of a priest and of the chief of the priests, that he is already experienced in the reading of the books; and when it shall have been sent to the Cell [i.e., the Patriarchate or the residence of the bishop], it shall be signed, giving to him the permission to officiate; and he shall take the rank (*taxis*) in conformity with what is stated by the writings of the priests. And the deacon who officiates shall not go away until he shall have finished communicating the people, and shall have dismissed (them). And the priest shall communicate him with the Despotikon (*Isbādikun* [i.e., the central square of the consecrated Host]), and the priest shall raise the chalice; and it is not allowed to him who officiates to raise the chalice at all, until he shall have finished communicating the people. . . .

"6. None of the priests shall go forward to read anything from the books, nor shall any of them go up to th Haikal (altar) without the sticharion (*Istikhārah* [*i.e., the stoicharion*]), and none of them shall communicate at the Altar with his head covered, and likewise, none of them shall pray with a priest or read the Gospel with his head covered."[11]

Canon 7 determines the distribution of celebrants in accordance with succession of feasts.[11a]

It must be admitted that what we derive from these texts is rather little. We do learn at least of the concern for order and dignity in the celebration of the various offices and in the distribution of roles. We also see something that is surely more important and worthy of our attention: the care given to the formation of deacon and priest in the matter of correct reading and the proclamation of the Scriptures. When all is said and done, the abuses requiring correction are rather minor.

This last point seems all the more significant when we recall how wide-ranging and varied the liturgical activity of Gabriel II was. His biographers tell us that with the collaboration of the monks of St. Macarius he had the texts of the Bible and the liturgy translated into Arabic so that the celebrations might be more intelligible to the people. Also attributed to him is a reorganization of the Holy Week lectionary and a new formulary for the consecration of the Myron (chrism). And yet he apparently did not think it necessary to intervene in regard to the actual execution of the rites. This means that the tradition was firmly established and correctly maintained; only a few points dealing chiefly with protocol had to be clarified.

A century later (April 19, 1240), Patriarch Cyril (Kirollos) III ibn Laqlaq issued a set of regulations that prescribed in a more detailed way the distribution of functions according to the rank of the feasts, and the allocation of offices. The chief of the priests (archpriest) and the chief of the deacons (archdeacon) were to officiate on the twelve major feasts, the priests and deacons of the second rank on five less important feasts, and the priests and deacons of the third rank on five other secondary feasts. These further directives are also given:

"As regards the Prayers [i.e., the Canonical Hours and the Service of the Evening and Morning Offering of Incense] on the eves of feasts, he who celebrates the Liturgy (*Kuddâs*) shall perform the Prayer of the eve of the feast, and the Prayer of the morning (shall be performed) by him who comes after him.

"As regards the Sundays of the whole year, the Sundays of the Fast [i.e., Lent] are begun by (the priest) highest (in rank) according to turn.

"If a great feast falls on (one of) the remaining Sundays, he to whom the feast is reserved shall celebrate the Liturgy (on it). The ministering shall revert during the rest of the year to the order of the first rank (*taxis*), so that the Second Sunday of Paschaltide shall be to him who has the seventh rank (*taxis*) who did not have the Sundays of the Fast.

"As regards the feasts of the churches [i.e., patronal feasts], the feast of Martyrs or Angels or of other (Saints), if the church is dedicated in their name, (shall be) for the chief of the priests.

"As regards the Absolution (recited) over the celebrant, it shall be (recited) by the chief priest who is present after the bishop [i.e., if the bishop is present, he recites it].

"As regards the prayers (recited) together with the bishop in sanctuary (*haikal*), and at (the services) of baptism and marriage and funerals and the sanctification of the water, they are especially for the the archdeacon (*archidiakonos*), and in like manner, the prayers in Holy Week and (at times) other than it, and the prayers of consecrations also.

"As regards the ranks (*taxis*) which is fixed for every day (on which there is) the Liturgy (*Kuddâs*), the Morning Prayer is for the second (priest) after the celebrant, and likewise the Epistle of St. Paul (*Paulos*) in the Liturgy (*Kuddâs*), and the Acts (*Praxeis*) is for the third (priest) after him, and the reading of the Catholic Epistles (*Katholikon*) is for the celebrant.

"The Sundays in Kyahk [i.e., November-December, Old Style] are great, and they are begun by the chief (*arch-* [i.e., priest]), as is done in the Great Fast.

"As regards the commentary of the Books [Pauline Epistles, Catholic Epistles, and Acts] in Arabic, it is not a rite (*taxis*) in the

146

church, for it is for every one to know what he (the reader) is saying, and (let him) comment well, be he priest or deacon.

"It is not allowed that anyone replace another by reason of his rank (*taxis*) on the feasts for a Liturgy (*Kuddas*) or a reading of a Book [i.e., a Lesson], unless the priest or deacon who comes after him in rank (*taxis*) be willing.

"None of the priests shall celebrate a marriage without the permission of the bishop.

"As regards the rest of the functions on weekdays, each priest or deacon shall serve one week in his rank (*taxis*), and if a feast fall on it, it (the service) shall be for him (who) is higher than he, (and) he to whom it (the feast) belongs shall celebrate it, and the rank (*taxis*) shall (then) revert to him to whom (the week belongs).

"He who is suspended shall not (serve), and he who (serves) with him without the permission of him who suspended him, shall be suspended with him, both together. Likewise, the priests shall not communicate any of the laity who is interdicted, without that he who interdicted him has absolved him, and he who does this shall be suspended with him, both together.

"The priests shall present themselves in the morning of every day at the Cell (*kellion*) of the bishop before the Prayer [i.e., the Canonical Hours and the Office of the Morning Offering of Incense], and they shall depart from it again to their affairs."[12]

We do not know the precise reason for these directives or the circumstances in which they were promulgated (although we do know that the authoritarian interventions of Cyril III in the organization of ecclesiastical life antagonized many bishops). We can say at least that the directives show the importance attached to respect for protocolary rules and to decorum in liturgical celebrations.

It was at this time that the Coptic Church entered upon the darkest period of its existence. It was reduced for several centuries to a life of semi-clandestinity and was frequently subjected to harassment, partly by the distrust and hostility of those who regarded Christians as infidels and suspected them of being collaborators of the hated "Franks," and partly by the arbitrary exactions of the Mamluk authorities. Yet it was in this very situation of wretchedness verging at times on despair that Patriarch Gabriel V in 1411 set down in detailed form the regulations governing the liturgical celebrations of baptism and chrismation, the anointing of the sick, marriage, the morning and evening office of incense, the eucharistic celebration, ordinations, monastic clothing, funerals, and the consecration of liturgical furnishings and altars: in short, an almost complete code of rubrics to accompany liturgical ritual. (Vansleb, who in 1673 found a copy of Gabriel V's *Liturgical Regulations*, confused this patriarch with his great predecessor, Gabriel II ibn Turaïk.)

In view of the Church's situation at the time, it is not likely that Gabriel's regulations were widely broadcast. In fact, we have only two manuscripts of them: Paris B.N. Arab. 98 (the one Vansleb brought back), and Vatican Copt. 46, copied in the seventeenth century. And yet the celebration of the offices in the modern Coptic Church corresponds rather faithfully (when allowance is made for local variations) with the descriptions given in Gabriel V. We may therefore conclude that, given the state of desolation in which his Church was living, this patriarch's intention was not to enact a new code of rubrics but simply to record traditional practice in writing, lest it fall into disuse because the clergy lacked an adequate formation.

As a matter of fact, the tradition has proved as indestructible as the very rocks of the country. When we are privileged to take part in a present-day Coptic liturgical celebration, we know that the structure of the ritual, the gestures of the officiants, the formulas they use, and the very melodies they sing are rooted in a past that stretches back many centuries. The tradition has been fed by many contributions over the years, but these have been so perfectly assimilated as to form part of an utterly Egyptian whole.

In concluding, I would like to dwell briefly on certain traits that I think characterize a Coptic celebration, and specifically the distribution of roles in such a celebration.

Let us turn to a privileged occasion: a pilgrimage (*mouled*) at one or other venerable sanctuary of the Blessed Virgin, for the celebration of the patronal feast. A *mouled* may bring together many tens of thousands of the faithful, people of all conditions and ages, to say nothing of the sheep that would be slaughtered and shared after the liturgy in joyous, fraternal agapes. Ordinarily there will be a good number of baptisms, since the people like to make such a pilgrimage the context for the sacrament of rebirth and entry into the Church. Priests and deacons are present; most of the time there is even one or more bishop.

On this occasion the transition is made almost without noticing from the popular festival to the liturgical celebration and back again. If there are not too many baptisms they will be conferred in the usual way: by immersion and in a great community celebration in which bishops, priests, deacons and other servants (*chammas*) carry out the functions which liturgical tradition assigns to them and which each individual knows thoroughly. The elders of the community are the attentive and often scrupulously careful guardians of this tradition and would not allow any major innovations although they do leave room for any adaptations which the situation of the moment renders necessary or at least desirable. Thus, for example, if the children, newborn or already somewhat grown, who are presented for baptism are numerous, baptism will be conferred by aspersion. The sprinkling will undoubtedly be abundant enough to make sure that all receive a generous amont of the purifying and regenerative water.

The ceremony is marked by the many summonses and appeals of the deacons, the singing led by the *arifs* (usually blind men who from childhood have faithfully memorized the traditional texts and melodies; these are familiar to the entire assembly which repeats them or joins in), the cymbals, triangles and sistrums which punctuate the ceremony. All these serve to stimulate the attention of the people when the length of the service and the heat of the day threaten to relax it.

The eucharistic liturgy (*Kiddas* = Sanctification) that is the heart and high point of this gathering is preceded by a lengthy preparation, first on the previous evening, then in the early morning of the day itself, in the form of the purifying offering of "morning and evening in-cense." At least in this form, the rite is peculiar to the Coptic tradition, although it is somewhat analogous to the *houssaye* which the Churches of the various Syrian traditions have enshrined in their morning and evening offices. The penitential aspect of purification by means of the incense has an important place in the Coptic tradition; in this tradition the "office of incense" is closely associated with the morning and evening "psalmody" which in turn has made its own the psalmody of the monastic tradition.

Two aspects of this office of incense seem characteristic: the importance and arrangement of the scripture readings in relation to those of the eucharistic liturgy; the role assigned to intercessions and especially to the three universal prayers which have been faithfully maintained in the Coptic tradition, in accordance with canon 19 of Laodicea. While the incensing of the assembly has a primarily penitential meaning (everyone knows the controversies that arose within the Coptic Church regarding "confession at the censer"), the offering proper of the incense is done in a perspective in which intercession takes first place. This aspect is emphasized by the very expressive ceremony in which each officiant places a few grains of incense in the censer while voicing his particular intentions. Moreover, ancient canonical directives which were retained in the compilation of ibn al-Assal and have sometime been attributed to St. Athanasius, forbid the priest to proceed to the offering of the incense unless he is assisted by a servant (*chammas*), who is not necessarily a deacon.

Evidently, the traits which I have presented as characterizing the Coptic tradition are best manifested in the course of the eucharistic liturgy: the intensely communal character, the active and varied participation of all orders in the assembly. Thus the lengthy proclamation of the eucharistic prayer, which in its entirety is sung in a manner that is regarded as a constitutive element of the celebration, is frequently interrupted by the calls of the various *chammas* and the acclamations and petitions of the choir and the entire assembly. One must have taken part in such celebrations, whether during a *mouled* or in a community of ordinary people, if one is to know from experience the magnificent way in which a Christian people who live the mystery of their communion in God with Christ and his saints can give expression to their faith.

Institut Supérieur de Liturgie
Paris

APPENDIX

The Three "Catholic" Prayers of the Coptic Liturgy
First Prayer: For the peace of the Church

Priest: Let us pray.
Deacon: Stand for the prayer.
Priest: Peace be with you.
People: And with your spirit.
Priest: Let us again pray to Almighty God, Father of our Lord, God and Savior, Jesus Christ. We invoke and petition your goodness, O friend of the human race.

Be mindful, Lord, of the peace of your one, single, holy, universal and apostolic Church.
Deacon: Pray for the peace of God's orthodox Church, which is one, single, holy, universal and apostolic.
People: Lord, have mercy!
Priest: On your Church which extends from one end of the world to the other.

Bless all peoples and all the faithful; grant the peace of heaven to our hearts, and grant us peace in this life as well. Bestow full peace on the president, the armed forces and the civil officials, on our neighbors and our allies. You have bestowed every favor upon us: make us your own, for we acknowledge no one but you and we ceaselessly call upon your holy name. Let your spirit give life to our souls, and do not allow the death of sin to rule over us, your servants, or over your entire people.
People: Lord, have mercy!

Second Prayer: For the hierarchy; that is, a prayer for the pope, the diocesan bishop and the entire Orthodox episcopate.

Priest: Let us again pray to Almighty God, Father of our Lord, God and Savior, Jesus Christ. We invoke and petition your goodness, O friend of the human race.

Lord, remember His Holiness the Pope (Shenoute III), Patriarch of the places where St. Mark preached, and of Alexandria, all Africa and the Near East; remember, too, his colleague in the sacred ministry, our bishop N.

Deacon: Pray for His Holiness the Pope (Shenoute III), Patriarch of the places where St. Mark preached, and of Alexandria, all Africa and the Near East.

People: Lord, have mercy!

Priest: Preserve them for many peaceful years. Let them carry out, in accordance with your holy and blessed will, the sacred ministry you have entrusted to them: may they exercise judgment uprightly through the word of truth; may they pasture your people in purity and justice.

To the Orthodox bishops, priests and deacons and to your entire Church which is one, single, holy, universal and apostolic, grant peace and salvation in every place. *The prayers they address to you for us and for your people,* [13] as well as the prayers we address to you for them [*here the deacon gives the censer to the priest, who puts a pinch of incense into it and then continues*] deign to receive on your holy altar (your baptistry), which is spiritual and heavenly, just as you deign to receive the fragrance of this incense.

Be quick to humble and crush beneath their feet all their enemies, visible and invisible, and preserve these men themselves in peace and justice within your holy Church.

People: Lord, have mercy!

Third Prayer: For Christian assemblies.

The priest recites the prayer, which is called the prayer "of the presence," i.e., a prayer for the people present.

Priest: Let us again pray to Almighty God, Father of our Lord, God and Savior, Jesus Christ. We invoke and petition your goodness, O friend of the human race.

Be mindful, O Lord, of our assemblies. [*He makes the sign of the cross over the people and says:*] Bless them.

Deacon: Pray for our gathering in this holy church and for those who have joined us.

People: Lord, have mercy!
Priest: [*He takes the censer in his hand and continues:*] Grant that there may be no disturbance, no shortcoming, in these holy places, so that in accordance with your holy and blessed will [*he holds the censer over the altar (or font) and swings the censer in four directions—east, west, north, south—each time in the form of a cross, while he continues the prayer:*] we may be able to make them houses of prayer, houses of purity, houses of blessing. Protect these places, Lord, and let them be a joy to your servants who will come after us to the end of time.

[*He holds the censer in his hand and continues:*] Eradicate idol worship utterly from the world. Be quick to crush beneath our feet the devil and all his deadly forces. Do away with doubt and those who foster it; put an end to the sad divisions caused by heresy. Lay low the enemies of your holy Church, O Lord, now as you have at all times. Break their pride and, without delay, teach them their weakness. Render vain their envy, their endeavors, their madness, their malice, their calumnies, and all their plots against us. Reduce them all to impotence and block their plans.

[*To an ancient air, he sings:*] O God who brought to naught the plans of Ahithophel (the enemy of your servant David).
People: Lord, have mercy!
Priest: [*He raises his hand, incenses three times toward the east, over the altar (or font), and continues:*] Rise up, Lord our God, and let all your enemies be scattered. Let all who hate your holy name flee from before your face.

[*He turns to the west and three times incenses the priests, deacons and people, saying:*] By the power of your blessing may your people be multiplied and become thousands of thousands and millions of millions, all of them doing your holy will.

[*He turns to the east and says:*] Do all this through the grace, mercy and love of your only Son, our Master, our God and Savior, Jesus Christ. [14] For to you belong all glory, all honor, all kingship, all power and all adoration: Father, Son and Holy Spirit, lifegiving and consubstantial, now and at the beginning and through endless ages. Amen.

Serge HEITZ

Reflections on the Contemporary Liturgical Assembly

I shall restrict my remarks to the Orthodox world, which almost everywhere uses the rite generally designated as "the Byzantine rite."

The liturgical assembly in our time—such is my subject—calls to mind certain theological principles from which I shall attempt to draw some concrete conclusions bearing on the concrete practice of our communities. It is not my intention to say anything very new, but rather to sum up what has already been said in various places and to add to this what I have been able to learn from experiences that seem cogent. I shall focus my attention on three points: what an assembly is; what a liturgical assembly is; and, finally, what a liturgical assembly in our day is.

1. First all, then, what is an assembly? It is an event involving the Church. Who summons this assembly? The paschal Christ, in his pentecostal Holy Spirit, summons it in order to make us sharers in the *Eschaton*, i.e., his everlasting kingdom. Part of the commission which the Word gave to his apostles and their legitimate successors is that the hierarchy should convoke this assembly here and now. In this sense the term "hierarchy" implies a holy origin (*archē* = origin), which is the holy origin of our assemblies.

What is it that makes an assembly an assembly? It is the worship that is offered by Christ, who is at the Father's right hand, in union with all his angels and heavenly saints: a worship that descends from heaven and enters this divine extraterritorial enclave of salvation that is the earthly spot where they are assembled who bear the name of Christ and dare unite themselves to the prayer of the eternal high priest. Thus the assembly obtains its existence from above and from below. From below it is constituted by the various roles played in the assembly: those of the bishop, the priest, the deacon, the lesser ministers, the choir, and each member of God's chosen people. For, as St. Peter says, in continuity with the prophecies of Exodus, Isaiah and Hosea: "But you are a chosen race, a royal priesthood, a holy nation, God's own people" (1 Pet 2.9).

What is the role of the assembly as such (a role which has the above mentioned roles as its integral parts)? The role of the assembly as such is kerygmatic and ethical, and most specifically, a role of prayer or worship.

At this point I would like to dwell for a moment on the concrete structure of the Christian reality we call "Church." Christ himself, in his hypostatic union, is the "religion" or bond between God and man, man and God. He speaks of himself as the way, the truth and the life; in other words he makes his own the three functions of the Messiah: he is pastor (shepherd) or king, he is prophet or teacher, he is high priest.

Christian ecclesial reality is thus composed of three concentric circles, as it were. The most important circle is the innermost one, upon which everything in the other two circles *converges* and from which everything in the other two circles *derives*. This central circle corresponds to the priestly role of Christ. It is the sphere of prayer and the sacraments, the sphere of grace, the sphere whence the Christian derives his very being.

The circle around this center is the one connected with the prophetic role of Christ and therefore of the Church and her members. What Christ proclaims, he brings to fulfillment in the mysteries of his economy. The Gospel proclaims the redemptive actions of the Man-God. This is to say, in terms of the Church, that her kerygma and faith represent the objective social grasp and consciousness of what has been accomplished and brought to fulfillment in the historical and liturgical mystery of Christ. This is the sphere of dogma and doctrine, on the one hand, and of personal faith, on the other.

The third circle corresponds to the pastoral role of Christ. It is the circle of royal commandments and of Christian ethics based on the Gospel. It is the sphere in which we are made to become what we are. Around this entire reality, i.e., around all three circles, runs the fence of canon law, which prevents what is within from being scattered and prevents what is outside from entering and mingling with what is within.

If we draw a line across these circles or spheres, or, in other words, if we take them in a kind of chronological order, we may say that the catechumen begins by presenting himself for enrollment in the list of candidates. He accepts, as it were, the statutes of the "association," that is, the prescriptions of canon law. He then enters the outermost circle, the third: he provides a minimum pledge that his intentions are serious, by practicing in at least a rudimentary way what Christian morality requires. Then he enters the second circle, the circle of faith. Here he begins to learn the catechism, and already adheres to the truths of faith. Finally, the catechumen receives Christian initiation: the baptism that immerses him in the death of Christ and causes him to rise with Christ and the seal of the gift of the Holy Spirit that enables him to share in the royal priesthood and in the communion of the divine liturgy.

The catechumen is now at the very heart of Christian reality, in the innermost circle. He is not simply called but in fact is a child of God (1 Jn 3.1). As a result this child of God moves back, but in a higher degree and fuller measure, into the second circle, which is that of the Gospel, dogma and doctrine. In this second circle his faith is now a divinely given virtue. The Christian acquires a deeper and fuller knowledge of the Gospel and commits himself fully to the teaching of Christ. Then, returning again to the third circle he gives concrete expression to the love of Christ that is poured out on him and crowns the life he has received in his Christian initiation. Finally, the bulk-head established by canon law protects himself from what lies beyond.

2. This outline enables us better to grasp the importance and significance of the liturgical assembly and thus brings us to our second point. The liturgy too has as its focus an ever new and ever deeper participation in the ontological Christian mystery. *In tantum vivimus in quantum oramus:* we live to the extent that we pray (St. Augustine). Furthermore, the liturgy brings the kerygma into play: the proclamation of Christ's death and the confession of his resurrection (Liturgy of St. Basil). Finally, it motivates and gives strength to our moral activity.

Participation in the liturgy is thus proper and indeed essential to our exercise of the love of God, for in the liturgy we unite ourselves to Christ's act of love on the cross and his act of victorious love on Easter; being made one with Christ and each other "just as the Father and I are one" (Jn 17), we are united with the divine exchange of love between the divine hypostases. This act of love in turn creates the space for true love toward those whom the Father loves; love of God and for God undergirds and supports love of neighbor. This is why (consistently with my outline above) the central liturgical action is preceded by the forgiveness that fraternal love inspires (Mt 5.23-24) and by the exchange of the kiss of peace before the confession in the form of the Creed (second circle), while the Creed in turn precedes the anaphora at the center (third circle).

Liturgical action is the expression of supreme fraternal love, because it is inserted into Christ's prayer of redemptive self-sacrifice for all human beings and especially for all who dwell with him in one house of faith. This liturgical act of love embraces the sick, the afflicted, the imprisoned, and those who bear the burden of responsibility for the common good. Understandably, then, the Fathers could not believe that if the Church did not pray in and with Christ, if she

158

did not pray for the cosmos and the human race, cosmos and human race would straightway collapse.

What, then, is the meaning of our liturgical assembly? It expresses ortho-doxy and makes it real and concrete here and now. We must look beyond the historical origin of the word "ortho-doxy" if we want to understand its true meaning, for the word now signifies the authentic, proper and correct way of glorifying God, of giving him the glory that belongs to him (*doxan anapempomen*). In this glorification we profess the true, correct and right faith. In other words, orthodoxy is most fully and deeply achieved in the act of the liturgical assembly.

What, then, is the purpose of this liturgical assembly? Its purpose or goal is our increasingly complete incorporation into the paschal and pneumatic (spiritual) body of Christ, our conformity to him, our imitation of him, our rootedness in his victory and glorification, our *theosis* or divinization.

What place does the liturgical assembly occupy? It is truly central. In it the kind of ecclesiology that has rightly been called "eucharistic" lives and achieves fulfillment. The essential work of the Church is the *leitourgia*. This term has a twofold movement because it reflects a twofold movement. First of all, the word *leitourgia* as used by scripture refers to the service or *work which God does* in Christ for his people and their salvation. At the same time, liturgy refers to the service or *work which the people do in Christ* for the glory of God. In the books of the Old and New Testaments liturgy refers to cultic service or public worship (Num 1.50; Lk 1.23; Rom 15.16; Heb 8.2). St. Paul also uses it to mean the service rendered by love (2 Cor 9.12; Phil 2.30). In the history of the Church the term liturgy was reserved strictly for the divine liturgy, i.e., the celebration of the eucharist. At the time when the Reformation in the West brought a breakdown in the ritual of the Holy Supper, the word "liturgy" was extended to the whole of public worship. The Catholic Church finally adopted this use of the term. This accounts for such paradoxical combinations as "the liturgy of baptism," "the liturgy of burial," and so on.

3. Our third point concerns the liturgical assembly today, in our time. The "today" of which we speak is the eternal today of God in the today of concrete human time. And it is the lifegiving Holy Spirit, the

"leader of the dance" of life, who joins the eternal today of God to the fragile today of our concrete times. It is he who brings our anamnesis—that of the assembly—into the eternal present of the anamnesis celebrated by the Most Holy Trinity and of its mysteries of salvation; it is he who links our epiclesis—that of the assembly—to his own real descent upon us and the gifts on the altar, to which gifts we ourselves are assimilated. Just as the Holy Spirit effected the incarnation of the Word in the womb of the Theotokos (Mother of God), so he gives the Word a body in the form of the human race–Church, which is the mystical body, or rather the mysterious and therefore pneumatic body, of the glorified Christ. Anamnesis and epiclesis (the words are to be taken in their strict and full sense) are inseparably, divinely connected; each exists within the other. The liturgical assembly here and now gives concrete form and expression to the mysteries contained in the one mystery of Christ; it bodies forth the meaning of these mysteries and causes us to experience their spiritual effect.

I would say—but without any intention of canonizing a particular philosophy—that the liturgical assembly is characterized by what I might call the primacy of being. That is, it transcends the psychological, intellectual, volitional and emotive levels, whether individual or social, although it certainly gathers these up and integrates them into the ontological sphere. This is why the liturgical assembly is so closely connected with divine Tradition, the pneumatological nature of which it also shares. The divine Paradosis (Tradition) is revelation itself, i.e., the handing over, the delivery, of the divine mysteries of salvation to the Church. In other words, it is the act of handing over in which God, in the person of Christ Jesus, puts himself into the hands of men by taking a human nature to himself.

Tradition and the sacraments, especially the divine liturgy, are based on the incarnation and share in the mystery of the latter. The Tradition must therefore be understood in the light of the doctrine of the two natures that are unconfused and unchanged yet also undivided and unseparated. This means that we can possess divine Tradition only in the form of traditions. Tradition is life with Christ in the Holy Spirit. The movement of this life can be glimpsed in the communion of the praying Church with the Father, the Son and the Spirit. Where the Spirit is at work, growth in Christ takes place. "The whole structure is joined together and grows into a holy temple in the Lord" (Eph 2.21).

Like Tradition, however, the mysteries of worship that have been handed on do not grow or evolve. For Christ is perfect, just as his act of handing on and that which he hands on are perfect. The historical dimension of the liturgical Tradition finds expression in traditions. The latter share in Tradition, though Tradition itself is one. Despite their relativity, however, these traditions, which have their birth in history, cannot be regarded as *adiaphora* (indifferent things), which we are free to interchange or get rid of. They are the forms in which the Church lives her life and renders divine Tradition visible and in which the communion of saints is carried on. Once again, in the liturgical assembly the Church *lives divine Tradition today* by means of the historical traditions which express it. For our part, we cannot dismantle traditions, break them up into parts as it were, in order to make a choice of components in accordance with abstract ideas and principles and then to construct a liturgy and a worship according to the more or less preconceived ideas of contemporary man as seen through the spectacles of philosophies now popular.

Here is another example of what I am trying to say: Icons, with their presuppositions in the areas of sacraments, kerygma and ethical ideals, are another instance of divine Tradition and how this Tradition is mediated and grasped through various pictorial traditions. Icons are an integral part of public worship, with the Word expressing himself therein in colors. The painting or sculpture of an ordinary religious artist only gives expression to human views and feelings about themes that are selected more or less arbitrarily. Look around: do we not see people—well-intentioned, indeed, but not very talented—creating "liturgies" out of whole cloth?

Another remark seems important with regard to the respect we should have for our liturgical tradition. The entire content of the liturgy is always present in the component parts of the assembly's liturgical celebration. The whole is accessible and reflected in the details. To tamper with certain details is to lay hands on the very substance, on the unity of the whole.

Does all this mean that our assemblies leave nothing to be desired? Not at all! Their concrete form always requires evaluation in the light of divine Tradition. Consequently there is nothing to prevent the elimination (in the case of icons, for example) of influences exercised therein by the Baroque and even the Gothic ages.

The today of the liturgical assembly gives the mystery of Christ a concrete existence here and now in space and time.

In space, first of all. We should devote great attention to the arrangement of the liturgical space, unless serious obstacles leave us no choice. By their very nature our places of worship emphasize the sanctification of space, with the place being set off as holy over against what is profane. The mystery, as something mediated and communicable yet also retaining a sense of reserve, finds protected expression there, as does the mission of the Church in concentrated form. It is through the Church that the work of Christ affects us. The word of God is addressed first and foremost to the Church which it brings together in assembly. The Holy Spirit descended first on the apostles, who then communicated him by building the Church, the spiritual body of Christ. The place where the Church is gathered is the high place of the word and the high place of the Spirit. In this context many texts from the dedication of a church and many hymns for the anniversary of dedication might be cited. I shall limit myself to the following: "Just as in the heights of heaven you have shown forth the splendor of the firmament, so on earth you have shown forth the beauty of the holy place where your glory dwells, O Lord"; "You have made the Church a heaven of dazzling light that illumines all of the faithful; for this reason, as we stand in this holy dwelling place, we cry to you: 'Make this House firm, O Lord!'" (troparion and kondakion for the dedication of the Basilica of the Resurrection, September 13).

The arrangement of our churches should show an increased respect for the function proper to the narthex. The narthex is not meant for the celebration of the liturgy and the Church's public prayer, but is for the prayers of catechumens and penitents. The nave should be the symbol of the Church as the ark of Noah. The royal doors, as we find them for example in the churches of Rumania, provide the entry way for the assembly which has previously gathered for the enarxis or *statio* in the narthex, for example, or for the celebration of the sacra-

162

ments, except the eucharist, crowning (marriage), and imposition of hands, essential parts of the Church's prayer the importance of which is not always appreciated.

The walls of the nave could be hung with icons representing the cycle of festal mysteries and thus allow certain types of iconostases to be made less massive. Finally, the sanctuary (or altar) should be made more clearly distinct from secondary locales such as the proskomidion and diakonikon. We should not underestimate the contribution this kind of clear demarcation makes to the understanding and exercise of the various roles played in and by the liturgical assembly.

I must not overlook the part played by processions. The manner in which the Greeks, for example, carry out the processions of the Little and Great Entrances brings out their rich meaning more clearly: when the clergy, in the name of the assembled people and in union with them (this is why the procession should pass through the entire nave), process with the word or with the sacred gifts, they symbolize the people's earthly pilgrimage and their ascent to the holy of holies in the heavenly city.

A procession like a dance moves through time as well as through space. So too the liturgical assembly of our day takes concrete form in time. There is a good deal that might be said on this point. Time means first of all the period of a day. When new communities are being founded and conditions permit, a very great effort should be made to have the rhythm of redeemed time follow the rhythm of created time. In other words, evening services should not be held in the morning or vice versa. If the nocturnal part of this rhythm cannot be followed, as it is in monasteries, at least the eothinon, lauds and matins should be celebrated, although the final ekteies should not be allowed to do double duty with those of the liturgy.

There is also room for ecclesial reflection on the possibility of introducing differentiation into, or even abridging, certain services, according as we find ourselves dealing with elements that are specifically monastic or with those that are ecclesial in the strict sense. But endless caution is needed in making such needed distinctions. Take vespers or matins for an example. The psalmic kathismas at the beginning of these offices should not be completely eliminated in parish churches. Why not, instead, use the appointed psalms one after another in successive offices? Why have two canons on feastdays and Sundays when one might be used one year, the other the next?

And the divine liturgy! One may legitimately think that it would be profitable to return to the primitive practice of singing the anaphora aloud and of saying aloud (responsorially from time to time) one or other part of the synapties or collects, with their doxological ekphonesis, which is, of course, always proclaimed. On the other hand, we must not forget that our rite has preserved and still preserves the other aspect of the mystery, namely, that it veils even as it reveals. This is why the elimination of the iconostasis or of the custom of saying the so-called mystical parts in a low voice (I am not referring to such prayers as regard only the person of the priest) is not desirable; we want to keep a proper balance, and this not least for pastoral reasons.

There is one point I want to emphasize: the rectification of the horarium for the offices of Holy Week and especially of the Easter Vigil. (In this context, popular terminology, which is often phenomenological and not strictly accurate, needs careful revision.) I shall limit my remarks to the Great Saturday. Why should not the eothinon and the synaxis, where feasible, be celebrated on the morning of this day rather than on Friday? The Easter Vigil is made up, of course, of vespers and the Liturgy of St. Basil, celebrated at nightfall on the Great Saturday. Its simple and massive character is much appreciated nowadays. The prophecies should stand out clearly by the way they are read and by their being given a subsequent explanation. The canticles, with their refrain in which all join, have a biblical flavor and an unparalleled spiritual richness. The change in adornments and floral decoration speaks for itself. The holy shroud may be carried in front of the Gospel for enthronement on the altar. The entire lighting may already be or can be made appropriate to Easter. During the reading of the prophecies baptism can be celebrated in the nave (the catechumenate having been celebrated during Lent).

My long experience enables me to say that if the Easter Vigil is carefully celebrated as I have suggested, it can be the high point of the Christian year. What about Easter matins? For pastoral reasons we pause briefly and then celebrate matins after the Liturgy of St. Basil. Matins then function like a kind of fireworks in which that which was begun in the liturgy bursts out in its full splendor. In addition, these matins are attended by what I might call "the general public" that does not receive communion but does take part in the agapes. We then celebrate the liturgy of the first Sunday after Easter, just as we do any other Sunday's liturgy. Families which, because they were traveling or for any other reason, could not come for the nocturnal service now take part in the divine liturgy and share the joy of Easter.

We may note other concretizations of the liturgical assembly. There are, for example, the acclamations that precede or follow the proclamations. Thus the celebrant proclaims: "Peace to all," that is, he is asserting that all *have* the peace of Christ and, at the same time, he is asking that all *may have* the peace of Christ. Then all speak the acclamation "And with your spirit." Originally, too—and not just in the East, for the Latin tradition attests the same—the trisagion consisted of a proclamation: "God is holy . . ." and not a vocative, "O holy God," and an intercessory acclamation: "Have mercy on us!" There is an acclamation that follows upon the proclamation of the Gospel: "Glory to you!" that is, glory *belongs* to the Word, and, may the Word *be glorified*. The calls and summons of the deacon—"Wisdom!" "Give heed!"—also belong in our category of concretizations.

But the essential acclamation of ratification, in which the assembled people of God reaches its highest pitch of concreteness in exercising the priestly function of its universal royal priesthood, is the "Amen"—it is so; so be it—after the epiclesis and the "Amen" after the reception of holy communion. The other "Amens" during the celebration should likewise not be reserved for the cantors. The same must be said of the responses to the intentions proclaimed by the deacon during the ektenies, and indeed of everything that does not belong specifically to the choir. The choir has its specific role which is analogous to that of the chorus in ancient drama: it calls the faithful, and itself gives expression, to meditative reflection and to sentiments that are true to the meaning and permanently valid content of what is done in and through the liturgical celebration of any given feast or mystery of the Christian year.

By way of conclusion let me ask: Should we seek liturgical reforms in our Church?

Hardly any Orthodox Christian would want reforms of the kind the Western confessions introduced in the sixteenth or eighteenth or twentieth centuries. The doctrinal as well as pastoral fruits of those reforms (taken as a whole) bid us exercise a prudent reserve if a not a complete avoidance of reform. The Orthodox idea of Tradition, as I explained it earlier, prevents us from moving in certain directions. In addition, we cannot afford to adopt an anthropocentric perspective in our attempts to build up the faithful and exercise the care of souls. After all, it is not permissible to shift emphases in a unilateral manner. Our salvation is the glorification of God. God became incarnate and suffered in order to bring us back to himself.

Our duty in every age, therefore, is to make the divine Light of Christ in the Most Holy Trinity shine forth resplendently and to let the light of the divine mysteries of salvation likewise shine forth brilliantly in the pure crystal of a transparent liturgical assembly. Thus the component crystals, which are the authentic and untainted structures of the celebration, must convey this light undimmed. Our task is to make these structures permeable to the action of the Holy Spirit.

In this way the liturgical assembly of our day will be united to the communion of saints in the Holy One; the "whole Christ" will make its own, and be caught up in, the priestly prayer of the Head as he sits at the Father's right hand. As the anaphoras of St. John Chrysostom and St. Basil bid us say: With him, in the Holy Spirit, we sing, we bless, we praise, we give thanks to the Lord our God.

Düsseldorf

Alexander KNIAZEFF

The Role of the Deacon
in the Byzantine Liturgical Assembly

The deaconate is one of the oldest institutions in the Church. Everyone is familiar with the apostolic and early Christian texts that speak of deacons, and there is no point to our citing them here. But while the deaconate as an institution is attested from the very beginning of the Church's history, its role has undergone considerable change in the course of the centuries. The deacon was initially the secretary and possible successor of the bishop; his role was precisely that of *diakonia* or service. In time, however, he lost his administrative and social functions and retained only a purely liturgical role.

In some Churches, moreover, the liturgical functions of the deacon underwent progressive restriction and finally almost completely disappeared. As a result, the deaconate became simply a theoretical step on the hierarchic ladder, with individuals being obliged to stay on it

167

for only a brief moment of the journey toward priestly ordination. At the present time, these same Churches have undertaken a renewal of the diaconate and are attempting to restore it to its proper place in the liturgy, administration and social work of the Church. But what of the Churches that have kept the full liturgical role of the deacon, and even if this be his only role? Is a reform of the diaconate to be desired in these Churches? If so, what kind of reform?

These brief remarks regarding the liturgy and other activities provide the starting point for my examination here of the role of the deacon in the Byzantine liturgical assembly, in keeping with the theme of our Twenty-third Week of Liturgical Studies. As everyone knows, the deacon continues to play an important part in this liturgy, not only in countries where the Churches of the Byzantine rite have traditionally been established Churches, but even in others where these Churches have experienced persecution or banishment.

I

The Byzantine liturgical texts describe the deacon's liturgical role, but they do not give any precise statement on the meaning of his ministry. The Typikon, the Euchologion, and the Pontifical tell the deacon what he is to say and do during the services or other liturgical functions in which he is called upon to participate. The very ancient ritual of ordination in the Pontifical gives details on the liturgical and ecclesial role of bishop and priest. The prayers of deaconal ordination recall St. Stephen, the first martyr, in whom they see the first deacon as well and in whose person "the law of the diaconate has been made known."[1]

The ritual goes on to give, in a very general way, the meaning of *diakonia* or service; it is summed up in this precept of the Gospel: "Whoever would be great among you must be your servant, and whoever would be first among you must be your slave" (Mt 20.26-27). The prayers then ask that through the descent of the Holy Spirit the ordinand may be filled with an unalloyed faith, with charity, courage and holiness, in order that "as one free of every sin, he may stand unashamed before God on the fearful day of judgment and receive the full reward God has promised."

These prayers thus evidently have in mind *diakonia* in the Church and emphasize the interior dispositions the person must have who exercises this ministry. After the *Axios* ("He is worthy!") acclamations and the vesting of the ordained, the bishop gives him the *rhipidion* (fan). The new deacon then takes his place beside the altar in order to wave the fan over the sacred species. I must add that this is practically the only moment in his liturgical service in which the deacon uses this fan and waves it over the sacred species. Apart from the rite of deaconal ordination, the custom of thus fanning the sacred species has fallen into disuse in the Byzantine liturgy. What, then, are the Byzantine deacon's liturgical functions in our day?

As I indicated above, these functions are set down in the Typikon, the Euchologion and the Pontifical. These books show that the deacon plays an important role in the eucharistic liturgy just as he does in the offices of vespers and matins. The deacon plays no part in compline, in the nocturnal office, or in the little hours of prime, terce, sext and none, unless we are speaking of the Royal Hours that are celebrated on Good Friday and on the Vigils of Christmas and Epiphany.

The Byzantine deacon has a function in the celebration of baptism, in the rites of espousal and crowning (i.e., marriage), in the blessing of the holy oils, in all the funeral rites, and in the consecration of water. He also takes part in all the functions of the Russian *Kniga molebnykh pienij*. The deacon likewise plays a role in extraordinary pontifical ceremonies such as the rite of the Exaltation of the Cross (September 14), the so-called rite of Orthodoxy on the first Sunday of Lent, and the washing of the feet after the eucharistic liturgy on Holy Thursday.

We should note at this point that the participation of the deacon is neither obligatory nor indispensable on most occasions. This is why in the second half of the nineteenth century the Russian Church adopted a policy of reducing the number of deacons in parishes; the stimulus to this policy came from Count A. D. Tolstoy, the Imperial Procurator to the Holy Synod. The reason for the move was financial: the savings effected by reducing the number of unneeded deacons would make it possible to raise the salaries of priests. As one way of eliminating deacons, it was decided that a cantor could be ordained a deacon only at the express wish of the members of the parish and after the latter had pledged themselves to pay his salary.

The result was that the number of deacons dropped off sharply in small or medium size parishes. But the numbers increased again on the eve of the First World War. One reason was that deacons were sought as teachers of catechism in the parochial schools. The main reason, however, was that the Orthodox faithful have traditionally set a high value on the deacon as liturgical figure. The faithful love their liturgical celebrations and are quite sensitive to the additional solemnity the ceremonies acquire from the participation of a deacon. In addition, the place which the Byzantine deacon occupies in the praying assembly turns him into an authentically liturgical personality; for this reason the faithful regard his participation as desirable. What form does this participation take?

II

In the Byzantine liturgical assembly the deacon does most of the incensing. At vespers and matins he does all the ordinary incensing, while at the eucharistic liturgy he incenses the sanctuary, the iconostasis and the people. There are solemn incensings at the beginning of vespers on vigils, at the polyeleos and during the offices of Easter week; these are done by bishop and priest, but the deacon precedes the latter and carries a large lighted candle.

The deacon is also the minister who does the reading. He reads the Gospel at the eucharistic liturgy; if there is a second deacon present, he should, in principle, read the epistle. At matins and vespers, at which the Gospel is read, the bishop or a priest reads the liturgical pericope, but the deacon proclaims the prokimenon or the other biblical verses which precede or follow the reading of the Gospel. The deacon carries the book of the gospels in the processions of the little entrance and of the entrance at vespers. When the Gospel is to be read from the center of the church the deacon brings it there in a solemn manner and brings it back to the sanctuary again when the reading is finished and places it on the altar. The deacon also urges the faithful to listen attentively to the sacred scriptures; he does so by means of such exhortations as: "Wisdom!" "Pay attention!" "Let us stand," "Let us listen to the holy Gospel," etc.

At the proskomide the deacon exhorts the priest to proceed to all the actions which make up the extraction, beginning with the first prosphora of the large cube of bread that is called the "Lamb of God" and that will be consecrated and used for communion. At the end of the liturgy of the word, which the Byzantines call the liturgy of the catechumens, the deacon bids the catechumens withdraw and urges the faithful to pray for them. Before the profession of faith he invites all those present to exchange the kiss of peace and orders the porters to keep careful watch at the doors of the church; then he urges all: "Let us be attentive in wisdom."

After the profession of faith the deacon announces the prayers of the anaphora and bids the faithful stand with attentive hearts and in a spirit of reverential fear of God. During the Sanctus the deacon takes the aster or asteriscus, which rests on the dish or paten, and raises it up, making motions which imitate those of the angels who are mentioned in the priest's prayer and who fly through the heavenly regions "singing, crying, shouting the triumphal hymn and saying: Holy, Holy, Holy . . ." At the words of institution the deacon uses his orarion to point to the elements that are to be consecrated: first to the paten, then to the cup.

At the words "We offer thee thine own from what is thine (*ta sa ek ton son*), the deacon takes the cup and paten and, with arms extended and crossed, traces a sign of the cross in the air. Among the Slavs, at the moment of the epiclesis, while the priest recites the troparion from terce, the deacon repeats verses 12 and 13 of Psalm 50 (51). He then urges the priest to consecrate the sacred species, and after each act of consecration he says "Amen," an acclamation originally meant to be uttered by the people. The priest incenses the eucharist, then returns the censer to the deacon who incenses the altar and the entire sanctuary. In Russian pontifical ceremonies, at the moment of the anamnesis the deacon pronounces a lengthy proclamation in which he mentions the name and title of the celebrating bishop and lists the various orders and categories of faithful for whom the eucharist is being offered.

After the Lord's prayer, the deacon urges the priest to proceed to the breaking of the consecrated bread, and pours the zeon into the cup. He then bids the clergy approach for communion; next he issues the same invitation to the faithful. Formerly—and still in the rubrics for the Byzantine liturgy of St. James—the deacon presented the chalice to the faithful, while the priest presented to them the dish with the body of Christ. The introduction of the liturgical spoon meant the disappearance of this diaconal activity from the other Byzantine liturgies. But the deacon does assist the priest during communion by holding a cloth in front of the chalice so that the faithful may wipe their mouths after receiving the sacred gifts. In Russian usage the deacon must still ask the name of each person who comes for communion; he then whispers it to the priest, and the latter then says, for each communicant: "N, servant of God, partake of the body and blood of Christ for the forgiveness of sins and for eternal life."

From what has been said it is clear that in the Byzantine liturgy the deacon, while being minister of the word, is also called upon to serve the bishop or priest and the people as well. He serves the people by leading and directing them in their participation. His exhortations and actions tell them the attitudes, exterior and interior, they should have. The Byzantine deacon mediates between altar and nave. He goes back and forth between celebrant and people. These comings and goings of the deacons in Byzantine celebration have often led to these ministers being compared to the angels who in Jacob's vision (Gen 28) ascend and descend the ladder that stands on the earth with its top reaching to the heavens, or with those other angels who are depicted on the side doors of the iconostasis (called "diaconal" doors because the deacon uses them to enter and leave the sanctuary as the parts of the service require).

In the Byzantine liturgy the deacon is not only the minister of reading and proclamation; he is not only the leader of the people and the intermediary between celebrant and nave. He is also a minister of prayer. He is this because, in addition to prescribing the attitudes and postures of the congregation, he also suggests the intentions for which the people should pray. He does this in litanies to which Russian usage has given the name ektenies. We must therefore turn our attention now to the diaconal litanies that are so characteristic of the Byzantine liturgy, and to the role they play in the prayer of the assembly.

III

Litanies bulk very large in Byzantine liturgical celebrations. They are to be found even in the text for the various services and offices, that is, in the Euchologion, the Hieratikon, the Pontifical and in the Slavic Sluzebnik and Trebnik. At the present time, litanies take three main forms: the collect, the litany of petition, and the ektenie. The Russian uses the name of the third type for the other two forms as well.[2]

The collect or synapte is a short prayer. But it also exists in a more developed form, the "great collect," also called the eirenika or, in Slavic, *mirnaja,* because of its opening words: "In peace let us pray to the Lord." According to the liturgists,[3] the little collect can be regarded as the beginning of a prayer that is introduced by the deacon. The prayer may be psalmic or said by a priest. In the latter case, it is generally said in a low voice[4] and ends with an ekphonesis that is said aloud. The little collect may also be found after the psalmody, after a stanza, a series of torparia and odes, as in the canon at matins. This allows these litanies to play a part in the structure of the office and to set off the major divisions of the latter.[5]

The great collect consists in a series of formulas in which the faithful are urged to pray for the peace that comes from on high, for the salvation of their souls, peace throughout the world, the prosperity of God's holy Churches, the union of all, and also for the bishop, the clergy, the country in which one is at the moment and the civil authorities, as well as good weather, abundant harvests, travelers, seamen, prisoners, the sick, the afflicted, and the salvation of all. The faithful, or the choir which represents them, answer each petition with a *Kyrie eleison*. In our day, the great collect is found at the beginning of the offices of vespers and the great collect is found at the beginning of vespers and matins, many offices of the Trebnik and of the Book of the Molebens, and also at the beginning of the liturgy of the catechumens. The great collect which comes at the beginning of vespers and matins, after the psalmic part, has been shifted to this place because of the psalmic petitions that now terminate these offices; the great collect used to come before the litany of petition.[6] The displacement has had the beneficial result of freeing up the litanic part and allowing it to be distributed in an orderly way throughout each of these offices; another result has been a more uniform distribution of the deacon's entrances and exits.

An ektenie, which the Slavs call *sugubaja,* i.e., "strengthened," is a fervent supplication and urgent prayer. The deacon proclaims its formulas and the choir or the faithful answer with a triple *Kyrie eleison.* The ektenie has two parts. The first three formulas of the deacon are connected with Psalm 50 (51) and call upon God for mercy. The second part is a prayer for the authorities of the country and of the Church, for priests, faithful, benefactors, and deceased: i.e., for specific groups of individuals who, generally speaking, have special links with the community in whose name the deacon leads the ektenie. We may note here that in the ektenie the deacon himself addresses God, whereas in the collect he simply announces the intentions to be prayed for.[7] The formulas used in the ektenie have varied greatly in the course of time.[8]

The litany of petition, aitesis to the Greeks, *prositelnaja* to the Slavs, completes the litanic prayer at vespers and matins at which the doxology is sung instead of being read by the reader. In nonfestive vespers and matins the litany is said after the ektenie. In the formularies for the anaphoras of St. Basil and St. John Chrysostom a litany of petition occurs twice: after the great entrance and after the prayers of consecration, or, more accurately, after the anamnesis and before the Lord's Prayer. In a liturgy of the Presanctified this litany is said only once: between the great entrance and the Lord's Prayer. It is chiefly a prayer for spiritual blessings: for peace; for the sending of a guardian angel[9] as faithful guide and protector of our souls and bodies; for pardon and the forgiveness of sins; for protection in every area of life; and, above all, for a Christian death and a successful defense before the awesome tribunal of Christ. To each petition that the deacon proclaims, the people or the choir answer: "Grant it, O Lord!"

Throughout this section I have been presenting, as I indicated, only the many forms of the litanies that are so abundant in the Byzantine rite. This rite has other categories or forms of litany, such as the litany of the deceased, the litany said at the lite, or at the ceremony of the exaltation of the cross, and so on. Sometimes special formulas are added to the regular formulas of the great collect, as is the case at baptisms, the blessing of the water, and the vespers of the Holy Spirit which are celebrated on the evening of Pentecost Sunday.

Nowadays the deacon leads the litanies while standing on the solea, in front of the royal doors and facing east, i.e., in the same direction as priest and people. Only the formulary for the Byzantine anaphora of St. James prescribes that the deacon should face the people as he leads the litanies. For the litanies themselves the same formulary has a text that is quite different from the one which has become current in the Byzantine rite used today. The litanies certainly originated in the context of a cathedral. The Kyries with which the assembly answers the deacon can have the ring of a popular acclamation, as in the Kyries of the lite or in the five hundred Kyries for the exaltation of the cross.

The diaconal litanies thus set up a kind of dialogue between people, deacon and priest, a collaboration in prayer that gives an impetus to the entire service. Moreover, the litanies fill in a desirable way the silences that became inevitable with the now solidly established practice of "secret" prayers. In fact, an examination of the offices shows that every litany, and not just the little collect, is connected in one way or another with a prayer of the priest that, in current practice, is regularly said in a low voice.[10] Moreover, as I pointed out for the little collects, all the litanies introduce divisions into the office and thus make its structure more readily visible. They introduce language that is more intelligible to the people than the language of the hymns and psalms and even, generally speaking, of the translations of scripture (except for the gospels) that are used in the liturgy. They also bring in objects of prayer that are more concrete and immediate and more directly accessible to the average religious mind than those we find in the prayers of the liturgy; in any case, the praying assembly does not hear the latter since today the priest says these prayers in a low voice for the most part.

By the way in which he says the litanies the deacon also gives the office a certain rhythm. The litanies as presently distributed throughout the service, alternate with the more compact parts, such as the psalmic parts, or with sections which are made up of troparia and are sometimes (the canon, for example) very erudite hymnographical compositions. The litanies thus allow the attention of the people to

175

relax, even while maintaining it in an atmosphere of prayer and thus preparing it for a subsequent period of greater spiritual effort.

The *Didascalia* compares the deacon to the Holy Spirit, while it sees the bishop as representing the Father and the priest the Son. The comparison is a legitimate one, for the Holy Spirit is the Spirit of prayer, and the role of the deacon, especially in the Byzantine liturgy, is to lead the prayer of the assembly and give it rhythm and vitality. Making our own the traditional comparison (traditional at least among the Russians) of the deacon with the angels, we may say that in the Byzantine liturgical assembly the deacon is the angel of prayer. This very concrete and well-defined role explains why in the Churches of the Byzantine rite there have always been and still are deacons who choose to remain deacons throughout their lives and who refuse priestly ordination even when their bishop insists they should accept it. The deaconate brings full satisfaction to devout men who love to pray and who are unwilling to become priests either out of humility or because they do not feel called.

We may add that the liturgical role of the Byzantine deacon is such that the believing people have a profound love and veneration for him, precisely as a deacon. His attractiveness reaches beyond the walls of the liturgical assembly; with the help of literature, the deacon has become a kind of popular hero. All Russians and lovers of things Russian are familiar with the famous deacon Achilles who appears in the well-known novel of Nikolai Leskov, *The Cathedral Clergy*. The author depicts him as a likeable and picturesque character, but at the same time he makes us feel the love a deacon could elicit from the people in a church-centered milieu, by reason both of his liturgical functions and his human qualities.

The world in which the Church must live today is no longer the world Leskov describes. It bears less and less the mark of the Church and quite often has lost that mark entirely. New mentalities are making their appearance even within the Church. Must the Churches of the Byzantine tradition entertain the idea of changes in order to enable the liturgical role of the deacon to retain its religious importance?

IV

To begin with, there can be no question of eliminating or changing the function of the deacon in the liturgical assembly. It is not only useful but necessary that there be someone to lead the people in prayer and help them to participate in the liturgy (the *Kyrie eleisons* and other responses originally belonged to the people and not to the choir, and a return to this practice is to be desired). What does need changing is a role sometimes given to the deacon but which does not belong to him. The popularity of a deacon is sometimes due not to the role he should play in the assembly or to his liturgical qualifications but to things that are purely external. Folklore sometimes becomes more important than prayer, and then bad taste forces its way in. It is possible then to value a deacon primarily for his voice (the Russians like a deacon to have a bass voice), his stature, his bearing and presence, his physical strength that enables him effortlessly to carry heavy evangeliaries in processions. The deacon himself, feeling flattered and admired, may then yield to the temptation of indulging in theatricality and may come to think of his liturgical role in terms of vocal effects, elegant gestures, and esthetic charm in doing the incensing or carrying the diaconal candle. Thus the deacon himself is sometimes the victim, and this not only at the spiritual level, of the folkloric personality which the people seek to force upon him in some circles.

At times, new deacons have trouble adapting immediately to their place in the diaconal celebration. Then they are hastily ordained priests, and are thus deprived forever of the experience—liturgical, spiritual, parochial—they might have acquired in the diaconate. On the other hand, when a deacon fits perfectly into his liturgical image and role, efforts are made to keep him in the deaconate as long as possible. Consequently some men have remained deacons all their lives when in fact they really aspired to the priestly ministry and apparently had the qualities and education required for this ministry.

All these aberrations and abuses can be avoided to the extent that we can educate the ecclesial sense of the faithful and the deacon himself, and also to the extent that the bishop can be kept from acting in an arbitrary manner. But in all this we are discussing points external to the liturgical role as such. Should we also be making changes in this role as well?

I spoke above of the litanies and emphasized the value these have for the Christian people who gather in the liturgical assembly. Now, in the present state of affairs, the litanies are frequently repeated; even in the course of a single service the same litanies may be said two or three times. Should an effort be made to cut down on these litanies?

The Greek liturgical reform of 1838 completely eliminated the litanies that ended the orthros. As a result, if this service is followed by the celebration of the eucharist, there is a direct transition from the great doxology to the ekphonesis of the priest, "Blessed be the reign. . ." and the liturgy of the catechumens. Within the celebration of the eucharist the Greek reform suppressed the ektenie after the Gospel, the litany of the catechumens, and the two litanies of the faithful. This means we go directly from the Gospel to the Cherubikon and the great entrance. The Greeks no longer say the second litany of petition and recite the Lord's Prayer almost immediately after the prayers of the consecration and the anamnesis.

These excisions in the litanic component certainly effect a notable shortening of the entire office. But as far as the orthros is concerned they also mean the loss of what for the people was one of the most prayerful parts of this office. As for the celebration of the eucharist, the cuts made after the Gospel means that the priest hardly has time (especially if he must be the reader of the Gospel) to say the prayer for holiness and the two prayers of the faithful before the Cherubikon. Yet these two prayers of the faithful are required by the overall structure of the service, as is proved by the fact that they are found in all the anaphoras.

As for the suppression in the liturgy of the second litany of petition, its effect has been to eliminate, after the epiclesis, a period of relatively easy prayer that would prepare the faithful for the next spiritual high point: the Lord's Prayer and communion.

The results of the Greek reform show that cuts in the litanic component tend to make the service unbalanced, to deprive it of something that creates a rhythm and makes the structure of the service stand out more clearly, and to deprive the praying assembly of restful periods within the overall effort at prayer, periods in which they might prepare for new spiritual fervor. Clearly, then, reforms aimed at lightening and shortening the services should not take the form of suppressing the diaconal litanies; such reforms should not even begin with these litanies. They should always keep in mind the service as a whole, i.e., its structure, composition, and overall development.

They should rethink each component part of the service, its place in the overall structure, and its importance for the movement of prayer.

More specifically, a primary need is to solve the problems created by the contemporary practice of saying inaudibly the very prayers whose content is the richest in the entire service, as well as the problems created by the language of the liturgy, the translations of the Bible, and all the other things that put a barrier between people and service and prevent the people from participating fully in the service.

Above all, we must not forget that in the Byzantine liturgical tradition the deacon is and should continue to be the angel of prayer. In order to emphasize still further the importance for prayer of the part played by the deacon in Byzantine liturgical celebrations, we may recall the fact that while the people like celebrations in which a deacon takes part, some devout priests prefer to celebrate without a deacon. Why? Because then they themselves have more prayers they can say aloud, and because by means of the ektenies, which they now say in the absence of the deacon, they themselves direct the prayer of the assembly in accordance with their own personal spiritual rhythm!

Thus it is still difficult to imagine reforms that affect what the deacon is called upon to do and say during the various offices. On the other hand, it is relatively easy to see what further role it would be desirable to give the deacon over and above his liturgical role. Modern life is too difficult and complicated; we cannot continue to confine the deacon to a purely liturgical role and refuse to use the institution of the deaconate as a way of supplying the Church with new means of action. It would be very desirable and profitable to restore to the deaconate its ancient administrative and social functions.

In addition to revitalizing and extending the scope of the deaconate in this way, there is another step we might take. With our eye precisely on what the liturgical figure of the deacon represents for the Church, we think it very desirable to open the deaconate to men who would participate as deacons in the liturgical assembly but would continue their professional, social and even political activity in the world: as lawyers, teachers, doctors, industrialists, managers, workers, employees, etc. There are precedents—admittedly, isolated cases until now—to show how valuable the Church would find a policy for the deaconate that led to this kind of men being ordained. Such men would bring the presence and witness of the Church into quite varied circles and widely divergent social classes.

This policy would also enable the Church to give a "real life" formation to many future priests and would awaken vocations to the priesthood in men who would later make excellent pastors after their years of liturgical and parochial practice as deacons involved in the life of the community. In short, to ordain such men would be to make liturgical prayer produce effects outside the assembly, to prolong that prayer in range and in depth. Should not the liturgical assembly influence the world around it not only through prayer but also through the men who lead that prayer? Is it not the vocation of the assembly to act upon the real world around us by flooding it with the light which the mystery of Christ brings to men?

Institut de Théologie Orthodoxe
Saint-Serge de Paris

Nicolas KOULOMZINE

Liturgical Roles in the Assembly of the Primitive Church according to Father Nicolas Afanassieff

It is my pleasure today to evoke the memory of Father Nicolas Afanassieff. He was not himself a specialist in matters liturgical; nonetheless, along with Dom Bernard Botte, Dom Olivier Rousseau, Dom Lambert Beauduin and his own long-time friend Father Cyprien Kern, he was a founder of the Saint-Serge Liturgical Weeks, the twenty-third of which we are celebrating this year. These are men whom we keep alive in our memories and whom we honor.

Father Nicolas Afanassieff was always an unpretentious man, but within there was a soul open to study and indeed a fervent praticioner of it. In the twenties, while still a young man, he found himself at Belgrade, where he devoted himself to theology and abandoned the exact sciences he had been studying in Russia. He finished his studies in the Faculty of Theology at Belgrade; there, just as later

181

on in Paris, he was drawn first and foremost to the study of church history and worked under the direction of Professor A. Dobroklonsky. From 1930 on, he taught at the Institute of Orthodox Theology in Paris. There, at the beginning of his career as a professor, he came under the influence of his spiritual father, Father Serge Boulgakov, although he did not adopt this master's views on "sophiology."

We see that during his lifetime Father Nicolas Afanassieff had to make an intensive study of several theological disciplines. At the same time, however, almost all of his thinking was focused on a single theme: the Church as actualized, or made real and effectively present here and now, in the eucharistic assembly of a local Church. In ecumenical circles during the sixties the name of Father Nicolas Afanassieff was closely associated with the concept of "eucharistic ecclesiology."

Father Afanassieff devoted relatively little attention to the Old Testament origins of the New Testament people of God. He was interested less in the continuity between the two covenants[1] than in the radical newness of the Church of Christ. This is the reason why, although he was a specialist in canon law and church history, he drew his inspiration chiefly from the New Testament. It is in this area that we shall try to trace out his thinking today.

I. THE CHURCH

Our subject is the roles played in the liturgical assembly of the primitive Church. Father Afanassieff turns to this question in his book *L'Eglise du Saint Esprit* [The Church of the Holy Spirit].[2]

In Father Afanassieff's view the Church cannot exist unless the eucharist is celebrated: "Wherever a eucharistic assembly is held, the Church is to be found because Christ is there. The Church cannot exist without the eucharistic assembly, and the eucharistic assembly cannot but manifest the fullness and unity of the Church. Consequently, the structure and order of the Church come from the eucharistic assembly which contains all the foundations of the Church's organization."[3]

This assertion underlies all the further study done by Father Afanassieff. It is easy enough to see how this conception of the Church differs from that of Rudolf Sohm, from whom Father Afanassieff is accused of having borrowed certain views or conclusions.[4] In the Protestant scholar's view, "Where two or three are gathered in the name of Christ, the people of God, the Israel of the New Testament, is present; present is the whole of Christianity with all of its partially fulfilled promises, for Christ, who is all in all, is present in the midst."[5] For Afanassieff, on the other hand, the Church in its innermost essence is not to be identified with just any *Gemeinde* [community] that gathers in the name of Jesus, any more than it is to be identified primarily with an institution governed by a hierarchy.[6] No, for him, the Church is, first and foremost, a sacramental entity; consequently its structure is to be grasped only in function of the eucharistic action.

Principles Guiding the Thinking of Father Nicolas Afanassieff

From this conception of the Church Afanassieff derives three conclusions which he subsequently treats as principles for his further thinking.

The Local Church

First of all, Afanassieff asserts that the very idea of Church or *ekklēsia* applies to a local community. At Corinth, Thessalonika, or elsewhere, the people of God, as assembled by the Spirit and communicating in the eucharistic body and blood of Christ, formed the ecclesial body of Christ, or Church of God, in the full sense of the term. It is easy to see that, from the viewpoint of eucharistic ecclesiology, the very idea of a universal Church, of which a local community would be a "part," has no meaning, since it is impossible to have a eucharistic assembly in which all Christian believers would come together. Afanassieff appeals to the well-known words of Ignatius: "Where Christ Jesus is, there is the catholic Church,"[7] and claims that every local Church is the catholic Church. He maintains that the very notion of a Church structured in universalist terms appears only in the third century and comes from Cyprian of Carthage, who says: "The Church that is one throughout the entire world is divided into many members."[8] For Cyprian, the unity of this universal Church finds its concrete expression in the unity of the episcopal college.[9]

Afanassieff's claim seems fully substantiated by the writings of Paul and John, as well as by the second half of the Book of Acts (chap. 13 to the end). In these sources it is very clear that "Church" means "local community."[10] I even think it possible to say that the more developed and fully elaborated ecclesiology of the Letters to the Ephesians and the Colossians presupposes the spiritual experience of an author who has lived in local communities, and that it does not seem to reflect any ecclesiology of a universalist type.[11]

The first part of Acts (1–12), however, where Luke, the presumed author, depends on various sources,[12] seems to offer a certain objection to the view I have stated. Is it possible to maintain that the first communities established in Palestine were, from the beginning, independent local Churches in the Pauline sense? Acts 9.31, in particular, is a stumbling block. If we adopt the *lectio difficilior,* the text reads: "So the church [singular] through all Judea and Galilee and Samaria had peace and was built up; and walking in the fear of the Lord and in the comfort of the Holy Spirit it was multiplied."[13]

If this reading (preferred by the [French] Ecumenical Translation of the Bible) is correct, we have before us a text that is unique in the New Testament, with the word "Church," in the singular, referring to all the communities of an entire region. (The other reading in Acts 9.31, which the Jerusalem Bible and others prefer, causes no difficulty: "The churches throughout Judaea, Galilee and Samaria were now left in peace . . .") And yet a reading of chapters 6–12 of Acts suggests that the first communities established in the Hellenistic Jewish world came into existence somewhat after the manner of the Jewish Diaspora and thought of themselves as independent of Jerusalem and of the Twelve who lived in Jerusalem during those years.

These remarks in no way detract from the importance of Father Afanassieff's basic insight into the sacramental and, specifically, the eucharistic character of the Church and, consequently, into the primordial importance of the Church of God as a local entity. This does not mean, of course, that we can shut our eyes completely to the universal aspect of the Church, for this too was something the first Christians were aware of. (Paul the Apostle, who saw the Church of God in every local community, was also intent on maintaining unity between the Churches he had founded and the older Churches of Antioch and Jerusalem. Clement, the bishop of Rome, thought it necessary to intervene in the affairs of Corinth in about the year 90,

184

while Ignatius, bishop of Antioch, felt himself obliged to write exhortations to a whole series of Churches.)

The Singleness of the Ecclesial Assembly
The second conclusion Afanassieff draws from his basic conception of the Church has to do with the oneness or singleness of the eucharistic assembly in a given place. Ignatius of Antioch saw this singleness as a necessary consequence of his teaching on the local Church: "Be careful, then, to participate in only a *single* eucharist, for there is but a *single* flesh of our Lord Jesus Christ and a *single* chalice that unites us to his blood, and a *single* altar, just as there is but a *single* bishop with his presbytery and deacons."[14]

In Afanassieff's view, a eucharistic assembly is an assembly of all who live in one place and gather for one and the same purpose: "This principle flows from the very nature of the eucharist as instituted by Christ."[15] Why? Because Christ is one and the Church is one. There can only be one eucharist for the entire local Church; otherwise Christ is divided.[16]

The pertinent texts of the New Testament do not explicitly affirm this unicity or singleness. On the other hand, as Afanassieff remarks, they do not support a contrary view.

In regard to the Pauline communities a difficulty arises in connection with the "church that gathers in the house" of Aquila and Prisca at Ephesus (1 Cor 16. 19) and at Rome (Rom 16.4),[17] and in the house of Philemon and Archippus at Colossae (Philem 2).[18] The phrase *hē kat' oikon ekklēsia* has been understood in different ways. The French *Bible du Centenaire* and the various Russian translations understand "church" here as being "a family community," but the (French) Ecumenical Translation of the Bible (TOB) says in a note on Philemon 2 that "the early Christian community gathered in the house of a well-known Christian." This was Afanassieff's interpretation.[19]

Philemon and Archippus, moreover, seem to have exercised a ministry in the Church of Colossae.[20] It would be natural, then, for the entire local Church to meet in their house. Then, too, Clement of Rome tells us that "the apostles, as they went preaching in the cities and rural areas, tested in the Spirit the first-fruits of their work [i.e., the earliest converts in each community] and appointed them overseers and deacons for future believers."[21] Now, Aquila and Prisca were in fact the first-fruits at Ephesus.[22]

A single eucharistic assembly must have remained the rule in Asia Minor as long as John the Apostle lived there, but it is probable that beginning in the time of Ignatius of Antioch there was a tendency to relax this rule; this would account for Ignatius' reaction.

Here again, Afanassieff's arguments seem less convincing in regard to the early community in Jerusalem. A text in the Book of Acts provides the basis for discussion: "Day by day, attending the temple together and breaking bread in their homes (kat' oikon), they partook of food with glad and generous hearts."[23] It is possible, of course, to think with Afanassieff that the entire community of Jerusalem faithful gathered in the homes of one after another of the members of this Church. But the smallness of houses in Jerusalem and the large number of the faithful would create a difficulty here of which Afanassieff was not unaware.[24]

Pentecost

The mention of the primitive Church in Jerusalem brings us to the third conclusion which Father Afanassieff drew from his basic conception of the Church. Since in his view the very existence of the Church was unthinkable without the celebration of the eucharist, he was logically forced to maintain and did in fact maintain, that the Church was instituted during the Last Supper when the Lord himself gave thanks (eucharistēsas) in the midst of the Twelve.[25] However, the Last Supper was not yet the eucharist in the Christian sense of the term, inasmuch as Christ was not yet glorified and the Spirit was not yet given. This is why Afanassieff adds that the Church which has been instituted at the Supper was "actualized" on Pentecost.

On Pentecost, according to the Book of Acts, "they were all together in one place" (ēsan pantes homou epi to auto).[26] The phrase epi to auto is generally understood by translators to be an adverbial phrase meaning "together." Afanassieff, however, sees in it a clear reference to the eucharistic action. The phrase does occur a few times in a eucharistic context,[27] but Afanassieff goes further and frequently takes it as a quasi-technical term for the eucharistic action itself.[28]

As Afanassieff interprets the event, on Pentecost the Spirit descended upon the disciples as they were gathered in eucharistic assembly. On that day the Church which had been instituted during the Supper was actualized, inasmuch as the meal taken by the disciples became, through the grace of the Spirit, a "eucharistic assembly"[29]: "This first eucharistic assembly on the day of Pentecost was an exact reproduction of the Lord's Supper; there can be no doubt on this point."[30]

Afanassieff subsequently rethinks the entire structure of the Church, taking as his point of departure this first eucharistic assembly, in which Peter, in the midst of the Twelve, occupies for the first time in the history of the Church the place that the Lord occupied at the Supper. This vision of Pentecost controls Afanassieff's conception of the Petrine primacy.

II. MINISTERIAL FUNCTIONS

Role of the Laity
On the basis of the classic New Testament texts (1 Pet 2.9: "You are a chosen race, a royal priesthood, a holy nation, God's own people"; Rev 1.6; 5.10) Afanassieff maintained the royal priesthood of the faithful. "And like living stones be yourselves built into a spiritual house, to be a holy priesthood (*eis hierateuma hagion*), to offer spiritual sacrifices acceptable to God through Jesus Christ."[31] In the spiritual house which is the Church, says Father Afanassieff, "all the faithful are members of the priesthood, and not merely some of the faithful, as was in the case in the manmade temple where only priests could enter the sanctuary."[32] "The ministry of lay people, members of the Church, finds expression in various ways in various areas," says our author; but he adds that it takes its most active form in the area of liturgy. There the lay people in their entirety are liturgical co-celebrants with their *proestotes* ("directors": cf. below). Father Afanassieff continues: "In the Church the entire people of God officiates, since in the Church the officiant is the Church herself, who has for her head Christ," the sole high priest.[33]

The diversity of ministries is likewise an important fact in the life of the early Church. Paul said that all these ministries are charisms of the Spirit.[34] Yet, as Afanassieff remarks, "none of the Pauline lists of gifts and ministries mentions the charism of priesthood or the priestly ministry or those who exercise these ministries."[35] In his view, all the assembled lay people officiated in the early Church; the difference between those who had specialized ministries and those who did not was functional and not ontological.[36]

Ministries

"From a comparison of the New Testament with the Didache theologians since the time of Adolf van Harnack have concluded to the existence in the very early Church of two main types of organization: on the one hand, what they call the charismatic institution and, on the other, an organization of a secular kind which administered each local Church."[37]

Afanassieff formally rejected this view of the situation since, as he saw it, "all the ministries of the Church were based on charisms."[38]

Prophets

According to Paul the Apostle,[39] the prophets who are mentioned along with the teachers and immediately after the apostles seemed to have occupied a very important place in the early communities.

According to Rudolf Sohm, the prophets exercised, to begin with, the ministry of the word.[40] Then too they occupied the upper level in the system of ecclesial government.[41] It was they who pronounced the eucharistic prayer[42] and administered the Church's material possessions.[43] R. Sohm sums up: "He [the prophet] is at once preacher, lawgiver and chief administrator of the community."[44] In this analysis Sohm does not restrict himself to the information given in the New Testament, but clearly depends as well on the Didache, a document which he considers to have been composed in the first century and in which prophets have a very exalted position.

In seeking light on the role of the prophet Afanassieff concentrates solely on the texts of the New Testament. In his view, the duty of the prophet was to build up the Church by means of his words.[45] Most importantly, the prophet had to proclaim to the Church the will of God in accordance with which the Church was obliged to "live and act."[46] As a result, the charism of prophecy was indispensable to "the life of the Church."[47] If Agabus predicted a famine, then help had to be sent to the Christians of Jerusalem.[48] If the prophets at Antioch imposed hands on Paul and Barnabas, it was in order that these men might launch out on a mission.[49] The mystery (*mysterion*) which the Spirit revealed to the holy apostles and prophets had to do with the historical course of the Church, which had an obligation to admit pagans no less than Jews.[50] But in any event New Testament prophecy could not add any new revelation in regard to the truths of faith or "what we now call dogmatic truths."[51] "The notion of a new revelation would undermine the tradition of the Church."[52] According to R. Sohm, on the contrary, "Prophecy is a new revelation of the divine word."[53]

Afanassieff emphasizes the point that the word a prophet speaks in the Christian assembly is to be judged by others: "Let two or three prophets speak, and let the others weigh what is said."[54] But this New Testament injunction is formally contradicted by the *Didache*: "You are not to test or pass judgment on any prophet who speaks when inspired; every sin will be forgiven except this one."[55]

The *Didache* also sees the prophets as appearing on the scene before the bishop and deacon did, and as remaining superior to these two. First-fruits were to be brought to the prophets because, says the text, they are your high priests (*autoi gar eisin hoi archiereis hymōn*).[56] "Choose for yourselves bishops and deacons who are worthy of the Lord: men who are gentle, unselfish, truthful and reliable. For they too (*kai autoi*) exercise among you the office of prophets and teachers."[57]

This preeminence given to prophets over bishops is characteristic of the *Didache*. Afanassieff thinks the little book may be a piece of Montanist writing; he is not the only one to have suggested this hypothesis.[58]

Presbyters; Church Government
"The opinion that early Christianity, or at least non-Palestinian Christianity, was in a permanent state of charismatic anarchy has taken profound root in theology," says Father Afanassieff. He adds: "The end of this charismatic anarchy supposedly marks the end of the charismatic era and the beginning of a detailed organization of ecclesial life. This outward organization came on the scene (it is said) with

the rise of episcopal power that either did not exist during the charismatic era or was manifested in ways quite different from those we find at the end of the second century."[59]

In a book by Auguste Sabatier which Afanassieff cites we find the following significant words in connection with 1 Corinthians: "How spontaneously all its members act! What brotherly equality we see, what an abundance of spiritual gifts and expressions of enthusiasm—with no official organization as yet to moderate and channel, no legal authority to dominate or regulate!"[60] Afanassieff's reply is that, in his own view, all first-century ministries, whether of prophets or of administrators, were based on gifts given by the Spirit. The contemporary Catholic ecclesiologist Hans Küng observes that there never was "an original Church-less, enthusiatic period, which was only gradually succeeded by a Church with all its limitations."[61]

From the very beginning of its historical existence the Church was an organized body: that is Afanassieff's view. In connection with it he likes to repeat the words of Paul the Apostle: "All things should be done decently and in order,"[62] "for God is not a God of confusion but of peace."[63] "The organization of the second century Church did not make its appearance like a deus ex machina but, on the contrary, was inherited from the primitive Church. From the very beginning the local Churches show themselves to be well ordered and organized."[64] Ecclesial organization was thus not a regrettable consequence of a gradual disappearance of the prophetic charism.

Afanassieff takes us to the next step in his thinking when he says: "The Church as assembly of God's people cannot exist *without the person or persons who stand before God at the head of this people*. Without the ministry of these *proestotes* an ecclesial assembly would be a shapeless mob. An ecclesial assembly is impossible without a *proestos;* this is to say that without him there is no Church."[65]

Where does the term *proestos* that is used so frequently in *L'Eglise du Saint Esprit*, the French version of Afanssieff's book come from? In the Russian original the author uses the Russian term *predstoïatel* which is difficult to translate into French (or English) by any single word. In the Greek text of the New Testament the word *proestos* or its equivalent *proïstamenos* occurs eight times and means: (1) the person who governs (his house)[66]; (2) the person who excels (in the practice of good works)[67]; (3) the person who presides over, directs, is at the head of (the Church).[68]

In 1 Thessalonians, the first letter which Paul the Apostle wrote, he addresses the brethren and says: "We beseech you, brethren, to respect those who labor among you and are over you in the Lord (*tous proïstamenous hymon en kyrio*) and admonish you."[69] In Afanassieff's interpretation, we have here the *proestotes* without whose presence it would be impossible for the people of God to form a eucharistic assembly in the Lord.[70]

Since there are only three texts in the entire New Testament in which *proestotes* or *proïstamenos* refers to authority exercised over the Church, Father Afanassieff looked for other terms that might be regarded as equivalent. In the list of charismatic ministries which Paul the Apostle gives we find the charism of *kybernesis* ("administrators," RSV, NAB; "good leaders," JB; "those who have power to guide others," NEB).[71] The Letter to the Hebrews speaks of the *hegoumenoi* ("leaders," RSV, NAB, JB, NEB)[72]: these are the persons to whom the faithful owe obedience, who watch over the flock,[73] and whose faith is to be imitated.[74] The Pauline churches have presbyters, whose presence is attested by Luke[75] and the Pastoral Letters,[76] and who are to be identified with the *episkopoi,* as a comparison of Acts 20.17 with 20.28 or of Titus 1.5 with 1.7 makes clear. At a later period the presence of presbyters is attested in the Catholic Letters.[77] In Ephesians we have the *poimenes.*[78]

Afanassieff writes rather at length about these ministries, specifies the functions proper to each, and emphasizes the ministry of ecclesial administration[79] (in the Russian original: *oupravlenie*[80]). His analysis is similar to that of Jean Colson, who writes: "Each Christian community has ministers who preside over (*proïstamenoi*) the liturgical assemblies . . . at which the Lord's Supper is celebrated again. . . . These ministers exercise judicial authority over the community of the faithful . . . like pilots (*kyberneseis*) in charge of a ship. . . . They see that the flock of Christ is fed, and are like shepherds (*poimenes*) . . . who keep watch (*episkopoi*) over it."[81]

"He who gives thanks"

Since the *proïstamenoi* have the charism and therefore the responsibility of governing the local Churches, they preside over the liturgical assemblies. This, according to Afanassieff, is their chief activity.

The government of the Church might be carried on in a collegial manner by a number of presbyter-*proestotes*, but *only one* could be assigned to "give thanks" at a eucharistic assembly. At the Last Supper Christ himself was "the one who gave thanks" (*eucharistesas*). On Pentecost Peter represented Christ in the midst of the Twelve, who themselves acted as *proestotes* in the first community at Jerusalem. Later on, James, the brother of the Lord,[82] functioned among the presbyters of Jerusalem as Peter had among the Apostles.[83]

Afanassieff supposes that from the very beginning of each Pauline church there was one and only one *proestos* who "gave thanks in the eucharistic assembly." He bases this hypothesis on the passage, already cited, in Clement of Rome, in which we read that wherever the Apostles went, they "tested in the Spirit the first-fruits of their work and appointed them overseers and deacons for future believers."[84]

Among these *episkopoi* (or *presbyteroi* or *proestotes*: the particular term used is unimportant), the oldest among them, i.e., the first one appointed by the Apostles, became chief presbyter and automatically took the place Peter had had among the Twelve.[85] In the letters of Ignatius of Antioch it is this chief presbyter who becomes the monarchical bishop.

I call a halt here to my sketch of Father Nicolas Afanassieff's basic ideas regarding the Church and the roles played by the Church's ministers. I am leaving out a number of questions, inasmuch as I have said nothing about Afanassieff's quite original views regarding the role of the Seven in the Book of Acts, nor about the role of the teachers (*didaskaloi*) and the deacons, nor have I analyzed our author's ideas regarding the role of the bishop in the time of Ignatius. I have, however, endeavored to present what I regard as the essential points of Afanassieff's thought in respect to the way the Churches were organized in the first century.

Maxime KOVALEVSKY

The Role
of the Choir in the Christian Liturgy

I

Role of the choir as directly defined in canonical documents and, more generally, in every document that has come down to us describing liturgical institutions.

Until the fourth century no document mentions the schola or choir as an "actor" in the liturgy. The great collections such as the *Apostolic Tradition, Apostolic Canons, Testament of Our Lord Jesus Christ,* and so on say nothing of the choir.

From the fifth century on ecclesiastical documents begin to speak of the "schola," i.e., a monastic or cathedral school in which individuals were trained to do certain kinds of singing, solo or group, of which the congregation was incapable. These documents are concerned, however, primarily with the material organization and the methods used in these schools. No precise definition of the *liturgical role* of the persons thus trained has yet been found in texts of a canonical nature from this period. As far as singing and the choir were concerned, we seem to be dealing with a de facto situation (in the second part of this essay we shall see how we can verify the factual situation) and not with an institution that answers a theological need inherent in the structure of the liturgy as such.

The same state of affairs continues in the sixth century. St. Germain of Paris, for example, seems to be aware of no other "actors" in the liturgy apart from the celebrating bishop, the clergy, and the people. We should not find this too surprising. Throughout the Christian world the body of the faithful still understood the language they heard spoken and sung in the services of the Church. The Church still followed the principle that the liturgy should be in the language of the country. Thus when Koine, the Greek in which the sacred scriptures and earliest liturgical texts were written, became unintelligible to most of the uneducated people in the western part of the Church, it was replaced by the end of the third century with "Church Latin," a language very close to the Latin spoken at Rome and in Italy, Gaul and North Africa. As a result spontaneous participation by the people was still possible. There was no line drawn as yet between a choir singing in a foreign (sacred) language and the people who could only listen without understanding the exact meaning of the words and who therefore participated only emotionally, if at all, in the liturgical action. At that period the action could find its full range of expression without the need of any intermediary between clergy and people in the form of a schola or choir.

Such an intermediary was not yet indispensable for the accomplishment of the liturgy; it was simply an ornament. But Church law gives precise definition to a liturgical role only if that role is indispensable. Thus the roles of bishop and major clergy were defined very carefully. Moreover, the canonical literature whether of "eastern" or of "western" provenance, is in agreement on the definition. Clerics in minor orders and their roles were less well defined. In fact, the various legislative texts do not even agree on the number of these orders. Thus some writings do not mention porters, exorcists and acolytes. These orders have completely disappeared in the Byzantine Church and have enjoyed only a theoretical existence in the Church of Rome down to our day. The only orders mentioned in all the sources are those of lector and subdeacon; the role of each is clearly defined.

From this period on there existed among the ministers active in liturgy a hybrid personage who was sometimes a cleric, sometimes a layman, sometimes half-cleric and half-lay. He was the cantor or "psalmist." The decrees of some councils located him among the minor clergy, between the porter (first step) and the lector (third step). Other decrees denied him any clearly defined clerical character. We shall return to him in the second section of this essay, because the Church's decrees regarding him will indirectly help us in attaining our goal, which is to discover the role of the choir in the liturgical action.

For the moment, we must not conclude from the absence of texts defining the choir's role that the Church did not raise the question in a practical existential way from the time of Constantine the Great on.

The situation changes noticeably in both the East and the West when we reach the Carolingian period.

In the western world, Gaul had its own ancient rite which the people and the local clergy had organically assimilated and of which they were very fond. By decree of Pepin III (Pepin the Short) this rite was now replaced by that of the city of Rome, this last being taken as the model for a single rite that was to be imposed on the entire West. In the Germanic lands, populations were converted en masse and received, along with baptism, a ready-made rite in a foreign language that was arbitrarily imposed on them. In the Latin-speaking countries the spoken language began to evolve; the Romance languages gradually replaced Late Latin.

Latin became the language of the Church and of educated people. A real line of division now separated the "kingly people" (a mass of individuals who were more or less christianized and who spoke various dialects and languages) and the clergy (a group of educated men who could speak the common language of the cultivated world, a world coextensive with the Church). An intermediary now became indispensable; that intermediary was the choir.

In the eastern world, the problem of a unified liturgical language did not arise. Each people that entered the communion of the Church received the sacred books and liturgical texts in a language sufficiently comprehensible to make their participation possible. This was the case with, for example, the Slavic peoples. There was no need of a choir as far as the chants of the Ordinary were concerned, i.e., the dialogues of the celebrant with the assembly and the unchanging texts of the service, which the faithful could learn by heart and sing. The existence of an organized choir became indispensable, however, due to the difficulty of singing variable texts that were becoming increasingly complex and at the same time contained the richest treasures of the Church's theological poetry and music, but that were impossible to learn by heart.

Thus it can be said that in both the East and the West, from the end of the eighth century on, a choir became an indispensable actor in the liturgy, and no longer a mere ornament.

This being the case, we might expect that the law of the Church and even of the empire would define in a positive way the precise role of this now indispensable agent. This did not happen. There were indeed many decrees of ecumenical councils, popes, and local councils that, as in the earlier period, regulated the formation, life, rights and obligations of the members of the groups called scholas or choirs. Other texts, even more numerous, attacked the abuses of every kind that were found in these groups, and specified the sanctions that would help eliminate the abuses. But the positive role of the schola in the liturgical action remained legally vague.

The same situation has held down the centuries to our own time. In the West, for example, the Constitution *Docta Sanctorum Patrum* of John XXII (Avignon, 1324), a very important text for our knowledge of the state of liturgical music in fourteenth-century Europe, starts with the fact that the institution known as the schola or choir exists, that it serves to beautify the services, and that it is also the source of many abuses which must be combatted without suppressing the institution itself. The same approach can be found in the decrees of the Council of Trent, the legislation of Benedict XIV, and the legislation of the popes of the early twentieth century, and, in the East, in the acts of local councils (in Russia the council of the Hundred Chapters in the fifteenth century, and the council of 1656) and in other texts that have been promulgated down to our day.

Only with the Second Vatican Council do we find some semblance of a definition, if not of the choir, at least of music in the liturgy: "The musical tradition of the universal Church is a treasure of inestimable value, greater even than that of any other art. The main reason for this pre-eminence is that, as a combination of sacred music and words, it forms a necessary or integral part of the solemn liturgy."[1] In this passage, however, the word "solemn" lessens the universality of the statement.

We are forced to conclude that an explicit definition of the role of the choir in the liturgy is not to be found in official documents. We must look elsewhere for such a definition.

II

Role of the choir as known indirectly from documents in which contemporaries describe the services they attended and from canonical literature in which the role of the choir is regulated, though not defined.

Until the fourth century contemporary descriptions of services do not mention the choir, any more than do canonical documents. The bishop and the priest celebrate, the deacon performs his office as coordinator, the reader reads the scriptures, and the people present do the singing. It is almost certain that this singing was limited to the dialogues with the celebrants and to the acclamations that punctuated the singing of certain psalms by a soloist. Who was this soloist? He might be a deacon or reader or other member of the clergy, but often he was the individual mentioned in the first section of this essay: the *cantor*.

If a deacon or reader sang a psalm, this was not part of his canonically defined role. The cantor on the other hand was appointed specifically to sing. He was chosen for his "artistic" abilities: he had to be able to chant the psalms in such a way as to be understood by all and "to delight the ears of the faithful and raise their minds to God." In all probability, his singing was usually an improvisation based on consecrated traditional formulas. He was a "charismatic." He was also somewhat difficult to locate in relation to other ministers. There was a desire to honor him by giving him a place in the hierarchy; at the same time others hesitated to subject him to too many formal canoni-

197

cal rules that might result in his being coopted into the clergy. Consequently, what we see in the first four centuries is the existence of two "liturgical actors" whose role will be taken later on by the choir: the kingly people, or stable basis for all else, and the cantor, who represented the element of inspiration.

From the end of the third century and especially after the Edict of Milan (315), descriptions begin to appear of services in cathedrals and parishes, in which between the clergy and the people there is a group of ascetics, male and female, who embody as it were the consciousness of the people and who stimulate the latter to respond to the celebrant and sing the acclamations. In addition, this group gradually begins to engage in the two-choir antiphonal singing that is being adopted at this time in the Eastern Church and will be adopted a little later in the Western Church as well.

The groups of ascetics thus formed quickly separate from the parish churches and settle in places specially chosen as conducive to a life of prayer. We are seeing the birth of monasticism. Monasteries of common life cultivate antiphonal singing, which calls for the formation of two monastic choirs in each community. This marks the beginning of monastic schools in which monks and nuns are taught the art of reading and singing liturgical texts.

At the same time, the cathedrals and parishes, being now deprived of the help of the ascetics, endeavor to replace them either with one or two official cantors or with choirs from a nearby monastery, the latter being often established precisely for this purpose (this is the case, for example, with the Lateran Basilica in Rome). This quest is seconded by the Church's efforts to channel and use in its service the capacity of children for memorization and spontaneity. Some bishops (e.g., St. Augustine) and priests take young children into their homes and accept the responsibility of raising and instructing them in the Christian faith by integrating them into the liturgical life of the community. The existence of these *pusinni* is already attested for fourth-century Jerusalem by Egeria. The sermons of St. Augustine, many papal documents, and, at a later date, St. Germain of Paris mention the participation of these children in the liturgy. The children thus educated and trained are elevated to the rank of reader when they reach the age of six, and from then on take an active part in the liturgy with their reading and singing. St. Athanasius the Great is an example of such children.

In the large cities, such as Constantinople and Rome, these first steps give rise to institutions called *scholae lectorum* (schools of/for readers), which are mentioned in many documents from the fifth century on. As ornate singing gradually develops for the services, the *schola lectorum* soon gives way to the *schola cantorum* or analogous institutions. Probably under Gregory the Great and certainly under his immediate successors, the *schola cantorum* becomes a fully defined and organized institution at Rome. It is made up not only of children but of adult singers as well (usually clergy) and is directed by a precentor who becomes a dignitary of the Church. Constantinople precedes Rome in this development. Thus in the time of Justinian the church of Santa Sophia already has a school and a group of singers (29 adults and children) who devote themselves exclusively to this liturgical function. Thus the inspired cantor of earlier times is gradually replaced by a group of trained singers who also begin to take over the role previously filled by the assembly.

The Carolingian period provides many descriptions of elaborate services at Rome, at the imperial court, and in the great monasteries (Saint-Riquier, for example). The "choir" (schola) plays an important part in all the ceremonies.

For reasons indicated in the first section of this essay, the "choir" becomes a necessity, while it is also a sign of cultural progress. Liturgical singing has entered upon its golden age. It is now an artistic skill; it can even—and this is something quite new—be written down and preserved in manuscript form. It is cultivated and performed by "artists" who receive a long, careful preparation for their function (nine years at least). This choir and these artists have almost completely taken over the role of the kingly people in solemn services and, to some extent, that of the cantor as well. The soloist still exists, but he is now simply a member of the choir, one of its dignitaries; his role as charismatic improvisor has almost completely vanished.

It seems, however, that in the parishes of the Latin and Romance countries as well as in the East, the chants of the Offertory continue to be sung by a group of fervent faithful, a kind of large choir, with the more difficult pieces among the variable chants being strictly reserved to the cantors. This state of affairs continues the traditional liturgical structure.

Polyphony. The end of the twelfth century brings another novelty in the West: the entrance of an abstruse type of polyphony into the services. The School of Notre Dame (Leonin [Leonius] and Perotin [Perotinus]) applies this new technique to the variable chants, especially to the Gradual which, in the "Gregorian" tradition, is already a piece of pure music, a time for listening and meditation. The School of Notre Dame does not touch the chants of the Ordinary; thus its work represents an innovation that enriches the services without detracting from their traditional structure.

A further innovation beginning in the fourteenth century is entirely different in that it represents an undermining of this structure. I am referring to the appearance of "polyphonic Masses," i.e., the polyphonic singing of the chants of the Ordinary. The Tournai Mass and later the Mass of Guillaume de Machaut thus inaugurate an entirely new and different period of liturgical music and consequently a new role for the choir in the liturgy.

The eucharistic liturgy (the "Mass") and then such major offices as "Solemn Vespers," the "Te Deum" and "Tenebrae" very quickly become *musical forms* which provide a pretext and a context for the creation and development of a new art: our Western European music.

We can see now that a significant evolution has occurred. Liturgical music originally acted as a sacralizing factor and served to give a greater impact to the words of which it was the vehicle. Now it had become an autonomous art with its own goals and technical problems. It was now words and forms sacralized by usage that would serve to give a religious or sacral dimension to an art that in itself was neutral. It is not unreasonable to assume that this evolution changed the attitude of Church and society to the "choir." For, if the primary function of music is no longer to sacralize the word, then it is natural to accept rhythms and melodic patterns different from those that had arisen out of cantillation or musical recitation, and to acknowledge musical instruments as collaborators, especially since these are more

200

flexible than the human voice in meeting the requirements of the new techniques.

The choir, as a group of clerical singers educated in a respect for the word, developed into a musical ensemble (choir and orchestra) trained in the techniques of what the nineteenth century will call "pure music."

There is a clear witness to this period of transition in the Constitution *Docta Sanctorum Patrum* of John XXII. A period was beginning in which the music of the Western Church existed on two levels which hardly intersected at all. On the one hand, traditional chant was still a living reality, even if one that was falsified by routine as well as by the zeal of reformers. On the other hand, a *musique figurée* (florid, ornate music) was developing independently of tradition. The former of these two levels became that of the "conservatives," who were willing to abandon any organic creative development. The other level became that of the innovators and a constantly evolving *ars nova;* from time to time people at this level tried to influence the conservatives and rescue them from what was regarded as a state of petrification.

A great deal of care must be taken in reading post-fourteenth-century canonical and juridical texts on music; it must be kept in mind, for example, that in these texts "music" always refers to the elaborate music of the innovators. The singing of the clergy and the traditional chants which were not "composed" by a "musician" continued to be the domain of the conservatives and are not treated under the term "music" in these texts.

In the area of Church music in the East there is no sign of any revolution comparable to the one that occurred in the fourteenth-century West. However, descriptions of fourteenth-century practice do show that there had been a simplification of rites, both at Byzantium and in Russia, by comparison with the rites of the tenth century. The explanation for this development must be sought in the political upheavals of the thirteenth century: the capture of Constantinople by the Crusaders (1204) and the Mongol invasion of Russia (1240). These upheavals led to a certain loss of outward splendor and a material impoverishment that were offset by a more intense spiritual life. Thus the description and commentary Cabasilas (1322–95) gives of a parish liturgy shows a service in which the texts are already

identical with those of the Liturgy of St. John Chrysostom as celebrated today in Greece and the Slavic countries, but in which there
are only two participants: the priest and the congregation. The choir is
not mentioned, nor is the deacon. Does this represent a return to the
simplicity of the early centuries? Possibly, but we may at least conjec-
ture that the vocal participation of the congregation was a vital part of
the liturgy in the fourteenth century.

Other descriptions that are accompanied by commentaries and
practical suggestions show that the variable chants (troparion, kondakion, etc.) were to be done by singers who should not be very
numerous lest the words not be "heard distinctly." The presence of a
cantor or a group of singers directed by him seems required.

In the fifteenth century, after the fall of Constantinople (1453), the
center of gravity of Church life shifts to Moscow, the "third Rome,"
where the cultivation of liturgical singing already had an important
place. Many documents mention the schools and the names of the
instructors in chant.

These masters do not accept the evolution that occurred in the West
from the fourteenth century on, when "traditional chant" became
identified with the "conservatives." Instead, they develop what they
have inherited from their predecessors of the thirteenth and fourteenth centuries. There is no question here of a birth of a new art, a
music independent of tradition. On the contrary: the tradition is
studied and its ultimate implications are seen and accepted; the result
is that in the late sixteenth and early seventeenth centuries the art of
liturgical singing in Russia reaches its high point.

The work of the cantor (as performer and as composer) is highly
valued. The group he gathers around him in a monastery or cathedral
will be called simply "the singers." Under Ivan the Terrible and his
successors the "Tsar's singers" are immensely famous; they are a
group of clerics in minor orders whose sole function is to provide the
singing in the Palace Chapel and in the Cathedral of the Assumption.

It is difficult to determine accurately how much of the service these
singers handled. Was there still room for singing by the faithful? The
Russian love for a regulated splendor in sacred functions suggests a
negative answer. And yet a recently discovered sixteenth-century
document[2] shows that the singing of the choir was repeated, in an

unobstrusive way, by the congregation; this is a practice that can at times be observed in present-day Russian churches.

The liturgical books published since the Council of Moscow (1656) suppose that the only "actors" in the liturgy are the clergy in major orders, the readers, and two choirs, one on the right, the other on the left. There is no reference to the kingly people, who are henceforth represented by the choirs.

The profound upheaval which the westernizing reforms of Peter the Great caused in Russian Church life at the beginning of the eighteenth century brought a rapid decay of traditional singing and the triumphant invasion of Italian-style four-part singing; this practice has continued dominant in the Russian Church down to the present time. The "singers" were replaced by musical ensembles (imperial, episcopal, manorial) composed of laymen and directed by a musician, likewise a layman (the "director") and a personage as important and often as difficult to get along with as the organist in the West.

Beginning then in the eighteenth century the situation in the East is similar to that found in the West since the beginning of the fifteenth century. Let us return now to the West.

Renaissance and Reformation in the West. The humanist renaissance and the reaction to it in the world of the Reformation found liturgical music in almost the same state as in the fourteenth century. On the one hand, there was a "traditional" music, fixed in the state in which it had been at the end of the twelfth century; in addition, there were some efforts to create a music accessible to the people, along with attempts to use the language of the country, especially in the German-speaking lands.[3] On the other hand, there was a *musique figurée*, an increasingly polished art that was exercised by professional musicians (singers and instrumentalists); this group of musicians was joined by an organist, who would soon dominate the ensemble.

The Reformers wanted to return to a primitive simplicity in which the only agents of the celebration would be the liturgical minister and congregation. They endeavored to eliminate both the cantor and the musical ensemble with its organist. However, especially because it was so difficult to involve the congregation in group singing, the organ very quickly came back on the scene. In other words, the agents of liturgy became the pastor, the organist and the congregation. Soon the musical ensemble likewise regained its place and continued the work of developing the great art of classical European music that had begun in the fourteenth century under the aegis of the Roman Church. The world in which the Reformation dominated made a priceless contribution to this work (Bach, Schütz, Handel, etc.).

The liturgical renewal in the twentieth-century West led the Roman Church, beginning in the late nineteenth century, to reexamine and revise its forms of celebration in accordance with traditional models. The same principle was applied to the revision of liturgical singing. The return, even if only partial, to a traditional type of singing, brought the formation of groups devoted to a study of the specific nature of such singing. The choir once more loomed large as a collective entity, and the problem of its function in the liturgy became an urgent one. Similarly, the kingly people as a collective person participating in the sacred action became a reality and had to be taken seriously.

As for the musical ensembles, their work in developing classical music under the tutelage of the Church had come to an end. It was no longer necessary to adapt music to Church services or to depend on the church as an auditorium. Music could be developed much better and more freely in concert halls built specifically to provide the best conditions for performance.

The Church, for its part, has finished its work of providing the masses with a musical education. The "great music" which the ordinary person could hear only thanks to the Church and within the walls of the church building was now available in the concert hall and, later, on records.

In the East and especially in Russia, the revolution of 1917 brought the Constantinian period of church history to an end. The Church was forced to return to simpler and more authentic forms of celebration; this was true both in the homelands and in the diaspora. The word, as supported and sanctified by singing, recovered its primacy and forced the singing to rediscover its own traditional forms which by now had often gotten covered by the dust of centuries. The question of the function of cantor and choir in the liturgical action presented itself with urgent novelty, as it did in the West.

Is the choir to recover function which have never been officially defined but can be specified from historical testimony? These functions are:

1. To be the fully alert sector of the people, whom the choir stimulates to take part in the dialogue with the celebrants and in the singing of the acclamations and hymns which are meant to be done by the congregation.

2. To sing the variable chants which the congregation cannot know by heart and which it cannot execute because of their difficulty.

3. To sing the texts which accompany sacramental actions (for example, the great entrance in the Eastern Church and the Introit in the Western Church) or those which *by their nature* are meant to be *listened to*.

Such a choir would have to be composed of members of the parish or diocese and directed by a musician who loves and has the best possible knowledge of liturgical singing, which is a special, difficult and mysterious art. It must be organized so as to avoid the abuses against which the canonical texts warn the singers of every age, and especially to avoid the attitude of "the artist" who stands aloof from the liturgical action.

In closing, I would like to point out a further role, or rather a further significance of the choir, and one that is usually passed over in silence. St. Ignatius of Antioch, back at the beginning, and, later on, St. Dionysius the Areopagite suggest that the choir represents the angels. John Chrysostom and many others mention the same point. The Liturgy of St. John Chrysostom does so quite clearly: in the chant that accompanies the great entrance, the *choir*, and not the clergy or the congregation, are bidden to sing: "We who mystically represent *the cherubim* . . ." The choir thus represents "the heavenly powers who invisibly celebrate with us" (Byzantine Liturgy of the Presanctified according to St. Gregory, Pope of Rome); through the choir we all share in the heavenly liturgy.

Burckhard NEUNHEUSER

The Relation
of Priest and Faithful
in the Liturgies of Pius V and Paul VI

I am not aiming here at any great novelty, but wish simply to call attention to the very great importance of the entirely new vision which the new Roman Missal (RM) presents of the role of the faithful. I shall do so by comparing the rubrics in the RM of Pius V with the *General Instruction of the Roman Missal* (GIRM) of Paul VI. Evidently, we would have to take many other factors and sources into account if we were seeking a rounded overview of the religious life of the faithful in the sixteenth century as compared with today. But the limits I have set myself do not prevent our seeing the new attitude as it emerges from a comparison of the two documents I have just mentioned.

We are dealing, of course, with the same Mass, the same eucharistic celebration. This identity, however, finds concrete embodiment in two quite different worlds.

I shall begin by reminding you briefly of the prehistory of the document that introduces the Missal.

The *Order of Mass,* [1] as we know it from, e.g., the Gregorian Sacramentary: "Qualiter Missa Romana celebratur" ("How the Roman Mass is celebrated"),[2] is extremely simple and clear; it deals with a celebration in which the entire community—celebrants, servers, people—participate. This *Order* in its most solemn form has been preserved in *Ordo Romanus I.*[3] But from the ninth century on, and even earlier, this *Order* was invaded by a large number of private prayers which properly belonged to the priest alone, the so-called "apologies."[4] The majority of these would disappear in the course of time, but some remained and, along with some norms for celebration, formed the *Ordo agendorum et dicendorum* (Order of actions and words) that was initially known as the *Ordo "Indutus planeta"*[5] and the *Ordo "Paratus (sacerdos)."*[6]

Subsequent to the quite elaborate description of the Mass according to these models, we find the word of Burchard of Strassburg,[7] the famous master of ceremonies of Pope Alexander VI: *Ordo servandus per sacerdotem in celebratione Missae sine cantu et sine ministris secundum ritum S. Romanae Ecclesiae* (Order to be followed by a priest in celebrating a Mass without singing and without ministers according to the rite of the holy Roman Church).[8] This represents the fullest development of the medieval *Ordines Missae* and describes how a priest who is practically all by himself is to celebrate a low Mass. Minute detail is given so as to provide all priests with an exact criterion for the uniform celebration of a Mass in which the faithful no longer participate actively. It is supposed, however, that the faithful do participate passively but devoutly; the *Ordo* mentions them from time to time.

Here are some of the points made in the *Ordo*. The priest should prepare and arrange the texts before the celebration begins "lest the Mass become irksome to the hearers." It is his responsibility to secure a server. Those present are to kneel throughout the Mass, except during the gospel; but they stand on Sundays and during the Eastertide. The faithful present at Mass should not recite other prayers, even if they do not understand Latin, but should "pay devout attention to the celebrant and direct their intention to what the celebrant says and does, while joining him interiorly in offering, petitioning and praying" (135). The servers and congregation answer the prayers which the priest says at the foot of the altar, and also give all the other responses during the Mass. The prayers and readings should be pronounced in such a way "that those present at Mass can hear the words clearly" (137). At the Offertory an announcement is made: "If there are any here who wish to make an offering. . .''; the priest accepts their gifts and says to each person: "May your sacrifice be acceptable to almighty God." The rubrics often prescribe that the priest is to turn to the people and show them the consecrated species. After the priest's communion and purification, the rubric reads: "If any are to receive communion, he gives them communion before he washes his fingers; the order regarding the time and manner of giving communion to the people, as given in the Presbyterale, is to be observed" (164).

Although we today find this *Ordo* of Burchard almost intolerable because it is so detailed in its explanation of the ceremonies, it became extremely successful in the sixteenth century. His final text of 1502 went through at least nine printings and, in addition, was often printed in the editions of the *Missale secundum usum Romanae Curiae* [Missal giving the practice of the Roman Curia] and in other editions.[9]

Pius V did not simply adopt Burchard's *Ordo* for the definitive 1570 edition of his own new Missal. On the other hand, he certainly drew inspiration from it; above all, he followed and even underscored further its rubricist and ceremonialist emphasis.[10] Worse still, he eliminated almost completely the references to the faithful. The *Ordo* of Pius V is and is meant to be essentially a guide for the priest who celebrates a low Mass all by himself. This low Mass (or "private Mass") thus becomes the norm for all eucharistic celebrations. Information necessary for the celebration of a sung or solemn Mass is added in the form of notes, appendices or supplements.

The RM of 1570 begins, then, with two series of rubrics under the overall title of *Ordo agendorum et dicendorum;* the first is *Rubricae generales Missalis,* and the second is *Ritus servandus in celebratione Missae.* These remained identical until Pius X added variations in 1911 and until John XXIII published the definitive version of a quite new *Codex Rubricarum* in 1960.[11]

The rubrics of Pius V represent an important part of the liturgical reform prescribed by the Council of Trent, for the universal Church.[12] No one should attempt to deny the real value of Pius' work at least for its day. But it must be noted that the value was accompanied by limitations which are equally undeniable. The sole intention of the rubrics and *Ritus* was to show the priest how to celebrate his daily Mass "secundum ordinem officii" ("according to the order of the service"),[13] that is, just how he should act, and to do so without making any reference (except an occasional chance one) to the faithful. In other words, the rubrics and *Ritus* reflect an extremely "clericalized" liturgy. Here are the references to the faithful in each part of the *Ordo*.

In the *Rubricae* title XVI speaks of the "hearers": the priest should say what he says "not too rapidly, so that he may advert to what he is reading; not too slowly, lest he irk his hearers; not in too loud a voice, lest he distract others who may be celebrating in the church at the same time, but in an audible and serious tone that will stir devotion and allow the hearers to understand what is being read."

In title XVII, 2, we read: "Those present at private Masses are to kneel throughout, even in the Easter season, except when the gospel is being read." The regulation is certainly less felicitous than the corresponding one in Burchard's *Ordo*.[14] In any case, these are the only remarks made about the faithful who are present at Mass.

The situation is pretty much the same in the *Ritus Servandus*.[15] Here are all the relevant passages:

II. Regarding the entrance, 3: "If he is to consecrate a number of hosts for communion . . . he puts them on the corporal."

III. Regarding the beginning of Mass, 9: "when the server and those present . . . respond." But the text seems in fact to be thinking chiefly of prelates who may be present: the Supreme Pontiff, a cardinal, a legate, a patriarch, a bishop, although, of course, the rest of the faithful are not excluded.

IV. Regarding the Introit, 2: "If a server or those present do not answer the celebrant, he is to say it [the Kyrie] nine times by himself."

V. Regarding the Oration, 1: "Having said the hymn *Gloria in excelsis Deo*, he turns . . . to the people"; 3: "If the altar faces East toward the people, the celebrant turns his face to the people without turning his back to the altar."

VI. Regarding the Epistle, 6: "If there is to be a sermon, the preacher delivers it after the gospel."

VII. Regarding the Offertory, 3: "If there are other hosts . . . on the corporal . . . to be consecrated for the people's communion . . ."; 7: "he turns to the people"; 10: "the censer-bearer afterwards incenses the servers and the people."

VIII. Regarding the Canon of the Mass, 3: "Lest he irk those present, the celebrant can also, before Mass . . . call to mind all those" for whom he wishes to pray; 5: "If there is a vessel on the altar that contains other hosts to be consecrated . . . he uncovers . . . the vessel." After the Consecration, "he reverently shows [the host] to the people for their adoration." He does the same for the chalice: "he shows it to the people for their adoration."

X. Regarding the Lord's Prayer, 3: "Then . . . if he is to give the gesture of peace, he kisses . . . the instrument of peace. If there is no one present to take this instrument from the celebrant the gesture of peace is not made"; 6. "If any are to receive communion at Mass . . . (the server) recites the Confiteor in their name"; 9: "At a pontifical Mass . . . he first gives communion to the deacon . . . then to the others in proper order . . . and the deacon offers them the purification."

XII. Regarding the blessing at the end of Mass, 1: "Turning to the people . . . he blesses them once"; 8. "A bishop blesses the people three times . . . ." In the following section, "On defects that may occur in the celebration of Mass," nothing at all is said of the people or those present!

From this survey we can conclude that these rubrics, which are very numerous, exact and detailed, concern only the priest who is celebrating. It is he and he alone who is meant to be helped by these rubrics to celebrate in a worthy, correct and proper way and in a uniform manner that is followed everywhere and by all.

Nothing is said of the faithful except to the extent that their presence is to dictate the action of the priest. In other words, any reference to the faithful here is accidental; their presence is not required. It is sometimes presupposed, but it always remains a passive presence.

At the time of the Offertory, nothing is said any longer about the collection (this is probably a quite deliberate omission, in order to avoid the offering of any money, which was frequently an occasion for the avarice so strongly condemned by the Council).[16] On the other hand, communion is explicitly mentioned, but again in a conditional way: "If any are . . ."; there is no emphasis on it. Similarly, there is no demand that the faithful sing or respond. As for "those present" (*circumstantes*) who are sometimes mentioned, they seem to be mainly prelates, and the relationship of priests and such prelates is described in a very detailed way. "Those present" may also, of course, be the faithful; but this is not said explicitly. We might say (with some exaggeration) that the point is of no interest.

Other sources tell us, of course, that the faithful readily attended Mass in great numbers, with regularity and devotion. They all regarded the Mass as an essential and central focus of their lives and their Christian piety.[17] It was precisely for the good of the faithful that the Tridentine Reform wanted priests to celebrate Mass in a worthy and uniform manner. But the faithful attended passively and in an entirely inward or spiritual way, by following the priest's actions from afar, absorbed in an interior realm of devotion, and helping themselves thereto by the allegorizing explanations of an Amalarius, to name an important interpreter of this type.[18] The only forms of a slightly more active participation were: to stand during the gospel, to adore the eucharistic elements after the consecration[19] (but this adoration did not properly belong to the eucharistic celebration as such!), and—rather rarely—to receive communion (from hosts consecrated at that same Mass).

Although these rubrics do not exclude a more active participation of the faithful (and the liturgical movement of the present century would make full use of these possibilities[20]), neither do they say much about it. It is not an exaggeration to conclude that for the authors of these rubrics the Mass had turned into an exclusively priestly, i.e., clerical, action, in which for practical purposes no thought need be given to the faithful.

It is the merit of the liturgical movement that it changed all that. It did so only slowly indeed, by starting with interior dispositions and then by taking advantage of the possibilities—real, even if not extensive—present in the rubrics themselves. There was no revolution, no elimination by destruction. The movement educated the faithful in an active participation: they gave the responses, they sang, they listened to the readings, they offered the sacrifice and received communion, in each Mass if possible.[21]

Vatican II gave its definitive and solemn approval to this change.[22] The Constitution *Sacrosanctum Concilium* on the Sacred Liturgy [CL] says: "The Church, therefore, earnestly desires that Christ's faithful, when present at this mystery of faith, should not be there as strangers or silent spectators. On the contrary . . . they should take part in the sacred action, conscious of what they are doing, with devotion and full collaboration."[23]

The new RM is meant as a response to the Council's desire; the effort to make it such takes shape above all in the GIRM.[24] This Instruction—as was said in connection with its first edition in 1969—"will take the place henceforth of the treatises *General Rubrics, The Rite to be Followed* and *Concerning Defects.*"[25] When the second edition appeared (in November of the same year), the fact was emphasized that the Instruction is not "a doctrinal or dogmatic document but a pastoral instruction on the ritual."[26] To this end it presents "the fundamentals . . . of catechetical instruction to be given to the faithful, and the chief . . . norms of eucharistic celebration for those who are present at the celebration in their various orders and ranks."[27] In the spirit of this statement, emphasis is put, from the very beginning of the GIRM, on the specific place of the two groups that come together for the celebration of Mass, namely, the priest and his assistants on the one hand, and the faithful or people of God on the other.

"1. The celebration of Mass is the action of Christ and the people of God hierarchically assembled. For both the universal and the local Church, and for each person, it is the center of the whole Christian life . . .

"2. It is of the greatest importance that the celebration of Mass, the Lord's Supper, be so arranged that the ministers and the faithful may take their own proper part in it and thus gain its fruits more fully. For this Christ the Lord instituted the eucharistic sacrifice of his body and blood and entrusted it to his bride, the Church, as a memorial of his passion and resurrection" (GIRM, nos. 1-2).

It is in this spirit that the GIRM speaks whenever it has occasion to touch on the faithful. The first edition of GIRM, no. 7, stressed the role of the faithful in strong terms: "The Lord's Supper or the Mass is a sacred synaxis or assembly of God's people in a single place, in order to celebrate the memorial of the Lord under the presidency of a priest."[28] The text had to be changed for reasons we need not go into here, but the new formulation did not reduce the emphasis on the participation of God's people: "The Lord's Supper or Mass gathers together the people of God, with a priest presiding in the person of Christ, to celebrate the memorial of the Lord or eucharistic sacrifice."

In addition, no. 14 says explicitly: "Since the celebration of Mass is a communal action, the dialogue between the celebrant and the congregation and the acclamations are of special value." For this reason the acclamations are to be used in every Mass "to express clearly and to develop the action of the entire community" (no. 15).

This "manifestation and development of active participation by the faithful" is emphasized on every possible occasion. Thus the introductory rites of the Mass have for their purpose "to make the assembled people a unified community and to prepare them properly to listen to God's word and celebrate the eucharist" (no. 24). The Mass begins "after the people have assembled" (no. 25).

The celebrant's greeting and the people's response "manifest the mystery of the Church that is gathered together" (no. 28).

Again, after speaking of the celebrant's opening prayer (Collect), the text adds: "The people make the prayer their own and give their assent by the acclamation, Amen" (no. 32).

Regarding the liturgy of the word the GIRM says: "In the readings, explained by the homily, God speaks to his people of redemption and salvation and nourishes their spirit; Christ is present among the faithful through his word. Through the chants the people make God's word their own and express their adherence to it through the profession of faith. Finally, moved by this word, they pray in the general intercessions . . ." (no. 33).

The same themes recur in the description of the eucharistic liturgy proper: "The offerings are then brought forward: it is desirable for the faithful to present the bread and wine" (no. 49).

The eucharistic prayer is "the center and high point of the entire celebration." At the beginning of it, "the priest invites the people to lift their hearts to God in prayer and thanks; he unites them with himself in the prayer he addresses in their name to the Father through

Jesus Christ. The meaning of the prayer is that the whole congregation joins Christ in acknowledging the works of God and in offering the sacrifice" (no. 54).

Even when the GIRM sets out to describe the characteristic points of the eucharistic prayer (no. 55)—which is a prayer reserved to the celebrating priest alone—it emphasizes the part the people are to play in it. One element in the prayer is "acclamation": "United with the angels, the congregation sings or recites the *Sanctus*. This acclamation forms part of the eucharistic prayer, and all the people join with the priest in singing or reciting it" (no. 55b). The eucharistic prayer is also "thanksgiving": "In the name of the entire people of God, the priest praises the Father" (no. 55a). It is also "offering": "The Church—and in particular the Church here and now assembled—offers the victim. . . . The Church's intention is that the faithful not only offer the spotless victim but also learn to offer themselves" (no. 55f.).

In the final doxology, the eucharistic prayer "is confirmed and concluded by the acclamation of the people. All should listen to the eucharistic prayer in silent reverence and share in it by making the acclamations" (no. 55h).

It is quite natural that the section on the communion rite should once again lay heavy stress on the participation of the faithful: the preparatory rites should "lead directly to the communion of the people" (no. 56). Even when speaking of the priest's personal, private preparation, the text adds: "The faithful also do this [i.e., prepare themselves] by praying in silence" (no. 56f.). Finally, "it is most desirable that the faithful should receive the body of the Lord in hosts consecrated at the same Mass and should share the cup when it is permitted" (no. 56h).

These same points are emphasized once again, from a different viewpoint, in Chapter III, "Offices and Ministries in the Mass." The following principle is set down as a general norm: "Everyone in the eucharistic assembly has the right and duty to take his own part according to the diversity of orders and functions. In exercising his function, everyone, whether minister or layman, should do that and that only which belongs to him . . ." (no. 58). The ministers themselves (i.e., the clergy) are asked to perform their functions for the good of the faithful: this applies to the bishop (no. 59), the priest (no. 60), and the deacon (no. 61). Through the ministry of these ordained individuals the faithful must acquire the ability to offer thanksgiving as a holy people, a chosen race, a royal priesthood. Moreover, they are invited to serve willingly "when asked to perform some particular ministry in the celebration" (no. 62).

Other valuable points are made in Chapter IV, "Different forms of celebration."

This chapter begins quite deliberately with "Mass with a congregation." In the introduction to this chapter pride of place is assigned to the Mass a bishop celebrates with his people: "First place should be given to Mass at which the bishop presides . . . with the people taking a full and active part. This is the principle sign of the Church" (no. 74).

Second place is given to Mass celebrated with a parish or other community (no. 75). Then, after these definitions, "Mass with a congregation" is described as being the normal and model case of a eucharistic liturgy. "Mass with a congregation" means here "one in which the people take part" (no. 77).

The clear intention of this chapter is to lay down rules for the president (*proestos*)[29] of the celebration. However, the celebration in question is a community celebration, and therefore the celebrant is always thought of precisely as presiding over a people who wish to celebrate the eucharist: "The priest and the ministers . . . when the people have assembled, go to the altar (no. 82); "[The general intercessions] in which the people take part" (no. 99). Even in the description of a concelebrated Mass, i.e., a description in which the focus is on the clerical celebrants, attention is called to the role of the entire congregation: "In a special way concelebration shows the unity of the priesthood and of the sacrifice, and the unity of the people of God" (no. 153). The concelebrants are expressly told to stand around the altar in such a way "that the people are able to see the rite clearly" (no. 167).

Finally, in third place, the GIRM speaks also of "Mass without a congregation," that is, the form of Mass that was normal and usual in the RM of Pius V. In the new RM it is described in last place and treated rather as an exception. As for its structure and course, "in general this form of Mass follows the rite of Mass with a congregation. The minister takes the people's part when suitable" (no. 210). A Mass at which there is not even a server present is allowed only "in serious necessity" (no. 211). In regard to this last kind of Mass the practice according to the RM of Pius V,[30] as confirmed by the Code of Canon Law,[31] was undoubtedly more strict; but it was undermined during the Second World War (for reasons of really extreme necessity). Unfortunately—and strangely—this kind of Mass without a server is still widespread in the houses of clerical communities, where individuals are unwilling to concelebrate.

Chapter IV; "General norms for all forms of Mass," focuses once again primarily on the celebrating priest. But he is always thought of as a priest who presides over a community, a group of faithful, a people gathered for the celebration of Mass. And when the text comes to speak of communion under both kinds the emphasis is once again on the people: the people are to take part with greater zeal in this form of communion (no. 241). The detailed way in which the different forms of this communion are described is due to the fact that the faithful are being addressed (nos. 240-252).

Chapter V; "Arrangement and decoration of churches for the eucharistic celebration," speaks again, and more extensively, of the people who assemble in a church or other place. These locales "should be suitable for celebrating the eucharist and for active participation by the faithful" (no. 253). The people of God who assemble at Mass should give expression to their calling as a holy people and royal priesthood "by the various ministries and actions for each part of the celebration. The general plan of the building should suggest in some way the image of the congregation. It should also help . . . the carrying out of each function" (no. 257).

In every case, all the factors considered should "clearly express the unity of the people of God" (ibid.). Everything should be so arranged that the contact of the faithful with what is going on at the altar is not hindered (no. 269). For example: "the celebrant's chair should express his office of presiding over the assembly and of directing prayer. Thus the proper place for the chair is the center of the sanctuary facing the people, unless the structure or other circumstances are an obstacle, for example, if there is too great a distance between the priest and the people" (no. 271). The lectern or ambo should be so located that the faithful may without difficulty direct their attention to it during the liturgy of the word (no. 272).

This chapter also has a special section on "places for the faithful." These "should be arranged so that the people may take part in the celebration by seeing and by understanding everything" (no. 273). The seats for the faithful should be so arranged that the latter "can easily take the positions required during the various celebrations" (ibid.).

Finally, there is a further interesting prescription in Chapter VI; "Choice of Mass texts." Priests are given great freedom in choosing the texts required for the celebration; this is true at least for simple weekdays and for other occasions that are important from a pastoral standpoint. But the priest must choose texts "which correspond to the needs, spiritual preparation, and attitude of the participants," and "consider the spiritual good of the assembly rather than his own desires"; he should also consult "the ministers and others who have a function in the celebration, including the faithful" (no. 313).

We may end with a summary. Although I would not want to deny that the faithful were rather deeply involved in the Mass even in the time of Pius V—this could be shown from other sources[32]—the Missal of Pius V was in fact concerned with the celebrating priest. It paved the way for him to celebrate in a worthy way that matched that of all other priests. Nothing was said of the faithful except now and then and in passing.

The Missal of Paul VI, i.e., the GIRM, is quite different. It speaks frequently, clearly and explicitly of the duty and right of the Christian people to take an active part in the eucharistic celebration, in accordance with the dignity of royal priesthood that they have all received in baptism. In organizing the celebration so that the faithful can, in keeping with their basic vocation, act along with the priest and under his leadership, the GIRM and the entire RM of Paul VI give an excellent response to the pastoral wishes of Vatican II, as expressed in the Constitution on the Liturgy:

"Mother Church earnestly desires that all the faithful should be led to that full, conscious, and active participation in liturgical celebrations which is demanded by the very nature of the liturgy. . . . In the restoration and promotion of the sacred liturgy the full and active participation by all the people is the aim to be considered before all else, for it is the primary and indispensable source from which the faithful are to derive the true Christian spirit.[33]

San Anselmo, Rome
Maria Laach

Charles RENOUX

Liturgical Ministers
at Jerusalem
in the Fourth and Fifth Centuries

By reason of its liturgical creativity and the influence of this, the Church of Jerusalem was the model church par excellence in the fourth and fifth centuries. This was also the period in which, as a result of regulations set down in the Council of Constantinople in 381, the organizational working of the ecclesiastical hierarchy came to be modeled on that of the administrative divisions of the empire. Two questions arise. How did the local churches behave as each saw its autonomy limited, controlled and integrated into a more comprehensive system: the province with its metropolitan, the provincial council and, at the top, the "diocese" (initial stage of the institution known as the patriarchate)? Did this organization lead each Church to adopt, in the area of liturgy which is our subject here, the hierarchic functions found in other churches of the province or "diocese"?

221

We do not lack sources of information about the ministers of liturgy at Jerusalem during this period of transformation. First, there are liturgical texts (*Pilgrimage of Egeria*,[1] *Armenian* and *Georgian Lectionaries*[2]), then the writings of Cyril of Jerusalem (*Catecheses*[3]), Epiphanius of Salamis (*Epitome of the Faith*[4]) and John Rufus (*Certainties*[5]). Hagiography in the form of the biographies written by Cyril of Scythopolis (*Lives of Euthymius, Theodosius,* and *Cyriacus*[6]) and Mark the Deacon (*Life of Porphyry*[7]), the letters of St. Jerome, history, and finally epigraphy also provide a good deal of material that gives us a glimpse of the Jerusalem clergy in the exercise of their liturgical functions.

1. MINISTERS IN THE LITURGY

The minister most frequently mentioned in liturgical descriptions of the holy city is the bishop. *Episcopus* is the only title given to him in Latin texts,[8] to the exclusion of *sacerdos* and *presbyter*. In Greek texts the usual technical term *episkopos*[9] is found alongside *hiereus*: the sacral man par excellence, the *pontiff*. This latter term is a favorite of the author of the *Mystagogical Catecheses*,[10] who carefully distinguishes its bearer from the priests, *presbyteroi*, who accompany him.

Those occupying the second rung in the hierarchic ladder are always called *presbyter, presbyteroi*[11] in the Latin documents. The word *sacerdos* does not appear in the *Pilgrimage of Egeria*. The Greek texts use the same term, *presbyteros*.[12] At least once in the sources I am using *presbyteros* is coupled with *didaskalos*, "teacher," thus calling attention to the doctrinal mission of the priest.

As a matter of fact, the Jerusalem community had its own teacher; this role emerges most clearly with the priest Hesychius of Jerusalem (active from 412[13]). Cyril of Scythopolis, in his *Life of St. Euthymius,* mentions the presence of Hesychius at the dedication of the laura of Euthymius in the wilderness of Judah; he tells us that "Archbishop Juvenal then went to the laura in the company of St. Passarion . . . and of the enlightened Hesychius, *priest and teacher* of the Church, and consecrated the church of the laura (May 7, 428)."[14] And in chapter 16 of his *Certainties*, John Rufus, a Monophysite, when speaking of the foreboding wonders (a rain of stones, for example) that preceded the "irregular" Council of Chalcedon, says that "Hesychius the preacher of Jerusalem collected a good many of them."[15]

Hesychius joined the function of exegete to that of preacher[16] and drew sustenance for his task from the scripture readings used in the celebration.[17] He preached during the liturgy and even in the presence of the bishop, for we find him preaching during the Easter Vigil which as the Jerusalem lectionaries show, was presided over by the bishop.[18] But the office of *didaskalos* or teacher was not something peculiar to the Church of Jerusalem; we find it also at Alexandria in the third century,[19] probably at Rome (according to chapter 19 of the *Apostolic Tradition*),[20] and finally at Antioch,[21] to limit ourselves to the best known instances.

As we shall see, an archdeacon (*archidiakonos*,[22] *archidiaconus*[23]) had a part in liturgical services, as did many deacons (*diaconus*,[24] *diakonos*[25]).

If we judge only by liturgical documents, there would seem to have been no office of *deaconess* in Jerusalem at this period; in describing the baptismal ceremonial the author of the first three *Mystical Catecheses* makes no reference to such a function.[26] And yet its existence is beyond doubt. Two funerary inscriptions from the period mention "the deaconess Sophia of Jerusalem, servant and bride of Christ,"[27] and "the deaconess Neoiketes,"[28] who served in a hospice near the holy city. In two churches not far distant from those of Jerusalem and following similar liturgical customs we meet with deaconesses. One is the Church of Gaza: the *Life of Porphyry* mentions "the devout Manaris, deaconess (*ton diakonon*), whose name has . . . a meaning in Greek and can be translated as Photina."[29] The other is the Church of Cyprus: according to the *Panarion* of Epiphanius deaconesses (*diakonissai*) are part of "the ecclesiastical order" (*ton ekklēsiastikon pragma*).[30]

As we continue with our list of liturgical ministers at Jerusalem, we must mention the function of *reader*. The Greek name *anagnōstes* occurs several times in the *Life of St. Euthymius*[31] and in the *Certitudes*[32]; on the other hand, the Latin name *lector*, does not occur in the *Pilgrimage of Egeria*,[33] although it was widely used in the West at that time.[34]

From the *Life of Theodosius* by Cyril of Scythopolis we learn that the churches of Jerusalem also had their cantors, male (*psaltēs*)[35] and female (*psaltria*).[36]

The language situation in the holy city, where the faithful might speak Greek or Syriac or even Latin required the presence of an *interpreter*. The *Pilgrimage of Egeria* simply mentions his existence[37] without telling us his name, probably because it was a priest who exercised this function. The office was known in other churches of the Greek world,[38] and Epiphanius, who mentions it in his *Panarion*, speaks of it under the title *hermeneutēs*.[39]

I have deliberately said nothing thus far of *exorcists*, since the literature of the holy city is not very explicit on the point. In his *Procatechesis* Cyril of Jerusalem assigns exorcism to *exorkizontes*, "exorcisers,"[40] and in the *Second Mystagogical Catechesis* the rite is described as accomplished through "insufflations by the saints" (*tōn hagiōn*).[41] Cyril does not use the technical term *exorkistēs* or *eporkistēs* found in Eusebius of Caesarea, Epiphanius, and the *Apostolic Constitutions* which mention this ministry. It is therefore possible that as with the functions of *teacher* and *interpreter*, exorcisms were done by a priest or cleric,[42] and that the function of exorcism had not yet become a specialized one at Jerusalem.

In the list of ministers I have drawn up there are neither *subdeacons* nor *porters*, although some churches of the Greek world had these ministries at this time.[43] It is true enough that the liturgical, patristic and hagiographical writings of the period are not as specific as we would like them to be. To speak only of Jerusalem, for example, we find frequent mention of a vague "cleric,"[44] or "clerics,"[45] or "ministers,"[46] or "clergy."[47] Do these terms include other ministries besides the ones I have listed? We cannot say for sure, since the purpose of such terms is always to distinguish the *bishop*, who is never called by the name of cleric or minister, from the orders of clergy beneath him, or the *priest* and sometimes the *deacon* from lower ranks in the hierarchy.[48]

In dealing with the ministers I have listed the hagiographical writings regularly indicate the place to which they are attached. The *Life of St. Euthymius* never fails to name the church with which a cleric is connected: Anastasius and Fidus are respectively "cleric" and "reader of the church of the Holy Resurrection."[49] Stephen, Cosmas and

Gabriel are "deacons and priest of the church of the Holy Resurrection."[50] Similarly, the *Certitudes* refer to "the archdeacon of the church of the Ascension."[51] A bishop could bestow a deaconal, priestly or other ministry only in function of a church, town or village, as canon 6 of the Council of Chalcedon decrees.[52] Jerusalem, then, was faithful to canonical discipline.

In these preliminary remarks I have mentioned only such ministers as played a part in the conduct of the liturgy. But the range of ministries was broader than that. When Archbishop Juvenal comes to consecrate the church in the laura of Euthymius, the *Life of St. Euthymius* mentions as part of his retinue not only Hesychius the teacher but also Passarion, at that time "chorbishop and archimandrite of the monks."[53] A few chapters later, the same *Life* speaks of a "certain Anastasius, cleric of the church of the Holy Resurrection . . . and chorbishop,"[54] this last being an office known in the East from the fourth century on.[55] The presence of the relic of the cross at Jerusalem required that an official be assigned to care for it; he was known as the *staurophylax* ("guardian of the cross"). We know of a whole series of these guardians, thanks to the *Lives* written by Mark the Deacon[56] and Cyril of Scythopolis[57]: Porphyry, Cosmas, Chrysippus and Cyricus, who successively held the office of "guardian of the precious cross," were priests, and two of them, Cosmas and Porphyry, became bishops.

II. LITURGICAL FUNCTIONS

In the writings that mention the ministers listed in the preceding pages the functions that emerge most clearly are those of bishop, priest and deacon. I shall first examine them separately and then speak of their mutual relations.

The Bishop

The bishop is the real leader and soul of his community. The thing that strikes us, however, in reading the Jerusalem liturgical texts is not so much the fact that he possesses authority as the fact that he is constantly with his people and leads them in prayer. Whenever he is mentioned, we find him surrounded by his people. The *Pilgrimage of Egeria* is studded with statements like these: "After this, singing hymns, they lead the bishop from the Anastasis to the Cross, and all the people go along also"[58]; "The bishop and all who are with him immediately enter the Anastasis"[59]; "When it is time, all the people and all the *aputactitae*, singing hymns, lead the bishop to the Anastasis."[60]

In this presence among his people the bishop stands at the summit of the ministerial hierarchy; he is the priest par excellence, the high priest. His primacy is signaled by the chair, the cathedra,[61] on which he sits, in an elevated location,[62] to the rear of the apse behind the altar[63] or sometimes at the center of the church.[64] Signs of respect are given to him: the faithful escort him,[65] or kiss his hand.[66]

There is a reason for all this: his position in the church and the signs of respect are undoubtedly due to the conviction that Christ is present in a special way in the bishop, the high priest. At the same time, however, the ritual that constantly surrounds the bishop bears the marks of an "historicizing" tendency which is very characteristic of the liturgy of the holy city. Since the bishop holds the place of Christ, he repeats, at appropriate times and places, the actions the Lord once did in these same places. This is clear, for example, in the Palm Sunday commemoration of Christ's entrance into Jerusalem.[67] Here, even more than elsewhere, the presence of Christ in his minister is brought out in the rite.

In addition to this desire to give dramatic form to the mystery being celebrated, it is also to be noted that actions heavy with symbolism are reserved to the bishop. For example, it is he who, each Sunday, reads the gospel of the resurrection at the end of the vigil office.[68] It is he who lights the paschal candle during the Easter Vigil.[69] The mystery of Christ's death and resurrection, which is recalled by this reading and this action, is thus communicated to the assembly with greater force through the person who holds the place of Christ.

The headship or presidency of the bishop also finds daily expression in the liturgy. It is the bishop who at the end of each office reads the prayer (*oratio*) and gives the blessing (*benedictio*),[70] for these are manifestations of his mission as mediator between God and the human race. It is he who presides over the growth of his Church, as he examines the candidates for baptism[71] and confers the sacraments of Christian initiation on them during the Easter Vigil.[72] Finally, he sanctifies his Church in the celebration of the eucharist. It is difficult to determine how often he celebrated; the liturgical texts show him celebrating in person on only four occasions.[73]

As sanctifier of his people, the bishop is also shown exercising his teaching mission. In his own church he often preaches at the Sunday eucharist,[74] in accordance with a rite to which we shall return shortly. He also preaches on the major feasts[75] and on the Wednesdays and Fridays of Lent.[76] He also has the charge of instructing the catechumens during Lent,[77] and then, during Easter week, of explaining to them the meaning of the sacraments they have received.[78] The frequency with which he preaches shows the importance attached to the ministry of the word, a ministry the bishop himself is regarded as exercising even when priests do the actual preaching, as we shall see.

Priests

The Jerusalem liturgical texts referring to priests are quite important theologically for they show priests in the same posture as the bishop: they are seated around him, whereas the other clerics are standing.[79] The priest's action in this regard is not merely ceremonial but accords with the prescription of the *Didascalia*,[80] the Apostolic Constitutions[81] and the *Testament of Our Lord*.[82] Priests and bishop are members of a single collegial group, the "rulers" as the *Didascalia* calls them in the passage cited.

The union of bishop and priests in a single priesthood is also shown in the exercise of other powers by the priests. The gospel, the reading of which is regularly reserved to the bishop at vigils,[83] is sometimes read by priests.[84] The priests celebrate the eucharist with the bishop,[85] share with him in the preparation of catechumens for baptism,[86] and even preach along with him.[87] We shall return to this last point below. All these facts and actions evidently have a dogmatic significance: they say that there is but a single ministry of sanctification and teaching and that in this ministry priests act as *collaborators of the bishop*. This becomes especially clear when the bishop is absent. In this church of the holy city, where the bishop presides over all functions, priests exercise presidency, together or with the deacons, when the bishop is away,[88] and they pronounce the blessing which the bishop usually gave.[89]

Deacons

There are many deacons at Jerusalem. The *Pilgrimage of Egeria* almost always refers to them in the plural, *diacones*,[90] as do other liturgical documents connected with the holy city.[91] Each church had several deacons. According to the *Pilgrimage of Egeria*,[92] the *Armenian Lectionary*[93] and the *Life of St. Euthymius*,[94] two or three, or even more, of them are on duty at the Anastasis. The *Certainties* mentions there being several at the church of the Probatic Pool.[95] Why so many? The number is doubtless determined by a deaconal mission on which the ecclesiastical regulations of the time lay great stress. Thus the *Didascalia* says that the number of deacons must be proportioned to the number of the faithful, so that necessary help may be brought as quickly as possible to all who are needy, sick or destitute.[96]

The liturgical ministry of deacons at Jerusalem involves carefully defined functions. Before the beginning of the office the deacons take charge of the crowd that is gathering[97]; they are probably seeing to it, as the *Didascalia* specifies, that the faithful go to the places assigned to them.[98] During the eucharist, as during other services, they "remain standing"[99]; that is their regular posture.[100] However, one of the deacons is stationed near the altar in order to be of service during the eucharistic sacrifice, by bringing water to the bishop or priests so that they may wash their hands or by stirring the faithful to attention or exhorting them to the kiss of peace.[101]

It is chiefly in the celebration of the Hours of the Office that the deacon appears as a leader of prayer. He directs the litanic prayer during the evening Office by formulating the intentions but also by occasionally giving admonitions needed for the participation of the community.[102] The duty of making announcements falls mainly to the archdeacon; he announces, for example, the hour and place of the next service.[103] The honor of being chief deacon is sometimes one that no one envies: John of Jerusalem sends his archdeacon to convey to Epiphanius the order to be silent after the latter has delivered an anti-origenist speech in the Rotunda of the Anastasis.[104]

Deacons probably also played a part, at Jerusalem as elsewhere, in the preparation for and administration of baptism. The texts concerning the holy city are unfortunately quite unexplicit, and I shall not dwell on this point.[105]

At the end of this brief sketch of deaconal service at Jerusalem, it is to be noted that—as far as the documents I have examined show— deacons do not enjoy the same prestige as those whose role the *Didascalia* describes (end of the third century). Only once do we find them standing by themselves (without any mention of the priests) around the bishop, and that is at the veneration of the cross on Good Friday.[106] They are at the service of the bishop but they are also at the service of the priests, for example, during the eucharistic celebration[107]; in this they follow the norm set down by Jerome in his *Letter to Evangelus*.[108]

III. A COLLEGIAL MINISTRY

In his *Procatechesis* Cyril of Jerusalem takes delight in depicting for his catechumens "the splendid discipline of the Church . . . her understanding of order . . . the presence of religious men and women."[109] And in fact the various liturgical ministries of which I have been speaking are all meant to make up a single action.

At Jerusalem, as everywhere else during this period, every assembly was conscious of being the agent of liturgical action. This would have emerged quite clearly if I had not excluded the various categories of the faithful (laity, monks, penitents, etc.) from my inquiry. I restrict myself to the roles of the bishop, priests and deacons: these are always presented to us as cooperating in one and the same ministry of sanctification and teaching.

We see this in the celebration of the Sunday eucharist in which the bishop is surrounded by the priests, while the deacons serve bishop and priests at the altar or superintend the people in the church.[110] We see it in the Liturgy of the Hours, in which clerics, deacons, priests, and bishop take part in the one celebration, each with his own function.[111] We see it again in the administration of baptism, in which the various ministers join with the bishop in bestowing a single sacrament.[112] We are familiar with the hierarchic yet communal character of these rites of the Christian liturgy,[113] and there is no need to insist on it. In concluding, I want to call attention to a less well-known rite of the holy city's liturgy in the fourth and fifth century, and one that is probably to be assigned a collegial value.

In Jerusalem, during the Sunday eucharistic liturgy, the reading of the gospel was followed by a type of preaching which surprised Egeria the pilgrim. "It is the practice here that as many of the priests who are present and are so inclined may preach; and last of all, the bishop preaches."[114] This procedure in the Sunday preaching is also followed on the feasts of the liturgical year: on the fortieth day after Epiphany, that is, on the feast of the Presentation of the Lord in the temple, "all the priests give sermons, and the bishop too."[115] "On the fortieth day after Easter . . . the divine service is celebrated in the prescribed manner, and as a result the priests and the bishop preach."[116] On Pentecost, at the first celebration of the eucharist, which takes place in the Martyrium, "the priests preach, and afterwards the bishop."[117] On the same day, at the celebration in the church of Sion, "there is read from the Acts of the Apostles that passage in which the Holy Spirit came down . . . and the priests take the passage which has been read as their basis."[118]

What information is given us in the four texts just cited? Multiple sermons were given on all Sundays and probably also on movable feasts. They were given after the reading of the gospel. Those doing the preaching were, first, the priests who accompanied the bishop[119] and concelebrated with him,[120] and finally the bishop himself.

A second but different example of this plurality of sermons is noted on the Wednesday and Friday of each week of Lent at the office of None. "So that the people will know the law, the bishop and a priest preach assiduously."[121] The reference is to instruction of a different kind than that given to catechumens[122]; here it is the bishop who preaches first.

The Church of Jerusalem was not the only one in the fourth and fifth centuries to have this kind of preaching. Many of St. John Chrysostom's sermons[123] tell us that the same custom existed at Antioch and Constantinople,[124] but Chrysostom says nothing about the reason for or origin of the practice. The *Apostolic Constitutions*, which reflect the customs of the same area, also tell us that a number of priests preach during the liturgy and that the bishop preaches after them, "as befits the pilot of the ship."[125] At Bethlehem St. Jerome's homilies to his monks attest that the same custom was followed even in Latin-speaking circles in Palestine.[126] For Alexandria, the historian Sozomen says that after the heresies of the priest Arius, the bishop was the only one to preach in church.[127]

Such explicit testimonies to this kind of preaching have come down to us only beginning in the fourth century. It is difficult to explain why this should be. But Anton Baumstark has endeavored to explain the practice in his book *Die Messe im Morgenland* (The Mass in the West).[128] In his view a succession of preachers giving sermons after the reading of the gospel is a survival of the charismatic preaching of which the First Letter to the Corinthians speaks: "You can all prophesy one by one, so that all may learn and all be encouraged."[129] We might rephrase Baumstark's explanation in contemporary language and say that this plurality of sermons shows how charism has given way to institution; how preaching which is not reserved to anyone in the First Letter to the Corinthians, has now become the business of priests and bishops alone.

Can we accept this explanation? Are we to connect the multiplicity of sermons that we find at Jerusalem and elsewhere in the fourth century with the practices of the first Christian communities? We may note, first of all, that we are dealing with a different problem than that of preaching or teaching done by a layperson (the Acts of the Apostles and Christian tradition provide many irrefutable testimonies to such a practice[130]). The members of the laity—the faithful and the monks—never take part in the preaching at Jerusalem; this preaching is always associated with the hierarchy, with priests, then bishop, or bishop, then priests, giving sermons.

Origen cannot be suspected of partiality, since he had occasion to preach before being ordained. Yet he speaks of the "teaching office of priests" and links ecclesiastical preaching with the apostles; this preaching has continued in the Church as the result of a succession.[131] It is, then, to the mission of proclaiming God's word which has been entrusted to the successors of the apostles and the bishop of each church, that we prefer to attach the custom of multiple sermons at Jerusalem. It was quite normal that priests, the institutional collaborators of the bishop, and sharers with him in the liturgical action and the Church's mission of sanctification, should also be united with him in his teaching mission, which is inseparable from that other

231

mission. Bishop and priests together have the duty of preaching. This rite of successive sermons was, then, a manifestation of the unity of their doctrinal mission.

Achille M. TRIACCA

Methexis
in the Early Ambrosian Liturgy

Contribution of Ambrosian Euchological Sources to an Understanding of a Contemporary Liturgical Problem: The Participation of the Assembly

Experience shows that human beings can carry on their intellectual activity only if they have recourse to the sensible world. So too we know that they cannot develop relations with God unless the body plays its part, with gestures, words and things becoming signs in which the mystery of God is manifested to men. Thus it is that worship, in its exterior manifestations, helps express divine realities, represent the truths of faith, and profess faith in an objective manner.[1]

If we adopt this perspective for discussing the participation of the assembly in the liturgy, the danger is that we may reduce it to something external, palpable and peripheral that does not really get to the inner truth of the matter. And in fact, in a good deal of current writing on the liturgy we can detect a certain stereotyped simplification: participation in the liturgy is seen as external as well as active, superficial as well as profound, individual as well as communal, misunderstood as well as habitual, and connected with the liturgical movement that has inspired so much pastoral effort in the Roman Catholic Church.[2]

It is clear, then, why the Second Vatican Council laid so much stress on an authentic participation in the liturgy.[3] It will be worth our while, then, to reflect on the similarities and differences between participation in the liturgy and participation in other human activities. The documents of the Council speak, do they not, of "participation" in the worlds of culture, education, the economy, work, social life, political life, public life, and even of participation in the lot of the international community?[4]

I have been led, then, to reflect on the meaning of the Latin word *participatio*, which is used as well in the various Romance languages,[5] and also on the fact that the same word is used to speak of participation in the liturgy and of participation in all kinds of other human activities. This reflection has stimulated me to explore the euchological resources of the early Ambrosian liturgy in order to determine what the reality is which we speak of today as "participation"; to discover how this participation was experienced in that past time; and, finally, to examine more closely the particular characteristics of this participation according to the early Ambrosian liturgy.

1. PARTICIPATION IN THE LITURGY:
MODERN THEORY OR PRACTICE OF EVERY AGE?

The study I am undertaking faces methodological difficulties that must be made explicit at the outset.[6]

Nowadays we never find the word "participation" used by itself in liturgical contexts. It is always accompanied by an adjective such as "external, internal, full, conscious, active, communal, etc." or with a complementary phrase: "participation of the faithful; participation in liturgical action; participation in the Church's worship; etc." This shows that participation is described in terms of external or internal factors, and is susceptible of various modalities and degrees of intensity. In addition, participation should be directed to goals that call for attention and an understanding of the rites or the mysteries of worship.

From the viewpoint of methodology, the attempt to project a modern problem into another historical age may seem an anachronism; after all, we are suggesting, are we not, that we read the euchological sources in light of a judgment passed in advance (*Vorlesung*)? Well, if we reflect carefully on the reality conveyed in the idea of participation in the liturgy, we realize that there is an essential connection between liturgy and participation and that consequently the question of participation is not a problem peculiar to one period but a problem for all times and places.

It follows that the study of participation in the liturgy during another historical period is not only possible but very meaningful, since the purpose is to show how that past time experienced participation. We must note, however, that attention to participation and attention to the problem of participation are two different things and that while our ancestors were concerned with participation they did not therefore share with us a reflexive concern with participation.[7] We shall be endeavoring, then, to highlight the essential elements of participation in the liturgy as seen in the early euchology of the Ambrosian synaxis. Such a study is perfectly legitimate.

The sources on which we shall be drawing are the Ambrosian sacramentaries.[8] More precisely, we shall limit ourselves to the *Sacramentarium Bergomense*[9] which is readily accessible in Paredi's edition and transcription.[10] This sacramentary is one of the most important, and the formularies in it are found without appreciable change in the other Ambrosian sacramentaries[11] that have been published in critical editions: the Sacramentary of Biasca,[12] that of Ariberto,[13] that of St. Simplician,[14] and the Triplex.[15]

The Bergamo Sacramentary does, however, have one difficulty in common with all those of the time: there are no rubrics to show the postures to be adopted and the actions to be done in the course of the liturgical celebration. Such information would tell us something about external participation. But to take this difficulty too seriously would be to misunderstand the rich complexity of participation by reducing it for practical purposes to an external participation; external participation is certainly not the whole of participation, and in fact it is not even the essential thing.

In this context we must add two subsidiary remarks.

We should always bear in mind that external attitudes and actions depend on an interior participation. They can be correctly understood only in light of the texts that accompany them. External rites and attitudes acquire their full meaning only from the words. Words are the means that enable us to enter into the action. They enable us to hit the target: not only the arrow, but the bow and the archer.

Words always call for a response. Interpersonal communication normally takes the form of dialogue.[16] This rule applies to liturgical language as to any other: the Church has established liturgical texts for particular peoples in order that as they celebrate the rites they may grasp the meaning of the celebration and participate in it fruitfully.[17]

With P. Alfonso we may add that "the prayers form a substantial part, indeed a preponderant part, even materially speaking, of the early liturgy, in which the rites themselves are extremely simple. A study of ancient liturgy is primarily a study of prayers."[18] Participation in the liturgy must be correlated with prayer texts. The permanent call for participation is intrinsic to the liturgical texts themselves, so that the expression and communication included in the prayers tend toward communion.[19] The literary art proper to the liturgy has always had for its purpose to make it easier for the faithful to identify with the prayer of the Church. Nor must we forget that the texts also have a pedagogical function[20] and that proclamation is one of their essential purposes.

From these various viewpoints, then, the study I am undertaking is possible.

Here is a further point of methodology. With regard to the Ambrosian sources there is a wide range of opinion on the chronology, the euchological schools, and the probable composer of the documents themselves.[21] In other words, the Ambrosian sources seem at first glance to be a heterogeneous amalgam; they seem to contain strata from various periods and redactional schools.[22] Thus we encounter a new methodological difficulty that may seem insurmountable, even if we limit our attention to the Bergamo Sacramentary, since the entire direction of this study would be significantly changed if we had to think of the document as a compilation and amalgam.[23] We would then have to distinguish the various formularies, classify them, and draw conclusions that would vary for texts from the first or second or third redaction.[24] That kind of work is almost impossible, given the present state of research. On the other hand, if we regard the Bergamo Sacramentary as a single whole, with an existence of its own, then this study is possible and meaningful.

From the viewpoint of methodology the present study is even more justified if we accept that at the period when the Bergamo Sacramentary was compiled, participation in the liturgy was an undeniable fact. In fact, it takes no lengthy reflection to realize that at that time there was a close link between the people and the liturgy, since a vital liturgy fed a fervent Christian life and vice versa. The people took part in the liturgy and drew life from it. Consequently it is possible to study the fact of participation in the liturgy as a function of the following varied factors.

As a human action participation in the liturgy implies:
participants (*nos, familia, populus,* etc.);
the reality in which they participate (*celebratio, festum, solemnitas, oblatio, munus, mysterium,* etc.);
the external and interior attitudes that are highlighted to a greater or lesser degree (*celebrare, offerre, cum gaudio, cum pietate*);
reasons for the action (*affectu–effecto, temporaliter–perpetuo*);
circumstances (*festum, solemnitas, quadragesima observatio*);
functioning: the commandment of Christ, "Do this . . ."[25]

If we were in addition to consider participation in the liturgy as an activity of the Trinity, the study would be even more fully developed and complex.

I shall restrict this study to certain points, with the terminology of the liturgy as my point of departure, and keeping in mind that the words of the liturgy are both the means and the expression of participation in the celebration. We can then move on to observe the nature of participation as seen in the context of the Ambrosian eucharistic liturgy. The study will then have a specific value, inasmuch as the Ambrosian liturgical patrimony, taken as a whole, has an inalienable and undeniable specific character of its own.[26]

2. ELEMENTS OF AMBROSIAN EUCHARISTIC EUCHOLOGY: CONTRIBUTION TO THE STUDY OF PARTICIPATION

If it be true that in the past, at the time when the celebration of the liturgy was being organized, the liturgy involved the people more than it has at other periods, then it must also be admitted that the forms of expression current among the people were clearly reflected in the liturgy. Popular culture was closely related to a vital liturgy and vice versa. Gestures, garments, songs, language, forms of expression: all that was part of the people's daily life became part of the liturgy as well, and everyone was familiar with the latter.[27]

I am not saying that the liturgy was made up only of elements drawn from local or daily life. It is certain, however, that the rites which the assemblies of the time celebrated as mysteries or events of salvation made use of forms of expression and methods of communication which were taken over from the cultural world of the faithful.[28] The religious climate in which the people lived was in complete harmony with the mentality expressed in liturgical prayer and song.

Clearly, then, it is very important for this study that we understand the *functioning of the euchological components*,[29] since their formulation was a basic reflection of the participation of the people. We should note, too, that the eucharistic assembly is formally constituted by formulas to be inserted into formularies whose primary characteristic is the varied but organic manner in which they function. The attitudes of the people differ depending on whether there is question of the opening prayer, the prayer *super sindonem* ["over the cloth": a prayer said immediately after the deacon has spread the cloth, *sindon*, on the altar at the offertory] or the prayer over the gifts, the postcommunion, or the preface.

Once we have recognized the importance of the way each prayer functions, we can ask what precise relation exists between the functioning proper to each prayer and the problem or reality of participation. In other words, we may reflect on the existence of a dynamic of participation in the overall celebration of the eucharistic synaxis. An analysis of the texts will show what agents are active in the celebration; in what sense and what degree these agents are called upon to participate in the celebration; and, finally, what awareness they have of their participation.[30]

Briefly, then: we shall first study the terminology which the Bergamo Sacramentary uses in relation to our theme; then we shall go on to consider the participating agents and to ask what they do; finally, we shall see to what conclusions the study leads.

The Terminology Used in the Bergamo Sacramentary for the Subjects Who Participate in the Liturgy

A first reading brings out a term which from a linguistic viewpoint is very generic, but which from the liturgical viewpoint is very concrete: the pronoun *nos* (we, us) with verbs in the first person plural. Other terms, in fact a whole series of ecclesial words, pinpoint and explicitate the sense of this simple pronoun.

The use of the first person plural in Ambrosian prayers. The prayers of the Amborisan liturgy make use of a plural which refers to the collection of persons who take part in the liturgy.[31] We find:[32]
nos (nominative case), either explicit or implicit, as subject of plural verbs[33]; direct or indirect objects: *nos* (accusative),[34] *nobis* (dative),[35] *u nobis* (ablative), and other complements as well.[36]

We must observe, however, that the use of this terminology in the opening prayer does not have precisely the same meaning as in other prayers. The difference is due to the function proper to each prayer. The opening prayer refers to the assembly, the *ecclesia*, in a general way, and it shows little reference to the liturgical season to which it belongs. On the other hand, in the prayers *super sindonem* and over the gifts, the same pronoun *nos* is more characterized by the liturgical season or the particular celebration; these prayers emphasize the action of the praying and offering community.

The postcommunions have still another character. First of all, almost all of them express the subject of participation in one or other manner, without any notable influence being exercised by the liturgical season. Furthermore, it is the passive aspect of participation that is emphasized; this is understandable, since the subject of participation (most often expressed by *nos* and the accusative *quos* [whom]) is seen as the object of divine benevolence. We may also note that these prayers which conclude the eucharistic synaxis are marked by an almost complete absence of explicitly ecclesial terms[37] such as *plebs* (the people of God, the body of Christians), *populus* (the people of God, the congregation), or *familia* (the assembly),[38] which occur so frequently in the opening prayers. Perhaps the postcommunions express a kind of "ec-stasy," in the etymological sense of the word, as if the participants, now utterly filled with the divine gift, could attend only to this *gift*.[39] A moment of this kind in the celebration would call, we might say, for a more personal or even individual type of participation. In my opinion, the texts validate this explanation as certain and not just as a working hypothesis.

In the prefaces participation is still expressed by the first person plural but is thrown into quite special relief. I need only refer to the quite enormous dimensions which the *nos* acquires as the prefaces contemplate the history of salvation. Then the *nos* represents the community of the redeemed as integrated into the divine order and roused to sing: "Let us give thanks to our God."[40] This is especially true of prefaces dealing with the history of salvation (*Heilsgeschichtliche-Präfationen*), but it also applies to prefaces that paraphrase the prayers (*Bitt-Präfationen*), which occur frequently especially on the weekdays of Lent, and to those which are centones of patristic texts (*Väterschrift-Präfationen*) or which are characterized by moral exhortation (*Moralpredigt-Präfationen*).[41] All these prefaces contemplate the *mirabilia Dei*, the marvelous deeds of God, and it is understandable that those who take part in the liturgy should be designated in the prefaces by the nominative and not the accusative: the *nos* is the agent who contemplates the plan of salvation which the Trinity predetermined and then executed. The content of the prefaces varies, of course, according to liturgical season and feast, but the terminology for the agent of contemplation is not thereby modified.[42]

In conclusion, we may say that there is a greater or lesser intensity of participation in the eucharistic celebration at various moments in this celebration and that this variation is reflected in the prayer texts. Consequently, we cannot speak in a purely general way of participation in the eucharist but must take this variation or diversity into account. As I said a moment ago, the liturgical season does not bring about any change in this respect. On the other hand, it is important to remark that, in relation to the participants, God has the initiative in the participation of his people. If we can offer gifts to him and receive his graces, this is only because he has first given us both what we offer to him and what we are asking from him. Given this perspective, it is natural that the community designated by *nos* should become more aware of itself at certain more significant points in the eucharistic celebration.

The use of other terms to designate the subject who participates; reflections on the nature of participation. After these remarks on the use of the first person plural, we must now turn to other terms that indicate the participating subject and try to discern from them the nature of the participation itself. But we must be honest and admit that this terminology does not differ from that used in the prayers of the Roman liturgy. This makes it rather difficult to find anything typically Ambrosian about it, and yet this Ambrosian character is real.

The Ambrosian euchology uses the words *ecclesia*,[43] *plebs*,[44] *populus*,[45] *famulus*,[46] *familia*,[47] *filii* (children),[48] *servitus, servus* (service, servant) and synonyms,[49] *fideles*,[50] *nova creatura* (new creature or creation),[51] and others,[52] which may be accompanied by characterizing phrase, attributes, explanations and complements, in order to designate the agents in the participation.

In the Bergamo Sacramentary the expression *ecclesia (tua)*[53] is clearly richer and more varied in its contents than are the other terms; the latter are sometimes rather stereotyped. *Ecclesia* names a body of the faithful whom the Father, acting through Christ, has called together for worship. This body of believers gives back to God, through Christ, what it has received from God through Christ in the Spirit. Knowing this, we can see the deeper meaning of the adjective *tua* (your) that regularly accompanies *ecclesia:*[54] the Church belongs to God the Father because it is governed by his goodness, and it is by means of his Church that God carries out his plan of salvation. Participation in the liturgy is thus the context par excellence in which God intervenes in a concrete way in the affairs of men. To celebrate the liturgy is to co-participate in the plan in which God takes the initiative. It is an apocritical participation or participation responsive (*apokrinein* = to respond) to God, a participation involving the whole person, who commits himself, in response to God, not only by words but by his life. These same ideas recur in other liturgical contexts.

In any case, since it is impossible here to analyze all the varied terms already mentioned, I shall concentrate on the word *populus*.[55]

Like *eccleisa, populus* is usually accompanied by the adjective *tuus*.[56] An examination of all the prayer texts in the Bergamo Sacramentary yields the following image of the people.

a) *A people belonging to God*. The position of the word at the beginning of prayers calls attention to the community that is gathered to celebrate the eucharist (general context) and that at this moment is praying and participating in communion with Christ and the Church (particular context). Within this framework the *populus* is seen in its special relationship with God, thanks to the adjective *tuus*, which signifies not only that the community belongs to God but also that the faithful are newly aware of their existential relation to God (subjective and communal aspect). Participation thus means the recognition and profession of the Church's belonging to God.

b) *A people at prayer*. This point is underscored by the verbs expressing petition: *fac* ("bring it to pass," i.e., grant), *concede* (grant), *da quaesumus* ("give, we beseech," i.e., grant), and so on.[57] By its petitions the community shows its awareness of its poverty but also its confidence in the Father's mercy.[57a] The source of this filial confidence is the initiative God has taken with regard to salvation; as a result of this initiative the community can associate itself in the eucharistic celebration with the prayer of Christ and can expect to obtain the completion of what has already been given. We may add that the explicit references to prayer show the *populus* to be clearly identified with the praying assembly and therefore with the local community. Participation in the liturgy provides the community with its best opportunity for manifesting itself as Church. This participation is the source of the Church's organic unity.

c) A careful analysis of the term *populus* shows that God exercises toward his people an action that can be called essential, sacramental, and dynamico-eschatological.

An essential action. This is indicated by such expressions as *adesto propitius* (be present in mercy),[58] *propitius respice* (look with mercy),[59] *intuere benignus* (look with kindness),[60] and so on. At first sight, such expressions may seem rather anthropomorphic. They serve, however, to call attention to various aspects of God's presence and action in the community. His presence is of an interpersonal kind: God's relation to the community is one of dialogue (cf. what was said just above about apocritical participation), marked by confident self-surrender on the part of the faithful and fatherly helpfulness on the part of God. Participation in the liturgy is thus a "koinonia" of love with the Father. This aspect of participation is emphasized in the first prayer of the formularies, viz., the prayer *super populum*.

A sacramental action. This is the supreme form of God's efficacious presence among his people. Thanks to the eucharist, God enters so closely into the faithful that he makes a new creation of them.[61] This aspect is brought out especially in the postcommunions, where the language of eating and the meal signifies repletion and the satisfaction of every human desire. At the same time, however, this language also emphasizes the attitude of joy and prayer that results from the abundance of God's gift and from the certainty of faith that this gift transforms our entire life from within by giving it the newness which is the sign and fruit of Christ's presence in us. Participation in the liturgy thus leads to a wholly new life because it is a participation in the life of Christ for the sake of each person's authentic fulfillment both as individual and as member of the community.

A dynamico-eschatological action. Thanks to God's intervention, the gift received gradually reveals all its virtualities and leads to an eschatological plenitude.[62] This divine action is carried on in the celebration, and the faithful ask that it may continue throughout their daily lives, so that the latter may be characterized by a continual passage to new life and may be crowned by a definitive transformation. Participation in liturgical action is inseparable from the participation of our entire lives in the liturgy; in this sense, participation is related to life.

d) The response of the Christian people to God's action occurs at a salvifico-existential level. The people of God enter into dialogue with God the Father not only by communion in a new life and by prayer but also by an active cooperation that tends to make the dialogue itself increasingly fruitful. The emphasis of the Ambrosian prayer texts on the theme of renewal is especially significant. It shows that the community of the faithful is aware of the danger of remaining prisoner of a past that was sinful or, at best, barren from a Christian point of view (*vetustas*). For this reason the people ask that the mysteries with which they have been fed may continue to nourish and inspire a life that is fruitful from the Christian standpoint (*novitas, renovare*).[63] Participation in the liturgy is the beginning, the deepening, and the advance in perfection and newness of those who participate in the mysteries.

In summary, the people of God can be described in the following terms: to God's initiative which invites the people to the eucharistic banquet and gives them power to lead a renewed Christian life, the community of the faithful responds with gratitude, prayer and trust in the power of the divine presence to bring to fruition the dynamic thrust of the eucharist toward eschatological fulfillment. Participation is the ontological deepening of awareness of the community's own reality as related to the mystery of salvation in which this reality originates and which the assembled people of God celebrates here and now.

The limitations which this essay must respect have forced me to discuss only the use of the first person plural and the use of the word *populus*. I have also discussed at various points the nature of participation as reflected in the prayers of the Ambrosian synaxis. I would like to turn now to the agents in this participation and to ask what it is that they in fact do.

The Agents of Participation and What They Do
As I have already indicated, the agents who participate are never individuals isolated from one another but a group of persons who act within an organic network of relations, namely, the community which is structured as *ecclesia, plebs, populus,* and whose members, the *fideles.* or *famuli,*[64] are called to celebrate, along with the celebrant, the memorial sacrifice of Christ. The Church that is gathered here and now engages in prayer that embodies specific attitudes.[65] After listening attentively to the word of God,[66] the Church penetrates ever more deeply to the heart of participation, until it reaches the summits to which the postcommunions bear witness.[67]

We may remind ourselves once again that the variety of liturgical seasons brings no difference in terminology. Only occasional phrases introduce a tone proper to a liturgical season.[68]

a) *Participation is unity and communion with Christ.* We may connect with this theme such expressions as emphasize the element of unity, communion of life, likeness and conformity, as resulting from the celebration. In a sense, everything referring to the community of the faithful is relevant here, since this community is based on and calls for unity.

This theme has its key words. Some terms[69] have a clear sacramental reference: *communio; frequentatio, frequentare; percipere; replere, satiare; sumere;* etc. Others emphasize more the relation to Christ: *coheredes, consortes (consortium), sociati, particeps,* [70] etc. The term *particeps*[71] has both a sacramental and an eschatological dimension.[72] Thus the unity and communion of the faithful have their source and concrete expression in participation in the eucharist. This participation is called a *communio*[73] because all who share in it enter into the communion of life with God and the brethren that is the foundation of ecclesial unity. We must note the insistence with which this *communio* is depicted as a source of purification, salvation, strength,[74] eternal happiness,[75] and blessing.[76] The result is that these effects are an inherent part of an authentic Christian life[77] that finds expression in the witness of love, in adherence to the things of God, and in a harmony with transcendent realities.

Participation thus appears as the fruit of the actions of the participants and as the cause of ecclesial union among these same participants. In other words, the union of the members of the Body of Christ is the fruit and result of participation in the body and blood of Christ,[78] in the one bread and one cup of the eucharist.[79] We become participants of Christ and the life of God; we take into ourselves the Christ who took us into himself in his incarnation.[80] Participation is therefore based not so much on harmony and friendship among the participants as on a common union with the eucharist (sacramental aspect) which calls for conformity and likeness to Christ (christological aspect), while the participants wait for the day when they can share his glory. These two aspects are joined in the Father's single plan of salvation which was carried out by Christ and is prolonged in the eucharist. I have already made it clear that the eucharist is an efficacious sign of vital communion with Christ and harmony with the brethren.

b) *Participation is conformity and solidarity with Christ.* All of the Ambrosian prayer texts that speak of *nos–ecclesia* imply a dynamism that has a complete and existential participation in the eucharist as its goal. We may take as an example the postcommunion for Saturday in the third week of Lent (Ber 386):

Quaesumus omnipotens deus
ut inter eius membra numeremur (=petitio)
cuius corpori communicamus et sanguini (=adiuncta). per.[81]

(We ask, almighty God, that we may be counted as members of him in whose body and blood we have communicated. Through . . .)

We find stated here a fourfold relation of causality between the petition and the circumstances of it; from this relation flows a triple solidarity (ontological, moral, eschatological) with Christ and in Christ, thanks to the sacrament. There is a compenetration of these three aspects of solidarity with the aspects of the unique relation that holds between the circumstances (participation in the body and blood of Christ) and the petition (to be counted among his members). This participation in the eucharist makes us increasingly disposed to celebrate it better, since it makes us more fully members of Christ the priest.

In the final analysis, the agent of participation is identified with Christ the priest: we are agents (*nos*) insofar as we concelebrate with him, and we become agents capable of celebrating only thanks to our union with him, the high priest and liturgical celebrant of the Father.[81a] This does not prevent our participation from being an active one, since it is up to us to continue, in our lives and our spiritual worship, a participation in the liturgy that becomes coextensive with our Christian life in its entirety. When we participate in the liturgy as its agents (*nos*), we show that the anthropological elements of the liturgy are in fact operative at the salvific level. For the assembly with which we are dealing is gathered for a cultic purpose, as the word *plebs*[82] indicates. God watches over this community by visiting, protecting and strengthening it. The faithful in turn manifest their collective belonging to God by preserving the salvation given them, by offering themselves in love, and by turning to the things of eternity.

It is clear, then that participation in the liturgy reveals a community's truest face as it acknowledges its poverty, seeks its fulfillment, and opens itself to the transcendent.

I am deeply regretful that I am unable here to give an exhaustive presentation of Ambrosian euchology. As it is, after some remarks on method I have indicated some aspects of Ambrosian prayer that have to do with participation, and I have spoken of aspects of participation

246

as seen in the Ambrosian liturgy. The reader is perhaps now in a position to see why the title of my essay speaks of *methexis* rather than *participation*. What we find in the early Ambrosian liturgy is better expressed by *methexis* than by participation, because the reality is ontological and marked by intimacy and profound inwardness; it is something more than what the term participation ordinarily conveys. To this final point I now turn.

3. MEANING OF PARTICIPATION (*METHEXIS*) IN THE AMBROSIAN LITURGY

I have no intention of repeating here what I have already said. My aim in this final section is rather to locate the word *participation* within its methodological coordinates and thus to reach a conclusion regarding the content of liturgical participation.

Methodological Coordinates for Situating the Term "Participation" in the Prayer Texts of the Ambrosian Liturgy
It is surprising that no one has as yet studied the use of the word *participatio* in these prayers. The term shows the following characteristics as it occurs in the various parts of prayers:

In the context of the invocation. The term can be found at the heart of the invocation, which is itself preceded by an explicit reference to God or by a petition or by a statement of fact.[83] The position of the word here calls attention to the divine initiative or gift that the term includes. It is this divine gift that grounds the request for a further development of what has already been received.

The term also shares in the dynamism of the *final prayer petition* (i.e., the postcommunion),[84] where it is either the logical subject or a presupposition. The immediate point of reference is called *mysterium*[85] or *sacramentum*.[86] The connection between participation and *mysterium* or *sacramentum* expresses—though still in a general way—our insertion into the plan of salvation via the sacramental economy. In the context of *mysterium* participation is described as "salutary."[87] In the context of *sacramentum* the emphasis is rather on the effectiveness of God's action, that is, the presence of grace.

In conclusion we may say that these few remarks show the reality and importance of the human person's encounter of God, which is described in a general way as "participation." Participation, then, is the symbiosis, the encounter, the *koinonia* (communion, fellowship) of man with the God who has taken the initiative and come to encounter him.

In the context of the ultimate goal. The word *participatio* always occurs in the ablative singular,[88] in a phrase which picks up what was said in the invocation and also justifies the petition that flows from the invocation. Thus the word links the two main parts of the prayer.[89] That to which reference is directly made in this context is described as a "mystery," and what the faithful receive they receive thanks to the benevolent goodness of God. Inasmuch as the participation takes place here and now it shows the actuality and intimacy of the experience of God which we have in the eucharist.

Thus, in the expression of the goal as well as in the invocation, *participatio* preserves its generic character, although with a eucharistic and theocentric orientation, as the next section will show.

In the context of the content. If we are properly to understand the word *participatio* we must attend to its immediate referent. The prayers emphasize the connection of *participatio* with the ideas of *sacramentum,*[90] *mysterium,*[91] *remedium,*[92] etc.,[93] *sumere,*[94] *percipere* and *accipere,*[95] and others,[96] *gaudere,*[97] and so on. Even a sketchy analysis of these words would involve us in digressions. I shall therefore point out simply that in Ambrosian prayer texts *methexis-participatio* includes:

union with God thanks to the sacrament, rather than participation in the sacrament itself;[98]

a purification or liberation that grounds the faithful once again in what is most real in them[99] and makes them the object of God's love and the locus of his efficacious presence;

a configuration to Christ that is brought about by participation in the liturgy; more specifically, a union with Christ in his paschal mystery, thanks to the eucharist and to the testimony of a life wholly directed to God.[100]

Without carrying the analysis any further, I shall propose a partial synthesis. The subject is one that I expect to return to on another occasion, when I shall deal with it in a more developed and complete way.

Synthesis of the Meaning of "methexis" in Amborisan Prayer Texts

The modality of participation. The modality is threefold: attention is focused directly on the present, i.e., the celebration itself. Since, however, we experience the celebration as taking place within the flow of time, we necessarily move from the present to the past and from the present to the future.

The movement from present to past shows how richly God nourishes the participants: we are called to receive the God who came to set us free and to make us new again in his paschal mystery.[101] This salvific past is present and operative in the attitude of the faithful. Participation thus implies that the salvific past is rendered present. This participation is in fact *sancta* (holy),[102] since encounter with God requires that the faithful be holy; it is also *divina* (divine), not only because it establishes a relation to God but also because of its effects, which are purification, increase of grace, joy in union with the Father.[103] Furthermore, the participation is a *communio* from which springs a desire for an increasingly deeper union;[104] it is a divine *donum* that is offered[105] to a praying community[106] and calls for a response in the form of a total gift (*plena devotio*) to the transcendent God. The fruit of participation, therefore, is the transformation of the whole person.

The movement from present to future, or, more accurately, the anticipation of the future in the present, is another aspect of participation. A number of prayers show that participation also exercises an influence on the future, since it is impelled toward the gaining of a completion or perfect state.[107] *Metnexis* teaches us to assign earthly realities their proper value and to make us attached to heavenly realities.[108]

The term and concept of *participatio* is the focal point of an entire edifice of thought which brings out the sacramental dynamism that enables the faithful to enter into the mystery of salvation by participating in it, and vice versa. This explains why, even in the post-communions, when the congregation has already participated in the eucharist, prayer is offered for the plenary reception of the effects of this participation.[109]

In conclusion we may say that as far as its modality is concerned participation has three aspects:

since participation implies an interpersonal relationship, it has two subjects: God, who acts through the sacrament, and the community, which responds to the divine initiative;

participation is a gift of God, but it is also the object of continual petition, and it affects man in his spatio-temporal existential condition, which is to say that it embraces past, present and future;

participation is the source and binding force of the community of believers, the latter being at present a community that is being formed and is growing toward its perfect form in an atmosphere both sacramental and christological. Every spiritual blessing is presented as a fruit of participation.

The true goals of "methexis." After speaking of the content of participation, we must now go on to point out its finalities or goals. These will help us understand the meaning of this participation which, as found in the Ambrosian liturgy, we prefer to call *methexis*. The nuances of intimate coparticipation, of vital adherence to and profound communion with the mystery thanks to the celebration, are such as to affect the entire existence of the faithful. The goals of participation are these:

a) Active participation is participation that is interior, close, deep. This interior participation must, of course, find ways of manifesting itself exteriorly. An analysis of the prayers shows the various attitudes the participants are to cultivate.[110] This amounts to saying that an external participation in worship is necessary because the very dynamics of participation call for it.[111]

But participation is the fruit of clearsighted reflection on and consciousness of the reality of the Church; this consciousness entails the perception of the communal nature of participation. There is not a text in the Bergamo Sacramentary that suggests an individual might be able to participate in isolation from the rest of the community.[112] The communal aspect and the personal aspect must, of course, always be taken together. If we are to understand *methexis*, we must keep this golden rule in mind: All of the faithful act together for the same end; participation has for its goal the rebuilding of the Church.

It is clear, then, that participation tends to a complete fulfillment: it tends to make the one authentic worship of God become part of the believer's life. It seeks to convert and transform Christians more each day into spiritual sacrifices that are offered to the Father in Christ by the power of the Spirit.

b) *Methexis* is a supremely vital activity. The agents of it are involved in it to the full so that they may offer Christ not only ritually but really: this is the existential *offerimus* that marks participation.[113] The ontological solidarity with Christ the God-man that has begun in baptism is deepened each day through a close ethico-moral solidarity with him; this new solidarity is at the same time a solidarity with eschatological overtones.[114] The *offerimus* leads to the reparation and restoration of one's total being, along with Christ. The idea and reality of participation imply a ceaseless possibility and need of liturgical action, because while we are *in via* we never attain to a complete possession but only to the partial possession which the very etymology of *participatio* (=*partem capere*, to obtain a part or share) asserts.[115]

CONCLUSION

I have presented, in a series of vignettes so to speak, the broad lines of the meaning of *participatio–methexis* as shown in the prayer texts of the Ambrosian eucharistic synaxis. In making the presentation I have tried to respect the limits set by a paper that aims at presenting information, as well as the framework and theme of this Twenty-Third Liturgical Week at Saint-Serge.

Despite the limits I have set on myself and the partial nature of the analysis I have made, I have shown how *methexis–participatio* embraces the moment of the liturgical action in order to pass thence into daily life conceived as a form of worship.

The faithful find sustenance for their lives in the saving event of Christ, who enters the history of each believer through the latter's interior, active, communal and integral participation in the supreme liturgical action, the eucharist.

The prayer texts show us a Christian liturgical life that participates in the life of Christ himself, so that participation becomes the prolongation in time and space of Christ's life.

Christ enters into the history of believers, begets divine life in them, nourishes and sustains them so that they may take ever deeper root in him. The effect of this salvific initiative is participation in the eucharist, which continues to make the new creation a reality in us, so that the entire existence of the faithful comes to bear this newness.

The development of Christian life is characterized, therefore, by a constant renewal, by the gift of self to God, and by the desire and commitment to live the saving mystery; it is marked, in other words, by an interior and profound participation in the eucharist that leads to a configuration to and a coparticipation in the life of the praying, offering, glorified Christ.

Pontifical Salesian University
Rome, May 24, 1976

Cyrille VOGEL

Is the Presbyteral Ordination
of the Celebrant a Condition
for the Celebration of the Eucharist?

Since the facts alone belong to history (underlying problems manifest themselves to theological reflection), the problem connected with the subject that concerns us here can be formulated quite simply: Do the documents that have come down to us show examples of eucharistic celebrants who were not also ordained ministers, ordained at least by presbyteral cheirotonia?[1]

A study of rituals, whether of the eucharist or of ordination, becomes possible starting only in about the year 200, and then only with reference to local communities. Before the break that occurs at the beginning of the third century literary evidence is too slight to permit an analysis that would differentiate between episcopate, prebyterate and deaconate, although these terms (without a clearcut context and without adequate delimitation) appear as far back as the apostolic period. The same must be said of the meaning to be assigned to such terms as "president of the community or assembly" (e.g., in Justin, *Apology I*, 65 and 67) and of the precise significance of some of these assemblies themselves (e.g., *Didache* IX, 1–X, 7, and XIV).[2]

A certain amount of evidence allows us to believe that, as far as ordination and the presidency of eucharistic gatherings was concerned, "heretical" groups such as the Marcosians, the Marcionites, and the Montanists, as well as the sects which make their appearance in some second- and third-century apocrypha differed very little, if at all, from "official" assemblies.[3]

I. RECALL OF CLASSICAL POSITIONS

A. *The Catholic Church*

Canon 802 of the Code of Canon Law reflects quite accurately the data of historical tradition: "Only priests have power to offer the sacrifice of the Mass."[4] From the end of the second century, even though there were at that time no traces as yet of ordination by cheirotonia as a specific rite, the celebrant of the eucharist has always and exclusively been a minister delegated thereto by hierarchic authorities. Thus Ignatius of Antioch says: "Do not regard any eucharist as authentic that is not celebrated under the presidency of the bishop or his delegate. Wherever the bishop is, let the community likewise be. . . . It is not permitted to baptize or to celebrate the agape apart from the bishop; on the other hand, whatever he approves God also approves. Everything done in this manner will be authentic and valid."[5]

This is not the place for examining once again the remarkably precise information given on cheirotonia and the eucharist in the Verona (or Hauler) Fragments, nos. LXVII to LXXII (a Latin version of the *Apostolic Tradition*, which is usually attributed to Hippolytus of Rome who died in 235).[6]

No ordination without cheirotonia, no celebrant of the eucharist without ordination: this seems indeed to be the universal practice, at least from the third century on. It is only the second part of this statement that will be discussed here.[7]

254

B. *The Eastern Church (both Orthodox and Non-Chalcedonian)*
All of the Eastern Churches are in complete agreement with the
Catholic Church in stating that the celebrant of the eucharist must
have received at least a presbyteral cheirotonia.

After a rather lengthy period of development, the tradition of the
Eastern Churches came to distinguish between *cheirotonia* (imposition
of hands with a view to episcopate, presbyterate and deaconate) and
cheirothesia (imposition of hands understood as a simple blessing for
ministers of less rank). The various euchologies ignore this verbal
distinction: the imposition of hands, whether we call it a cheirotonia
or a cheirothesia, is part of the ritual for ordination to all clerical ranks;
in this, the Eastern Churches differ from Latin practice. This factual
situation is of no importance here; it simply shows that the gesture of
imposing hands becomes nondeterminative if it is considered solely
from a ritual viewpoint and not given its ecclesial context.[8] The fun-
damental requirement remains: hierarchic ordination is required for
the celebration of the eucharist.

**C. *The Churches of the Reformation: Lutheran Church (Augsburg
Confession) and Reformed Church of France***
In keeping with their officially approved creedal books the two
Churches distinguish very clearly between *ordination* (also called consecration) of a pastor and *installation* of a pastor. Ordination is never
repeated, even after one or more interruptions of ministry, and it is
bestowed by the laying on of hands.[9] (In an Appendix, below, I cite,
for documentary purposes, the central part of the ordination of a
pastor. Oddly enough, this central part is highlighted in Prostestant
liturgical books by its typographical format; it is as though there were
a desire to call attention to the *verba essentialia*.[10])

The ritual of the Lutheran Church also states that "several candidates for the sacred ministry can be ordained in a single ceremony."
This is to accept the principle—which the early Church rejected—of
absolute ordinations (i.e., ordinations without relation to a concrete
and locally delimited ministry in a local church).[11]

We should add, however, that in the churches of the Reformation a
pastoral delegation is possible; in this case, the delegated pastor, *even if
he has received no cheirotonia,* is qualified to conduct the liturgy of the

word and to administer the sacraments. He receives a mandate, a pastoral mission, from hierarchic authorities, although the giving of the mandate does not find ritual expression in a laying on of hands; here, then, ordination and installation are one. The hypothesis that a baptized believer can be the minister of the Lord's Supper without having received at least this pastoral delegation seems to be excluded by all the decision-making bodies of the churches in question.

We know of only very rare exceptions to the remarkable constancy all Christian churches show when it comes to the ordination of the celebrant who presides at the eucharist. We shall review these exceptions here. Each document is located on a different plane. Strangely enough, there had not been, to my knowledge, any critical review of the dossier until Hugo Grotius (de Groot; died, 1645) undertook one.[12] Neither Gratian in his *Concordia discordantium canonum* nor Gregory IX in his *Decretales* nor Morin nor Thomassin cite the texts that are pertinent to our problem.[13]

II. A REREADING OF THE DOSSIER

The documents referring to a minister of the eucharist who is not ordained, at least by presbyteral cheirotonia, are few and of unequal value. Here is the list.

A. Eastern Versions of the Apostolic Tradition Attributed to Hippolytus of Rome

The passage in question is the well-known one on the "confessor." The text of this passage is available to us only in the Arabic, Ethiopic and Sahidic versions; it is missing in the Latin fragments edited by Hauler (the Latin version is from ca. 375-400). The Eastern versions are not completely in agreement among themselves; since this text, unique in the history of the Church, is so important, I shall give it here in the various versions at full length.

1. *Coptic (Sahidic) version*, ch. 34 (from W. Till and J. Leipoldt, *Der koptische Text der Kirchenordnung Hippolyts herausgegeben und übersetzt* [TU 58; Berlin, 1954], pp. 5-7):

256

"a) If a confessor (*homologetes*) has been put in chains for the name of the Lord, there is to be no imposition of hands on him for the ministry of deacon or presbyter, for *he possesses the dignity (time) of the presbyterate by the very fact of his confession (homologia)*.

"b) *But if he is to be appointed (kathistanai) a bishop, there is to be an imposition of hands*.

"c) On the other hand, if the confessor is one who has not been haled before the authorities and has not been condemned to chains nor imprisoned nor punished in any other way, but has simply been on occasion the victim of insults for the name of our Lord and has received some domestic punishment (*kolasis*), hands must be imposed on him for all the ministries (*kleros*) of which he is worthy, since he has confessed (his faith).

"d) When the bishop gives thanks (*eucharistein*) in the manner we have indicated, it is not necessary that he recite the identical formulas we gave above—as if he had to give thanks from memory—but each one is to pray as he can. If he is capable of pronouncing a solemn prayer in a fitting way, well and good. But if he is content with uttering a simpler prayer, nothing prevents him from doing so; his prayer must, however, be marked by solid orthodoxy."

2. *Arabic version*, ch. 24 (from J. and A. Périer, *Les 127 Canons des Apôtres* [PO 8; Paris, 1912]):

"a) If a confessor has been in chains for the name of the Lord, he is not to receive the imposition of hands when being invested with the functions of the deaconate or the priesthood, for *he has acquired the honor of the priesthood by his confession*.

"b) *But if he is raised to the episcopate, he is to receive the imposition of hands*.

"c) If he has borne witness to his faith without having been taken before the rulers, without having been condemned to chains or prison, and without having been placed in a very hard situation, but has received passing scorn on his person and been mistreated at home, then, having confessed his faith, he is to receive, by imposition of hands, all the degrees of priesthood of which he is worthy, and so is to be ordained.

"d) [Paragraph substantially the same as paragraph d of the Coptic version.]"

3. *Ethiopic versions,* cf. 24 (from H. Duensing, *Der aethiopische Text der Kirchenordnung des Hippolyt* [Abhandlungen der Akademie der Wissenschaften in Göttingen, Phil.-Hist. Klass, 3rd series, 32; Göttingen, 1946], pp. 37-39):

"a) If a confessor is put in chains at the tribunal for the name of Christ, they are not to impose hands on him for the ministry, since [the ministry] is the work of the deacon or rather of the presbyterium, and *he who confesses (the faith) already has the honor of the presbyterate* . . . [lacuna in the text].

"b) . . . *if the bishop is to install him, he [the bishop] is to impose hands.*

"c) If he who confesses (the faith) has not appeared before the judges and if he has not been afflicted in chains and has not been imprisoned nor fallen into suffering, but if they have derided him because of the Lord's name and he has suffered lesser torments, then if he is given the presbyteral ministry as suitable to him, then it is proper to impose hands on him and thus make him a presbyter, and the bishop is to give thanks in the manner we indicated earlier.

"d) [Paragraph substantially the same as paragraph d of the Coptic version.]"

The three versions are in agreement on the following points:

They distinguish very clearly between the "martyr" who has endured grave cruelty, and the "confessor" who has simply been humiliated or suffered less grievous vexations.[14]

The martyr is a presbyter by the fact of his confession; hands are not to be imposed on him, therefore with a view to this ministry. It follows, even if the text does not say so, that the martyr may exercise all presbyteral functions, the celebration of the eucharist among them, if the bishop is not present.

The "confessor" is not a presbyter by reason of his confession. If there is reason for doing so, hands are to be imposed on him in view of the presbyteral ministry.

Finally, all three documents agree that the imposition of hands is required for the episcopate, whether the candidate is a "martyr" or a "confessor."

If the martyr *is* a presbyter by reason of his confession and without any cheirotonia, this is very certainly because of the early Christian idea that without a special charism no one can endure torments for the faith. The martyr is thus, by definition, a charismatic being: he is a "perfect imitator of Christ," a person "possessed by Christ" and "filled with the Spirit." There is no room for conferring on him by cheirotonia a spirit he already possesses and without which he would not have been a martyr. As a matter of fact, the men who had suffered for the faith formed a real "stockpile" of presbyters on which the communities could draw at need.[15]

Apart from the presbyteral charism attributed to the martyr, the only other charism the *Apostolic Tradition* acknowledges is that of the healer, although this, of course, bears no relation to presbyteral functions. A complementary inquiry might well be made at this point to determine whether a martyr who later on *lost the Spirit* and therefore his charism due to sin, remained a presbyter.[16] A martyr who thus lost his presbyterate because he lost his charism would be in the same state of ritual destitution as the presbyter who "lost" his ordination because he had been deposed.[17]

The arrangement regarding the confessor appears later on only in documents that are closely connected with the *Apostolic Tradition*. I shall mention only one of these (because of its date): *The Canons of Hippolytus*, ch. 6, in the Arabic version (ca. 336-340) (edited by R. Coquin, PO 31/2 [Paris, 1966], p. 359):

"When a man has been worthy to appear before an assembly because of the faith and to endure suffering because of Christ, and then has been set free by acts of grace [Achelis: by gracious cancellation], he has in this manner been judged worthy of the dignity [or: responsibility] of the priesthood. Therefore he is not to be ordained by the bishop, since his confession was his ordination.

"But if he becomes a bishop, he is to be ordained.

"When a man has confessed and not undergone chastisement, he has indeed been judged worthy of the priesthood, but he is to be ordained by the bishop.

"If someone's slave has endured punishment for the sake of Christ, he too, in the same way, is a presbyter of the flock: although he has not received the mark (or: form, figure) of priesthood, he has nonetheless received the Spirit of the priesthood."[18]

This text introduces a distinction not founded in the Eastern versions of the *Apostolic Tradition,* a distinction based on the state of freedom or slavery. The free man who becomes a martyr is a presbyter by the fact of his confession, but the situation is different for a slave who becomes a martyr. The latter has indeed received the Spirit, but he does not therefore possess the "mark" or "figure" of the presbyterate. This *forma presbyteratus* can hardly refer to anything but the *state of freedom* required for the presbyterate. If this interpretation is correct, it follows, first of all, that by his martyrdom the slave attains both freedom and the presbyterate, and secondly, that as long as a slave remains a slave, he cannot receive the priesthood by a simple cheirotonia.[19]

The decisions in favor of the martyr were almost immediately, if not resisted, at least overridden by the hierarchy. This happened first and foremost in the North African communities, according to the testimony of Cyprian.[20] Approximately a century later, the *Apostolic Constitutions in Eight Books* are still emphasizing the hierarchy's control (this, despite the fact that the *Apostolic Tradition* is one of the *Constitutions'* sources), although the context is different. There is question now of confessing the faith, not before persecutors, but before "nations and kings."[21]

B. *The Testimony of Tertullian*

We shall look at two passages of Tertullian; they belong to two Montanist works (ca. 207-220) but do not deal with the Montanist priesthood. The question here is no longer of a presbyteral charism attributed to martyrs, but of presbyteral functions of a liturgical kind being exercised by nonordained laymen.[22]

1. *De exhortatione castitatis* VII, 2-6 (proposed translation):

"The Apostle directs that those chosen for priestly rank should be married only once. In fact, at the present time I know of digamists who have been stripped of their function. You may say to me: 'Well, the rest [the laity] are permitted to do what a certain number of individuals [the presbyters] are forbidden to do.' But we would be fools to think that what is forbidden to priests is allowed to laypersons. Are not we laypeople also priests? It is written: He has made us a kingdom and priests for God his Father (Rev. 1.6).

260

"The distinction between clergy and people is due to a decision of the Church, and the clerical office is sanctified [by God?] through the mediation of the assembled clerical order [i.e., the presbyterium]. *Where this order of the presbytery is not available, you, a layman, may celebrate the eucharist, you may baptize,* you may be your own priest; for, where two or three are gathered together, there the Church is, even if these three be laypersons.

"... *If then you have the right to do, in case of necessity, what a priest does,* then in the same way you must observe priestly discipline [i.e., monogamy], even when necessity does not give you occasion to use your priestly right. Or would you baptize once you had married for the second time? Would you celebrate the eucharist once you had married for the second time? How could a layman married for the second time be allowed to exercise priestly functions that are necessary for salvation, when this same right is taken from a digamous priest?

"But, you may say, it is precisely the necessity that excuses. No. There is no necessity that can excuse what is impossible. Therefore do not put yourself in the situation of a digamist, and you will not be in danger of doing, even in case of necessity, what a digamist is forbidden to do. It is God's will that we all be so disposed that in every circumstance we are able to perform the ritual actions. There is only one God and one faith; there must also be but a single discipline. . . . Besides, if laymen do not observe what is required of priest, how could there be priests chosen from among the laity?"[23]

2. *De monogamia* XII, 1-2 (proposed translation):
"At this point the other party advances a very clever argument. The clear proof, they say, that the Apostle permits remarriage [to the laity] is the fact that the Apostle imposes the yoke of monogamy [in the sense of a prohibition against *remarrying*] only on clerics. Therefore (they continue), what he prescribes only for some, he does not impose on all!

"But, is it not true that in this case he would not have imposed on bishops alone what he prescribes for all, unless at the same time he prescribed for all what he imposes on these same bishops? Did he not rather impose monogamy [in the sense of a prohibition against *remarrying*] on all because he imposed it on the bishops, and did he not impose it on the bishops precisely because he imposed it on all? After all, where do the bishop and clergy come from? Do they not emerge from the lay community? If, then, the obligation of being monogamous did not bind all, where would the monogamous men be found from among whom clerics are chosen? Would not a special order of monogamous laymen have to be established from among whom these clerics would be chosen? Of course, when occasion offers for resisting the clergy and swaggering at their expense, then we are quite ready to claim that we are all one and are all priests because (Christ) has made us all priests for God and the Father (Rev. 1.6). But, when we are urged to accept priestly discipline, *then we put aside our sacred vestments* and suddenly no longer regard ourselves as equals!"[24]

The two passages have the same polemical context, namely that monogamy, i.e., the prohibition against contracting a second marriage, is obligatory on all the faithful as well as being the rule for clerics. Tertullian develops his argument in a roundabout fashion, taking facts accepted by all as his starting point; otherwise his reasoning would lack not only force and relevance but even a foundation. The facts on which are all agree are these:

There certainly exists a difference between *ordo* and *plebs*, between clergy and laity, presbyters and faithful, but the difference is purely ecclesiastical in origin.

In case of necessity, when no presbyter is present, a layman exercises the liturgical functions of a presbyter: he baptizes; he celebrates the eucharist. In case of necessity he is a presbyter.[25]

It follows—and this is the goal of Tertullian's argument—that the obligations incumbent on presbyters are incumbent on the laity as well (therefore monogamy), precisely by reason of the presbyteral functions which a layman may be led to discharge in special circumstances.[26]

Nothing could be more alien to Tertullian's thinking than to imagine any distinction between *ordo* and *plebs* other than the one introduced by the Christian communities themselves. It is a purely functional viewpoint that calls for safeguarding the specific character of the various stages in the clerical *cursus* and maintaining the distinction between clergy and faithful people. The idea of the presbytery being a caste within the Christian community is not part of the African's vision of things. Even in his Catholic days Tertullian had acknowledged the right of laypeople to baptize in case of necessity. For the author of the *De baptismo,* however, baptism is the Christian sacrament par excellence, not to say the only Christian sacrament.[27] The ultimate consequence of maintaining that in certain circumstances all laypersons possess a ministerial presbyterate is a Church which, as a priestly body, is identical with an order made up exclusively of presbyters or else (and in Tertullian's thinking it amounts to the same thing) is composed exclusively of laypersons.

It is rather odd that the first liturgical function which the laity were historically recognized as having, in exceptional cases, namely, the right to baptize, should still be acknowledged today by all the Christian churches as belonging to all laypersons (even if not baptized), whereas the right to offer the eucharist is refused to these same laypeople. Moreover, these laypeople obtain without difficulty the right to teach, although this is a basic episcopal prerogative. It would seem that, from a theological viewpoint, the right to baptize and the right to teach should raise as many problems as does giving baptized believers the right to offer the eucharist.

APPENDIX

Ordination of a Pastor
[I offer here, by way of documentation, the central section of the ritual for the ordination of a pastor. The formulary and rubrics are common to both the Lutheran and the Reformed Francophone Churches. I follow the typographical format of the original: *Eglise réformée de France. Liturgie* (Paris, 1963), pp. 253-62; *Liturgie de l'Eglise évangélique luthérienne de France* 2 (1965), pp. 99-102.]

ORDINATION
Let us pray to God.
  The candidate kneels. The congregation kneels or bows:
  Lord God, heavenly Father, we thank you for the work of your Son, Jesus Christ, for his redemptive death, for his resurrection and for his ascension into glory. He it is who, through the Holy Spirit, has raised up apostles, evangelists and witnesses, and who, down the centuries, has given the Church the servants it needs. He it is who gives us this new pastor today. In thanksgiving and in joy we praise you, Lord.

The officiating pastor and his assistant(s) impose hands on the candidate:
WE PRAY YOU, ALMIGHTY FATHER, SEND YOUR HOLY SPIRIT ON OUR BROTHER N. WHOM WE CONSECRATE TO YOUR SERVICE AND ORDAIN A PASTOR IN YOUR HOLY CURCH, A MINISTER OF THE WORD AND THE SACRAMENTS.

When the imposition of hands has been thus accomplished, the officiant continues:

Lord God, who call weak and sinful men to so great a responsibility, let your strength be at work in the weakness of your servant. Keep him faithful, humble and courageous in proclaiming your gospel, undeterred by fear of men or moved by the desire to please them.

Grant that he may be fully human, a man who is able to hear and understand. Grant him prudence and discernment as well as all the gifts and aids he needs for the faithful exercise of his ministry.

Bless his home. Bless his work for your glory, for the building up of your Church and for the salvation of human beings. Then, after having served you in this world and having persevered to the end, may he be received with all your faithful servants into the joy of your kingdom.

Christopher WALTER

The Bishop
as Celebrant
in Byzantine Iconography

Ever since the sixth century the holy eucharist, in the form of the Communion of the Apostles, has been represented in Byzantine art. In addition to the famous miniature in the Rossano Gospels,[1] there exist two patens dating from the reign of Emperor Justin II, on which the Communion of the Apostles is represented.[2] Yet we must wait until the eleventh century before we find Byzantine art depicting the celebration of the eucharist by one or more bishops.[3] From this period on, however, the two subjects regularly appear together in the decorative art in the Byzantine apse. Before we examine further the iconographic theme of the bishop as celebrant, we will do well to recall quickly how eucharistic themes formed part of every apsidal program: the presence of Christ in his creation.

265

Christ's presence amid his creation takes two main forms: his physical presence to the eyes of angels and human beings, and his sacramental presence in the consecrated species. In the art of the pre-iconoclast period the emphasis is chiefly on the first of these two forms. The saints are those who saw Christ and acknowledged him to be God. The Blessed Virgin, St. John the Baptist and the Apostles acknowledged him during his earthly life; the angels see him in his glory, the prophets and martyrs saw him in a vision. Among the martyrs we may distinguish a special category: the iconodule martyrs who bore witness that the portrait of the God-Man that is painted on an icon is an authentic image of him.[4]

Over the centuries an important development took place in the teaching of the faith: the mystagogy or liturgical commentary replaced the sacramental catechesis. The purpose of the catechesis had been to give an exegesis of the biblical mysteries that are types of the eucharist; the mystagogy has for its point of departure the texts and ritual actions of the liturgy.[5] As a result, the commentator's focus of interest changes and he regards the liturgy as no less important than the scriptural stories as a source of knowledge (gnosis). Similarly, the second form of Christ's presence in his creation, namely through the sacramental species, acquires a new importance. And who makes Christ present in the eucharist? The celebrating bishop. Thus it is that in the *Historia Mystagogica*, the liturgical commentary attributed to Germanus, patriarch of Constantinople (died 733), we find this passage which is of great importance to us here: "The Church is heaven on earth, the place where the God of heaven dwells and acts. . . . It was prefigured in the person of the patriarchs, proclaimed in that of the prophets, established on that of the apostles, brought to perfection in that of the martyrs, and adorned in that of the bishops."[6]

In churches built or restored after the Triumph of Orthodoxy bishops no longer figure simply as martyrs or confessors; they constitute a new rank in the hierarchy of the saints. Initially, no location in the church is assigned especially to them, but in the course of the tenth century they find a place in the apse; since it is here that the altar is located, it is evidently the part of the church most suited to them. They are represented fullface; in most instances, among them are put John Chrysostom and Basil the Great, to whom the two principal versions of the Byzantine liturgy were attributed.

During the tenth and eleventh centuries the liturgy exercised a growing influence over the Byzantine soul. We see reflections of this in the various types of illuminated liturgical books: psalters, collections of homilies, lectionaries, and liturgy rolls. These last contained the prayers recited by the celebrant during the eucharist.[7] Other reflections are to be seen in the decoration of the churches. Let us look here at the decoration of the apse of Sancta Sophia at Ochrid.[8] I choose this church, which Bishop Leo rebuilt between 1037 and 1056, for two reasons: first, because the frescoes are well preserved, and second, because it contains the first dated example of an episcopal celebrant in Byzantine art.

The decoration in the apse of Sancta Sophia at Ochrid is especially rich from an iconographic viewpoint. The first form of Christ's presence, namely his physical presence to the eyes of creatures, is well represented: on the vault of the choir the Ascension; on the arch Christ being worshiped by the Blessed Virgin, the Prodromos (Forerunner) and the angels; on the calotte of the apse the Virgin and the Child Jesus. At the bottom of the calotte we see the Communion of the Apostles. Beneath this scene are numerous portraits of bishops, among them the patriarchs of Constantinople, Rome, Alexandria and Antioch.

The scene that particularly interests us is on the north wall of the apse; in the church of San Vitale in Ravenna they had used this wall, in the sixth century, for the Offering of Justinian. Above an altar there is a ciborium [baldachino]. Behind the altar are two deacons, each carrying a fan. On the extreme left are the laypeople attending the celebration, and, between them and the celebrant, three priests dressed in phenolion [chasuble] and epitrachelion [stole]. The bishop himself, wearing the omophorion [pallium] and epigonation [ornament suspended from the epitrachelion], is bending over the altar, on which are the chalice and the paten with the bread. In his hands he has a liturgy roll on which are written the words: *Kyrie ho Theos hemon ho ktisas hemas* . . . (Lord, our God, who made us). I need not tell you that they are from the proskomide prayer in the Liturgy of St. Basil.

The celebrant is therefore in the act of blessing the offerings. By way of comparison look at the image of Emperor Justinian making his offering at San Vitale; you will then be able to see the difference between a scene with imperial imagery and one with ecclesiastical imagery.

This picture of the blessing of the offerings in Sancta Sophia at Ochrid is the only one of its kind, as far as I know. But it does introduce a new stage in the development of apsidal decoration. At Ochrid the bishops painted on the wall of the chevet are seen fullface. In the church of St. Panteleimon at Nerezi, the bishops are no longer represented frontally but are turned toward a throne.[9] This church, commissioned by Alexius Comnenus, a member of the imperial family, was completed in 1164, or more than a century after the church of Sancta Sophia at Ochrid. There are some indications, in two other less well-preserved churches whose dating is also less sure, that this change took place during the second half of the eleventh century.

Let us look a little more closely at the frescoes in the church of St. Panteleimon. Eight bishops are represented. In the left-hand row are Gregory Thaumaturgus, Epiphanius, Gregory of Nazianzus, and John Chrysostom. In the right-hand row are Nicholas, Gregory of Nyssa, Athanasius and Basil. At the head of the two rows are the authors of the two great Byzantine liturgies. On their rolls are written texts that can be read rather easily. In each case the text is that of a prayer which the bishop reads during the eucharistic celebration; more specifically, it is a prayer found in the liturgy rolls. Gregory Thaumaturgus is reading the prayer of the catechumens: *Kyrie ho Theos hēmōn ho en hypsēlois katoikōn* (Lord, our God, who dwell in the heights). Epiphanius, the *Trisagion* prayer: *Ho Theos ho agios ho en hagiois anapauomenos* (Holy God, who take your rest among the saints). Gregory of Nazianzus, the prayer of the proskomide in the Liturgy of John Chrysostom: *Kyrie ho Theos ho pantokratōr ho monos hagios* (Lord God, ruler of all, who alone are holy). John Chrysostom, the prayer of the prothesis: *Kyrie ho Theos hēmōn ho ton ouranion arton* (Lord our God, who . . . the bread of heaven). Basil, the prayer at the Cherubikon: *Oudeis axios tōn syndedemenōn* (No one bound . . . is worthy). Athanasius, the prayer at the Lesser Entrance: *Despota Kyrie ho Theos hēmōn ho katasiēmas en ouranois* (Master, Lord, our God, who have established in heaven). Gregory of Nyssa, the prayer of the first antiphon: *Kyrie ho Theos hēmōn hou to kratos aneikaston* (Lord, our God, whose power is unmatched). Nicholas, the prayer of the second antiphon: *Kyrie ho Theos hēmōn sōson ton laon sou kai eulogēson tēn klēronomian sou* (Lord, our God, save your people and bless your inheritance).

The bishops, as I mentioned, are facing toward a throne. On the throne is a book; a dove is perched on the book, and behind the dove are the instruments of the passion. The usual iconographical name for this throne is the Hetimasia.[10] This kind of throne, empty of the deity but accompanied by a symbol of him, occurred in ancient art too. Christian artists easily adapted it to their purposes by introducing the symbols of Christ and the Holy Spirit.

From the twelfth century on, this manner of decorating an apse becomes widespread. Two converging rows of bishops, with each bishop carrying an inscribed roll, are depicted in the church of Kurbinovo, Macedonia, which was decorated around 1191.[11] This time, however, the rows of bishops converge not on a Hetimasia but on an altar. On the altar are the paten with the bread and the asteriscus; the artist has painted the Child Jesus in front of these. The proportions of his body are those of an adult rather than of an infant. Nonetheless, the cleaning of the fresco eliminated any doubt: the representation is of the Child Jesus and not of the dead Christ that is seen on an epitaphios.

It is not my intention to discuss in detail all the Byzantine churches which show, in their apses, two rows of bishops converging on an altar, with each bishop holding a liturgy roll. I propose rather to make a quick analysis of the components of this iconographic theme, and then to discuss the deeper meaning of the theme.

I. ANALYSIS OF THE ICONOGRAPHIC THEME

1. The Altar

The altar may be provided with a baldachino. Frequently, two angels dressed as deacons, or a single seraph stand there, waving a fan. In some twelfth-century representations Christ is not present; instead, on the altar are placed the chalice, the paten, the asteriscus and some times a roll. These liturgical utensils are also found on the altar when Christ is present. Christ may be resting on the paten; sometimes he is covered with a veil and the asteriscus. In some exceptional cases he is represented half-length, either in a chalice or directly on the altar. In some images his body is represented as excessively long, as at Kurbinovo, but usually natural proportions are observed. Whereas the dead Christ is regularly represented on the Epitaphios, examples of the dead Christ lying on an altar are rare and late.[12]

2. The Inscriptions

The word *melismos* (dismemberment, breaking) is written beside the Child Jesus for the first time in the church of St. Nicholas at Manastir (Macedonia), which dates from 1272.[13] From this time on, the word appears occasionally beside the Child. As far as I know, it is not translated into Slavic in representations of this scene that occur in regions settled by the Slavs. But in the church of Sts. Joachim and Anne at Studenica we do find the following inscription: "The Lamb of God is sacrificed and slain for the life of the entire world."[14] I do not know whether it is a liturgical text that is being cited.

In the church of the Holy Apostles at Seirikari (Crete), which is dated 1427, the Child Jesus is shown covered with the asteriscus and accompanied by this inscription: *Christos prokeitai kai melizetai Theos* (Christ is set forth and God is broken for us).[15] Again, I do not know whether this is a citation of a liturgical text. In any case, the reference to the *prokeimenon* or the laying out of a dead person is clear. This same inscription is found on an enamel in the Hermitage Museum, on which Christ is represented as dead, lying on a mat and guarded by two angels.[16]

3. The Liturgy Rolls

The texts on the liturgy rolls are taken in almost all instances from the Liturgies of John Chrysostom or Basil. In the vast majority of cases the words are the *incipit* of a prayer that is recited by the celebrant and written down in the liturgy rolls which he used during the service at this period. In collaboration with Gordana Babić of the Serbian Academy in Belgrade I have called attention to the Greek inscriptions in about forty churches.[17] We found about thirty different texts. The assignment of a text to a particular bishop usually follows no rule. Except for Basil and John Chrysostom whose respective rolls refer to the prayers at the Cherubikon and the prothesis, only Cyril of Alexandria has a monopoly on a prayer. However, in a good number of churches the text written on the rolls refers directly to the consecration.[18]

When a church is located in a region in which the language spoken at the time was Slavic, the texts were translated into the local language. The first example of a roll with a text in Old Russian is at Staraya Ladoga near Novgorod.[19] The paintings date from about 1167. The first example in Old Serbian is in the church of the Virgin at Studenica, dated 1208/9.[20] We did not undertake a systematic study of these Slavic inscriptions although they are very interesting in several respects. The first liturgical manuscript in Old Serbian dates from the second half of the fourteenth century, that is, almost two centuries after the first roll inscriptions in Old Serbian. The inscriptions are thus a valuable witness to the early state of the liturgy in a Slavic language.

4. *The Bishops*

How was the choice made of the bishops to be represented? The names of Basil and John Chrysostom needed no justification. Those of Athanasius, Nicholas, Cyril and Gregory of Nazianzus are invoked even today in the rite of the prothesis. This doubtless explains their presence. For the others we must look, I believe, to liturgical texts: either to the various *Hermeneia* and *Diataxis* or to the different versions of the prothesis rite that were current at the time. I shall cite only one example given by Trempelas. To the bishops already mentioned, this text adds Spyridion, Amphilochus, Epiphanius, Abercius, Gregory Thaumaturgus, Gregory of Armenia, Gregory of Agrigentum, and Gregory of Nyssa. But these are all bishops who are represented in apsidal decoration.[21]

The bishops, bowing and holding rolls in their hands, are turned toward the altar. Only the two leaders, John Chrysostom and Basil, at times make a noncustomary gesture. They may bless the offerings on the altar or be making ready to cut the child into pieces, as for example in the prothesis chapel at Ljuboten or in the chapel attached to Panagia Mavrotissa at Kastoria.

II. DEEPER MEANING OF THE ICONOGRAPHIC THEME

Now and then a historian of Byzantine art asks: What point in the liturgy is being represented in these pictures? The answers given vary rather widely: Great Entrance, the blessing at the proskomide, the breaking and distribution of the bread. These various answers can be justified by arguments, but in my opinion none of them hits the mark. The artist may doubtless have intended at times to *point to* a precise moment in the liturgical action, but I do not think he intended to *represent* it. I make an exception, of course, for the picture of the blessing of the offerings in Sancta Sophia at Ochrid, but the image here does not properly exemplify the iconographic theme of which we are speaking. I also exclude representations of the heavenly liturgy; in these the artist seems to have chosen the moment of the Great Entrance.[22]

The celebrating bishops, as depicted on the wall of the apse, constitute a special iconographic theme. If we are to grasp its underlying significance, we must study it in its physical context and then carefully follow its development. I have stressed the fact that from the very beginning the main theme of apsidal decoration was the presence of Christ in the world. Now, when an artist represents the bishops celebrating the liturgy, he is highlighting the presence of Christ in the liturgy. This iconographic theme should therefore be considered in conjunction with the Communion of the Apostles, which it often accompanies, and with the presence of Christ in the flesh and in heaven.

The presence of Christ in the liturgy is a dogma that lends itself to several interpretations. The liturgy is both figure and reality, and, at various moments in it the manner of Christ's presence can change. For example, Christ is present in figure in the bread of the prothesis, but he is really present in the consecrated bread. This real presence in turn can be explained in different ways. Some of the iconoclast theologians saw the consecrated species as being the true icon of

Christ. Gregory Palamas, however, uses a more nuanced language: "Whoever looks with faith upon the mystical table and the bread of life that is placed upon it sees there the subsistent Word of God who has become flesh for us and dwells among us."[23]

In studying these images, then, we must take the representation of Christ as our starting point. In the beginning, a symbol of Christ, namely, the Hetimasia, was preferred to a physical representation. When the incarnate Christ replaced the Hetimasia, a further choice had to be made: the Child Jesus or the dead Christ. It is difficult to explain why in the majority of cases the Child Jesus was chosen. An image with almost the same meaning as those we are examining exists in the church of the Source of Life at Samari in Messenia. Here the dead Christ is accompanied by a citation from John 6.54: "He who eats my flesh and drinks my blood has eternal life."[24]

It is also possible that in the iconography of the celebrating bishops the dead Christ preceded the Christ Child, for, as we have seen, in the first representation of this theme, the Child has the proportions rather of an adult. In the view of a commentator on the liturgy like Nicholas of Andida, who died shortly before the creation of this iconographic theme, the liturgy represents the entire life of Christ from birth to death.[25] Yet tradition perhaps favored the choice of an infant rather than an adult. In addition to the well-known text of the sixth-century Pseudo-Cyril of Jerusalem, in which he speaks of a child who brings to earth a sacrifice according to the Law (a text cited by Nicetas Chroniates in the christological controversies of the twelfth century), there is a less well-known story which I shall tell you.[26]

A fifth-century monk dared to claim that the consecrated bread is not the body of Christ but an "antitype" of the body. But then in a vision he saw an angel descending from heaven to an altar and there slaying a little child, cutting up the body and distributing the pieces to the communicants.[27]

For myself, I attribute the choice of the Christ Child rather than the dead Christ to the growing importance of the prothesis rite during the period when this new iconographical theme was created. In the central rites of the liturgy the primary emphasis is on the connection between the sacrifice of the cross and the eucharistic sacrifice, but in the rite of the prothesis the texts refer to the birth of Christ. In his commentary prior to the creation of the theme Nicholas of Andida likewise parallels the rite of the prothesis and the Nativity.

The underlying meaning of these images of the celebrating bishop is thus clearly christological. How then should we define the role of the bishop in these pictures? The bishops represented are always *holy* bishops. They are present by a twofold title: first, because by reason of their office they make Christ present in the consecrated bread; and, second, because they have borne witness to the presence of Christ in the bread.

Once the underlying meaning of the image has been established, we can call attention to details which add a secondary meaning. If the bishop has a knife in his hand and is getting ready to cut up the body of the Child Jesus, there is certainly an allusion either to the rite of the prothesis or to the Melismos. If the word Melismos is written near the body of the Child Jesus, it is in order to emphasize the point that all who receive communion eat the body of Christ. Finally, if the words of consecration are written on the liturgy rolls, the purpose is to underscore the fact that the celebrant's action makes Christ present in the consecrated species. Thus the Byzantine artist shows that his primary concern is always with the communication of a truth of Christology rather than the faithful representation of an event or ceremony.

Institut de études byzantines
Paris

Gaston WESTPHAL

Role and Limit
of Pastoral Delegation to Laymen
for the Celebration of the Eucharist
in the Protestant Reformed Churches

PRELIMINARY REMARKS

In their discipline the Reformed Churches of France acknowledge *ordination-consecration, installation* and *delegation*.

The first of these, as Michel Bouttier reminds us, involves "a life-long and full-time commitment (are these two conditions interconnected and indispensable?). It cannot be repeated and has for its object a ministry exercised throughout the Church and acknowledged by the entire Church.

"*Installation* looks to ministries of limited duration and circumscribed range. It is intelligible, I think, only with respect to a specific community.

"Finally, *delegation* would be for a particular short-term mission."*

275

When I speak of the "Protestant Reformed Churches," I exclude churches of the episcopal type, such as the Lutheran Church of Sweden, the Anglican Communion, and others, which have never envisaged even the possibility of a practice of delegation, since the principle of apostolic succession is what it is.

I shall be speaking above all of the situation in France from Calvin's time to our own, and principally in terms of the current ecclesiastical discipline. I have not come across any systematic studies of the question, and I speak as a pastor who has experienced one type of custom as compared to others.

Recent synods, both Lutheran and Reformed, have devoted their attention to the *Mission of the Church and the Variety of Ministries* (report of Lods, Deltheil, Bouttier and others); some solid studies of ministry have appeared (von Allmen, Ganoczy, Faith and Order, Dombes Group, Taizé) which will help us somewhat to put an often confusing state of affairs into perspective.

I excuse myself in advance for dealing with such a ticklish question. It is perhaps more from what I do not say than from what I say in my effort to gain a little clarity (the unanimous judgment of the synods is that we are really "in the soup" when we take up the question of ministries), that you will obtain some light on the matter.

Provisional Conclusion
As far as the synodal discussions in France are concerned: "The synodal documents bear traces of the thinking of J.-J. von Allmen, who sees the foundation of ministry as christological, and of Hébert Roux (an observer at Vatican II) who sees it as being ecclesiological. For the former, ministry is located at the point where head and body join, and depends directly on the head although it functions within the communion of the body. For the latter, ministries are part of the body and provide it with its articulations; they have no privileged relation to the head. Who will unwind the skein? Which comes first: the chicken or the egg? Thank God, we do not have any clarity on this point: the messianic community is in the service of him who is coming, and will never be able to enclose him within a system.

"Two poles thus emerge from the New Testament. One of them reminds the Church that she does not draw her life from any initiative of her own: it finds expression in the episcopate, along with ordination and aggregation to the universal college. The other bears witness to the outpouring of the Spirit on the entire community: it manifests itself in the responsibilities accepted by one or other person, *including delegation momentarily given to this or that member for a limited task.* Ecclesial functions gravitate between these two poles, but they are always subordinate to the primary goal of service, that of the gospel and reconciliation. . . . Our difficulty comes first and foremost from the fact that we do not see clearly the specific task of the Reformed communities that are scattered throughout France at the end of the twentieth century!"**

Theology will try in vain to settle and decide whether apostolic succession requires, in addition to its manifestation in the messianic people as a whole, a vertebral prolongation into "ministry." This question, which the Dombes agreement attempts to resolve, has left its mark on all the discussions.   *The Author*

"The practice of delegation to laymen, in some of the Reformed Churches, may obscure the real significance of the ordained ministry and be an obstacle to unity."[1] Thus speaks the second publication of the Dombes group in its work on the delicate problem of the reconciliation of ministries.

What precisely is the situation?

The Church is born of the Holy Spirit; it is gathered together and built up by the word of God; but its real foundation is the one perfect sacrifice which Christ offered, once and for all, on the cross. It is to be expected therefore that the action which renders this sacrifice present should also play an essential constitutive role. It is also right that this same action, more than any other, should be distinctive of the pastoral ministry. It is generally acknowledged that the pastor is the one with the right to baptize and to celebrate the Holy Supper; on this point the specific character of the pastoral ministry is clearest and least subject to challenge. In mission countries, it is the missionary and not the catechist or the evangelist who is authorized to perform these actions.

In France, however, we sometimes find the faithful asking: Why is it that we, the Church of the word, can at a moment's notice replace the pastor as preacher of the Sunday sermon, while when it comes to celebrating the eucharist we require a pastoral delegation from the synodal authorities?[2] In this whole matter the question puts a sure finger on the deepest, most sensitive and most crucial aspect of the problem.

We have the beginning of a reply in the fine text from the Second Helvetic Confession which Professor von Allmen uses in his admirable book *Le saint ministère* [The Sacred Ministry] as a basis for discerning the convictions and intentions of the sixteenth-century reformed churches:

"Furthermore, the Apostles of Christ give the title 'priest' to all who believe in Jesus Christ. They do so, not because all have a ministry, but because all the faithful have been made kings and priests, or sacrificers, by Christ and can therefore offer spiritual sacrifices to God. Priesthood and ministry are therefore two quite diverse and different things. Priesthood, as we have just said, is common to all Christians, but ministry is not. Consequently, we do not strip the Church of the ministry when we deny to the Church of Christ a priesthood as found in the Roman Church."[3]

The Catholic tradition—although very unyielding on the necessity of priestly power as a condition for sacramental validity—and the Orthodox tradition as well[4] admit that in case of pressing need an unordained believer, and even a non-Christian, can celebrate the sacrament of baptism. We must admit that this offends Protestant sensibilities. For, although one of the faithful can baptize by pastoral delegation, this occurs only very, very rarely. In fact, a child not baptized by a pastor would be felt by others to have been questionably baptized (and we do not have the problem of Limbo!).

As for the Lord's Supper, the eucharist, it is perfectly true that pastoral delegation may be temporarily given to a devout believer and good Christian (usually a lay preacher, a presbyteral councillor, a deacon, a parish assistant, a theological student who has completed his studies, or a candidate for the sacred ministry). But, in my view, Christ is so much the author of the eucharistic sacrament that it is he and he alone who presides and invites, while the ministry of the celebrant, no matter who he may be, should disappear in the dazzling light of the Lord who is really present in the mystery of his death, resurrection and intercession.

The real presence of Christ in the eucharistic celebration is possible:

1) by reason of the presence of the gathered Christian people who want to communicate;

2) by reason of the proclamation of the word that purifies and prepares;

3) by reason of the solidarity of this liturgy with the liturgy of other communities spread throughout time and space;

4) and not by reason of the presence of the celebrant alone. The latter exercises a function in the service of the Christian people.[5] A function creates its specific organ; the celebrant acts rather as the "herald" of the sacrament: that is, as a human instrument he correctly pronounces the words of institution and the epiclesis. In a sense, the sacrament is a mystery that remains external to him; the only thing that really counts is the authority behind his delegation.

In short: whereas in Catholicism (if I understand it correctly), the author of the sacrament, in the case of baptism, is the words of institution and the water, in Protestantism (but not in early Calvinism, as we shall see) the author of the sacrament of the Lord's Supper is primarily the memorial of the Lord's words, their actualization by means of the bread and the wine.

We must keep in mind that in Protestantism apostolic succession is a succession of doctrine, not of persons.[6] The Church exists, not where the bishop or pastor is, but in the well-known formula of the Augsburg Confession and almost all the Reformed confessions of faith, "where the word of God is preached with purity and the sacraments are rightly administered."

According to the medieval doctrine of the Mass, "sacrificers who have received power from a bishop daily offer the very body and blood of the Lord as a sacrificial victim for the living and the dead,"[7] instead of actualizing, along with the people, the one perfect sacrifice which the only supreme sacrificer, Jesus Christ, offered once and for all. This teaching stimulated the Reformers to rethink the ministry in terms of service and not of power; the eucharist in terms of a communal meal that requires the spiritual sacrifices of the entire believing people, and not as the personal property of a clergy who dispose of it for a financial consideration; apostolic succession in terms of a comprehensive apostolic succession involving a return to the sources, a doctrinal fidelity to the thinking of the apostles as set down in the Bible, the interior witnesses of the Holy Spirit, and a calling, and not of ordination to the episcopate.

But let us turn now to the texts. The idea of delegation is a relatively recent Reformed tradition, especially (I think) in France, since my German, Dutch and English colleagues of the European churches at Luxembourg do not seem to have this practice of delegation in their respective churches, chiefly, I fear because despite the undeniable eucharistic renewal of recent years, the Lord's Supper is often celebrated in those churches only four or five times a year. Consequently, there is rarely any need of replacement for the pastor.

Calvin was against delegation. We read in the *Institutes*:

"It is also pertinent here to know that it is wrong for private individuals to assume the administration of baptism; for this as well as the serving of the Supper is a function of the ecclesiastical ministry. For Christ did not command women, or men of every sort, to baptize, but gave this command to those whom he had appointed apostles. And when he ordered his disciples to do in the ministering of the Supper [Matt. 28.19] what they had seen him do—while he was performing the function of a lawful steward [Luke 22.19]—he doubtless willed that they should follow his example in it."[7a]

I turn now to a brief examination of the ecclesiastical discipline, ancient and modern, of the Reformed Churches of France and the *Coutumier* now in force. To begin with, we may remind ourselves, in the words of Crespin, that:

"this discipline is simply a set of spiritual statutes established by the express command of God for several purposes: that the word of God might be preserved in its integrity and not corrupted or falsified; that the sacraments might not be contaminated by sinners; that those who have *the responsibility of teaching the Church and watching over it might be called to their responsibilities in a lawful manner and might exercise them in due fashion*; that those who devote themselves to the preaching of the gospel might put it into practice by a good and holy life, observing obedience to God and the magistrates and every duty of charity to their neighbor. The purpose of it all is that God should be glorified, the reign of his Son promoted, and his Church built up and purified of all scandal. This, in summary, is the goal of all the steps taken and discussions held in ecclesiastical consistories and synods."[8]

In this kind of "Canon Law" the main principles of these spiritual statues point to a single goal: "The sacraments—this visible word of God— are in turn to be celebrated with the greatest care; they must be protected against all profanation."[9]

There is no valid baptism unless it is administered by a person who has received a call. There is to be no adult baptism that has not been preceded by religious instruction, the effectiveness of which is to be seen in the catechumen's profession of faith. Wherever a Church exists, baptism is to take place at the assembly of the faithful. Godparents who come from elsewhere must bring testimonials from their own Church. If the Church has not yet taken visible form in a place, the Lord's Supper may not be celebrated. Children are not admitted to the Lord's Supper before the age of twelve, and persons from elsewhere who take part in it must bring adequate testimonials from their own pastor. The Supper is celebrated only four times a year. The intention in this prescription was to elicit respect for the Supper and hedge it in with precautionary measures. But, says the ancient discipline, once this respect is secured, it is desirable that the Supper be celebrated more frequently, "because it is very profitable that the faithful be exercised and increase in faith through the reception of the sacraments; moreover, the example of the early Church urges us to this frequency."

As for Church government, there is to be no preeminence given to individuals. Instead of a hierarchy of individual persons there is to be a hierarchy of bodies: consistories, colloquiums, provincial synods, national synod. The last named "can decide and resolve all ecclesiastical issues in a definitive manner." Deacons were simply to serve the poorest of the poor. Elders were permitted to conduct public prayer, "following the regular formulary," when no pastors were present, but pastors alone could preach the word and administer the sacraments. Our forefathers liked to repeat the words of St. Paul: "Let everything be done in a seemly and orderly way. God is not a God of confusion." Du Moulin's *Traité de la vocation des pasteurs* [Treatise on the Vocation of Pastors] (1618) and various ordination sermons that have come down to us[10]—to take but a few examples—show us that this discipline was really put into practice.

The first changes date from 1685 after the revocation of the Edict of Nantes by Louis XIV and the arrest or exodus of the pastors. Jurieu writes as early as 1686: "The sending of one pastor by another is simply a form that should be observed in times when the Church is at peace but which may be bypassed in times of need. The abiding rule is that a true call comes from the people and from the choice made by assemblies."[11]

Claude Brousson and the Confession of Faith (article 31) tell us:

"We believe that no one may by his own authority presume to govern the Church and that government may be assumed only through election, as far as this is possible and God allows. We add this qualifying clause especially because it has been necessary at times and even in our day (when the Church was in a corrupt state) for God to raise up people in an extraordinary manner in order to restore a decayed and desolate Church."

We also have the testimony of a certain Colognac, surnamed Dauphine, whom the "people" appointed their pastor despite his protestations of inadequacy. Having been forced to accept, he justified his call when he was arrested later on and brought before Bâville. Question: "Who appointed you a preacher?" Answer: "God and those who heard me preach." "It was pointed out to him that he had preached without receiving a mission for it, even though the discipline of the 'reformed' religion forbade him to do so. He answered that he had an extraordinary mission, proper to an extraordinary time like the present."

Antoine Court, struggling against a type of fanaticism in about 1715 (an analogue today would be the charismatic movement) and Paul Rabaut in the period when the French Revolution was drawing near were to rediscover the ancient discipline.[12]

It is time for us to come to present-day practice. This practice is rather a deviation when viewed in the light of early Reformed thought. It is the especially tragic situation of the Reformed Churches in France that has contributed to make it a reality.

As a matter of fact, it was not until recent years that the current Discipline, which was largely taken over from the ancient Discipline, explicitly envisaged the case of a layman presiding at the Lord's Supper. When it did so, it spoke rather of a "delegation for parish duties" (*délégation de desserte*):[13]

"*Discipline of 1938, article 18:* Pastoral delegation confers the right to exercise fully the duties of the sacred ministry—but only for a time and for the care of a particular parish—on individuals who have not received ordination, and in particular on divinity students, candidates for the sacred ministry, and candidates in theology. They must be a least twenty-one years old, present testimonials to their religious character, and fulfill the conditions set down in articles 13 and 14. Pastoral delegation is never granted for longer than a year, but it can be renewed.

"The request for delegation is addressed by the person concerned to the Commission on Pastoral Ministry, along with a favorable decision by the Regional Council. However, delegation can be granted by the Regional Council if it is not to be valid for more than three months.

"*Modification of 1970:* Delegation for parish duties gives one of the faithful the right to exercise the ministry of word and sacraments in a specific place and for a determined period of time. In case of urgent need, Regional Councils have power to grant it for fifteen days."[14]

The limits set upon this delegation are immediately clear: temporary, for a particular place and not universal, and granted chiefly to persons already in the seminary and in process of becoming a pastor or something close to it.[15]

Apart from such persons as have just been mentioned, delegation is most frequently given to a presbyteral councillor, one of the well-known "elders" of our Churches, men chosen for a six-year term that can be renewed. The exhortation in the liturgy for the installation of these councillors (not a cheirotonia but a commitment and a blessing) shows the importance of this ministry which the Church confers through the pastor in charge:

"Councillors, in whom the Church has just placed its trust, you are to share with the pastor the burdens involved in the Church's ministry.

"You must discern, implement and coordinate the various special ministries which God gives to the Church for the carrying out of his plan.

"You must watch over the assembly of the faithful, *the celebration of the liturgy* and the instruction of children and adults.

"You must work for the rule of fraternal love and the maintenance of Church unity. You must keep the secrets entrusted to you.

"You must see to the management of the community's material possessions.

"In your daily life, in your profession, and in civic life you must try to be witnesses of your Lord.

"*You must be regular in attendance at worship and at the Lord's Supper, finding therein the strength and inspiration you need. You must help to celebrate the liturgy when you are called to do so.*

"You must be diligent in attending the meetings of the Council. You must take all measures to protect the life of the Church. You must prepare for and apply the decisions of synods.

"You are urged to continue your personal formation while on the Council and by all the means the Church puts at your disposal.

"Put at the service of the Lord and his Church the gifts and talents you have received from God. Carry out your mission zealously, so as to help the faithful to hear the word of God and bear witness by their lives to their fidelity to Jesus Christ in our world."[16]

The assembly then rises to welcome its councillors and possibly its new deacons as well (suitable liturgy). The pastor then extends his hands and says: "In the name of the Father, of the Son and of the Holy Spirit, we appoint you to the ministry of presbyteral councillors in the church of . . ., where, by the grace of God, you are to exercise its various responsibilities toward your brothers and sisters. May the Lord who is faithful make you likewise faithful in all things by the power of his Spirit. Amen."

Does not this blessing of a presbyteral councillor resemble somewhat "the presbyteral ordination of the celebrant" as "a condition for the celebration of the eucharist," of which Professor Vogel has spoken?[17]

Pastor Bruston, "protesting" president of the Dombes Group for several decades, wished that in addition to this "installation" of the councillors, a more specific cheirotonia be given to one or other member of the Council for the specific ministry of substitute celebrant for which that given individual might have greater gifts.

It is important to grasp the present reasons given for pastoral ordination as the latter is understood by Pastor Jean Bosc and Pastor Greiner in accord with the Reformed and Lutheran Churches of France (four of its regions). They understand it less in the line of the sacramentality of orders as Calvin did,[18] for the latter view explains the possible distortion of the specific character of pastoral ministry:

"The Lord Jesus Christ, who lives in and for his body which is the Church gives her various ministries so that she may be built up in him and carry out in the midst of the world the mission he entrusts to her.

"The ceremony of ordination is the liturgical action during which the Christian community publicly acknowledges these ministers, invests them with their office and, by means of the laying on of hands, calls down on them the help of the Holy Spirit. By doing this the ministers already in office receive the newly ordained into their ministry with the approval of the entire people of the Church. They acknowledge his responsibilities and the authority that goes with his office.

"Solemn ordination is *not an action* by which *ministers in office transmit a power to the newly ordained in virtue of a material succession*.

"Moreover, *neither does the act of ordination introduce the person who receives it into a clerical state that would set him apart from the people of the Church or confer a special character on him*. The Lord Jesus Christ is the only source of authority in a ministry, and the ministry, whatever it be, *is a function of the entire Church* that is entrusted especially to one member of the community.

"It remains true, however, that when in submission to the Lord Jesus Christ and in expectation of his gifts, they welcome a new minister, those who receive him into their ranks acknowledge him as thereby part of the succession of the Church's ministers, a succession guaranteed by the fidelity of Jesus Christ."[19]

The liturgy of ordination is fortunately much more christological. For in the explanation I have just quoted the impression is too much (in my opinion) that the pastor is a "permanent representative" of the priesthood of the faithful, the baptismal priesthood. It is this view of the pastorate that emerges in recent demands for the modification of the present ordination liturgy (the Lutheran-Reformed ritual), demands coming from the younger generation who often see the pastorate as simply one form of lay life. They argue for the change on the grounds that: there is not explicit reference in the preamble (of the ordination liturgy) to the universal priesthood; and the "life-long" commitment should not be made explicit.[20]

The extensive documentation which Michel Bouttier, president of the Theological Institute at Montpellier, gathered and explained a few years ago on the subject of the "Assembly of the Christian Community and its Ministries"[21] made it clear that there are two currents of thought. There is the *ecclesiological* line of thought: the pastor is needed for the "well being" of the Church and is simply a baptized Christian who lives his baptism full-time; and the *christological* line: the pastor is part of the very "being" of the Church and derives his ministry not from his baptismal priesthood (although he is first and always a baptized Christian) but from a distinct and different calling and from Christ. The laying on of hands is not renewable at each change of assignment but is definitive, being given once and for all.

Some persons rejoice at the present dearth of pastors, because they think this will force the laity to exercise their universal priesthood. For, note well, among us the laity are not like a great pile of well-stacked, carefully squared wood; they are a living tree with branches large or small that provide shade and fruit at the end of the year. Improvisation and spontaneity are relatively easy for them.

Experience shows that, while a parish without a pastor may get along fairly well for a while, in the long run there is no exercise of the ministry of unity; consequently, the parish is united to another and the pastorate suppressed.

CONCLUSION

The role of pastoral delegation to the faithful is to show that there is no impassable gulf between the baptismal priesthood and the priesthood of pastors. The emphasis is placed not on the being of the pastor, that is, on a dignity he would possess unconditionally, but on the aspect of service to a Christian community. The pastor is not a super-Christian; he does not say "his Mass"; he is consecrated solely in view of a ministry. As Jean Bosc puts it: "Baptism is not only the sign of the purification and regeneration of the person who receives it; it is also the anointing that appoints him to priestly, kingly and prophetic service. Consequently baptism gives the Christian a ministerial responsibility within and with the community."[22]

And the document of the World Council that was used at Nairobi reminds us:

"Baptism is both God's gift and man's commitment. It leads to a growth 'to mature manhood, to the measure of the stature of the fulness of Christ' (Eph 4.13). In and through this growth baptized believers must present to the world the new generation of liberated human beings. Their joint responsibility here and now is to bear witness together to the Church, the world, those who have not yet heard the gospel and those who reject it. It is in such a communion of witness and service that we shall learn once again the meaning of God's gift to his entire people."[23]

I do not have the time here to show that in a sense the monk's call to devote himself to the Absolute is at the bottom of every authentic Christian life and that the search for God in contemplation as distinct from the search for him in the neighbor is not a difference of nature, since the specific element in Judeo-Christian revelation is that the God we seek is found with the help of our neighbors, especially the least among them. Congar testifies: "While I was a prisoner I saw Protestant laymen celebrating the Supper in the absence of a pastor; I even helped them prepare their sermons. . . . It is also a fact that in some rural areas of France—Ardèche, Tarn, etc.—elderly Protestants who possess a deep biblical formation are fully capable of being excellent community leaders."[24]

The concern of the Reformers was to get back to the structure of the early Church with its profound sense of conciliarity. Just as in the language of the New Testament it is difficult to define precisely the meaning and scope of such terms as "elders" (Paul's farewell to the elders of Ephesus), "overseers" (*episkopoi*), etc., so also at a Synod of the Reformed Church of France it is often quite difficult to distinguish a layman from a pastor, except that the latter, who has studied theology, is in a better position than the layman to assert himself, at least verbally.

The limitation of this pastoral delegation, which Catholics sometimes think is a regular practice in Protestantism, is, on the contrary, that it exists only in certain parts of the Reformed Church, and that it is subject to strict ecclesiastical regulation and is used only in very precisely defined cases (an automobile accident on Christmas eve, for example).

Whereas an ordained pastor can celebrate at the call of any parish whatsoever, delegation given to one of the faithful is always temporary and can be used only in the parish in which this member of the Church lives or in its dependent chapels. The ancient discipline did not permit a pastor to celebrate before his ordination; nowadays, such a celebration is regarded as a "trial run": reliance is placed on the interior call and ongoing, controlled preparation of the future pastor or parish assistant.

And in fact there is need of knowing the congregation to whom one will give a share of the Supper. A layman knows the members of his parish, and although nowadays each individual accepts the responsibility of approaching the holy table or absenting himself from it, the danger of giving communion to just anyone is avoided.

Calvin wrote: "And here also we must preserve the order of the Lord's Supper, that it may not be profaned by being administered indiscriminately. For it is very true that he to whom its distribution has been committed, if he knowingly and willingly admits an unworthy person whom he could rightfully turn away, is as guilty of sacrilege as if he had cast the Lord's body to dogs. On this account, Chrysostom gravely inveighs against priests who, fearing the power of great men, dare exclude no one. 'Blood,' he says, 'will be required at your hands.'"[25]

A presbyteral councillor who moves away does not take his function with him. He must now make his qualities known in his new parish. The problem of distribution is as important as the problem of consecration. Here, once again, is Calvin: "He [the Lord] has therefore given us a Table at which to feast, not an altar upon which to offer a victim; he has not consecrated priests to offer sacrifice, but ministers to distribute the sacred banquet."[26] The food is a prefiguration of the heavenly banquet: "The manner of binding and loosing [power of the keys] is not only shown repeatedly in the whole of Scripture, but Paul best states it when he says that the ministers of the gospel have the command to reconcile men to God and at the same time to exercise vengeance upon those who shall reject this benefit [2 Cor. 5.18; 10.6]."[27]

Brother Max Thurian (who was kind enough to preach the sermon at my ordination at Le Creusot, eight years ago) has this to say:

"Preaching, baptism and the eucharist belong together in the ordained ministry of the Church, for these actions make up the embassy or mission of pastors. They are actions that make known the work of Christ as the Head who is active in his body the Church. Pastors receive the charisms they need in order to be the signs of this priestly activity of Christ among the people of God. This is the ordinary and normal situation of the ministry of word and sacraments in the Church.

"If pastoral or missionary necessity calls for more men in the ministry, we should not derogate from the presbyteral vocation and ordination by multiplying pastoral delegations to laymen for functions proper to the ministry. Rather we should consider the possibility of developing the deaconate or even developing a presbyterate that would be conferred on men who practice a profession and would work only part-time for the Church. . . . The presidency of the eucharistic celebration has always been reserved to the bishop or the presbyter, while the deacon has exercised only secondary functions. But would it not be possible, in urgent cases and the absence of pastors, for the Church to use its authority and grant deacons delegation to preside at the eucharist?"[28]

In its little work *Vers une même foi eucharistique?* [*Toward a Single Eucharistic Faith?*], the Dombes Group (I was a cosigner of this text) expresses itself quite well on the subject of the presidency of the eucharist.

"32. In the eucharist Christ gathers and feeds his Church by inviting it to the meal over which he himself presides.

"33. The sign of this presidency is a minister whom Christ has called and sent. The mission of ministers has its origin and standard in that of the apostles; it is passed on in the Church by the imposition of hands and the invocation of the Holy Spirit. This transmission implies the continuity of the ministerial responsibility, fidelity to apostolic teaching, and conformity of life to the gospel.

"34. *The minister shows that the assembly* [the same can be said of the clergy] *is not the proprietor of the action it is performing, that it is not master of the eucharist; it receives the eucharist from Another, namely Christ living in his Church. While continuing to be a member of the community, the minister is also the envoy who makes known God's initiative and the bond that unites the local community with the other communities of the universal Church.*

"35. In their mutual relations the eucharistic assembly and its president live out their dependence on the one Lord and High Priest. In its relationship with the minister the assembly exercises its royal priesthood as a gift from Christ the priest. In his relationship with the assembly the minister exercises his presidency as a service to Christ the Shepherd."[29]

On the Orthodox side, Father Afanassieff shows how in the course of history the laity were isolated from the sacramental action as a result of the doctrine that the ecclesial consciousness had absorbed: a doctrine that opposed the laity to the clergy and especially to the ecclesiastical hierarchy because they were not consecrated (according to the sixty-ninth canon of the Trullan Synod they could not even enter into the sanctuary [*thysiasterion*]—except, according to Balsamon in his commentary, by royal authority), that led to the separate communion of the priests behind the iconostasis and of the faithful in the nave, etc.[30] Afanassieff then writes:

"In its practice the Church has departed from its original customs in two ways: on the one hand, the real participation of the faithful in the eucharist has become the exception; on the other hand, this sacrament is celebrated more often than in the primitive Church. These two facts are quite significant for they show *the gradual elimination of the doctrine of the priestly dignity of the laity*. . . . We come back to what was said earlier: the sacramental realm is open to the laity, and without their participation the Church cannot accomplish her liturgical actions.

"The people officiate in a different way than their *proistamenoi* do, but everything in the Church takes place by their joint action. 'That they may all be one; even as thou, Father, art in me, and I in thee, that they also may be in us' (John 17.21)."

ABBREVIATIONS

AAS
Acta Apostolicae Sedis

AL
Archiv für Liturgiewissenschaft

Amb
Ambrosius

Bib
Biblica

CCL
Corpus Christianorum, Series Latina

CSCO Iberici
Corpus Scriptorum Christianorum Orientalium, Scriptores Iberici

CSCO Syri
Corpus Scriptorum Christianorum Orientalium, Scriptores Syri

CT
Concilium Tridentinum. Diariorum, actorum, epistularum, tractatuum nova collectio. Ed. Goerres Society.

CTom
Ciencia Tomista

Abbreviations

DACL
Dictionnaire d'archéologie chrétienne et de liturgie

DBS
Dictionnaire de la Bible: Supplément

DTC
Dictionnaire de théologie catholique

EL
Ephemerides Liturgicae

ETL
Ephemerides Theologicae Lovanienses

HBS
Henry Bradshaw Society

HJ
Historisches Jahrbuch

JL
Jahrbuch für Liturgiewissenschaft

JTS
Journal of Theological Studies

LBK
Lexikon für byzantinische Kunst

LJ
Liturgisches Jahrbuch

LQF
Liturgiegeschichtliche Quellen und Forschungen

LTK
Lexikon für Theologie und Kirche (2nd ed.)

MD
La Maison-Dieu

Mus
Le Muséon

OC
Oriens Christianus

OCA
Orientalia Christiana Analecta

OCP
Orientalia Christiana Periodica

OSyr
L'Orient Syrien

PG
Patrologia Graeca

PL
Patrologia Latina

PO
Patrologia Orientalis

QLP
Questions liturgiques et pariossiales

RAC
Reallexikon für Antike und Christentum

RB
Revue biblique

RBK
Reallexikon für byzantinische Kunst

REB
Revue des études byzantines

RevSR
Revue des sciences religieuses

RHE
Revue d'histoire ecclésiastique

RivL
Rivista Liturgica

RQ
Revue de Qumrân

RT
Revue Thomiste

Sal
Salesianum

SC
Sources chrétiennes

SE
Sacris Erudiri

Trad
Traditio

TU
Texte und Untersuchungen zur Geschichte der alchristlichen Literatur

NOTES

Preface (pp. ix–xi)

1. Cf. O. Cullman, *La foi et le culte de l'Eglise primitive* (Neuchâtel, 1963), p. 120.

2. Cf. A.M. Triacca, "Il Mistero dell Chiesa, communità di salvezza," in V. Miano (ed.), *Corso intriduttivo al Mistero della salvezza* (Zürich, 1971), pp. 93-114.

3. Cf. U. Valeske, *Votum Ecclesiae II. Interkonfessionelle ekklesiologische Bibliographie* (Munich, 1962), pp. 201-204, for bibliography on the "figures," "analogies," "metaphors," and "allegories" used in the effort to express the many-sided reality of the Church. See also L. Cerfaux, "Le immagini simboliche della Chiesa nel Nuovo Testamento," in G. Baraúna (ed.), *La Chiesa del Vaticano II. Studi e commenti alla Costituzione dommatica "Lumen Gentium"* (Florence, 1965), pp. 299-313.

4. Cf. the papers of the Sixteenth Week of Liturgical Studies at the Saint-Serge Center, *Le Saint-Esprit dans la Liturgie* (Bibliotheca Ephemerides Liturgicae, Subsidia 8; Rome, 1977).

5. Cf. on this subject the very important papers of the Twenty-second Week of Liturgical Studies at the Saint-Serge Center, *Liturgie de l'Eglise particulière et Liturgie de l'Eglise universelle* (Bibliotheca Ephemerides Liturgicae, Subsidia 7; Rome, 1976).

6. Cf. S. Lyonnet, "La nature du culte dans le Nouveau Testament," in *La Liturgie après Vatican II. Bilans, études, prospectives* (Paris, 1967), pp. 357-384.

7. Cf. 1 Cor 14, where St. Paul sets down the principle: "Omnia ad aedificationem fiant" (*panta pros oikodomēn ginesthō*) (v. 26).

8. Cf. Acts 2. 42.

9. Cf. Jn 11.51-52.

10. Cf. Eph 4.12-13.

11. Cf. E. Alberich, "Il Mistero della Chiesa e la Liturgia," in *La Costituzione dommatica "De Ecclesia"* (Reggio Emilia, 1963), pp. 76-110 at p. 107.

12. Only P.-M. Gy has not submitted his paper.

13. The interest aroused by this meeting may be judged by the reports about it: B. Neunheuser, "Liturgische Studienwoche in Saint-Serge, Paris, vom 28. Juni bis 1. Juli 1976," *Erbe und Auftrag* 52 (1976), 389-392; Ph. Harnoncourt, "Liturgische Studienwoche am 'Institut de Théologie Orthodoxe St. Serge' in Paris," *LJ* 26 (1976), 183-184.

Allmen, Jean-Jacques von (pp. 1-11)

1. *Le Catéchisme de Heidelberg* (1563), Question 103, explaining the sixth commandment (3rd ed.; Neuchâtel, 1963), p. 49. For the German original cf. W. Niesel, *Bekenntnisschriften und Kirchenordnungen der nach Gottes Wort reformierten Kirche* (Munich, 1938), p. 175.

2. Cf., e.g., *La Confession helvétique postérieure*, French tr. of 1566 (Neuchâtel, 1944), pp. 126-127.

3. Ibid., p. 128. Among the countless references that might be given cf., e.g., F. Schmidt-Clausing, *Zwinglis liturgische Formulare* (Frankfurt a. M., 1970), pp. 31, 67; J. Calvin, *La forme des prieres et chantz ecclesiastiques*, 1542, in *I. Calvini opera selecta* II (Munich, 1952), pp. 12-13; J.M. Barkley, *The Worship of the Reformed Church* (London, 1966), pp. 13, 21.

4. *Connaître Dieu et le servir* (Neuchâtel, 1945), pp. 188-189.

5. Cf. my study, *Le saint ministère selon la conviction et la volonté des Réformés du XVIe siècle* (Neuchâtel, 1968), p. 154, n. 67.

6. Schmidt-Clausing, op. cit., p. 79, n. 50; "Les Ordonnances Ecclésiastiques de l'Eglise de Genève, 1561," in Niesel, op. cit., p. 51.

7. This is also the tradition at Basel, St.-Gall, etc. Zürich will adopt it at the end of the sixteenth century, since in 1598 the organs which Zwingli had removed from places of worship were restored; cf. Schmidt-Clausing, *Zwingli als Liturgiker* (Göttingen, 1952), p. 83.

8. Cf. *La forme des prieres et chantz ecclesiastiques*, facsimile of the original edition with a short account by P. Pidoux (Kassel and Basel, 1959) no pagination.

9. Ibid. [ed. cited in n. 3, above], p. 13.

10. Ibid., p. 15.

11. R. Staehlin is right in saying that "the hymns of the Reformation are undoubtedly the most important contribution the movement made to the history of the liturgy": "Die Geschicte des christlichen Gottesdientes," in *Leitourgia* 1 (Kassel, 1954), p. 59.

12. *La forme des prieres*, p. 17.

13. V. Pollanus, *Liturgia sacra (1551-1555)*, ed. by A.C. Honders (Leiden, 1970), pp. 79 and 83.

14. Cf. Schmidt-Clausing, *Zwingli als Liturgiker*, pp. 76ff.; W.D. Maxwell, *The Liturgical Portions of the Genevan Service Book* (London, 1965), pp. 210ff.; H.O. Old, *The Patristic Roots of Reformed Worship* (Zürich, 1975), index under "Vestments."

15. Op. cit., p. 105.

16. *La forme des prieres*, p. 19.

17. The Reformers protested loudly against baptism administered by lay people, especially by midwives. Cf. my *Saint Ministère*, pp. 84, 152-153, nn. 40ff.

18. Pollanus, op. cit., pp. 239-263; cf. also *La forme des prieres*, p. 48.

19. I shall not discuss here the relationships between the order of reformed worship and the traditional order of the Mass. W.D. Maxwell, op. cit., and in his *An Outline of Christian Worship, Its Developments and Forms* (London, 1958), pp. 87-119, tries to show the two are connected, but I do not find his arguments fully convincing.

20. *La forme des prieres*, p. 20; and Pollanus, op. cit., p. 61.

21. *La forme des prieres* appeared in a format which enabled it to become the "prayerbook" of the members of the Church of Geneva. The same was probably the case with the other liturgies of the time, since the later custom had not yet arisen of printing the liturgies in such a voluminous form that for practical purposes only pastors have access to them.

22. See especially Schmidt-Clausing, *Zwingli als Liturgiker* and *Zwinglis liturgische Formulare*; H.G. Hageman, *Pulpit and Table* (London, 1926), especially pp. 13-36; E. Bersier, *Projet de révision de la Liturgie des Eglises réformées de France* (Paris, 1888), especially pp. VII-XVII; Barkley, op. cit., pp. 10-37; Maxwell, the two works cited. I refer the reader especially to Old, op. cit., which I regard as especially important.

23. Cf. Schmidt-Clausing, *Zwinglis liturgische Formulare*, pp. 31, 66-67.

24. Ibid., p. 30: "Danksagung und Frohlocken."

25. Oddly enough, in the editions of 1525 and 1529—and it is probably implied in the description Zwingli gave Francis I of the Zürich liturgy in 1531; cf. Schmidt-Clausing, op. cit., pp. 33, 59—in v. 26 Zwingli omits the words "until he comes" and replaces them with: "you recall and *you extol* the death of the Lord" (*auskünden und hoch preisen*). Why this change? Because the Greek word *achri* ("until") can also have a final meaning (*in order that* he may come) and if it were thus taken, the Mass could be interpreted as a sacrifice of intercession, which it is not in Zwinglian theology.

26. 1 Clem 40, 5; 41, 1.

27. The cups too are wooden. The bread is unleavened. The faithful who have scruples about taking the eucharistic bread for themselves can receive it from the hand of the deacon without touching it. Cf. Schmidt-Clausing, op. cit., pp. 71, 91, n. 113.

28. H.O. Old is right in saying: "It is not . . . primarily by means of the texts which are recited that the thanksgiving is expressed, but rather it is through an action. Nothing could be further from the truth than to say that Zwingli dissolves the worship into words, or that it is purely a matter of reflection" (op. cit., p. 44).

29. Cf. J. Schweizer, *Reformierte Abendmahlsgestaltung in der Schau Zwinglis* (Basel, n.d.), passim; J. Courvoisier, *Zwingli, théologien réformé* (Neuchâtel, 1965), pp. 68-84.

30. Barkley correctly observes that the aim of the Reformation was "to make the Church a worshipping community" (op. cit., p. 13).

31. *La forme des prieres*, p. 16.

32. Ibid., p. 129.

33. After the singing of the first table of the Law, the pastor greets the people: "The Lord be with you" (*La forme des prieres*, p. 19), but, since the people do not reply, "And with your spirit," the pastor says (ed. of 1545 and thereafter), "The Lord be with *us*." Cf. Pollanus, op. cit., p. 29.

34. Cf. Pollanus, op. cit., p. 93; *La forme des prieres*, p. 48.

35. Pollanus, op. cit., p. 61.

36. These deacons are often future pastors or pastors already ordained but as yet without a parish. Cf. Maxwell, *The Liturgical Portions*, p. 133; Pollanus, op. cit., p. 231. The custom will grow, starting, it seems, in the Churches of Scotland, of appointing readers whose task it is to read the scriptures until the congregation is fully assembled; the pastor becomes active only when the congregation is complete. Cf. Maxwell, op. cit., pp. 177ff.; Barkley, op. cit., p. 26.

37. Cf. Schmidt-Clausing, *Zwingli als Liturgiker*, pp. 81ff.

38. *La forme des prieres*, facsimile ed. [The French original is not only in verse form but in rhyming couplets; no effort has been made to reproduce the rhymes.—Tr.].

39. Cf. Hageman, op. cit., p. 21.

40. Cf. *La Liturgie ou la maniere de celebrer le Service Divin* qui est établie dans les Eglises de la Principauté de Neufchatel & Vallangin (Basel, 1713), and my book, *L'Eglise et ses fonctions d'après Jean-Frédéric Ostervald* (Neuchâtel, 1947), pp. 84-96.

41. *La Liturgie . . .*, Preface (no pagination).

42. Cf. Bersier, op. cit., passim.

43. Proof of this is the remarkable effort that has led to the publication of the collection *Psaumes, Cantiques et Textes pour le culte* (Lausanne, 1976), which was introduced into the Reformed Churches of French-speaking Switzerland in September 1976.

Andronikof, Constantin (pp. 13-27)

1. G. Florovsky, "Eucharistie et sobornost'," *Pout'* (Paris), no. 19 (November 1929), p. 14.

2. *De sacra liturgia*, 94 (PG 155:280-281).

3. *De virginibus velandis* II, 2.

4. *De unitate*, 4, and *Epistulae* 45, 59, 69, etc.

5. *Sermo* 227 (PL 38:1099).

6. *De Trinitate* VIII, 15 (PL 10:248).

7. Ibid., VIII, 17 (PL 10:249).

8. *Homiliae in 1 Corinthios* 24 (PG 61:200).

9. *Homiliae in Matthaeum* 83 (PG 58:744).

10. *Commentarium in Evangelium Joannis* XI, 11 (PG 74:560).

11. Ibid.

12. Ibid., X, 2 (PG 74:342).

13. Ibid., XI, 11 (PG 74:561); cf. *De SS. Trinitate Dialogus I* (PG 75:697).

14. Ibid.

15. *Catecheses Mystagogicae* 4, 3 (SC 126, p. 137).

16. *De imaginibus* III, 2 (PG 94: 1348).

17. *De fide orthodoxa* IV, 13, 86 (PG 94:1154).

18. Cf. especially Maximus the Confessor, *Mystagogia* 8 (PG 91:688), where he follows the text of the prayer for the "lesser entrance" in the ancient version of the Liturgy of St. John Chrysostom; cf. R. Bornert, *Les commentaires byzantins de la divine liturgie du VIIe au XVe siècle* (Paris, 1966), pp. 108-109.

19. Theodore of Mopsuestia, *Homiliae catecheticae* 15, 43.

20. Theodore of Studios, *Antirrheticus* II.

21. *Homilia* 60 (ed. Oikonomos, p. 250).

22. *De vita in Christo* IV, 4 (PG 150:585B); cf. Gregory Palamas, *Confessio fidei* (PG 151:765).

23. *De divina liturgia* 37, 6; 38, 1 (SC 4 bis; pp. 228-231; PG 150: 452CD).

24. Secret after the prayer "behind the ambo," Liturgy of St. Basil.

25. *Adversus haereses* IV, 14, 2 (SC 100, pp. 543-545).

26. Ibid., V, 14, 2 (SC 153, p. 191); cf. V, 1, 1 (SC 153, p. 21); V, 14, 2 (SC 153, pp. 187); etc.

27. Roman Liturgy, Secret for the ninth Sunday after Pentecost in the old Missal; now the prayer over the gifts for the second Sunday in Ordinary Time, for Holy Thursday, and for the votive Mass of the Blessed Sacrament.

28. Cyril of Jerusalem, *Catecheses baptismales* III, 16.

29. Cyprian, *De oratione dominica*, tr. Reveillaud, in *L'Eucharistie des premiers chrétiens* (Paris, 1970), II, p. 16.

30. Irenaeus, *Adversus haereses* IV, 18, 5.

31. Leo the Great, *Sermo 3 in Nativitatem* (PL 54:203).

32. Epiclesis of Addai, cited in Theodore of Mopsuestia; cf. B. Botte, "Les anaphores syriennes orientales," in *Eucharisties d'Orient et d'Occident* (Paris, 1970), 2, p. 16.

33. Athanasius, *Epistula ad Serapionem* IV, 19 (PG 26:665).

34. Cabasilas, *De divina liturgia* 37, 3 (PG 150:452B).

35. Irenaeus, *Adversus haereses* IV, 18, 4.

36. Narses of Edessa, *Homilia* 21: *De mysteriis Ecclesiae et de baptismo*, tr. by Ph. Gignoux, in *Initiation chrétienne* (Paris, 1963), p. 210.

37. Cf. Rom 8.24; Theodore of Mopsuestia, *Homiliae Eucharisticae* II.

38. Cyril of Jerusalem, *Catecheses mystagogicae* III, 3 (PG 33: 1097); cf. John Damascene, *De fide orthodoxa* IV, 13.

39. Cyril of Alexandria, *Commentarium in Evangelium Joannis* XI, 12 (PG 74:565).

Arranz, Miguel *(pp. 29-59)*

1. B. Botte, *La Tradition Apostolique de Saint Hippolyte. Essai de reconstitution* (LQF 39; Münster/W., 1963). See also Dom Botte's edition with translation: Hippolytus of Rome, *La tradition apostolique d'après les anciennes versions* (SC 11bis; Paris, 1968).

2. *La Liturgie d'Hippolyte* (OCA 155; Rome, 1959; new ed., 1970). Cf. also J. Magne, *Tradition Apostolique sur les charismes et Diataxeis des Saints Apôtres. Identification des documents et analyse du rituel d'ordination* (Paris, 1975). I regret very much that I did not learn of this last-named book until my study was completed and I did not have the time for a possible revision of some of my own inferences.

3. Cf., e.g., B. Altaner, *Précis de patrologie* (Paris–Tournai, 1961), p. 102; J. Quasten, *Patrology* 2 (Utrecht–Antwerp, 1953), pp. 185-186; E. Amann, "Testament de Notre Seigneur Jésus Christ," DTC 15:194-200; H. Leclercq, "Messe, XXVI: Le Testament de Notre Seigneur," DACL 11:622-624.

4. E. Renaudot, *La perpetuité de la foi* (Paris, 1782), 2, pp. 573ff. Cf. also J. W. Bickell, *Geschicte des Kirchenrechts* 1 (Giessen, 1843), pp. 183ff.

5. P. de Lagarde, *Reliquiae Juris ecclesiastici antiquissimae syriace* (Leipzig, 1856), pp. 2-19.

6. I.E. Rahmani, *Testamentum Domini Nostri Jesu Christi* (Mainz, 1899) [henceforth: Rahmani, with page number].

7. A. Vööbus, "Nouvelles sources de l'Octateuque Clémentin Syriaque," *Le Muséon* 86 (1973), pp. 105-109; *The Synodicon in the West Syrian Tradition* (CSOC Syri 161-162; Louvain, 1975).

8. R.-G. Coquin, "Le Testamentum Domini: Problèmes de tradition textuelle," *Parole de l'Orient* 5 (1974), pp. 165-188.

9. F.X. Funk, *Das Testament unseres Herrne und die verwandten Schriften* (Forschungen zur christlichen Literatur und Dogmengeschichte 2; Mainz, 1901). Cf. also his *Didascalia et Constitutiones Apostolorum* 1 (Paderborn, 1905).

10. For bibliography see J. Quasten, *Monumenta eucharistica et liturgica vetustissima* (Florilegium Patristicum 7), pars 5 (Bonn, 1936), p. 236.

11. F. Nau, *La version syriaque de l'Octateuque de Clément* (Paris, 1913) [henceforth: Nau, with page number].

12. E. Schwartz, *Über die pseudoapostolischen Kirchenordnungen* (Strassburg, 1910); R.H. Connolly, *The So-called Egyptian Church Order and Derived Documents* (Texts and Studies 8/4; Cambridge, 1916); cf. Botte, op. cit. (1963), p. X, and op. cit. (1968), pp. 12-13.

13. M. Skaballanovich, *Tolkóvy Tipikón* 1 (Kiev, 1970), pp. 72ff.

14. N. Uspensky, *Chin vsénoshchnogo bdénia v Gréchiskoi i Rússkoi Tsérkvi* (Leningrad, 1949), pp. 1ff. Cf. my review in OCP 42 (1976).

15. P. Vintilescu, *Incercari de istoria Liturghiei: Liturghia crestina in primele trei veacuri* (Bucharest, 1930), pp. 107-123; cf. Costin Vasile, "Scrierea pseudoepigrafa 'Testamentum Domini' ca izvor pentru istoria cultului crestin," *Studii Teologice* 17 (1965), pp. 204-218.

16. P. Chrîstou, "Diathîkî tou Kyriou hîmôn," in *Thrîskeutikî kai îthikî Egkyklopaideia* 4 (Athens, 1964), pp. 1136-1137.

17. M. Arranz, "Le 'Sancta Sanctis' dans la tradition liturgique des églises," AL 15 (1973), pp. 59-60.

18. L. Bouyer, *Eucharist: Theology and Spirituality of the Eucharistic Prayer*, tr. C.U. Quinn (Notre Dame, 1968), pp. 88-90, 119-135, and the whole of ch. 6, "The Patristic Eucharist and the Vestiges of the Primitive Eucharist," pp. 136-186.

19. Nau, 24-25; Rahmani, 18.

20. Nau, 25; Rahmani, 20.

21. Nau, 26; Rahmani, 22.

22. Nau, 28; Rahmani, 26.

23. Botte, op. cit. (1968), p. 42; henceforth I shall cite only this edition (SC 11bis).

24. See n. 2, above. N.b.: Hanssens always calls the *Tradition* the *Church Order*.

25. *The Ancient Church Orders* (Cambridge, 1910); cf. J. Cooper and A.J. Maclean, *The Testament of Our Lord translated into English from the Syriac, with an Introduction and Notes*

(London, 1902). N.b.: Maclean, like Hanssens, uses the name *Church Order* for the *Tradition*.

26. Botte, op. cit., p. 68.

27. Nau, 25; Rahmani, 20.

28. Nau, 28; cf. ibid., n. 5: most of the qualities demanded of a bishop are listed in 1 Tim 3 and Tit 1, and passed from there into the *Didascalia,* ch. 6 and the *Apostolic Constitutions;* Rahmani, 26.

29. Nau, 28; Rahmani, 26.

30. Nau, 20; Rahmani, 32. In the specification of the hours for prayers we deliberately depart from Nau whose translation is excessively free and inaccurate.

31. Nau, 32; Rahmani, 34.

32. Nau, 36; Rahmani 46.

33. Nau, 37; Rahmani, 50.

34. Cf. n. 14, above.

35. Nau, 40; Rahmani, 58.

36. Nau, 44; Rahmani, 66.

37. Nau, 44; Rahmani, 66.

38. Nau, 44; Rahmani, 68.

39. Nau, 45; Rahmani, 70.

40. Nau, 47; Rahmani, 76.

41. Nau, 49; Rahmani, 78.

42. Nau, 49; Rahmani, 80.

43. Nau, 50; Rahmani, 82.

44. Nau, 52; Rahmani, 88.

45. Nau, 53; Rahmani, 90.

46. Ibid.

47. Botte, op. cit., p. 62.

48. Nau, 54; Rahmani, 92.

49. Botte, op. cit., p. 64; cf. p. 27, where Botte is of a different opinion.

50. Hanssens, op. cit. (1970), p. 88.

51. Ibid.

52. Ibid., p. 22.

53. Nau, 54; Rahmani, 94.

54. Nau, 56; Rahmani, 98.

55. Botte, op. cit., p. 66.

56. Nau, 57; Rahmani, 100.

57. Ibid.

58. MSS *Barberini gr. 336, Leningrad gr. 226, Coislin gr. 213* (A. Dmitrievsky, *Euchologia* [Kiev, 1901], p. 996), *Grottaferrata B.b.I.*

59. Nau, 58; Rahmani, 104.

60. Hanssens, op. cit., pp. 90-91.

61. Ibid., pp. 22-23.

62. Botte, op. cit., p. 67.

63. Hanssens, op. cit., p. 88.

64. Ibid., p. 91.

65. Nau, 59; Rahmani, 104. N.b.: Rahmani thinks the Syriac text has been altered in order to place the subdeacon ahead of the reader.

66. Nau, 59; Rahmani, 106.

67. Nau, 60; Rahmani, 108.

68. Botte, op. cit., p. 68; Hanssens, op. cit., pp. 92-93.

69. The division of the *Testamentum* into two books—the first two of the *Octateuch*—is peculiar to the Syriac recension of the work; it forms but a single book in the Coptic and Arabic versions. The Coptic and the Arabic *Octateuch* have the *Apostolic Order* as a second book and the *Church Order* or *Tradition* as a third. Since the Syriac *Octateuch* omits the *Church Order* it is obliged to divide the *Testamentum* into two books in order to make up an *Octateuch*; cf. Hanssens, op. cit. (1959), pp. 53ff.

70. Nau, 61; Rahmani, 110.

71. Hanssens, op. cit. (1970), pp. 94-95.

72. Nau, 64; Rahmani, 116.

73. Nau, 64; Rahmani, 118.

74. Nau, 65; Rahmani, 120.

75. Nau, 67; Rahmani, 126.

76. Nau, 69; Rahmani, 130.

77. Nau, 70; Rahmani, 130.

78. Nau, 70; Rahmani, 132.

79. Botte, op. cit., p. 100.

80. Nau, 71; Rahmani, 134.

81. Botte, op. cit., p. 102.

82. Nau, 72; Rahmani, 136.

83. Nau, 73; Rahmani, 138.

84. Nau, 74; Rahmani, 140.

85. Nau, 74; Rahmani, 142.

86. Ibid.

87. Ibid.

88. Nau, 75; Rahmani, 144.

89. Nau, 76; Rahmani, 147.

90. Botte, op. cit., p. 118.

Botte, Bernard (pp. 61-72)

1. B. Botte, *La Tradition apostolique de saint Hippolyte. Essai de reconstitution* (LQF 39; Münster/W., 1963[1], 1972[4]); idem, *Hippolyte de Rome. La Tradition apostolique* (SC 11bis; Paris, 1968). The numbering of the chapters is the same in all three editions. In the following footnotes, the first page number refers to the editions of 1963 and 1972, while the page number in parenthesis refers to the Paris edition of 1968.

2. Ch. 1, p. 3 (39). Cf. also pp. XXIV-XXV in the Münster editions and p. III in the Paris edition.

3. Ch. 2, pp. 5-7 (41-43).

4. 1 Cor 12.28.

5. 1 Cor 13.13.

6. Ch. 2, p. 5 (41).

7. For the bishop, ch. 2, p. 9 (45): "Pour out the power that comes from you, the power of the sovereign Spirit." For the priest, ch. 7, p. 21 (57): "Grant him the Spirit of grace and counsel proper to the presbyterium." For the deacon, ch. 8, p. 27 (63): "Grant the Spirit of grace and zeal."

8. Ch. 21, pp. 47, 51-53 (83, 87-89).

9. Ch. 3, p. 9 (45).

10. Ch. 4, p. 11 (47).

11. Ibid., p. 13 (49).

12. Ibid., p. 17 (53).

13. Ch. 35, p. 83 (119); ch. 41, p. 89 (125).

14. Ch. 25, p. 65 (101).

15. Ch. 41, pp. 91-97 (127-133).

16. Ch. 15, p. 33 (69).

17. Ch. 20, p. 43 (79).

18. Ch. 19, p. 41 (77).

19. Gal 3.16.

20. Pliny the Younger, *Epistulae* X, 96-97.

21. Ignatius of Antioch, *Ad Philad.* 4, ed. by P.-Th. Camelot (SC 10; Paris, 1951), pp. 142-144 and p. 142, n. 4.

22. Cf. Jn 3.5.

23. Ch. 21, p. 55 (91).

24. Ch. 17, 18, 19, pp. 39-41 (75-77).

25. Ch. 20, pp. 43-45 (79-81).

26. Ibid., p. 43 and p. 42, n. 1 (79 and n. 1).

27. Cf. Gen 22.18.

28. Gal 3.16.

29. Alleluia for the fourth Sunday of Advent in the Missal of Pius V. Used in the new *Ordo lectionum* in the list of Alleluias for the season of Advent. Cf. Ps 39.18; 69.6.

30. Ch. 21, p. 45 (81).

31. Ibid., p. 47 (83).

32. Cf. 1 Sam 10.1-2.

33. Cf. Ex 29.7; Lev 8.12.

34. Cf. Gen 28.18.

35. Is 61.1 (LXX); Lk 4.18.

36. Is 11.1-2.

37. Cf. Mt 3.16; Mk 1.10; Lk 3.22; Jn 1.32.

38. Cf. Jn 3.5.

39. Cf. Mt 3.11; Mk 1.8; Lk 3.16.

40. Eph 1.13; 4.30.

41. Ch. 21, p. 47 (83).

42. Ibid., pp. 51-53 (87-89).

43. Ibid., pp. 49-51 (85-87).
44. Ibid., p. 51 and n. 1 (87 and n. 1).
45. Tertullian, *De resurrectione carnis* 8, 3 (CCL 2:931).
46. Ch. 21, pp. 51-55 (87-91).
47. Ibid., p. 55 (91).
48. Ibid., pp. 55-59 (91-95).
49. 1 Pet 2.2.
50. Ex 3.8; etc.
51. Ch. 16, pp. 35-39 (71-75).
52. Ch. 20, p. 43 (79).
53. Cf. Rom 6.3-4; Col 2.12.
54. Cf. Rom 8.15; Gal 4.6.
55. Leo the Great, *Sermo 1 in Nativitatem Domini* (PL 54:192-193).
56. 1 Cor 6.20.
57. Cf. 1 Cor 10.16-17.
58. Jn. 17.22.

Braniste, Ene (pp. 73-100)

1. J. Tixeront, *A Handbook of Patrology*, tr. by J. Gummersbach (from the 4th French ed.; St. Louis, 1920), pp. 213-215. F. Cayré, *Manual of Patrology*, tr. by H. Howett (2 vols.; Paris, 1935-40), 1, pp. 373-374. J. Quasten, *Monumenta eucharistica et liturgica vetustissima* (Bonn, 1935-37), pp. 179-180, 186, 196-197. B. Altaner, *Patrology*, tr. by H. Graef (from the 5th German ed,; New York, 1960), pp. 57-59. I. Coman, *Patrology* (in Rumanian) (Bucharest, 1956), pp. 118-120. C. Iordachescu, *History of Early Christian Literature* (in Rumanian), I (Iasi, 1934), pp. 28-29.

2. *Constitutiones Apostolorum* [= CA] VI, 18, 11; VIII, 46, 13; in F.X. Funk, *Didascalia et Constitutiones Apostolorum* (Paderborn, 1905; reprinted: Turin, 1962), 1, p. 345, 560.

3. The best studies, which also indicate editions and translations: F.X. Funk, *Die apostolischen Konstitutionen. Eine literarhistorische Untersuchung* (Rottenberg, 1891). F. E. Brightman, *Liturgies Eastern and Western*, 1: *Eastern Liturgies* (Oxford, 1896; reprinted: 1965, 1967), pp. XVII-XLVII. E. Schwartz, *Über die pseudo-apostolichen Kirchenordnungen* (Strassburg, 1910). F. Nau, "Constitutions Apostoliques," DTC 3/2 (1908), cols. 1520-1537. H. Leclercq, "Constitutions Apostoliques," DACL 3/2 (1914), cols. 2732-2795.

Critical ed. of text: F.X. Funk, *Didascalia et Constitutiones Apostolorum* (2 vols.; Paderborn, 1905; reprinted: Turin, 1962) [henceforth: Funk, with page reference to vol. 1]. Some of the liturgical texts (in Greek and a Latin translation), together with the more important bibliography to 1935 and critical notes, in Quasten, op. cit., pp. 179-233. The text of the eucharistic anaphora of the "Clementine" liturgy is given (in Greek and Latin) in A. Hänggi and I. Pahl (eds.), *Prex Eucharistica: Texts e variis liturgiis antiquioribus selecti* (Spicilegium Friburgense 12; Fribourg, 1968), pp. 82-95. There is a complete Rumanian translation by G. Nitu in the collection *Les écrits des Pères Apos-*

toliques avec les Constitutions et les Canons Apostoliques 2 (Kishinev [formerly Chisinau], 1928).

4. *Biblioteca*, cod. CXII-CXIII, cited in PG 1:548-559.

5. Funk's edition of the *Didascalia* includes the Latin translation as well as the oldest Latin fragments preserved. Fragments in a Latin translation in Quasten, op. cit., pp. 34-36, who also lists the editions of the Syriac version, its translation into modern languages, and studies published down to 1935.

6. The *Didache* was discovered and edited for the first time by Metropolitan Philotheos Bryennios in 1883, and later reedited a number of times. More recent editions: J.-P. Audet, *La Didachè: Instruction des Apôtres* (Paris, 1958); H. Lietzmann, *Die Didache, mit kritischem Apparat* (Kleine Teste für Vorlesungen und Ubungen 6; 6th ed.; Berlin, 1962), with bibliography, notes and a Latin translation; Quasten, op. cit., pp. 8-13. A Rumanian translation with an introductory study in the collection cited in n. 3, above, pp. 81-94. Cf. also S. Giet, *L'énigme de la Didachè* (Paris, 1970).

7. Cf. especially Schwartz, op. cit., and R. H. Connolly, *The So-called Egyptian Church Order and Derived Documents* (Cambridge, 1916). Information on the origin, content, author and date, versions and reworkings of the *Didache* in J. Quasten, *Initiation aux Pères de l'Eglise*, tr. by J. Laporte, 2 (Paris, 1966), pp. 216-232, with extensive bibliography (the French tr. represents an updating, to some extent, of the English original, *Patrology* 2 [Leiden, 1953], pp. 180-194). Selection of texts, in Latin translation, in Quasten, *Monumenta*, pp. 26-34. English ed. by G. Dix, *Apostolike Paradosis. The Treatise on the Apostolic Tradition of St. Hippolytus of Rome* (London, 1937). A more recent edition with a reconstitution of the Greek text by B. Botte, *La Tradition apostolique de saint Hippolyte. Essai de reconstitution* (LQF 39; Münster/W., 1963; 3rd ed., 1966). Cf. also *Hippolyte de Rome. La Tradition apostolique d'après les anciennes versions*, with introd., French translation, and notes by B. Botte (SC 11bis; Paris, 1968). J.-M. Hanssens, *La Liturgie d'Hippolyte, ses documents, son titulaire, ses origines et son caractère* (OCA 155; Rome, 1959; reprinted, 1965), with extensive bibliography on pp. XXV-XXXV. Idem, *La Liturgie d'Hippolyte. Documents et études* (Rome, 1970).

8. Cf., e.g., II, 57 (functions of clerics of all ranks in the liturgical assemblies); III, 9–11 (officiants in baptisms, cheirotonias and cheirothesias); III, 16–17 (role of deacons in baptism); VIII, 20 (liturgical functions of priest and deacon); VIII, 28 (functions of members of the clergy in the liturgical office); VIII, 46 (disciplinary measures against those who do not respect the rights and duties of each rank of the clergy in the administration of the sacraments).

9. II, 57 (description of a church with its various annexes that are used in worship).

10. Cf., e.g., V, 8 (veneration of the martyrs); V, 13–20 (rules for the celebration of Easter); VII, 23 (days of fast and the Saturday celebration); VII, 30 (celebration of Sunday); VIII, 33 (a list of the feasts to be observed).

11. VII, 57, 59; VII, 24, 47–49; VIII, 6–15, 34–39.

12. VIII, 16–17 (description and short explanation of baptism and confirmation); VII, 22 (baptismal service); VII, 26 (prayer formula for chrism); VII, 39–45 (baptismal service, including the prayers to be said); VIII, 4ff. (rite for the consecration of a bishop);

VIII, 29–31 (various services); VIII, 40 (prayer for the blessing of the offerings); VIII, 41–42 (prayers and services for the deceased).

13. Hanssens, *La liturgie* (1959), p. 52.

14. Cf. especially St. John Chrysostom, *Huit catéchèses baptismales inédites*, critical text, introd., tr., and notes by A. Wenger (SC 50; Paris, 1957).

15. Edition of the Syriac version, with English translation by A. Mingana, *Commentary of Theodore of Mopsuestia on the Lord's Prayer and on the Sacraments of Baptism and the Eucharist* (Woodbrooke Studies 6; Cambridge, 1933). Selection of texts on baptism and the eucharist, in Latin translation, in A. Rücker, *Ritus Baptismi et Missae quem descripsit Theodorus ep. Mopsuestenus in sermonibus catecheticis* (Münster, 1933). Theodore of Mopsuestia, *Les homélies catéchétiques*, tr., introd., index by R. Tonneau and R. Devreesse (Studi e testi 145; Vatican City, 1949).

16. PG 5:729-872. Cf. especially G. Bareille, "Ignace d'Antioche (Saint)," DTC 7/1 (1922), cols. 695-697.

17. E. Schwartz, in *Zeitschrift der Savigny-Stiftung für Rechtsgeschichte. Kanonische Abteilung* (Weimar, 1936), p. 41 (cf. B. Altaner, *Précis de patrologie*, tr. and adapt. by H. Chirat [Paris, 1961], p. 101).

18. Th. Zahn, *Ignatius von Antiochien* (Gotha, 1873), p. 141. Cf. also G. H. Turner, "Notes on the Apostolic Constitutions," JTS 31 (1930), pp. 130-131.

19. O. Perler, "Pseudo-Ignatius aund Eusebius'von Emesa," HJ 78 (1958), pp. 73-82.

20. For example: the Holy Spirit is a *hyperetes* (servant) of the Son; the birth of the Son *ek tou Patros* (from the Father) depended on the will of God the Father to create the world; the Son and the Paraclete are listed at the head of the heavenly powers that adore God the Father; a religious rationalism that is expressed chiefly in the heaping up of terms for the knowledge of God which is the object of the Church's prayer (*gnōsis, epignōsis, katalēpsis, agnoia*, etc.).

21. *De viris illustribus* 120 (PL33:709–711).

22. G. Wagner, "Zur Herkunft der Apostolischen Konstitutionen," in *Mélanges liturgiques offerts au R.P. Bernard Botte, O.S.B., de l'abbaye de Mont César, à l'occasion du 50ᵉ anniversaire de son ordination sacerdotale (4 juin 1972)* (Louvain, 1972), pp. 525-537.

23. Cf., e.g., N. Milas, *Les canons de l'Eglise Orthodoxe accompangés par des commentaires*, Roumanian tr. by U. Popovici and U. Kovincici, I, Part 2 (Arad, 1931), pp. 312-316, where a list is given of many directives in CA VIII that have passed into the various Orthodox canonical collections in the form of canons attributed to one or other of the holy Apostles.

24. L. Duchesne, *Christian Worship: Its Origin and Evolution*, tr. by M.L. McClure (from 3rd French ed.; London, 1903), pp. 55-64. 376-378. Cf. I. Mihalcescu, in the collection mentioned at the end of n. 3, above, 1 (Kishinev, 1927), p. 48.

25. This description is an amplification of the one in the corresponding chapter of the *Didascalia* (Quasten, *Monumenta*, pp. 34-36).

26. Botte, *Hippolyte de Rome. La Tradition apostolique*, p. 16.

27. Cf., e.g., J.-M. Hanssens, *Institutiones Liturgicae de Ritibus Orientalibus* 3 (Rome, 1932), pp. 642-643; Brightman, op. cit., pp. XVII, XXIII.

28. Duchesne, op. cit., pp. 55-64 (description of a fourth-century liturgical assembly in Syria; Duchesne's sources are CA, the fifth *Mystagogical Catechesis* of St. Cyril of Jerusalem, and the homilies of St. John Chrysostom). Cf. S. Salaville, *An Introduction to the Study of Eastern Liturgies*, tr. by J.M.T. Barton (London, 1938), pp. 11-12; E. Lanne, "Les ordinations dans le rite copte et leurs relations avec les *Constitutions apostoliques* et la *Tradition apostolique* d'Hippolyte," OSyr 5 (1960), pp.81-107.

29. Cf., e.g., F. Probst, *Die Liturgie der ersten drei Jahrhunderten* (Tübingen, 1870), pp. 258-295 (Probst thought that the "Clementine" liturgy reflected the liturgy of the early second century and that the latter was the only one used throughout the Christian world until the end of the fourth century); Brightman, op. cit., pp. XXVII ff.; P. Drews, *Untersuchungen über die sogennante Clementinische Liturgie* (Tübingen, 1906) (in Drews' view the Clementine liturgy reflected apostolic practice); H. Lietzmann, *Mass and Lord's Supper: A Study in the History of the Liturgy*, tr. by D.H.G. Reeve (Leiden, 1979), p. 108; H. Leclerq, art. cit. (n. 3 above), col. 2748f; A. Fortescue, *The Mass: A Study of the Roman Liturgy* (London, 1912), pp. 57-67; Hanssens, op. cit. 2 (Rome, 1930), pp. 437-440; P. Trampela, *The Liturgical Rites of Egypt and the East* (in Greek) (Athens, 1961), pp. 109-113.

30. Cf. 1 Cor 11.22: "Or do you despise *the church of God?*"

31. Cf. Eph 1.22-23: "And he [God] has put all things under his [Christ's] feet and has made him the head over all things for *the church, which is his body."*

32. "It is the function in its nascent state that calls forth the ministry" (J. Colson, "Désignation des ministres dans le Nouveau Testament," MD, no. 102 [2nd quarter, 1970], p. 22).

33. Cf. especially A. Lemaire, *Les ministères aux origines de l'Eglise. Naissance de la triple hiérarchie: évêques, presbytres, diacres* (Paris, 1971), with extensive bibliography.

34. Cf., e.g., canon 18 of the first ecumenical council, and canons 20-23 of the local synod of Laodicea (ca. 362-363).

35. Cf. the references given in n. 8, above.

36. F. Heiler, *Urkirche und Ostkirche* (Munich, 1937), p. 455.

37. See the texts in Funk, pp. 530, 556-562.

38. Cf. Paul Evdokimov, *L'Orthodoxie* (Neuchâtel, 1965), p. 266: "The bishop, acting in the name of Christ, is the one who transforms an assembly into a eucharistic synaxis and a manifestation of the Church of God." Cf. also B. Marliangeas, *Introduction à la Constitution sur la liturgie,* p. 18: "The liturgical assembly should be a manifestation, *an epiphany of the Church* in its visible aspect and in its underlying mystery" (cited by H. Holstein, *Hiérarchie et peuple de Dieu d'après "Lumen gentium"* [Paris, 1970], p. 138).

39. Cf. the anaphora of the Byzantine Mass of St. John Chrysostom: "We offer you again this spiritual and bloodless worship (*tēn logikēn tautēn kai anaimakton latreian*) . . ." (*La divine Liturgie de notre Père S. Jean Chrysostome*, Greek text and French tr. with introd. and notes by Placide de Meester, O.S.B. [3rd ed.; Rome–Paris, 1925], pp. 74-75).

40. Cf. *Apostolic Tradition*, chs. 4-5 (Botte, op. cit.[1968], pp.46-47).

40a. A. Bergère, *Etude historique sur les chorévêques* (Paris, 1925). E. Kirsten, "Chorbischof," RAC 2:1105-1114.

41. The comparison of the Church with a ship and of the bishop with its pilot occurs rather often in early Christian literature. Cf. F.J. Dölger, *Sol salutis* (2nd ed.; Münster, 1925), pp. 272-286.

42. In the great litany of the Clementine liturgy (VIII, 10), four bishops of the apostolic age are mentioned by name: James of Jerusalem, Clement of Rome, Evodius of Antioch (predecessor of St. Ignatius and ordained by St. Peter), and Anianus of Alexandria.

43. Cf. also canon 33 of the Fourth Council of Carthage, cited in the *Statuta Ecclesiae Antiqua* and in the *Didascalia* (II, 58) (Funk, p. 168).

44. On the practice of having several priests preach during the same liturgy cf. also *Egeria: Diary of a Pilgrimage*, tr. by G.E. Gingras (ACW 38; New York, 1970), ch. 25, 1 (p. 93): "Indeed it is the practice here that as many of the priests who are present and are so inclined may preach; and last of all, the bishop preaches. These sermons are given every Sunday."

45. Cf. *Apostolic Tradition* 7 (Botte, 1968, pp. 57-58).

46. Cf. the letter of Pope Cornelius (251) to bishop Fabius of Antioch, in Eusebius, *Historia ecclesiastica* VI, 43, in which it is said that there were seven deacons at Rome in those days.

47. Cf. *Didascalia* II, 44, and III, 13 (Funk, pp. 138, 216). The wording shows the subordinationist theology of the compiler (probably Eunomius).

48. Cf. *Apostolic Tradition* 8 (Botte, 1968, pp. 58-63).

49. II, 58 (Funk, p. 167): *sustasin (epistolen)* or *grammata sustatika* (canonical letters or letters of peace), of which St. Paul speaks in 1 Cor 16.3 and 2 Cor 3.1. Cf. also the letter of St. Ignatius to the Philippians, ch. 14; the 33rd or the *Apostolic Canons*; canons 7-8 of the council of Antioch (341); canons 41-42 of the council of Laodicea, etc. (cf. Funk, p. 166, n. 1).

50. Cf., e.g., *Apostolic Tradition* 13 and 34 (Botte, 1968, pp. 58, 116); various letters of St. Cyprian; the letter of Pope Cornelius to Bishop Fabius of Antioch (in Eusebius, *Historia ecclesiastica* VI, 43), which says that Rome at that time had seven subdeacons. But subdeacons are not mentioned in the *Didascalia*, which is generally considered as coming from the same century.

51. *Hyperetai legontai hoi hypodiakonoi. . . . Hyperetas tous hypodiakonous legei* (Balsamen and Zonaras in their commentary on the 21st canon of Laodicea, in G. Ralli and M. Potli, *La collection des divins et saints canons* 3 [Athens, 1853], p. 190). In his collection of canons Dionysius Exiguus regularly translates the Greek *hyperetas* by the Latin *sub-diaconos*, while other Latin translators of the canons usually translate it by *ministros*.

52. Cf., e.g., III, 11, 1; VI, 17; VII, 10, 9: *hyper pases . . . hyperesias* (Quasten, *Monumenta*, p. 207).

53. Cf., e.g., VIII, 11, 11; VIII, 12, 43; VIII, 21 (prayers for the cheirothesia of subdeacons); VIII, 28; VIII, 31.

54. In this essay I shall follow the usual language of Orthodox theology and use *cheirothesia* for the bestowal of all minor orders and *cheirotonia* only for major orders. But the ancient theology of the Church did not make this distinction; this is why the compiler of the *Apostolic Constitutions* will use *cheirotonia* and *cheirotonein* throughout for

the ordination of all ministers of worship (cf. especially VIII, 16ff.), while *cheirothesia* means simply the *imposition of hands*, which does not always imply the bestowal of ecclesiastical office (cf. especially VIII, 28; Funk, p. 530: *presbyteros . . . cheirothetei, ou cheirotonei,* "the priest imposes hands but does not ordain"). Moreover, in modern Catholic theology even the verbal distinction (which is juridical in origin) between *cheirotonia* and *cheirothesia* is not made, since the *imposition of hands* is used in ordination only for major orders, while "minor orders" are given by a simple blessing. Cf. C. Vogel, "L'imposition des mains dans les rites d'ordination en Orient et en Occident," MD, no. 102 (2nd quarter, 1970), pp. 57-72; idem, "Chirotonie et chirothésie, Importance et relativité de l'imposition des mains dans la collation des ordres," *Irénikon* 45 (1972), pp. 7-21 and pp. 207-238.

55. Cf. *Apostolic Tradition,* 13: "The bishop is not to impose hands on the deacon, but simply to appoint him to follow the deacon" (Botte, 1968, p. 68).

56. Cf., e.g., John Chrysostom, *Exhortation à Théodore. Lettres à Olympias,* introd. and tr. by Ph.-E. Legrand (Paris, 1933). *Jean Chrysostom. Lettres à Olympias,* ed. by A.-M. Malingrey (SC 13bis; Paris, 1967). On Olympias cf. also Sozomen, *Historia ecclesiastica* VIII, 9. St. John Chrysostom speaks generally of deaconesses, especially in his commentary on 1 Timothy, Homily 11 (PG 72;553D).

57. Cf. Egeria, *Peregrinatio ad loca sancta* 23, 3.

58. *Vita et miracula Sanctae Theclae* (PG 85:6 17B).

59. Cf., e.g., Tertullian, *Ad uxorem* I, 7, and *Exhortatio ad castitatem* 13 (both *widows* and *deaconesses* are regarded as clerical "orders"); canon 19 of Nicaea I; canon 44 of St. Basil the Great who speaks of "the deaconess's *sanctified* body" (Ralli and Potli, op. cit., IV [Athens, 1854], p. 192); and others.

60. Cf. Nau, art. cit., cols. 1521, 1525, and Leclercq, art. cit., col. 2737 (both in n. 3, above).

61. VIII, 17.

62. Later on, some canons set the minimum age at forty (canon 15 of the Council of Chalcedon, and canons 14 and 40 of the Council *In Trullo*).

63. Cf. also III, 6: "We do not allow women to teach in church; they are simply to pray and listen to those who teach."

64. But in the Clementine liturgy (VII, 11) it is the subdeacons who are entrusted with watching the doors for women.

65. They are not mentioned, however, among the lesser clergy when there is question of distributing the offerings brought for the agapes (II, 28). On the Syrian deaconesses cf. A. Kalsbach, "Die altkirchliche Einrichtung der Diakonissen bis zu ihrem Erlöschen," *Supplementheft 22 der Römischen Quartalschrift* (Freiburg im Br., 1926), pp. 19-31.

66. Cf. I.-H. Dalmais, "Ordination et ministres en Orient," MD, no. 102 (2nd quarter, 1970), pp. 79-80.

67. The names of two readers, *Favor* and *Claudius Atticianus,* are to be found in inscriptions in the Roman catacombs (Duchesne, op. cit., p. 347, n. 1). Cf. also Tertullian, *De praescriptione haereticorum* 41 (PL 2:69); Hippolytus, *Apostolic Tradition* 11 (Botte, 1968, p. 66); Cyprian, *Epistulae* 24; 29; 33; 34; and others (PL 4:294, 310, 328, 329); the

council of Sardica, canon 10; the council of Laodicea, canons 23 and 24; the 28th of the *Canones Apostolorum*; etc.

68. In the *Testamentum Domini* I, 23, the order is: readers, subdeacons, deaconesses (Quasten, *Monumenta*, p. 249).

69. Cf. *Apostolic Tradition* 11: "The reader receives his office when the bishop gives him the book, for he does not receive any imposition of hands (*ou de gar cheirotheteitai*)" (Botte, 1968, p. 66).

70. The chapter on the agape meals in the CA is taken over from the *Didascalia* (Funk, pp. 108-109) and is an echo of Christian antiquity; by the end of the fourth century the agape had everywhere been separated from the Mass and was held outside the churches, where it still survived in the East in different forms and under different names; cf. H. Leclercq, "Agape," DACL 1:775-848).

71. But no prayer is given for the conferral of this office in the chapters on the ritual for ordaining clerics (VIII, 16ff.).

72. See especially the description of the "Clementine" liturgy in Book VIII, where nothing is said about the cantors as singing the liturgical hymns.

73. "Let another sing the psalms of David, while the people sing the *akrosticha* or refrains" (II, 57, 6). On the method of chanting the psalms in the early Church cf. P. Vintilescu, *On the Hymnographical Poetry of the Liturgical Books and on Ecclesiastical Chant* (in Rumanian) (Bucharest, 1937), pp. 185ff. J. Mateos, S.J., *Le célébration de la Parole dans la liturgie byzantine. Etudes historiques* (OCA 191; Rome, 1971), pp. 7-13.

74. At Rome, in about the year 251, there were no less than fifty exorcists (letter of Pope Cornelius to Bishop Fabius of Antioch in Eusebius, *Historia ecclesiastica* VI, 43). For the fourth century, cf., e.g., canon 10 of the council of Antioch (341), and canon 24 of the council of Laodicea.

75. Cf. also *Apostolic Tradition* 14 (Botte, 1968, p. 68), and Duchesne, op. cit., p. 344. There may be an echo of the competition between charismatics and clergy in the apostolic period; cf. J. Colson, "Désignation des ministres dans le Nouveau Testament," MD, no. 102 (2nd quarter, 1970), pp. 21-29.

76. On the scriptural expression "people of God" as a name for the Church, cf. especially M. Keller, *"Volk Gottes" als Kirchenbegriff. Eine Untersuchung zum neuren Verständnis* (Zürich–Einsiedeln–Cologne, 1970); H. Asmussen *et al.*, *Die Kirche, Volk Gottes* (Stuttgart, 1961); A. Vonier, *The People of God* (London, 1937).

77. Cf. L. Kotzoni, *The Place of the Laity in the Ecclesiastical Organism* [in Greek] (Athens, 1956).

78. Cf. St. Justin Martyr, *Apologia I*, 65, 5.

79. Cf., e.g., Tertullian, *Apologeticum* 39, 14: "We form a 'corporation' by reason of our common religion, our unity in discipline, and the bond of a single hope. We hold reunions and assemblies in order to lay siege to God with our prayers, approaching him like a tightly knit army, if I may so put it. . . . In these gatherings we also hear exhortations, corrections and reprimands in the name of God. Our judgments in this circumstance are weighty ones for we are sure that we are in God's presence; it is a terrible mark against a person in the judgment to come if he has committed a sin serious enough to warrant his exclusion from the common prayers, from the assemblies, and from all connection with holy things."

80. Cf., e.g., Ignatius of Antioch, *Ad Trallianos* 7: "He who is within the altar is pure, but he who is outside the altar is impure; that is, he who does something that separates him from the bishop, presbyters and deacons is not pure in his own conscience." On the bishop and the eucharist as principles of Church unity cf. I. Zizioula, *The Unity of the Church through the Eucharist and in the Bishop during the First Three Centuries* [in Greek] (Athens, 1965), and N. Afanassiev, "L'assemblée eucharistique unique dans l'Eglise ancienne," *Klēronomia* (Thessalonika) 6 (1974), pp. 1-36.

81. Cf. Evdokimov, op. cit. (n. 38, above), p. 266: "In it [the eucharist] the Church reaches fulfillment and manifests itself; all other sacraments are in function of the eucharist and operate by its power which is that of the Church itself. *The Church exists wherever the eucharist is celebrated, and the person who takes part in the celebration is a member of the Church,* for it is in the eucharist that Christ remains with us to the end of the world, as he promised. Excommunication, on the other hand, has for its primary effect to deprive a person of the cup; it cuts him off from the *koinōnia.*"

82. Cf. E. Braniste, *Participation in the Mass and Methods for Achieving It* [in Rumanian] (Bucharest, 1949; originally in the journal *Etudes Théologiques*, 1949, nos. 7-8).

83. On the participation of children in liturgical singing cf. also Egeria, *Peregrinatio ad loca sancta*, 24, 5: "Every time the deacon mentions the name of someone, the many children standing about answer: *Kyrie eleison,* or, as we say, 'Lord, have mercy,' and their voices are legion" (tr. Gingras, op. cit., p. 90).

84. See the similar but somewhat more fully developed description in the *Testamentum Domini* I, 19 (Quasten, *Monumenta,* pp. 237-239).

85. I.e., in the nave, separated from the sanctuary by a low lattice work (*cancelli*).

86. *Testamentum Domini* II, 4 (Quasten, Monumenta, p. 238, n. 5), specifies that men are to sit in the right-hand side of the nave and women in the left, as is still customary today in most Orthodox churches, especially in the cities. Cf. also H. Selhorst, *Die Platzordnung im Gläubigenraum der altchristlichen Kirche* (dissertation; Münster, 1931), pp. 12ff.

87. These four groups are mentioned in the Clementine liturgy (VIII, 6–9); in the liturgy described in II, 57, only *catechumens* and *penitents* are mentioned, and then only in passing: "After the catechumens and penitents have left . . ." (Quasten, *Monumenta,* pp. 184-185).

88. This formula was also used in other parts of the Christian world, for example, at Rome, where the deacon would say: "Let Jews, pagans and heretics leave!" (*Judaei, pagani, haeretici recedant*) (S. Salaville, *Les liturgies orientales. La Messe* 1 [Paris, 1942], p. 90, n. 2). It still persists, though in different forms, in modern Eastern-rite liturgies. In the Armenian liturgy, for example, the deacon says in a loud voice, before the Cherubikon: "Let no unbaptized person, no unbeliever, no penitent or unclean person approach this divine mystery" (Z. Baronian, *Liturgie de l'Eglise Arménienne dans le cadre des autres rites liturgiques orientaux* [Bucharest, 1975], p. 78).

89. The text of these litanies and prayers and the ritual for dismissal are among the formularies of the Clementine liturgy (VIII, 6ff.).

90. The CA do not mention the presentation of the offerings by the faithful at the beginning of the Mass of the faithful, but it is abundantly attested in other contemporary documents.

91. Cf. canons 24 and 30 of the council of Laodicea; Egeria, op. cit., 20, 11.

92. Cf. especially, Egeria, op. cit., 23, 3; 24, 1, 12; 25, 7, 12; and Cyril of Jerusalem, *Catecheses* 4, 24; 12, 33; 16, 22 (PG 33:485, 768, 949).

93. Cf. A. Lambert, "Apotactites," DACL 1:2610-11.

94. Canon 11: "Those who are called *elderly women* or *front-seaters* (*tas legomenas presbytides etoi prokathemenas*) are not to be ordained in the Church." Cf. J. Hefele and H. Leclercq, *Histoire des Conciles* 1/2 (Paris, 1907), pp. 1003-5. Cf. also N. Afanassiev, "Les presbytides ou 'présidentes,'" *Messager Ecclésial,* 1957 (Special number: Hommage à S. E. le Métropolite Wladimir; in Russian).

95. VIII, 24: "Virgins are not ordained, since this crown is voluntarily assumed and is intended not as a condemnation of marriage but as a stimulus to piety." VIII, 25: "The widow is not ordained. . . . she is included among the widows only if she has been found worthy for a long time after the death of her husband" (Funk, p. 528). Cf. *Apostolic Tradition* 10 and 12 (Botte, 1968, pp. 66-68). Cf. also J. Viteau, "L'institution des diacres et des veuves," RHE 21 (1926), pp. 513-536.

96. Cf. also III, 6: "Let a *widow* realize that she is an altar of sacrifice for God."

97. Cf. also *Testamentum Domini* I, 23, where "canonical widows" (*viduae canonicae*) and charismatics are listed among the clerics, while in church the widows sit directly behind the presbyters on the bishop's left (Quasten, *Monumenta,* p. 249).

98. The same directive with regard to widows in *Traditio Apostolica* 30 (Botte, 1968, p. 111).

99. But according to *Testamentum Domini* I, 35, widows receive communion immediately after the deacons, which means before all others in minor orders (Quasten, *Monumenta,* p. 258).

100. Cf. VIII, 23: "a confessor is not ordained, because his state is due to an act of the will and to perseverance." Cf. also *Apostolic Tradition* 9 (Botte, 1968, pp. 27-28, 64-65).

101. Cf. n. 83.

102. Everyone will remember how St. Ambrose, bishop of Milan, barred emperor Theodosius the Great from entering the sanctuary of the cathedral because of the massacre for which he was responsible at Salonika (Sozomen, *Historia ecclesiastica* VII, 25).

103. Cf. especially, Lemaire, op. cit. (n. 33, above); Y. Congar, "Ministéres et structuration de l'Eglise," MD, no. 102 (2nd quarter, 1970), pp. 7-20; J. Colson, "Désignation des ministres dans le Nouveau Testament," ibid., pp. 21-29.

104. In the East, the Council of Chalcedon (canon 6) forbade the cheirotonia and cheirothesia of any minister of the Church unless he was to exercise a definite function and was assigned to a definite church. Cf. C. Vogel, *"Vacua manus impositio,"* in *Mélanges Botte* (n. 22, above), pp. 511-524. On the present situation of the Catholic Church in this respect, cf. J. Lécuyer, "Les ordres mineurs en question," MD, no. 102 (2nd quarter, 1970), pp. 97-107.

Cazelles, Henri (pp. 101-113)

1. R. de Vaux, *Ancient Israel: Its Life and Institutions*, tr. by J. McHugh (New York, 1961), p. 382.

2. Ibid., p. 356.

3. The Book of Nehemiah shows the importance of thus storing up consecrated tithes (Neh 12.44-47, especially v. 47; cf. 10.35-40). It is not only nonperishables that are thus kept in special storerooms, but also consecrated food that is intended for the ordained personnel, i.e., priests and Levites (or, in the New Testament, all Christians); cf. Lev 22.7, 10-16. This storeroom is regarded as especially important by Nehemiah who expels Tobiah from it (Neh 13.4-9). Of course, such consecrated offerings intended for the temple personnel must not be allowed to go bad; this accounts for prescriptions regarding consecrated food that has been kept for a certain length of time and is in danger of going bad (*piggul*; Lev 7.18; 19.7; cf. 22.31).

4. The latter part of this verse ("and according . . . Levites") is based on the (French) Ecumenical Translation of the Bible (TOB).

Cothenet, Edouard (pp. 115-135)

1. J. Daniélou, *The Theology of Jewish Christianity*, tr. and ed. by J.A. Baker (Chicago, 1964), pp. 173-204. We may note in particular the interpretation given of the two seraphim in Isaiah: they represent the Only Son of God and the Holy Spirit. Origen echoes this interpretation and follows it in commenting on Hab 3.2 (LXX: *en meso duo zoon gnosthese*, "You shall be known between the two living creatures"), in *Principia* I, 3, 4; IV, 3, 14.

2. T. Holtz, *Die Christologie der Apokalypse des Johannes* (Texte und Untersuchungen 85; Berlin, 1962); J. Comblin, *Le Christ dans l'Apocalypse* (Paris–Tournai, 1965).

3. P. Prigent, *Apocalypse et Liturgie* (Cahiers théologiques 52; Neuchâtel, 1964). There is a brief survey of the question in my article, "La prière dans l'Apocalypse," *Carmel* (1966), pp. 85-104. On the ecclesiology of Revelation see my essay in *Le ministère et les ministères dans le Nouveau Testament*, ed. by J. Delorme (Paris, 1974), pp. 264-77.

4. Pliny the Younger, Epist. X, 96: "stato die ante lucem . . . carmenque Christo quasi deo dicere secum invicem."

5. Prigent, op. cit., pp. 14-45.

6. Compare with *Testamentum Levi* III, 5-6.

7. J. Comblin, "La liturgie de la Nouvelle Jérusalem," ETL 29 (1953), pp. 5-40.

8. Quoted in R. de Vaux, *Ancient Israel: Its Life and Institutions*, tr. by J. McHugh (New York, 1961), p. 496.

9. Prigent, op. cit., pp. 37-45.

10. A. Jaubert, *La notion de l'Alliance dans le Judaïsme aux abords de l'ère chrétienne* (Paris, 1963), pp. 189-98.

11. According to *Jubilees* II, 18-19, God prescribes the sabbath for the two highest classes of angels, that is, the angels of the Presence and the angels of Sanctification. In the same way, through the sign of circumcision God "sanctified Israel in order that it might be with him and his holy angels" (*Jubilees* XV, 27).

12. *Hodayôt* III, 19-23, tr. by G. Vermes in his translation of A. Dupont-Sommer, *The Essene Writings from Qumran* (Cleveland, 1967; reprinted 1973), p. 209.

13. G. Jeremias, *Der Lehrer der Gerechtigkeit* (Göttingen, 1963).

14. 1 QS VI, 2-3. On the antithesis "to separate–to unite," see my article "Pureté et impureté, III: Nouveau Testament," DBS 9:513-15.

15. M. Delcor, *Les Hymnes de Qumrân (Hodayôt)* (Paris, 1962).

16. 1 QH XI, 10-14, in Dupont-Sommer, op. cit., p. 237.

17. M. Delcor supports his interpretation with citations from *Joseph and Asenath*, a Jewish-Hellenistic novel which speaks of a proselyte's conversion as follows: "Bless this virgin too! Renew her with your holy spirit! May she eat your bread of life and drink of your cup of blessing. Number her among your people" (ed. Batiffol, p. 49).

18. *Hagigah* 2, 1; tr. in H. Danby, *The Mishnah* (Oxford, 1933), pp. 212-13.

19. Palestinian Talmud, Y 77a; text in J. Bonsirven, *Textes rabbiniques des deux premiers siècles chrétiens* (Rome, 1954), p. 280, no. 1102.

20. Dupont-Sommer, op. cit., pp. 333-34.

21. Ibid. [J. Carmignac's French translation, quoted here by E. Cothenet, has "recruits" for "numbered ones" in the last lines. —*Tr.*]

22. "L'attitude de l'Eglise naissante à l'égard du Temple," in *Liturgie de l'Eglise particulière et Liturgie de l'Eglise universelle* (Rome, 1976), pp. 89-111.

23. I QS X, 8-11, in Dupont-Sommer, op. cit., p. 98.

24. See my critical review of G. Klinzing, *Die Umdeutung des Kultus in der Qumrangemeinde und im Neuen Testament* (Göttingen, 1971), in RQ 8 (1972-75), pp. 291-94.

25. On Ex 19.6 see most recently H. Cazelles, "Royaume des prêtres et nation consacrée," in *Humanisme et foi chrétienne* (Paris, 1976), pp. 541-45. According to him this text is postexilic; in introducing the covenant it shows the role of priests in preserving the specific character of Israel in the midst of the nations. On the use of Ex 19.6 in the New Testament, I refer the reader to my essay in *Le ministère et les ministères* (n. 3, above), pp. 139-44.

26. J. Carmignac, "L'utilité ou l'inutilité des sacrifices sanglants dans la 'Règle de la communauté' de Qumrân," RB 73 (1956), pp. 524-32; A. Jaubert, op. cit., pp. 148-50.

27. *Rule of the Congregation* II, 10-21, in Dupont-Sommer, op. cit., pp. 108-9.

28. Op. cit., pp. 46-76: "Apocalypse 4 et 5: Une liturgie juive adaptée au christianisme." The hypothesis formulated in the title of this section is verified, in fact, only for ch. 4.

29. Cited ibid., p. 52. There are further amplifications in II Henoch (or *Livre des Secrets d'Hénoch*, tr. into French by A. Vaillant, Paris, 1952; in English in R.H. Charles [ed.], *The Apocrypha et Pseudepigrapha of the Old Testament in English* 2 [Oxford, 1913], pp. 425-69), and III Henoch (or *The Hebrew Book of Henoch*, ed. and tr. by H. Odeberg, Cambridge, 1928).

30. Cf. D. Flusser, "Sanktus und Gloria," in *Abraham unser Vater (Festschrift O. Michel)* (Leiden, 1963), pp. 129-52.

31. Cf. M. McNamara, *The New Testament and the Palestinian Targum to the Pentateuch* (Rome, 1966), pp. 101-12.

32. The French version is from L. Bouyer, *Eucharistie: Théologie et spiritualité de la prière eucharistique* (Paris–Tournai, 1966), pp. 66-67. [I have translated directly from this French text instead of using the translation in the English version of Bouyer's *Eucharist.* —Tr.]

33. A. Feuillet, "Les vingt-quatre vieillards de l'Apocalypse," RB 65 (1958), pp. 5-32.

34. J. Colson, *Ministre de Jésus-Christ ou Le sacerdoce de l'Evangile* (Paris, 1966), pp. 199-203.

35. The book in Rev 5.1 is to be compared with the books in Dan 7.10 (although their content is different); coming and receiving (Rev 5.7; Dan 7.13); authority over every tribe, tongue, people and nation (Rev 5.9; Dan 7.14); reigning over the earth (Rev 5.10; Dan 7.27); multitude of angels (Rev 5.11; Dan 7.10). Rev 5 is a rereading of Dan 7; in the rereading, the image of the Lamb is superimposed on the figure of the son of man. This step profoundly transforms the meaning of the vision.

36. A. Vanhoye has studied the systematic rereadings of the Book of Ezekiel in Revelation, and has observed that the same symbol may be used several times (thus in Rev. 10.8-9 the seer must eat the *open* book); cf. "L'utilisation du Livre d'Ezéchiel dans l'Apocalypse," Bib 43 (1962), pp. 436-76, especially p. 462.

37. Gen 49.9 was used at Qumran in the *Book of Blessings* (V, 29); the title "Root of David" occurs in the *Florilegium* (I, II) and the *Patriarchal Blessings* (I, 3).

38. M.-Al. Chevalier, *L'Esprit et le Messie dans le Bas-Judaïsme et le Nouveau Testament* (Paris 1958).

39. Cf. my article "Prophétisme dans le Nouveau Testament," DBS 8.1255-57; and A. Jaubert, *Approches de l'Evangile de Luc* (Paris, 1976), pp. 135-39.

40. "Les chrétiens prêtres et rois d'après l'Apocalypse," RT 75 (1975), pp. 40-66, at p. 54.

41. Bibliography in S. Lyonnet and L. Sabourin, *Sin, Redemption and Sacrifice: A Biblical and Patristic Study* (Rome, 1970), pp. 264-67.

42. *Neofiti I,* ed. by A. Macho, with English tr. by M. McNamara, I: *Genesis* (Madrid, 1968), p. 552.

43. Ibid., III: *Levítico* (Madrid, 1971), p. 394.

44. Jerusalem Targum I on Genesis 22; French tr. in R. Le Déaut, *La nuit pascale* (Rome, 1963), pp. 138-39.

45. Lyonnet and Sabourin, op. cit., pp. 110-19.

46. "Les chrétiens prêtres" (n. 40, above), p. 52.

47. There is a good bibliographical introduction in R.P. Martin, *Carmen Christi. Philippians II, 5-11* (Cambridge, 1967), and J.-F. Collange, *L'Epitre de saint Paul aux Philippiens* (Neuchâtel, 1973), pp. 75-97.

48. DBS 9:336-81.

49. Cf. M.-E. Boismard, *Quatre hymnes baptismales dans la Première Epître de Pierre* (Paris, 1961), pp. 81-94.

50. E. Käsemann, "Kritische Analyse von Phil. 2, 5-11," in his *Exegetische Versuche und Besinnungen* 1 (Göttingen, 1970), pp. 51-95; French tr. by D. Appia, *Essais exégétiques* (Neuchâtel, 1972), p. 102.

Dalmais, Irénée-Henri (pp. 137-153)

1. *Contra Celsum* VI, 48 (SC 147:300).

1a. L. Bouyer, *L'Incarnation et l'Eglise-Corps du Christ dans la théologie de saint Athanase* (Unam Sanctam 11; Paris, 1943).

2. Some indication of the wealth of material can be found in E. Mersch, S.J., *The Whole Christ,* tr. by J. R. Kelly (Milwaukee, 1938), ch. 8.

3. Cf. Emmanuel-Pataq Siman, *L'expérience de l'Esprit par l'Eglise d'après la tradition syrienne d'Antioche* (Théologie Historique 15; Paris, 1971).

4. Cf. O. H. E. Burmester, "The Canons of Gabriel ibn Turaīk, LXX Patriarch of Alexandria," Mus 46 (1933), p. 44.

5. B. Botte, "L'euchologe de Sérapion est-il authentique?" OC 48 (1964), pp. 50-56.

6. A. Veilleux, O.C.S.O., *La liturgie dans le cénobitisme pachômien au quatrième siècle* (Studia Anselmiana 57; Rome, 1968).

7. Ibid., pp. 167, 176-78, 197. Cf. H. Bacht, "Pachôme et ses disciples," in *Théologie de la vie monastique* (Paris, 1961), p. 39.

8. Cf. Veilleux, op. cit., pp. 138-60.

9. Alfonso Abdallah, *L'Ordinamento Liturgico di Gabriele V, 88° Patriarca copto* (Studia Orientalia Christiana Aegyptica; Cairo, 1962).

10. O. H. E. Burmester, "The Canons of Christodulos, Patriarch of Alexandria (A.D. 1047-1077)," Mus 45 (1932), p. 82.

11. Burmester, "The Canons of Gabriel ibn Turaīk," pp. 51-53.

11a. Ibid., p. 53.

12. O. H. E. Burmester, "The Canons of Cyril III ibn Laklak, 75th Patriarch of Alexandria, A.D. 1235-1250," *Bulletin de la Société d'Archéologie Copte* 14 (1950-57), pp. 142-45.

13. If the Pope or the Bishop is present he recites these words.

14. As he says the words, "For to you, etc.," he incenses three times to the East and then returns the censer to the deacon.

Kniazeff, Alexander (pp. 167-180)

1. The prayers of ordination are in the Pontifical (Slavic: Ciovnik). There is a French translation in F. Mercenier and F. Paris, *La prière des Eglises de rite byzantin* 1 (Amay, 1937).

2. For details cf. *Prière des Heures* (Chevetogne, 1975), pp. 68ff.

3. Ibid., p. 69.

4. One of the rare instances in which these prayers are still said aloud today is the genuflection prayers which the priest says at vespers on Pentecost.

5. In the little hours the little collect is replaced by a triple *Kyrie eleison.* The same is done when vespers or matins are celebrated without deacon or priest.

6. J. Mateos, "La synaxe monastique des vêpres byzantines," OCP 36 (1970), p. 267; idem, *La célébration de la Parole dans la liturgie byzantine. Etude historique* (OCA 191; Rome,

1971), pp. 29-33; A. Strittmatter, "Notes on the Byzantine Synapte," Trad 19 (1954), pp. 85-108; *Prière des Heures*, p. 69.

7. This is true at least of the initial formulas of the ektenie. In the formulas inserted into it for the celebration of one or other Russian *moleben* we find both prayer intentions and prayers addressed directly to God by the deacon.

8. Mateos, *La célébration de la Parole*, pp. 150-52.

9. This petition for the angel of peace is probably the nucleus of the oldest prayers before the final blessing and dismissal. The petition was already present in the fourth century, in *Apostolic Constitutions* VIII, 36, 3; 38, 2 (Funk, 1:544-46) and in St. John Chrysostom (*Prière des Heures*, bibliography p. 70, n. 2).

10. Thus seven prayers at vespers and twelve at matins have been shifted to form a unit in the first, or psalmic, part of these offices. The priest says them in a low voice while standing on the solea before the closed Royal Gates, while Psalm 103 (104) is being read at vespers and the Hexapsalm at matins. Cf. M. Arranz, "Les prières sacerdotales des vêpres byzantines," OCP 37 (1971), pp. 85-124; idem, "Les prières presbyterales des matines byzantines," OCP 37 (1971), pp. 406-36; 38 (1972), pp. 63-115.

Koulomzine, Nicolas (pp. 187-192)

1. On the theme of "the Church as people of God" cf. L. Cerfaux, *The Church in the Theology of St. Paul*, tr. by G. Webb and A. Walker (New York, 1959); Y. Congar, "The Church and the People of God," in K. Rahner and E. Schillebeeckx (eds.), *The Church and Mankind* (Concilium 1; New York, 1965), pp. 11-38.

2. Archpriest Nicolas Afanassieff, *L'Eglise du Saint-Esprit* (Cogitatio fidei 83; Paris, 1975). Russian original: *Tserkov Doukha Sviatogo* (Paris, 1971). I shall cite this work as ESE, with the page number of the French version and, in parentheses, the page number of the Russian original.

3. ESE, p. 196 (143). The same conception of the Church is developed in *Trapeza Gospodina* [The Lord's Supper] (in Russian) (Paris, 1952). This work is to be published in an English translation. Cited henceforth as TG.

4. L. Bouyer, review of ESE in *Istina* 23 (1976), pp. 97-101.

5. R. Sohm, *Kirchenrecht* 1. *Die geschichtlichen Grundlagen* (Leipzig, 1892). A Russian translation of this book was published in 1906.

6. *Catéchisme à l'usage des diocèses de France* (published in the diocese of Paris; Paris, 1941), p. 36.

7. *Ad Smyrnaeos* 8, 2.

8. N. Afanassieff, "Two Conceptions of the Church" (in Russian), *Pout'*, no. 4 (1934), p. 17, and "L'Eglise qui préside dans l'amour" in *Primauté de Pierre dans l'Eglise orthodoxe* (Neuchâtel, 1960).

9. In the decrees of the 1917 Council of Moscow we read: "A diocese is a *part* of the Russian Orthodox Church and is governed by a diocesan bishop in accordance with the canons."

10. *Ekklesia* may mean: (1) a local assembly (1 Cor 14.4); (2) a local community (1 Cor 1.1; 1 Thess 1.1; Rom 16.1; Col 4.16; Acts 14.23; etc.); (3) in the plural, a group of local Churches (1 Cor 16.1; Gal 1.1; etc.).

11. In Eph 1.23, e.g., we read: "the church, which is his body, the fulness of him who fills all in all." Several translations of this verse are possible, but none of them invokes the specifically universalist vision of the Church to which the note on this passage in the Jerusalem Bible seems to refer; there is no such reference in J. Colson, *L'évêque dans les communautés primitives* (Paris, 1951), p. 48.

On Acts 20.28 cf. J. Dupont, *Le discours de Milet* (Paris, 1962), p. 180: "A favorite topic of discussion among exegetes is whether 'Church of God' (Acts 20.28) refers to the universal Church or to a particular Church. . . . The Church is not an abstraction; it is concretely made up of all the Christian communities in a place, and these are not simply a portion of the Church."

12. Cf. J. Dupont, *Les problèmes du livre des Actes d'après les travaux récents* (Analecta Lovaniensia Biblica et Orientalia, Series II, no. 17; Louvain, 1950).

13. This reading is accepted not only in the RSV, cited here, but in the New American Bible and the New English Bible.

14. *Ad Philad.* 4.

15. TG, p. 19.

16. Ibid., p. 20.

17. The presence of Aquila and Prisca at Rome and not at Ephesus is a difficulty; some scholars suppose that chapter 16 of Romans was part of a separate letter: cf. M. J. Lagrange, *Epitre aux Romains* (Paris, 1950), notes on pp. 362-64.

18. The text in Col 4.15 is uncertain from the standpoint of textual criticism.

19. TG, pp. 19-28.

20. Col 4.17.

21. Clement of Rome, *Epist. I ad Corinthios* 42, 4. The statement is confirmed by Eusebius, *Historia ecclesiastica* III, 4, 10; III, 23, 3, and by Athenian local tradition which makes Dionysius the Areopagite (Acts 17.34) the first bishop of that city.

22. Acts 18.26, at Ephesus prior to Paul's activity.

23. Acts 2.46.

24. TG, pp. 22-23.

25. Mt 26.26 and parallels.

26. Acts 2.1.

27. Acts 2.46; perhaps in 1 Cor 14.23; surely in Ignatius of Antioch, *Ad Ephesios* 13, 1; etc.

28. TG, p. 47, and elsewhere.

29. ESE, p. 246 (188).

30. Ibid., p. 248 (189).

31. 1 Pet 2.5.

32. ESE, p. 40 (but cited in accordance with the Russian original, p. 13).

33. Ibid., p. 120 (but cited in accordance with the Russian original, p. 81).

34. 1 Cor 12.

35. ESE, p. 128 (87).

36. Ibid., p. 44 (16).
37. Ibid., p. 130 (89).
38. Ibid., p. 151 (108).
39. 1 Cor 12.28; Eph 4.11.
40. Sohm, op. cit., p. 36.
41. Ibid., and also p. 46.
42. Ibid.
43. Ibid.
44. Ibid.
45. 1 Cor 14 *passim*.
46. ESE, p. 172 (125).
47. Ibid.
48. Acts 11.27-28.
49. Acts 13.1-3.
50. Eph 3.1-6.
51. ESE, p. 173 (125).
52. Ibid., p. 174 (127).
53. Sohm, op. cit., p. 38.
54. 1 Cor 14.29; cf. also 1 Jn 4.1 and 1 Thess 5.20.
55. *Didache* XI, 7.
56. Ibid., XIII, 3.
57. Ibid., XV, 1.
58. Cf. Colson, op. cit., p. 125.
59. ESE, p. 192 (139).
60. A. Sabatier, *Les religions d'autorité et la religion de l'Esprit,* (Paris, 1909), p. 133.
61. H. Küng, *The Church,* tr. by R. and R. Ockenden (New York, 1967), p. 75.
62. 1 Cor 14.40.
63. 1 Cor 14.33.
64. ESE, p. 194 (142).
65. Ibid., p. 196 (143).
66. 1 Tim 3.4; 3.5; 3.12.
67. Tit 3.8; 3.14.
68. Rom 12.8; 1 Thess 5.12; 1 Tim 5.17.
69. 1 Thess 5.12.
70. ESE, p. 201 (148).
71. 1 Cor 12.28.
72. Heb 13.24.
73. Heb 13.17.
74. Heb 13.7.
75. Acts 14.23; 20.17.
76. 1 Tim 5.1; 5.17; Tit 1.5.
77. Jas 5.14; 1 Pet 5.1; 5.5.
78. Eph 4.11.
79. ESE: "Those who preside in the Lord," pp. 191-237 (139-80).

80. This term may signify rather "government" or "direction."

81. Op. cit., p. 53.

82. And not "James the Greater," as the French translation mistakenly puts it: ESE, pp. 262, 264 (202, 204).

83. Acts 21.18.

84. Cf. n. 21, above.

85. ESE, p. 283 (222). The Russian original has "the oldest presbyter" rather than "the chief presbyter."

Kovalevsky, Maxime (pp. 193-205)

1. Constitution on the Sacred Liturgy, no. 112, tr. in A. Flannery (ed.), *Vatican II: The Conciliar and Postconciliar Documents* (Collegeville, 1975), p. 31.

2. The "golden chain," a document cited by the Soviet musicologist Rogoff in his book *Russian Musical Esthetics from the Eleventh to the Eighteenth Century* [in Russian] (Moscow, 1973), p. 49.

3. Cf. Philipp Harnoncourt (cf. Bibliography).

BIBLIOGRAPHY

In French

Dictionnaire d'archéologie chrétienne et de liturgie, ed. by F. Cabrol and H. Leclercq, vol. 3.

Porte, J. (ed.), *Encyclopédie des musiques sacrées* (Paris, 1968—), vol.3.

Pons, André, *Droit ecclésiastique et musique sacrée* (St. Maurice, Switzerland, 1958—), 5 vols.

Corbin, Solange, *L'Eglise à la conquête de sa musique* (Paris, 1962).

Gelineau, Joseph, *Voices and Instruments in Christian Worship: Principles, Laws, Applications*, tr. by. C. Howell (Collegeville, 1964).

Le chant liturgique après Vatican II (Paris, 1966).

Rousseau, Olivier, O.S.B., *The Progress of the Liturgy: An Historical Sketch*, tr. by the Benedictines of Westminster Priory (Westminster, Md., 1951).

In German

Harnoncourt, Philipp, *Gesamtkirchliche und teilkirchliche Liturgie* (Freiburg im Br., 1974). The second essay.

In Russian

Ouspensky, *The Art of Early Russian Singing* (Moscow, 1965).

Rogoff, *Russian Musical Esthetics from the Eleventh to the Eighteenth Century* (Moscow, 1973).

Neunheuser, Burckhard (pp. 207-219)

1. Cf. J. A. Jungmann, *The Mass of the Roman Rite: Its Origins and Development (Missarum Solemnia)*, tr. by F. A. Brunner (New York, 1951-55), 1:92-103; cf. also 1:44-60 (in the 5th German ed. of 1962, pp. 122-37; 57-77).

2. H. Lietzmann, *Das Sacramentarium Gregorianum nach dem Aachener Urexemplar* (LQF 3; Münster, 1921; 1968), nos. 1-53, pp. 1-5; J. Deshusses, *Le sacramentaire grégorien* (Spicilegium Friburgense 16; Fribourg, 1971), nos. 1-20, pp. 85-92.

3. M. Andrieu, *Les Ordines Romani du Haut Moyen Age* 2 (Spicilegium Sacrum Lovaniense 23; Louvain, 1948), pp. 65-108.

4. Cf. Jungmann, op. cit., 1:78-80 (5th German ed., pp. 103-6); F. Cabrol, "Apologies," DACL 1/1:2591-2601.

5. Haymo of Faversham, *Ordo agendorum et dicendorum,* in S. J. P. Van Dijk, *Sources of the Modern Roman Liturgy* (Leiden, 1963) 2:3. This *initium* remains unchanged in all editions of the Missal "according to the practice of the Roman Church" until the sixteenth century.

6. This is very close to the beginning of the *Ordo iuxta Romanam consuetudinem* described by Bernold of Constance in his *Micrologus* 1 (PL 151:979A): "When the priest prepares for Mass. . . . Having made his preparation (*Paratus autem*) he advances to the altar." Cf. S. J. P. Van Dijk and J. Hazelden Walker, *The Origins of the Modern Roman Liturgy* (London, 1960), pp. 248-53.

7. On Burchard, cf. F. Wasner, "Burckard, Johannes," LTK 2 (1958), pp. 784-85.

8. J. Wickham Legg, *Tracts on the Mass* (HBS 27; London, 1904), pp. 121-78. The title cited is on p. 126.

9. Cf. ibid., pp. XXV-XXVIII.

10. Cf. Jungmann, op. cit., 1:135-36 (5th German ed., p. 179).

11. For the Missal of Pius V I have consulted an edition published in the last century. The *Codex Rubricarum* of John XXIII is in AAS 52 (1960), pp. 593-740.

12. Cf. H. Jedin, "Das Konzil von Trient und die Reform des Römischen Messbuches," *Liturgisches Leben* 6 (1939), pp. 30-66, especially pp. 65-66.

13. Introduction to the Rubrics of the Roman Missal (no division into numbered paragraphs). For the rubrics themselves I shall follow the traditional numbering.

14. Cf. Burchard's *Ordo* in Legg, op. cit., p. 134.

15. Again, in citing I shall follow the traditional and official numbering.

16. Cf. Council of Trent, Session XXII, the *Decretum de observandis et vitandis in celebratione missarum,* in CT VIII, pp. 962-63, espec. p. 963; also in *Conciliorum Oecumenicorum Decreta,* ed. by J. Alberigo et al. (3rd ed.; Bologna, 1972), pp. 736-37 (at paragraph 2 on p. 736).

17. Cf., e.g., A. Franz, *Die Messe im deutschen Mittelalter* (Freiburg, 1902), passim, but especially pp. 3-35 and 739-40.

18. Cf. Jungmann, op. cit., 1:86-91 (5th German ed., pp. 114-20).

19. For the rather late development of this rite, cf. P. Browe, "Die Elevation in der Messe," JLw 9 (1929), pp. 20-66.

20. Cf. my article, "Die klassische Liturgische Bewegung (1909-1963) und die nachkonziliarische Liturgiereform," in *Mélanges liturgiques offerts au R.P. Dom Bernard Botte* (Louvain, 1972), pp. 401-16, especially pp. 404-5.

21. Cf. ibid.

22. For details see the major commentaries on the Liturgy Constitution; these are listed in R. Kaczyinski (ed.), *Enchiridion Documentorum Instaurationis Liturgicae* (Turin, 1976), p. 1.

23. Constitution on the Liturgy, no. 48, tr. in A. Flannery (ed.) *Vatican II: The Conciliar and Postconciliar Documents* (Collegeville, 1975), p. 16 [henceforth references will be to Flannery with page number].

24. In the *Editio Typica* of 1970, pp. 17-92. The text can also be found with the variants of the first (1969) edition of the *Ordo Missae* and second *Editio Typica* of the RM (1972), in the *Enchiridion* mentioned in the preceding note. [The English translation of the final version of the GIRM will be that of the International Committee on English in the Liturgy, as given in *The Sacramentary* (Collegeville, 1974). References will be by numbers, not pages. Texts not given in the Sacramentary, and the (divergent) text of the first edition of the GIRM will be translated from the text as given in the *Enchiridion* (reference by number, not page).]

25. *Enchiridion,* no. 1373.

26. Ibid., no. 1375.

27. Ibid.

28. Ibid., no. 1402 and note *j*.

29. The term is from St. Justin, *Apologia I* (PG 64:429C).

30. Cf. Jungmann, op. cit., 1:225-30 (5th German ed., pp. 295-303).

31. *Codex Iuris Canonici,* c. 813.1.

32. Cf. above, n. 17.

33. Constitution on the Liturgy, no. 14 (Flannery, pp. 7-8).

Renoux, Charles (pp. 221-232)

1. *Itinerarium Egeriae,* ed. by A. Franceschini and R. Weber (CCL 175; Turnhout, 1965).

2. A. Renoux, *Le Codex Arménien Jérusalem 121* (PO 36/2; Turnhout, 1971) [henceforth: *Lectionnaire arménien*]; M. Tarchnischvili, *Le Grand Lectionnaire de l'Eglise de Jérusalem (V-VIII s.)* ((CSCO Iberici 189 and 205; Louvain, 1959-60) [henceforth: *Lectionnaire géorgien*].

3. PG 33:332-1125.

4. PG 42:773-832.

5. *Jean Rufus. Plérophories: Témoignages et révélations contre le concile de Chalcédoine,* Syriac version and French translation edited by F. Nau (PO 8/1; Paris, 1912) [henceforth: *Plérophories*].

6. E. Schwartz, *Kyrillos von Skythopolis* (TU 49/2; Leipzig, 1949) [henceforth *Vita Euthymii, Vita Theodosii, Vita Cyriaci*].

7. Mark the Deacon, *Vie de Porphyre, évêque de Gaza,* text, tr. and comm. by H. Grégoire and M.-A. Kugener (Collection Byzantine; Paris, 1930) [henceforth: *Vita Porphyrii*].

8. Cf. *Itinerarium Egeriae* 25, 2ff., p. 67.

9. Cf. *Vita Euthymii* 15, p. 25.

10. PG 33:1109ff.

11. Cf. *Itinerarium Egeriae* 24, 1, p. 67.

12. *Catecheses Mystagogicae* 5, 2 (PG 33:1109).

13. Hesychius of Jerusalem, Basil of Seleucia, John of Berytus, Pseudo-Chrysostom, and Leontius of Constantinople, *Homélies Pascales (cinq homélies inédites),* with introd., critical texts, trans., commentary and index by M. Aubineau (SC 187; Paris, 1972), pp. 37-38.

14. *Vita Euthymii* 16, p. 27.

15. *Plérophories* 16, p. 13. "Preacher" and not "speaker" is doubtless the correct translation of the Syriac *omouro* (the one who gives the *memro* or homily).

16. On the exegetical work of Hesychius cf. Aubineau, op. cit. (n. 13, above), p. 41.

17. Ibid., pp. 56-60, 113-15.

18. Cf. *Lectionnaire arménien,* n. 44, pp. [157-173].

19. A. Vilela, *La condition collégiale des prêtres au IIIe siècle* (Théologie Historique 14; Paris, 1971), pp. 60, 128-36, 160.

20. B. Botte, *La Tradition Apostolique de saint Hippolyte: Essai de reconstitution* (LQF 39; Münster, 1963), p. 40. Cf. Vilela, op. cit., pp. 364-65.

21. P. Rentinck, *La cura pastorale in Antiochia nel IV secolo* (Analecta Gregoriana 178; Rome, 1970), p. 176.

22. *Plérophories* 44, p. 95. The Syriac word *archidiacoum* which John Rufus uses is evidently taken over from Greek. In the Life of St. Sabas the archdeacon is called *diakonos ton proton* (Schwartz, op. cit., p. 184).

23. *Itinerarium Egeriae* 29, 3, p. 76.

24. Ibid., 24, 1, p. 67.

25. *Catecheses Mystagogicae* 5, 2 (PG 33:1109).

26. PG 33:1065-1093.

27. P. Thomsen, "Die lateinischen und griechischen Inschriften der Stadt Jerusalem und ihrer Umgebung," *Zeitschrift der deutschen Morgenländischen Gesellschaft* 45 (1922), no. 130.

28. J. Germer-Durand, "Epigraphie chrétienne de Jérusalem," RB 1 (1892), pp. 560-88

29. *Vita Porphyrii,* p. 78.

30. PG 42:744-46; cf. also *Epitome* (PG 42:824-25).

31. *Vita Euthymii* 22, p. 35: "Fidus . . . a young boy and reader in the Church of the Holy Resurrection." The rather widespread practice of having children exercise this function seems thus to have been followed at Jerusalem; cf. H. Leclercq, "Lecteur," DACL 8/2:2247-49.

32. *Plérophories* 18, p. 35.

33. "Dicitur et tertius psalmus a quocumque clerico [a third psalm is said by one of the minor clerics]": 24, 10, p. 69.

34. Cf. H. Leclercq, "Lecteur," DACL 8/2:2247-54.

35. *Vita Theodosii,* p. 236. See also Cyril's *Catecheses* 13, 26 (PG 33:804), where he refers to the *spoudaioi tes Ekklesias psalmodoi* (diligent singers of the Church), and *Catecheses Mystagogicae* 5, 20: *akouete tou psallontos* (listen to the singer) (PG 33:1124).

36. Mary, a recluse, was singer in the church of the Holy Resurrection; cf. *Vita Cyriaci,* p. 233.

37. *Itinerarium Egeriae* 47, pp. 88-89.

38. Cf. H. Leclercq, "Interprète," DACL 7/1:1205.

39. PG 42:825.

40. PG 33:349.

41. PG 33:1080.

42. *Itinerarium Egeriae* 46, 1, p. 87.

43. For the subdeaconate, cf. *Didascalia* IX, 34 (tr. by R. H. Connolly, *Didascalia Apostolorum* [Oxford, 1929], pp. 96-97); Synod of Antioch (341), canon 10, in P.-P. Joannou, ed., *Discipline générale antique (II-IX s.)* (Pontificia Commissione per la redazione del codice di diritto canonico orientale. Fonti 9; Grottaferrata, 1962 ff.), I/2, p. 112; Epiphanius (PG 42:824); *Apostolic Constitutions* VIII, 11; etc. (Funk, *Didascalia et Constitutiones Apostolorum* [Paderborn, 1905], 1:494). For the function of porter cf. Epiphanius (PG 42:825); *Apostolic Constitutions* II, 26; etc. (Funk 1:103).

44. *Itinerarium Egeriae* 24, 9 (*clerico*), p. 69.

45. Cyril of Jerusalem, *Catecheses baptismales* 2 (*tōn klērikōn*; PG 33:377); *Itinerarium Egeriae* 44, 23, p. 86; 45, 2 and 46, 1 (*clerici*), p. 87; Jerome, *Contra Johannem* (PL 23:374); *Lectionnaire arménien* 44bis, p. [159]; Zachary, *Historia ecclesiastica* III, 3 ("the communities of monks and clerics returned to Jerusalem") (CSCO 87; Louvain, 1953), pp. 107-8.

46. *Lectionnaire arménien* 52ter, p. [189].

47. *Itinerarium Egeriae* 39, 3, p. 83.

48. Cf. A. A. R. Bastiaensen, *Observations sur le vocabulaire liturgique dans l'Itinéraire d'Egérie* (Latinitas Christianorum Primaeva 17; Nijmegen–Utrecht, 1962), pp. 12-14.

49. *Vita Euthymii* 22, p. 35.

50. Ibid., 20, p. 32; 37, p. 56.

51. *Plérophories* 44, p. 95.

52. Joannou, op. cit., I/1, pp. 74-76.

53. *Vita Euthymii* 16, p. 26.

54. Ibid., p. 35.

55. Cf. R. Aigrain, "Chorévêques," *Catholicisme* 2 (Paris, 1949), cols. 1072-75.

56. *Vita Porphyrii* 10, pp. 9-10; 14, p. 13.

57. *Vita Euthymii,* 20; 22; 30; 37; and 48, pp. 33, 35, 48, 55, and 69; *Vita Sabae* 20, p. 104.

58. *Itinerarium Egeriae* 24, 7, p. 68; tr. in G. E. Gringas, *Egeria: The Diary of a Pilgrimage* (Ancient Christian Writers 38; New York, 1970), p. 91 [henceforth: Gingras, with page reference].

59. Ibid., 25, 7, p. 71 (Gingras, p. 94).

60. Ibid., 40, 1, p. 84 (Gingras, p. 116).

61. Ibid., 37, 1, p. 80.

62. Ibid., 24, 4, p. 68.

63. Ibid., 46, 5, p. 88.

64. Ibid., 45, 2, p. 87.

65. Ibid., 24, 7, p. 68.

66. Ibid., 24, 2, p. 67.

67. Ibid., 31, 3, p. 77.

68. Ibid., 24, 10, p. 69.
69. *Lectionnaire arménien* 44bis, p. [159].
70. *Itinerarium Egeriae* 24, 2, pp. 67-68.
71. Ibid., 45, 3, p. 87.
72. *Lectionnaire arménien* 52ter, p. [189].
73. *Offertur, agitur, fit: Itinerarium Egeriae* 29, 3, p. 76; 35, 2, p. 79; 38, 2, pp. 82-83; *Catecheses Mystagogicae* 5 (PG 33:1109). The letter of Epiphanius of Cyprus to John of Jerusalem (*Saint Jérôme. Lettres*, ed. by J. Labourt, 2 [Paris, 1951], p. 171) tells us that the two bishops celebrated together at Bethel.
74. *Itineraruim Egeriae* 25, 1, p. 70.
75. Ibid., 26; 42; 43, 2, pp. 72, 84, 85.
76. Ibid., 27, 6, p. 74.
77. Ibid., 46, pp. 87-88.
78. Ibid., 47, pp. 88-89.
79. Ibid., 24, 4 and 45, 1, pp. 68 and 87.
80. *Didascalia* II, 57, 2-5 (Connolly, op. cit., pp. 119-20).
81. *Constitutiones Apostolorum* II, 57 (Funk, p. 159).
82. *Testamentum Domini Nostri Jesu Christi* (ed. Rahmani, p. 25).
83. *Itinerarium Egeriae*, 24, 10, p. 69.
84. Ibid., 29, 5, and 34, pp. 76 and 78.
85. *Catecheses Mystagogicae* 5, 2 (PG 33:1109).
86. *Itinerarium Egeriae* 45, 1, p. 87.
87. Ibid., 25, 1; 26; etc., pp. 70, 72.
88. Ibid., 24, 1 and 12, pp. 67 and 70.
89. Ibid., 24, 1, p. 67.
90. Ibid., 10, 3; 24, 1; 24, 8; etc., pp. 50, 67, 69.
91. *Lectionnaire géorgien*, no. 709, p. 107 (cf. the apparatus as well).
92. *Itinerarium Egeriae* 24, 1, p. 67.
93. *Lectionnaire arménien* 44bis, p. [159].
94. *Vita Euthymii* 20, p. 32.
95. *Plérophories* 18, pp. 35-37.
96. *Didascalia* II, 27, 3 (Connolly, op. cit., p. 96).
97. *Itinerarium Egeriae* 24, 8, p. 69.
98. Didascalia II, 57 (Connolly, op. cit., p. 120).
99. *Itinerarium Egeriae* 31, 7; 37, 2; 37, 3, pp. 77, 81.
100. In his *Epist. 146 ad Evangelum* St. Jerome is indignant at seeing a deacon seated among the priests (Labourt, op. cit., 8, p. 118).
101. *Catecheses Mystagogicae* 5, 2 (PG 33:1109).
102. *Itinerarium Egeriae* 24, 5-6, p. 68.
103. Ibid., 29, 3; 30, 2; 35, 1; 43, 3, pp. 76-77, 79, 85.
104. Jerome, *Contra Johannem* (PL 23:380).
105. Cf. *Catecheses Baptismales* 17, 35 (PG 33:1009). Are we to regard the functions attributed to the "saints" or to clerics as in fact done by *deacons* (*Catecheses Mystagogicae* 2, 3 [PG 33:1080]; *Itinerarium Egeriae* 45, 2, p. 87)?

106. *Itinerarium Egeriae* 37, 2, p. 81.

107. *Catecheses Mystagogicae* 5, 2 (PG 33:1109).

108. Jerome, *Epist. 146* (Labourt, 8:115-19).

109. *Procatechesis* 4 (PG 33:340).

110. *Catecheses Mystagogicae* 5, 2 (PG 33:1109-12); *Itinerarium Egeriae* 25, 1-2; 30, 2; 42; 43, 2, pp. 70, 76-77, 84, 85.

111. Cf. *Itinerarium Egeriae* 24, 9-12, pp. 69-70.

112. Ibid., 46, 1; *Catecheses Mystagogicae* 2, 3 (PG 33:1080); *Lectionnaire arménien* 44ter, p. [169].

113. Cf., e.g., Y. M. J. Congar, "L''Ecclesia' or communauté chrétienne, sujet intégral de l'action liturgique," in J.-P. Jossua and Y. Congar, eds., *La liturgie après Vatican II: Bilans, études, perspectives* (Unam Sanctam 66; Paris, 1967), pp. 241-82.

114. *Itinerarium Egeriae* 25, 1, p. 70 (Gingras, p. 93).

115. Ibid., 26, 1, p. 72 (Gingras, p. 97).

116. Ibid., 42, 1, p. 94 (Gingras, pp. 117-18).

117. Ibid., 43, 2, p. 85 (Gingras, p. 118).

118. Ibid., 43, 3, p. 85 (Gingras, pp. 118-19). [I have modified Gingras' translation to fit Renoux's interpretation of the Latin text.—*Tr.*].

119. "Qui sedent," says the Latin text (ibid., 25, 1, p. 70). In fact, these are probably *seated* around the bishop, as the text indicates elsewhere (24, 4, p. 68).

120. *Catecheses Mystagogicae* 5, 2 (PG 33:1109).

121. *Itinerarium Egeriae* 27, 6-7, p. 74 (Gingras, p. 99).

122. Ibid., 46, 1, p. 87.

123. PG 49: 314 and 358; 50: 618 and 626; 56:111-12 and 119.

124. Texts listed in V. van De Paverd, *Zur Geschichte der Messliturgie in Antiocheia und Konstantinopel gegen Ende des vierten Jahrhunderts* (OCA 187; Rome, 1970), p. 131.

125. *Constitutiones Apostolorum* II, 57, 9 (Funk 1:163).

126. *Sancti Hieronymi Presbyteri Tractatus sive Homiliae in Psalmos* (Anecdota Maredsolana 3/2; Maredsous, 1897), pp. 140, 342, 343.

127. Sozomen, *Historia ecclesiastica* VII, 19 (ed. Bidez and Hansen; Berlin, 1960), p. 330.

128. A. Baumstark, *Die Messe im Morgenland* (Kempten–Munich, 1906), pp. 96-97.

129. 1 Cor. 14.29-31.

130. Cf. Acts 18.27-28; Eusebius, *Historia Ecclesiastica* IV, 19, 16-18 (ed. G. Bardy in SC 41; Paris, 1955), pp. 117-19; *Constitutiones Apostolorum* VIII, 32, 17-18 (Funk 1:538).

131. Cf. Vilela, op. cit., pp. 133-36.

Triacca, Achille M. (pp. 233-252)

1. Cf. P. Fernandez-Rodriguez, "La liturgia, profesion de fe," CTom 94 (1967), pp. 586ff; J. Lécuyer, "Réflexions sur la théologie du culte selon saint Thomas," RT 55 (1955), pp. 339-62.

2. On the question and subject of liturgical participation cf. at least the following (in alphabetical order): G. Baraúna, "La partecipazione attiva principio ispiratore e direttivo della Costituzione," in G. Baraúna (ed.), *La Sacra Liturgia rinnovata dal Concilio:*

Studi e commenti alla Costituzione Liturgica del Concilio Ecumenico Vaticano II (Turin, 1964), pp. 135-99; B. Botte, "La participation active et le sacerdoce des fidèles. L'idée du sacerdoce des fidèles dans la Tradition," in *Cours et conférences des semains liturgiques* 11 (Louvain, 1934), pp. 21-28; F. Cabrol, "Comment nos pères participaient à la liturgie de la Messe," ibid., pp. 75-94; B. Capelle, "Que faut-il entendre par 'participation active'?" ibid., pp. 7-19; idem, "'Mediator Dei' et la participation active," QLP 31 (1950), pp. 77-81; J. Espeja, "El poder cultural del bautizado," *Salmanticensis* 11 (1964), pp. 147-93 (on this theme in St. Thomas Aquinas); idem, "El sacerdocio del pueblo cristiano," CTom 55 (1964), pp. 77-130; G. Lercaro, "Partecipazione attiva, principio fondamentale della riforma pastorale-liturgica," in *Cours et conf*érences 11 (1934), pp. 73-81; A. Lupp, *Der Begriff "Participatio" im Sprachgebrauch der römischen Liturgie* (Munich, 1960); F. Nakagaki, S.D.B., *Partecipazione attiva dei fideli secondo il Sacramentario Veronese. Un importante aspetto dell'ecclesiologia in prospettiva liturgica* (doctoral dissertation at the San Anselmo Pontifical Liturgical Institute, unfortunately not published as yet; Rome, 1969), pp. XIX + 398; P. Parsch, *Volksliturgie* (Klosterneuburg–Vienna, 1952); A. Pascual, "La participatión activa de los fieles en la liturgia eucarística en los textos litúrgicos de los seis primeros siglos," *Liturgia* 7 (1952), pp. 131-42; J. Pascher, "Das Wesen der tätigen Teilnahme. Ein Beitrag zur Theologie der Konstitution über die heilige Liturgie," in *Miscellanea liturgica in onore di S.E. il Card. G. Lercaro* 1 (Rome, 1966), pp. 219-29; etc.

We may also mention the published acts of various congresses and important "weeks" held prior to the Constitution on the Sacred Liturgy and dealing with the subject of participation in the liturgy: e.g., *Participation active des fidèles au culte: Cours et conférences de semaines liturgiques* 11 (Louvain, 1934); *Partecipazione attiva alla liturgia: Atti del III Convegno Internazionali di Studi Liturgici. Lugano 14-18 Settembre 1953*, ed. by L. Agustoni and G. Wagner (Lugano–Como, 1953); *Active Participation of the Faithful in the Liturgy of the Church* (Madras, 1959); *Participation in the Mass: 20th North American Liturgical Week* (Washington, 1960); on Heeswijk, *14-16 Janvier 1962*, cf. QLP 43 (1962), p. 36; *Participating in the Mass: Eighth Irish Liturgical Congress, April 1961*, cf. V. Ryan, *Studies in Pastoral Liturgy* 2 (Dublin, 1963); issue of *Liturgica* 3 (Rome, 1963), on "La partecipazione dei fideli alla Messa: Dottrina e pastorale."

3. Cf. *Sacrosanctum Concilium*, nos. 11, 12, 14, 17, 19, 26, 27, 28, 33, 41, 48, 50, 55, 56, 79, 90, 106, 113, 114, etc. See G. Baraúna, op. cit., espec. pp. 136-39; C. Vagaggini, "Idee fondamentali della Costituzione," in *La Sacra Liturgia rinnovata* (n. 2, above), pp. 59-100, espec. pp. 60-61, 83, 90; E. (=H.) Schmidt, "Il popolo cristiano al centro del rinnovamento liturgico," *Civiltà Cattolica* 115 (1964), I, pp. 120-31, espec. p. 123.

4. Cf. X. Ochoa, *Index verborum cum documentis Concilii Vaticani Secundi* (Rome, 1967), pp. 356-59. The documents of Vatican II speak of:

participation in cultural life: cf. *Gravissimum Educationis*, no. 6; *Gaudium et Spes*, nos. 31, 56-57, 60; *Inter Mirifica*, no. 11.

participation in social life: cf. *Gravissimum Educationis*, no. 1; *Apostolicam Actuositatem*, no. 13; *Gaudium et Spes*, nos. 57, 68.

participation in the world of work and the economy: cf. *Apostolicam Actuositatem*, no. 13; *Gaudium et Spes*, no. 13.

participation in political life and public life: cf. *Apostolicam Actuositatem,* no. 9; *Gaudium et Spes,* nos. 31, 75.

participation in the international community: cf. *Gaudium et Spes,* nos. 79, 84, etc.

5. Nakagaki, op. cit., p. 11, writes: "In the context of liturgy these words translate the well-known phrase of St. Pius X in his Motu Proprio *Tra le sollecitudini,* which was written in Italian"; in n. 39 he adds: "The word used by Pius X was translated into Latin as *actuosa communicatio* because the Roman Latinists could not find the term *participatio* in classical Latin. The pope probably had some liturgical expression in mind, and specifically the one in the Roman Canon: 'ut quotquot ex hac altaris participatione sacrosanctum Filii tui Corpus et Sanguinem sumpserimus.'" Cf. also Paschar, art. cit., pp. 212-20.

6. In developing the first part of my paper I shall take the doctoral dissertation of my confrere F. Nakagaki as my starting point (especially pp. 70-76). I thank my Japanese colleague for permission to use his work.

7. An appropriate method is of course required in studying the sources. Cf. F. Nakagaki, "Metodo integrale. Discorso sulla metodologia nell'interpretazione dei testi eucologici," in *Fons vivus. Miscellanea liturgica in memoria di Don Eusebio Maria Vismara* (Bibliotheca Theologica Salesiana, Sectio 1, Fontes 6; Zürich, 1971), pp. 269-86.

8. For a list of the sources of the early Ambrosian liturgy, cf. K. Gamber, *Codices Liturgici Latini Antiquiores* (2nd ed.; Fribourg, 1968), pp. 259-86, nos. 501-95 [henceforth: CLLA]; C. Vogel, *Introduction aux sources de l'histoire du culte chrétien au Moyen Age* (Biblioteca degli "Studi Medievali" 1; 2nd ed., Spoleto, 1975), pp. 27-29, 92, 230-31, 300-2, 333, 349-50, 357, 365; A.M. Triacca, *I prefazi ambrosiani del ciclo "De Tempore" secondo il "Sacramentarium Bergomense." Avviamento ad uno studio critico-teologico* (Rome, 1970), pp. 112-13.

9. Cf. A. Paredi (ed.), *Sacramentarium Bergomense. Manoscritto del secolo IX della Biblioteca di S. Alessandro in Colonna in Bergamo* (Monumenta Bergomensia 6; Bergamo, 1962); CLLA, no. 505. . Henceforth I shall refer to Paredi's work thus: Ber + number in the edition-transcription, e.g., Ber 1234.

10. For studies of the Bergamo Sacramentary cf. the bibliography in CLLA, no. 505, and especially F. Combaluzier, "Sacramentarium Bergomense. L'édition Paredi (1962)," SE 13 (1962), pp. 56-66; F. Dell'Oro, "Sacramentarium Bergomense (a proposito di una edizione," Sal 25 (1963), pp. 74-80; and O. Heiming in AL 9/1 (1965), pp. 331-36.

11. Cf., e.g., the tables of formulas and concordances in F. Combaluzier, *Sacramentaire de Bergame et d'Ariberto. Tables des matières. Index des formules* (Instrumenta Patristica 5; Steenbrugge, 1962) (on this work cf. F. Dell'Oro, "Indices sacramentarii Bergomensis et Eriberti," EL 77 [1963], pp. 109-14). Cf. also J. Frei, "Konkordanztabellen" in idem (ed.), *Das ambrosianische Sakramentar D. 3-3 aus dem mailändischen Metropolitankapitel. Eine textkritische und redaktionsgeschichtliche Untersuchung der mailändsichen Sakramentartradition* (Corpus Ambrosiano-Liturgicum 3; Münster, 1973), pp. 469-542 (CLLA, no. 510). We should bear in mind what A. Paredi wrote in Amb 40 (1964), p. 255, regarding the *Sacramentarium Bergomense* and the other Ambrosian sources: "One point is certain: the earliest Ambrosian Missals are surprisingly uniform. The Bergamo

Sacramentary was written shortly after the middle of the ninth century: for almost all the feasts and all the prayers it is identical not only with the sacramentaries of Biasca and Lodrino, which are a little later, but also with the Sacramentary of Ariberto, from the eleventh century, and the other Missals of the twelfth and later centuries."

12. Cf. O. Heiming (ed.), *Das ambrosianische Sakramentar von Biasca. Die Handschrift Mailand Ambrosius A 24 bis inf. I. Text* (Corpus Ambrosiano-Liturgicum 2; Münster, 1969) (CLLA, no. 515).

13. Cf. A. Paredi (ed.), "Il Sacramentari di Ariberto. Edizione del ms. D. 3.2. della Biblioteca del Capitolo Metropolitano di Milano," in *Miscellanea Adriano Bernareggi* (Monumenta Bergomensia 1; Bergamo, 1958), pp. 329-488 (CLLA, no. 530).

14. Cf. J. Frei's ed. (n. 11, above) (CLLA, no. 510).

15. Cf. O. Heiming (ed.), *Das Sacramentarium Triplex. Die Handschrift C 43 der Zentral-bibliothek Zürich I. Text* (Corpus Ambrosiano-Liturgicum 1; Münster, 1968) (CLLA, no. 535).

16. Cf. Nakagaki, *Partecipazione attiva* (n. 2, above), pp. 73-74.

17. Cf. J. Pinell, *Cursus methodologicus. Principia methodologica studiis scientificis liturgicis aptata* (Lecture notes at the San Anselmo Pontifical Liturgical Institute; Rome, 1965-66), pp. 34-37; M. Augé, "Principi di interpretazione dei testi liturgici," in *Anamnesis* 1. *La liturgica momento nella storia della salvezza* (Turin–Rome, 1974), pp. 159-79, especially pp. 167ff.

18. P. Alfonso, *L'eucologia romana antica (Lineamenti stilistici e storici)* (Subiaco, 1931), pp. 7-8.

19. Cf. L. Eizenhöfer, "Untersuchungen zum Stil und Inhalt der römischen *oratio super populum*," EL 52 (1938), pp. 258-311, especially pp. 261-63.

20. Cf. A.M. Triacca, "La liturgia educa alla liturgia? Riflessioni fenomenico-psicologiche sul dato liturgico globalmente considerato," RivL 58 (1971), pp. 261-75, especially pp. 264-67; J.A. Jungmann, *The Early Liturgy to the Time of Gregory the Great*, tr. F.A. Brunner (Notre Dame, 1959), pp. 164-74.

21. Cf. A.M. Triacca, "Per una migliore ambientazione delle fonti liturgiche ambrosiane sinassico-eucaristiche (Note metodologiche)," in *Fons vivus* (n. 7, above), pp. 163-220, with the bibliography cited there.

22. Cf. A.M. Triacca, "Liturgie ambrosienne: Amalgame hétérogène ou 'specificum' influent? Flux, reflux, influences," in *Liturgie de l'Eglise particulière et liturgie de l'Eglise universelle. Conférences Saint-Serge, XXII Semaine d'etudes liturgiques, Paris 20 juin–3 juillet 1975* (Rome, 1976), pp. 289-327.

23. On the subject of the redactional stratification proper to the Ambrosian liturgy, cf. the synthesis of problems in A.M. Triacca, "Le rite de l'*Impositio manuum super infirmum* dans l'ancienne liturgie ambrosienne," in *La maladie et la mort du chrétien dans la liturgie. Conférences Saint-Serge, XXI Semaine d'etudes liturgiques, Paris 1-4 juillet 1974* (Rome, 1975), pp. 339-60, espec. pp. 340-42, and passim.

24. I have already dealt with the difficult subject of the prefaces in the Bergamo Sacramentary and have distinguished the various redactions of them. Cf. Triacca, *I prefazi ambrosiani* (n. 8, above), espec. pp. 49-100; idem, "Riflessioni teologiche su alcuni prefazi del *Sacramentarium Bergomense*," Sal 33 (1971), pp. 455-98.

25. Cf. Nakagaki, op. cit., p. 14.

26. Cf. my conclusions (passim) in the article cited in n. 22 and the works cited in nn. 23-24.

27. Cf. Jungmann, op. cit., pp. 164-67.

28. Cf. A. Verheul, *Introduzione alla liturgia* (Milan, 1967), pp. 214-16.

29. Cf. Augé, art. cit. (n. 17, above) and the bibliography he gives. Cf. also A.M. Triacca, "La strutturazione eucologica dei prefazi. Contributo metodologico per una loro retta esegesi," EL 86 (1972), pp. 233-79, especially pp. 243-44 (existential expression), pp. 264-65 (associative expression); pp. 266-68 (existential expression), p. 278 (existential function).

30. Cf. Nakagaki, op. cit., pp. 192-93.

31. Cf. Chapter 7 of Nakagaki's work (pp. 193-211), on which this section is based.

32. I am, of course, simply giving some examples of each point. All examples for this paper are taken from the *Proprium de tempore*.

33. Cf. Ber 54, 56, 57, 58, 60, 65, 66, 67, 68, 69, 71, 72, 73, 76, 79, 81, 82, 83, 85, 86, 87, 90, 91, 92, 95, 96, 97, 98, 99, 100, 101, 102, 104, 105, 106, 107, 110, 112, 113, 114, 115, 116, 117, 120, 123, 126, 127, 130, 137, 146, 147, 148, 176, 178, 179, 180, 181, 182, 183, 190, 191, 193, 195, 196, 197, 198, 201, 202, 203, 204, 205, 206, 208, 211, 212-14, 215, etc.

34. Cf. Ber 52, 60, 61, 62, 64, 76, 88, 90, 91, 92, 94, 98, 106, 107, 110, 112, 131, 150, 182, 183, 184, 185, 201, 204, 208, 209, 212, 213, etc.

35. Cf. Ber 59, 61, 65, 66, 68, 69, 83, 86, 87, 92, 104, 108, 111, 118, 120, 121, 122, 127, 128, 180, 185, 191, 199, 210, 216, etc.

36. Cf. Ber 78, 106, 146, 197, 211, etc.

37. In the *postcommunion* prayers of the *temporal* cycle ecclesial terms (except for *nos*: cf. nn. 33-36) are used only in: Ber 564, 597, 1240, 125, 625, 136, 1235, 632.

We may add: Ber 219, 269, 411, 455. This is the sum total!

38. Cf. *populus:* Ber 62, 67, 72, 77, 174, 207, 265, 270, 300, 309, 330, 437, 451, 456, 462, 558, 569, 586, 616, 650, 660, 680, 686, 770, 860, 865.

Familia: Ber 57, 290, 320, 427, 593, 755.

Famulus (servant): Ber 280, 355.

Plebs: Ber 179, 275, 305, 353.

Fideles (faithful): Ber 216, 645.

Ecclesia (Church): Ber 315, 387, 407, 412, 422, 581, 628, 645, 680, 755, 783, 792, 855.

39. The words for *gift* that are used in the *postcommunion* prayers of Ber are:
Donum (gift): Ber 219, 269, 279, 319, 411, 436, 441, 548, 644, 685, 724, 782, 864, 869.

Munus (gift): Ber 56, 71, 542, 178, 211, 289, 329, 476, 638, 649, 749, 769, 774, 782.

To this terminology we may add *mysterium* and *sacramentum* since the context of the postcommunion highlights the theme of God's free giving. See, e.g.:

Mysterium (here: especially sacred rites or sacred species): Ber 61, 76, 201, 294, 304, 308, 367, 446, 466, 481, 548, 557, 659, 690, 749, 864.

Sacramentum (here: especially ritual action or sacred species): Ber 66, 136, 150, 206, 211, 215, 284, 299, 344, 348, 357, 377, 381, 401, 406, 426, 431, 455, 578, 590, 610, 654, 760, 786, 854.

40. Cf. my essay cited in n. 29 on the existential dimension in the prefaces.

41. Cf. the works cited in n. 24.

42. The importance of the embolisms or inserts in the prefaces is well known. See what I wrote earlier in EL 86 (1972), pp. 268-75, especially pp. 269-70: "From a structural viewpoint the embolism is usually connected with the opening phrase and appears as the *ratio* [motive] for it; it is in fact an explanatory statement that gives the motive for the *gratiarum actio*. This *ratio*, explicit or implicit, is directly or indirectly accompanied by the *adiuncta* [circumstances], i.e., the expressions referring to the circumstances of God's action or to theological truths, and quite often to liturgico-celebrational circumstances as well. From these *adiuncta* the embolism takes on a specific coloring or tone in the liturgical context. . . . In addition it should be noted that the embolisms are constructed from the stylistic viewpoint, according to the classic norms of poiesis and, more specifically, are related to the *genus demonstrativum*."

43. Cf. n. 37, above, and n. 53, below.

44. Cf. *Plebs* in:

Super populum [*oratio super populum:* prayer over the people]: Ber 179, 275, 305, 353, 628.

Super sindonem: Ber 383, 443.

Super oblata [over the gifts]: Ber 218, 555, 576.

VD [*Vere dignum:* It is truly right = preface]: Ber 55.

Postcommunion: Ber 136, 1235.

Alia [i.e., *oratio:* alternate prayer]: Ber 91, 179, 506, 507.

45. Cf. n. 55.

46. Cf. *Famulus* in:

Super populum: Ber 280, 335, 581.

Super sindonem: Ber 133, 478, 582, 594, 641.

Super oblata: Ber 327, 453, 857.

VD: Ber 376.

Postcommunion: Ber 125.

Alia: Ber 95, 98, 351, 533, 55, 709, 717, 718, 719.

And cf. *Famulari* (to serve): Ber 557.

47. Cf. *Familia* in:

Super populum: Ber 57, 290, 320, 427, 593, 755.

Super sindonem: Ber 266, 345, 281, 359, 433, 539.

Super oblata: Ber 385, 630.

VD: nothing.

Postcommunion: Ber 632.

Alia: Ber 350, 538, 592, 627, 734, 735.

48. Cf. *Filius* in:

Super populum: Ber 451, 628, 645.

Super sindonem: Ber 634, 671.

Super oblata: Ber 767.

VD: Ber 405, 445, 636, 781, 1234.

Postcommunion: nothing.

Alia: Ber 520, 527, 639, 725.

49. Cf. *Servus, servitus, subditus* (subject), *servitium* (service) in:

Super populum: nothing.

Super sindonem: Ber 539.

Super oblata: Ber 176, 214, 267, 307, 360, 399.

VD: nothing.

Cf. *Infra actionem* [during the *actio,* i.e., the Canon]: "This offering, therefore, of our *servitus*" (cf. e.g., Ber 759, 817).

Postcommunion: nothing.

50. Cf. *Fidelis* in:

Super populum: Ber 202, 645, 650.

Super sindonem: Ber 428, 559, 634, 646, 651.

Super oblata: Ber 317, 623, 635.

VD: Ber 303, 631.

Postcommunion: Ber 219, 269, 411, 455.

Alia: Ber 350, 529, 679, 763, 1230, 1331.

51. Cf. *(Nova) creatura* in:

Super populum: Ber 52.

Super sindonem: Ber 18 (same initium as in Ber 52), 766, 861.

Super oblata: Ber 213.

VD: nothing.

Postcommunion: Ber 602.

Alia: Ber 498.

52. Cf. also similar terms such as *proles* (offspring: Ber 451, 513, 638, 766, 855, etc.), *suboles* (offspring: Ber 451, 507, 639, etc.), *progenies* (offspring: Ber 539, 755), and also *christianam imperium* (Christian kingdom or rule: Ber 511).

53. Cf. *Ecclesia* in:

Super populum: Ber 387, 407, 412, 422, 581, 628, 656, 680, 755, 783, 792, 855.

Super sindonem: Ber 291, 331, 570, 629, 766.

Super oblata: Ber 134, 188, 272, 409, 588, 747.

VD: Ber 55, (cf. 768), 781, 1234, 1239.

Postcommunion: Ber 564, 597, 1240.

Alia: Ber 88, 89, 506, 509, 513, 516, 521, 525, 527, 638, 639, 751, 776.

Laetare Sunday in Lent: Ber 314, 352.

54. There is an exception, though only an apparent one, in Ber 155 (*super populum*); 1234 and (1239) (*VD*); 509, 516, 525, 638 (*Alia*).

55. Cf. *Populus* in:

Super populum: Ber 62, 67, 72, 77, 123, 174, 207, 265, 270, 300, 309, 330, 397, 437, 456, 462, 558, 569, 586, 616, 660, 865.

[*Populi*]: Ber 103, 301, 451, 650, 680, 681, 770, 860.

Super sindonem: Ber 187, 203, 276, 341, 408, 423, 571, 617, 656, 721, 746, 1237.

Super oblata: Ber 370, 540, 571.

[*Populi*]: Ber 464, 608.

VD: nothing.

Postcommunion: Ber 625.

Alia: Ber 99, 113, 130, 195, 461, 506, 528, 529, 530, 699, 702, 732, 736, 741, 742, 744, 752, 1226.

[*Populi*]: Ber 194, 526, 531.

56. There are some apparent exceptions (i.e., *populus* without *tuus*), Ber 62, 174, 437, 456, 600, 301, 451, 686, 860 (=*super populum*); 617 (=*super sindonem*); 464 (=*super oblata*); 506, 530, 741, 852, 531 (=*Alia*).

57. For a study of these terms, which have the same meaning in the Ambrosian liturgy as in the Roman, cf., e.g., M.P. Ellebracht, *Remarks on the Vocabulary of the Ancient Orations in the Missale Romanum* (Latinitas Christianorum Primaeva 12; Nijmegen, 1963), passim, with the bibliography given there.

57a. For the *theme of the Father's mercy,* cf., e.g., Ber 52, 66, 174, 175, 182, 208, 213, 265, 276, 331, 345, 364, 371, 388, 395, 397, 402, 423, 433, 451, 456, 433, 549, 569, 571, 595, 651, 686, 717, 718. Cf. also the expression *misericors Deus* (merciful God) in, e.g., Ber 362, 363, 439, 449, 613, 649, 690, etc., and Ber 438 (God, who show mercy [*miserator*] to the hearts of your faithful), 544 (God . . . who act with kindness [*benignus*]), 645 (merciful consoler and teacher of your faithful).

58. For *adesto (propitius)* (be [mercifully] present) and similar terms, cf. Ber 86, 87, 100, 132, 187, 208, 316, 321, 305, 447, 335, 383, 446, 455, 331, 627, 664, 665, 678, 714, 1232.

59. For *respice (propitius)* (look [with mercy] on) and similar terms, cf. Ber 52, 77, 88, 94, 131, 134, 174, 176, 290, 309, 330, 332, 351, 375, 380, 423, 427, 553, 617, 625, 626, 642, 651, 699, 718.

60. For *intuere benignus* (look with kindness), *intende placatus* (be appeased and look) and similar terms, cf. Ber 63, 64, 74, 686, 705, 717, 1237.

61. See n. 51 for the term *nova creatura* and n. 63 for the theme of renewal. I add here: Ber 116, 150, 473, 482, 483, 422, 602; cf. also Ber 424, 539, and P. Borella, "*Vetustas et novitas* nella liturgia dell'Avvento," Amb 39 (1963), pp. 347-59.

62. The theme of eschatological fulfillment is found especially in the postcommunions, as in the Roman liturgy.

63. On the theme of renewal which comprises many subthemes, cf., e.g., Ber 52, 53, 61, 62, 64, 76, 82, 87, 146, 179, 196, 197, 208, 209, 212, 287, 289, 313, 320, 330, 340, 370, 387, 412, 424, 473, 539, 541, 542, 565, 569, 570, 602, 612, 620, 638, 641, 656, 755. Cf. also nn. 51 and 61.

64. See nn. 44, 46, 50, 53, 55 and also 47 (=*familia*) and 48 (=*filius*) for references to the terminology mentioned.

65. The praying community adopts specific attitudes. E.g., Ber 53, 58, 63, 66, 71, 73, 74, 75, 76, 79, 81, 105, 106, 107, 108, 110, 113, 120, 125, 147, 149, 174, 175, 177, 203, 298, 373, 392, 409, 439, 548, 434.

And also: Ber 57, 459, 454, 465.

66. The structure of the eucharistic liturgy had the same form then as today: the proclamation of the word of God, followed by the liturgy of sacrifice. For the proclamation of God's word there were doubtless readings from both testaments. See e.g., Ber 753.

67. The theme of participation is expressed with different nuances in the postcommunion prayers:
a) by the word participation: Ber 76, 136, 396, 416, 431, 859. See also n. 71.
b) by other words, e.g., by the word *participes* (sharers).
Ber 201, 304, 348, 426, 685. See also n. 71.
Cf. also with *percipere* (receive) in Ber 269, 304, 219, 441, 597, 610, 689, 690, 724, 791, 859—all of them postcommunion prayers.
And with *perceptio* (reception) in Ber 284, 299, 377, 381, 410, 590, 602, 791, 753.
68. For example, for the Nativity cycle see the phrases in Ber 71, 86, 120, 125, 190, etc.
69. It would be enough to examine only the postcommunion prayers: Ber 56, 61, 71, 76, 81, 86, 107, 178, 211, 274, 284, 289, 299, 294, 304, 319, 324, 796, 854, 334, 343, 348, 357, 362, 372, 377, 381, 386, 391, 396, 401, 406, 411, (416), 426, 431, 450, 455, 460, 466, 476, 494, 542, 548, 571, 590, 602, 610, 620, 654, 664, 674, 685, 690, 724, 749, 775, 782, 791, 854, 864, 869. Cf. also nn. 93-96.
70. Cf. also n. 67 and, furthermore, e.g., Ber 59, 57, 68, 73, 76, 103, 104, 120, 147, 179, 270, 304, 426, 460, 578, 796, 1240.
71. Cf. n. 67b where *particeps* is a term proper to postcommunion prayers. I add here: Ber 59 (*=super oblata*). In n. 67a, *participatio* too is a term in postcommunion prayers. I add here: Ber 449 (*=super oblata*), 753 (*=Alia*).
72. See the sacramental dimension connected with the word *particeps* (sharer) especially in Ber 201: in the mystery (eucharist); 348: in the sacrament; 685: in the gifts. See the eschatological dimension in Ber 304: in the reality of heaven. And both the sacramental and the eschatological dimensions in Ber 426: in the sacrament and in eternal life.
73. The eucharist is called *communio* in postcommunions: Ber 324, 796, 854, 852; cf. also Ber 386 (*communicare*).
74. Simply as examples I recall here: Ber 107, 215, 454, 620. Ber 206, 276, 625, 367, 372, 377.
75. *Communio* as a source of eternal happiness. Cf., as examples: Ber 343, 372, 381, 401, 615, 620, 632, 669, 436.
76. For *communio* in relation to *benedictio,* cf., e.g., the postcommunions: Ber 125, 441, 859, 1235.
77. Cf. the postcommunion prayer Ber 396, in which liturgy and life are identified: "Lord our God, we ask that, filled with your generous divine gift, we may always live in this participation."
78. This is explicit in Ber 107, 494, 854, 386.
79. Cf., e.g., Ber 460, 548.
80. Cf. the very significant expression in Ber 68: "Grant us that, as we deserved to have him *share* our bodily nature through birth from the Virgin, we may also deserve to be his fellows in the kingdom of his grace."
81. This prayer is found in many non-Ambrosian sources (cf. P. Siffrin, *Konkordanztabellen zu den römischen Sakramentarien*. I. *Sacramentarium Veronense* [*Leonianum*] [Rerum ecclesiasticarum documenta. Series minor: Subsidia studiorum 4; Rome, 1958], p. 97) and also in *Ambrosian sources* (cf. Frei, "Konkordanztabelen," in op. cit., [n. 11,

above], p. 477). Our reflections here are based on the fact that Bergamo Sacramentary is an *unicum*. Cf. nn. 9-13 and 15.

81a. Cf. Ber 601: "It is truly right . . . because the day of our resurrection and of the glory of our Lord Jesus Christ has shone forth with an eternal light. He acted as worthy priest and worthy victim, not only to sanctify the people but, once sanctified, to commend them to your Majesty." Cf. also Ber 609: "One man volunteered to die lest all die. One deigned to die that all of us might live forever."

82. Cf. n. 44.

83. As in Ber 416, 431.

84. Cf. n. 67.

85. The immediate point of reference is called *mysterium* in Ber 79 and also Ber 201, 304. *Participatio* is parallel in meaning to *percipere mysteria (gloriosa)* in Ber 204. Cf. also Ber 690.

86. The immediate point of reference is called *sacramentum* in Ber 136, 416, 431, and also Ber 348. *Participatio* is equivalent in meaning to *perceptio*. For *perceptio sacramenti (tui)* cf. Ber 299, 377, 602; (*huius*): 381, 401; (*paschalis*): 590. For *percipere sacramenta*, cf. Ber 610 and 540.

87. Ber 431; and in Ber 377 and 602.

88. Cf. Ber 76, 136, 396, and also Ber 859, 449.

89. Namely, the invocation and the petition.

90. Cf. n. 86.

91. Cf. n. 85.

92. As in Ber 859; cf. Ber 620.

93. Various terms are used; e.g.,

dona (gifts): Ber 724, 219 and 269;

sancta (holy things): Ber 791;

desiderata (things desired, longed for): Ber 669;

munera (gifts): Ber 753, etc.

Also with: *satiare* (sate, fill, feed): Ber 71, 289, 426, 460, 542, 578, 854, 869;

communicare (to communicate in, share in): Ber 386 (also *communio*: Ber 324, 796, 854);

replere (fill): Ber 76, 178, 476, 782;

vegetare (feed, nourish): Ber 107, 211, 637;

innovare (renew): Ber 629;

reficere (restore, refresh): Ber 274, 357, 455, 749;

libare (taste, take nourishment): Ber 548. Also *libatio* (taste, nourishment): Ber 348, 372, 585.

94. Cf. *sumere* (take, receive): Ber 86, 284, 334, 406, 654, 451, 466, 775, 494, 674, 864, 664.

95. Cf. *accipere* (receive): Ber 294, 343.

percipere (receive): Ber 304, 610, 690, 724, 791.

Also *perceptio* (reception): Ber 299, 377, 381, 401, 590, 602.

And *participatio*: Ber 416, 431.

96. For example: *frequentare* (to perform a ritual action, to celebrate a liturgical feast): Ber 61, 81, 319. Cf. also Ber 301. Also *frequentatio* (celebration): Ber 56.

97. Explicitly in Ber 136. Cf. also Ber 331, 83, 275, 72. Especially Ber 79, 91, 81, 120, 284, 289, 331, 403, 428, 443, 468, 548, 555, 573, 598.

98. Cf., e.g., Ber 56, 57, and the references in n. 69.

99. Cf. Ber 61, 62, 64, 66, 76. Cf. also Ber 82, 87, 88, 90, 91, 97, 107. Cf. also n. 63.

100. Cf. n. 67 and also Ber 68, 73, 103, 134, 121, 147, 270, 548, 578, 585, 590.

101. Cf., e.g., Ber 548, 576, 578, 585, and especially 474.

102. Cf. nn. 87, 88, 93.

103. Cf. nn. 97, 99 and 63, 98 and 69, 74.

104. Cf. nn. 75, 70.

105. Cf. n. 39.

106. Cf. n. 65.

107. But there is also the attainment of a completion during the liturgical action, as Ber 148 says: "Lord, may the *offering* made in today's celebration be acceptable to you, because it has been preceded by our reconciliation through its *perfect expiation,* and because the *fullness of divine worship* has been given to us."

108. This theme is common to all the western liturgies. Cf., e.g., Ber 76 and parallels (Filled with the food that nourishes the spirit, we humbly pray you, Lord, to teach us, through participation in this mystery, to scorn the things of earth and love those of heaven). Cf. P. Bruylants, *"Terrena despicere et amare caelestia,"* in *Miscellanea liturgica in onore di Sua Eminenza il Cardinale Giacomo Lercaro* 2 (Rome, 1967), pp. 195-206.

109. Cf. nn. 67 and 72.

110. Cf. the references given in n. 65. These show a whole series of attitudes proper to participants: trusting, confessing, praying humbly, glorying, rejoicing, being glad, shining, presenting, proclaiming, believing, offering prayers, entering the fellowship of the redeemer, sacrificing, begging, recalling, receiving instruction, meeting Christ with just deeds, strewing before him the branches of uprightness, singing melodiously, etc.

111. This point is well made in a *Super oblata* prayer, Ber 311 (Lord, through this sacrifice sanctify our fasting, so that *what* our observance *professes externally* it may effect *interiorly*).

112. Ber 218 (that what each has brought may be profitable for his salvation) is not an exception to this statement, since hermeneutical principles show that the ecclesial dimension is always present in the euchological sources.

113. See also, e.g., the terminology equivalent to *offerimus* (we offer) in Ber 759 and 817 and also Ber 74, 117, 148, 123, 176, 198, 204, 218, 297, 332, 335, 360, 389, 394, 409, 429, 434, 458, 588, 672, 682, 785, 1238, and also 183, 188, 277, 419, 424, 439, 449, 453, 464, 479, 484, 652, 688, 789, 867.

God completes the offering along with us; e.g., Ber 84, 214, 267, 209, 287, 327, 767, and also 292, 307, 311, 322, 370, 375, 380, 414, 545, 555, 576, 600, 608, 623, 635, 642, 657, 672, 705, 780, 794, 857, 862, 867.

114. Cf. Ber 540 (God, by whose generosity the *venerable mysteries of baptism have been celebrated,* grant that your people, cleansed now through the sacred font from the error of original sin, may *enter your promised land* and so even now receive the *sweet food* of your sacrament).

115. Cf. *s.v. participatio* in A. Forcellini and V. de Vit, *Totius latinitatis lexicon* (Padua, 1865); *Thesaurus linguae latinae*; A. Blaise, *Dictionnaire latin-français des auteurs chrétiens* (Strasbourg, 1954); A. Blaise and A. Dumas, *Le vocabulaire latin des principaux thèmes liturgiques* (Turnhout, 1966); Ellebracht, op. cit., pp. 132-33.

Vogel, Cyrille (pp. 253-264)

1. The term "minister" is used here in its general liturgical meaning and not in its medieval juridical meaning; that is, "minister" is "celebrant" or "president" of the liturgy. On the other hand, with reference to the ordination of ministers, it is appropriate to use the technical term *cheirotonia*, as distinct from *cheirothesia*; the former signifies the imposition of hands, together with a verbal formula that specifies the meaning of the imposition at the making of a bishop, presbyter or deacon. On cheirotonia see C.H. Turner, "Cheirotonia," JTS 24 (1923), pp. 496-504; M. Siotis, *Classical and Christian Cheirotonia and Their Relationship* (in Greek) (Theologia XX-XXII, 1949-51; Athens, 1951); C. Vogel, "Chirotonie et chirothésie," *Irénikon* 45 (1972), pp. 7-21, 207-35. It must be said that etymology and philology by themselves are inadequate resources for analyzing the concept of the imposition of hands.

2. Cf. on this point A. Lemaire, *Les ministères aux origines de l'Eglise. Naissance de la triple hiérarchie: Evêque, presbytres, diacres* (Lectio Divina 68; Paris, 1971); J. Dupont, "Les ministères de l'Eglise naissante d'après les Actes des Apôtres," in *Ministères et célébration de l'Eucharistie. 1. Sacramentum* (Studia Anselmiana 61; Rome 1973), pp. 94-148. A study paralleling the one I am presenting here was published in the same volume, pp. 181-209: C. Vogel, "Le ministère charismatique de l'Eucharistie. Approche rituelle "

3. In the absence of more detailed studies cf. A. Hilgenfeld, *Die Ketzergeschichte des Urchristentums* (Leipzig, 1884; photographic reprint, Hildesheim, 1963); K. Adam, *Der Kirchenbegriff Tertullians* (Forschungen zur christlichen Literatur- und Dogmengeschichte 6/4; Paderborn, 1907), pp. 151-225, On the general problem as applying to official communities and unofficial communities cf. W. Bauer, *Orthodoxy and Heresy in Earliest Christianity*, translated and edited by R.A. Kraft and G. Krodel (Philadelphia, 1971).

By way of an example, here is a ceremonial for ordination in the Marcosian sect as given by Irenaeus, *Adversus haereses* I, 13, 3 (Harvey 1:118; Stieren, pp. 148-51; PG 7:581-85): "He [Marcos] deals above all with women and chiefly those who are cultivated, well-bred and wealthy. . . . He tells them: 'I want you to share in the grace that is mine. . . . The place of his greatness is in us; we must attain to unity. Receive grace first from me and through me. Adorn yourself like a bride ready for her bridegroom, that you may be what I am and I may be what you are. Welcome the seed of light to your marriage bed. . . . Behold, grace is descending on you. Open your mouth and begin to prophesy.' The woman answers: 'I have never prophesied and do not know how.' Marcos then utters further invocations and, to the woman's astonishment, says to her: 'Open your mouth, say anything, and you will prophesy.' The woman swells with pride . . . and begins to utter nonsensical words about the future, words without coherence but full of ardor as her spirit warms to the task. . . . Finally she thinks she is a prophetess and thanks Marcos for giving her a share of his peace. She is ready to show her gratitude not only with gifts of money but by allowing him fleshly union with her. She desires a complete union with Marcos so as to be fused with him." We may compare this passage with Acts 8.9-24 (episode of Simon the magician). Irenaeus' account is contemporary with the ordination ritual in the *Apostolic Tradition*.

4. On the problem of a return of a presbyter to the lay state cf. the pieces of a dossier that I have brought together in my essay, *"Laica communione contentus,"* RevSR 47 (1973), pp. 56-122.

5. *Ad Smyrn*. 8. The same idea is already to be found in *1 Clement* 40; 41; 42, 2-5.

6. In order to avoid any discussion of the attribution of the *Apostolic Tradition* to Hippolytus of Rome (an attribution generally accepted by historians, but not completely unchallenged), I shall cite this document as found in the Latin version that has been preserved in the Verona Fragments (also called the Hauler Fragments), nos. LXVIII-LXXII and that was made in the time of Pope Damasus (ca. 380) and thus closer in time to the original Greek than the other versions for which there is paleographic testimony.

7. For the first part of the proposition, i.e., "No ordination without cheirotonia," I refer the reader to my essay cited above in n. 2: "Le ministère charismatique."

8. For Eastern practice and the doctrine that underlies or is derived from this practice, cf. Vogel, art. cit., pp. 207-9, along with the corrective observations made by L. Ligier and C. Vagaggini; cf. C. Vagaggini, "Possibilità e limiti del riconscimento dei ministeri non cattolici," in *Ministères et célébration* (n. 2, above), pp. 250-320.

9. *Confessio Augustana*, ch. 14: "Regarding ecclesiastical orders they teach that no one may publicly teach in the church or administer the sacraments *unless he be duly called"* (*Die Bekenntnisschriften* [3rd ed.; Göttingen, 1956], p. 69). *Apologia confessionis*, ch. 13: "If [priestly] orders be thus understood, *we do not take it amiss that the imposition of hands should be called a sacrament*. For the Church is commissioned to establish ministries" (ibid., p. 294). *Articuli christianae doctrinae (Smalkaldenses*, ch. 10: "Therefore, as ancient examples of the Church and the Fathers teach us, we *should ordain* those who are suited to the office, and this we intend to do" (ibid., p. 458). The reader will have caught the surprising similarity of the Latin vocabulary of these Lutheran creedal documents and that of the Council of Trent on the same point.

10. See the Appendix, where the typographical format of the original is followed in the English translation.

11. The action is in violation of the decision of the Council of Chalcedon (451), canon 6, which formally condemns absolute ordinations. On this point cf. C. Vogel, *"Vacua manus impositio. L'inconsistance de la chirotonie absolue en Occident,"* in *Mélanges Liturgiques B. Botte* (Louvain, 1972), pp. 511-24.

12. H. Grotius, *Dissertatio de Coenae administratione ubi pastores non sunt,* in his *Opera theologica* 4 (Basel, 1722), pp. 507-9.

13. J. Morin, *Commentarius de sacris Ecclesiae ordinationibus* (Paris, 1655); L. de Thomassin d'Eynac, *Ancienne et nouvelle discipline de l'Eglise* 2 (Bar-le-Duc, 1884); Gregory IX, *Decretales* (ed. Friedberg 2:6-928). None of these have anything to say on our subject.

14. On the distinction established toward the end of the second century between martyr and confessor cf. E. Jungklaus, *Die Gemeinde Hippolyts* (Leipzig, 1928), pp. 44-45; W.H. Frere, in H.B. Sweet, *Essays on the Early History of the Church and the Ministry* (ed. Turner; London, 1921), p. 290.

15. Cf. W. Hellmanns, *Wertschätzung des Martyriums in der altchristlichen Kirche bis zum Anfang des IV. Jhs.* (Breslau, 1912), p. 31; R. Reitzenstein, *Historia Monachorum und Historia Lausiaca* (Göttingen, 1916), p. 88; Jungklaus, op. cit., p. 44.

16. Some data for this complementary inquiry are given in V. Fuchs, *Der Or- dinationstitel* (Kanonistische Studien und Texte 4; Bonn, 1930), pp. 46ff., in succession to Adam, op. cit., p. 206.

17. On deposition, which is not simply a juridical act but a liturgical act inasmuch as it "takes back" what ordination had given, cf. Vogel, art. cit. in n. 4, above.

18. Cf. some observations on the term *forma* in Th. Michel, "*Forma iustitiae,*" in the collection of his writings, *Sarmenta* (Münster, 1972), pp. 172-79.

19. It is not possible to understand the expression "form of the priesthood," in the Arabic *Canons of Hippoytus,* as meaning "presbyteral qualification" or "ordination," or "presbyteral character"; the context *ante* and *post* exclude this.

20. Writing in the autumn of 250, Cyprian says of the martyr Aurelius: "Know, then, dear brothers, that *I* and my colleagues who were present *ordained* him" (Epist. 38); of the martyr Celerinus: "Know, moreover, that *we planned* the honor of priesthood for them [Celerinus and Aurelius]" (Epist. 39); of the martyr Numidicus: "Know that we have been instructed . . . by the divine honor done him that Numidicus the priest should be *enrolled among the priests of Carthage*" (Epist. 40).

21. *Constitutiones Apostolorum* (ca. 380), VIII, 23-24 (Funk, 1:527-28), with reference to Acts 9.15.

22. I am deliberately not taking any positions on the texts concerning the priesthood which is called "universal" or "priesthood of the faithful." These texts have been the occasion for well-known controversies with uncertain results. The texts I am translating here have to do with very specific *liturgical functions*: the celebration of baptism and the eucharist by laymen, i.e., by unordained ministers.

23. There is no doubt that the terms Tertullian uses, *tinguere* and *offerre,* refer to the actions of baptizing and celebrating the eucharist. For the same view cf. Grotius, op. cit., p. 507; Adam, op. cit., p. 192; and R. Berger, *Die Wendung "offerre pro" in der römischen Liturgie* (LQF 41; Münster, 1965), pp. 42-65.

24. The translation proposed for the final phrase is the only possible one despite the divergent Latin variants: "Cum ad peraequationem sacerdotalis disciplinae provoca- mur, deponimus infulas et *pares non sumus* [variants: *pares sumus; impares sumus; partes sumus*]." The various recensions show the hesitations and perplexity of the copyists in the presence of a passage that had no concrete relevance at the time they were tran- scribing it.

25. In his Catholic period Tertullian had already acknowledged the right of laypeople to baptize in case of necessity; but in his view baptism is the sacrament par excellence and perhaps even the *only* Christian sacrament; cf. *De baptismo* 17. If presbyters are the usual celebrants of the eucharist, this is due simply to custom and not to a divine law; cf. *De corona* 3.

26. The texts I have translated are in no way contradictory to others that strongly affirm the distinction between *ordo* and *plebs,* the institutional organization of the clergy, the specific character of the various stages in the clerical *cursus* (but without thereby turning the clergy into a caste); on this point cf. Vogel, "Le ministère charismatique" (n. 2, above), pp. 203-4 and n. 20.

27. *De baptismo* 17. The anomaly resulting from the fact that the Christian church recognizes the right of laypeople to baptize but refuses them the right to celebrate the eucharist seems to have been perceived, but not formulated, in *Notes de pastorale liturgique,* no. 120 (1975), in speaking of Sunday assemblies without a priest. The even more surprising anomaly of granting the laity the right to engage in catechesis or to perform the liturgy of the word (a privilege of bishop!) while denying the same laity the right to preside at the eucharist under any circumstances, is felt in every place where *ordained* celebrants are lacking.

Walter, Christopher (pp. 265-274)

1. A. Munoz, Il codice purpureo di Rossano (Rome, 1907), f.3ᵛ-4.

2. One is in the Archeological Museum of Istanbul; cf. Erica Cruikshank Dodd, *Byzantine Silver Stamps* (Washington, 1961), p. 108. The other is at Dumbarton Oaks; cf. ibid., pp. 12-15, and M.C. Ross, *Catalogue of the Byzantine and Early Medieval Antiquities in the Dumbarton Oaks Collection* 1 (Washington, 1962), pp. 12-15, pl. XI-XIII.

3. Gordana Badić and C. Walter, "The Inscriptions upon Liturgical Rolls in Byzantine Apse Decoration," REB 34 (1976).

4. C. Walter, "Two Notes on the Deësis," REB 26 (1968), pp. 324-36.

5. R. Bornert, *Les commentaires byzantins de la divine Liturgie du VII au XV siècle* (Paris, 1966).

6. Cf. F.E. Brightman, "The *Historia mystagogica* and Other Greek Commentaries on the Byzantine Liturgy," JTS 9 (1908), pp. 257-58; C. Walter, "La place des évêques dans le décor des absides byzantines," *Revue de l'art* 24 (1974), p. 83.

7. L.W. Daly, "*Rotuli:* Liturgy Rolls and Formal Documents," *Greek, Roman and Byzantine Studies* 14 (1973), pp. 333-38.

8. Djuric, *Vizantijske freske u Jugoslaviju* (Belgrade, 1974), pp. 9-11 and 179, n. 3.

9. Gordana Babić, "Les discussions christologiques et le décor des églises byzantines au XII siècle," *Frühmittelalterliche Studien* 2 (1968), pp. 375-76; Djuric, op. cit., pp. 13 and 182, n. 8.

10. Th. von Bogyay, "Hetoimasia," RBK 2:1189-1202.

11. Lydie Hadermann-Misguich, *Les fresques de Saint-Georges et la peinture byzantine du XII siècle* (Brussels, 1975), pp. 78-86.

12. I.D. Stefanescu, "Le voile de calice brodé de Vatra Moldovitei," in *L'art byzantin chez les Slaves* 1 (Paris, 1930), pp. 303-9.

13. D. Koco and P. Miljkovic-Pepek, *Manastir* (Skopje, 1958), pp. 47-49.

14. V. Petkovic, *Menastir Studenica* (Belgrade, 1924), p. 70; Djuric, pp. 51 and 203, n. 52.

15. K. Lassithiotaki, "Ekklēsias tēs Dutikēs Krētēs Lassithiōtakē," *Crētika Chronika* 21 (1969), pp. 192-93, fig. 30.

16. Alisa Banck, *Byzantine Art in the Collections of the USSR* (Leningrad–Moscow, 1965), figs. 186- 189. For the restoration of the inscription cf. G. Millet, *L'iconographie de l'Evangile* (Paris, 1916), p. 499, n. 4.

17. Babić–Walter, op. cit.

18. For example, in the Bezirana Kilisesi at Paristrema (Cappadocia), at Sv. Nikita, Cucer (Macedonia), and in the church of the Taxiarches at Kastoria (cf. Babić–Walter, op. cit.).

19. V. Lazarev, *Freski Staroy Ladogi* (Moscow, 1960), pp. 22-23, figs. 1-3.

20. Djuric, op. cit., pp. 31-33 and 191, n. 29.

21. P. Trempelas, *Hai treis leitourgiai kata tous en Athēnais kodikas* (Athens, 1935), p. 225.

22. K. Wessel, "Himmlische Liturgie," LBK 3:119-31.

23. *Homiliae* (PG 151:272D).

24. Hélène Grigoriadou-Cabagnols, "Le décor peint de l'église de Samari en Mes-sénie," *Cahiers archéologiques* 20 (1970), pp. 182-85, figs. 4-5.

25. Cf. Bornert, op. cit., p. 202.

26. Cf. Walter, "La place des évêques" (n. 6, above), pp. 87 and 89, n. 39.

27. PG 65:157A-160A.

Westphal, Gaston (pp. 275-290)

*M. Bouttier, President of the Protestant Institute of Theology and chief reporter to the National Synod at Grande Motte on the theme that had been studied for two years: in "Mission de la communauté et diversité des ministères," *Information Evangélique*, nos. 2-3 (1973), p. 137.

**Ibid., pp. 122-23.

1. Dombes Group, *Pour une réconciliation des ministères* (Paris, 1973), p. 54.

2. Cf. Bouttier, op. cit., p. 135: "I do not think we can lay down rules. He who presides at the meal is not so much the representative of Christ [position of the Dombes Group] as the one responsible for the ecclesial character of the meal shared. If he has not been ordained, then it is important that he receive 'delegation' according to our usage."

3. Jean-Jacques von Allmen, *Le saint ministère* (Neuchâtel, 1968), p. 56.

4. Cf. N. Nissiotis, "L'unité du laïcat et du clergé dans la tradition orthodoxe," *Verbum caro*, nos. 71-72 (1964), p. 168. The issue is on "Ministères et laïcat."

5. Cf. the 37th decree of the Synod of the Reformed Church of France (1973): "the presence of Christ is connected not with an individual, even the pastor, but with the entire community, whose life is inseparable from the word which it proclaims and the eucharist which it celebrates. The function of ministers is to be constantly at the service of this mission, to face it in the light of the biblical witness, and to show solidarity with the Church that is universal in space and time."

6. Von Allmen, op. cit., p. 196: "Apostolic succession in Reformed ecclesiology." Cf. John Calvin, *Institutes* IV, 15, 20.

7. In Calvin's view pastors continue the work of the apostles (Rom 15.16): "Especially in the organization of the church nothing is more absurd than to lodge the succession in

personalities to the exclusion of teaching" (*Institutes of the Christian Religion,* tr. by F.L. Battles [Library of Christian Classics 20-21; Philadelphia, 1960], 21:1045).

7a. *Institutes* IV, 15, 20 (Battles 21:1320).

8. F. Méjan, *Discipline de l'Eglise Réformée de France annotée et précédée d'une introduction historique,* with a preface by Marc Boegner (Paris, 1947), p. 12.

9. Ibid., pp. 14-15.

10. Cf. Bruno Hubsch, *Le ministère des prêtres et des pasteurs* (doctoral dissertation; Lyons, 1965). Sections published in *Verbum caro,* no. 77 (1966).

11. Méjan, op. cit., p. 30.

12. Ibid., p. 32.

13. *Coutumier de l'Eglise Réformée de France* (Paris, 47 rue de Clichy), D. 15 (Discipline, article 15).

14. Méjan, op. cit., p. 78.

15. The reference is to the many young pastors who refuse ordination, because (it seems) they respect the baptismal priesthood. Despite the exhausting debates of recent synods on this matter the current Discipline has been retained: "Only pastors who have received a consecration have a right to the title of pastor of the Reformed Church of France" (art. 10, p. 73).

16. *Liturgie de l'Eglise Réformée de France* (Paris, 1963), p. 231.

17. V. Vajta, "Priests and Laymen," in W.A. Quanbeck (ed.), *Challenge . . . and Response: A Protestant Perspective of the Vatican Council* (Minneapolis, 1966): "The transferal of the offices of Christ to the hierarchy is the result of a special interpretation by Catholic theology. This Catholic emphasis is closely connected with the narrowing down of the concept of the Church" (p. 84); "This sacramental concept of ordination has come into conflict in the documents of the Council with the ecclesiology of the people of God" (p. 93).

18. Cf. Leopold Scummer, *Le ministère pastoral dans l'Institution chrétienne de Calvin, à la lumière du troisième sacrement* (Wiesbaden, 1965); M. Thurian, *Sacerdoce et ministère* (Taizé, 1970), ch. 3.

19. *Coutumier de l'Eglise Réformée de France,* M.P. IIb: Ordination. I prefer the following definition given by F.J. Leenhardt: "Incorporation of the ministry and of the minister who receives the office into the succession of those through whom Christ carries on, through the centuries and to the ends of the earth, the same ministry that was once his own."

20. *68ème Synode national E.R.F., Carry-le-Rouet (May, 1975)* (Valence, 1975), p. 253.

21. M. Bouttier, *Rapport synodal,* op. cit.

22. J. Bosc, *L'unité dans le Seigneur,* p. 97.

23. Faith and Order, *La réconciliation des Eglises: baptême, eucharistie, ministère* (Taizé, 1974), p. 17.

24. In *Jean Puyo interroge le Père Congar* (Paris, 1975), p. 202.

25. *Institutes* IV, 12, 5 (Battles 21:1232-33), citing Chrysostom, *Homilies on Matthew* 82, 6 (PG 58:742).

26. Ibid., IV, 18, 12 (Battles 21:1440).

27. Ibid., IV, 4, 3 (Battles 21:1104).

28. Thurian, op. cit., p. 197.

29. Dombes Group, *Vers une même foi eucharistique?* (Paris, 1972), p. 26.

30. Archpriest Nicolas Afanassieff, *L'Eglise du Saint-Esprit* (Paris, 1975), pp. 72 and 95 (title of the chapter: "Ministry of the laity in the area of the sacraments").